Uncle Sam's Farmers

Donald Holley

Uncle Sam's Farmers

The New Deal Communities
in the Lower Mississippi Valley

University of Illinois Press

Urbana   Chicago   London

This book is a winner of the Agricultural History Society Book Award.

LIBRARY OF CONGRESS CATALOGING IN PUBLICATION DATA

Holley, Donald, 1940–
  Uncle Sam's farmers.

  Bibliography: p.
  Includes index.
    1. Land settlement—Mississippi Valley.
  2. Mississippi Valley—Rural conditions.
  3. Farmers—Mississippi Valley—History. I. Title.
HD210.M55H64   333.1′0976   75–20091
  ISBN 0–252–00510–4

For Bankie and Stephen

Contents

Preface

In the grim days of the Great Depression the federal government built almost two hundred resettlement projects, mostly farm colonies and subsistence homesteads. They were model rural communities, complete with neat, white-frame houses, picket fences, red barns, vegetable gardens, flower beds, and fruit trees. Here poor farm families could escape the rural slums they occupied and get a fresh start in life. A comprehensive program of loans, farm management and home economic training, cooperative services, medical care, and debt adjustment insured that no family would fail for lack of technical assistance.

These communities were part of a dramatic effort to rebuild rural life through the use of good sense and scientific planning. The idea itself was simple: the government would take impoverished families off land too poor to yield a decent living and convert it to forest, recreational, or other nonagricultural uses. The displaced families would be resettled on productive soil, and eventually they would become owners of their own farms.

A number of New Deal agencies experimented with community building. The Federal Emergency Relief Administration launched several community projects as part of a rural rehabilitation program. The Division of Subsistence Homesteads of the Department of the Interior resettled low-income families on small plots where they could farm and hold part-time jobs. The efforts of both agencies soon merged in America's first war against poverty. In 1935 the Resettlement Administration, headed by Rexford G. Tugwell, absorbed the old subsistence homesteads and most of the rural rehabilitation projects, and initiated a more ambitious series of communities. Two years later, operating under the Bankhead-Jones Farm Tenant Act, the Farm Security Administration replaced Tugwell's agency, inherited its organization and personnel, and completed the re-settlement program.

The Resettlement Administration attacked the fundamental problems of rural America: land misuse, inadequate credit, bad management, and poor tenure arrangements. It brought together tasks that complimented each other. The suffering of millions of rural families in the Great Depression made action necessary. Their plight struck the nation's conscience, and the federal government was willing to invest funds in their rehabilitation. A grand scheme—logical, necessary, seemingly feasible. But it never lived up to expectations.

This book is an attempt to reconstruct the resettlement program at the regional and local levels. The states of Arkansas, Louisiana, and Mississippi made up the Resettlement Administration's Region VI, and I have used them as a case history of the resettlement agencies in action. Arkansas in particular was the source of sharecropper agitation; and on the principle that the squeaky wheel gets the most grease, it was the scene of a disproportionate amount of resettlement activity.

The local perspective suggests its own questions. What bureaucratic machinery existed to administer the program? Who were the officials running it and what kind of people where they? What were the mechanics of launching the community projects and operating them on an everyday basis? What problems did local officials face in winning acceptance and dealing with opposition? What was the influence of the small town and rural people, civic clubs, chambers of commerce, businessmen, large planters, and powerful farm organizations that made up the environment in which these agencies moved? What of the men, women, and children who were the objects of so much attention? How much did such programs really do to help them change their old attitudes and habits?

Although contemporary critics of the Farm Security Administration accused it of practicing Socialism and even Communism, the recent trend in historical scholarship has been to depict the New Deal as overly cautious and its accomplishments as very limited, particularly where such groups as sharecroppers, unskilled workers, and Negroes were concerned. Those who needed the most, it is now clear, got the least, while the major New Deal benefits went to middle-class people or to groups with effective lobbying power. The local perspective dramatizes the federal government's shortcomings in dealing with the chronic poor; but it also suggests, as I have pointed out, some of the limitations which held back any effort at genuine social reform. The surprising thing is not that the resettlement agencies accomplished little, but that they managed to do as much as they did.

While researching and writing this book, I received assistance from many people. Burl Noggle of Louisiana State University introduced me to the topic, and I am profoundly grateful for his guidance and inspiration. My thanks go to two participants in this story, H. L. Mitchell and E. B. Whitaker, who read the manuscript and made helpful comments. Among other people who gave the manuscript a critical reading were Merrill R. Pritchett and John L. Shelby, who read the final draft. Thanks are also due two very patient and efficient typists, Jody Brookings and Janet Matherly.

Some of the material in this volume previously appeared in *Louisiana History* (Spring 1970), *Agricultural History* (July 1971), and the *Arkansas Historical Quarterly* (Autumn 1973).

The dedication goes to my wife, who tolerated me while I worked on this book, and my son, who made all of the labor worthwhile.

—D. H.

Abbreviations

The following abbreviations have been used in the interest of brevity:

FDR, *Public Papers*

Samuel I. Rosenman, ed., *The Public Papers and Addresses of Franklin D. Roosevelt*, 13 vols. (New York: Russell and Russell, 1969).

FDR Papers, OF

Franklin D. Roosevelt Papers, Franklin D. Roosevelt Library, Hyde Park, N.Y. The collection cited is the President's Official File with the file number indicated.

FERA Records, NA, RG 69

Records of the Work Projects Administration, Record Group 69, National Archives, Washington, D.C.

FSA, "Resettlement Projects, Region VI"

United States Department of Agriculture, Farm Security Administration, "Resettlement Projects, Land and Source of Acquisition, also Status of Unit Development, Vendor, Acreage and Number of Units Developed or Undeveloped, Region VI," 1 January 1941, mimeographed, in FSA Records, NA, RG 96.

FSA Records, NA, RG 96

Records of the Farmers Home Administration, Record Group 96, National Archives, Washington, D.C. This record group includes the records of the Resettlement Administration as well as the Farm Security Administration.

HHFA Records, NA, RG 207

Records of the Housing and Home Finance Agency, Record Group 207, National Archives, Washington, D.C.

Hopkins Papers

Harry L. Hopkins Papers, Franklin D. Roosevelt Library, Hyde Park, N.Y.

Ickes Papers, NA, RG 48

Records of the Office of the Secretary of the Interior, Record Group 48, National Archives, Washington, D.C.

RA, "Project Description Book"

Resettlement Administration, "Project Description Book, March–December, 1936," mimeographed, FSA Records, NA, RG 96.

Sharp Papers

Works Progress Administration Papers, Special Collections, University of Arkansas Library, Fayetteville, Ark.

Socialist Party Papers

Socialist Party of America Papers, Farm Labor File, Manuscript Division, Duke University Library, Durham, N.C.

STFU Papers

Papers of the Southern Tenant Farmers' Union, Southern Historical Collection, University of North Carolina Library, Chapel Hill, N.C.

Tugwell Papers

Rexford G. Tugwell Papers, Franklin D. Roosevelt Library, Hyde Park, N.Y.

USHR, *FSA Hearings*

United States House of Representatives, Select Committee of the Committee on Agriculture, *Hearings on the Farm Security Administration*, 78th Cong., 1st sess. (Washington: Government Printing Office, 1943–44).

USHR, *USDA Approp. Hearings*

United States House of Representatives, Subcommittee of the Committee on Appropriations, *Hearings on the Agricultural Department Appropriation Bill*, with the fiscal year, congress, and session indicated.

USS, *USDA Approp. Hearings*

United States Senate, Subcommittee of the Committee on Appropriations, *Hearings on the Agriculture Department Appropriation Bill,* with the fiscal year, congress, and session indicated.

US Stat.

United States Statutes at Large, preceded by the volume number and followed by the page number.

Wallace Papers, NA, RG 16

Records of the Office of the Secretary of Agriculture, Record Group 16, National Archives, Washington, D.C.

WPA Records, NA, RG 69

Records of the Work Projects Administration, Record Group 69, National Archives, Washington, D.C. Until 1939 the agency's name was Works Progress Administration.

Uncle Sam's Farmers

Chapter I

Prologue: "The Farmer in the Dell"

One mild winter Saturday in January 1931, England, Arkansas, an obscure rural community twenty miles below Little Rock, enacted a scene symptomatic of the early depression years. Some three hundred farmers swarmed into town and threatened to loot the stores unless they were given food for their families. They had just come through the worst drought year on record in the South and Southwest. Crops had been poor that fall. With their gardens burned up, many families had already emptied their pantries. Agricultural prices had been declining sharply since 1929, and were still nosing downward. The Citizens Bank and Trust Company of England had closed only a few days before, and farmers found their accounts impounded. That Saturday morning, when Red Cross officials refused to give out additional provisions because their supply of application blanks was exhausted, a reservoir of fear and frustration suddenly exploded into rage.

Within a few hours the town was thronged with people who came from all directions—in cars, on horseback, in buggies, and on foot—all milling about, uncertain as to what they intended to do. Some of them were reportedly armed, but the crowd was orderly. "Now then," their organizer, a man named Coney, had said, "when we gets to town, we'll ask for food quiet-like, and if they don't give it to us, we'll take it, also quiet-like."[1]

While the excitement was running high, a local attorney, George E. Morris, tried to calm their fears. He was sympathetic with their predicament. They were prosperous, hard-working citizens who had fallen on a little bad luck, and he promised that the people of England would work with them to feed their families. The crowd was in no mood for a speech.

1. Lement Harris, "An Arkansas Farmer Speaks," *New Republic* 67 (27 May 1931): 41.

There were continuous interruptions: "We want food! Our children are crying for food, and we're going to get it!" "We're not beggars!" someone shouted. "We will work for any amount if we can get it. We're not going to let our families starve!"[2]

England merchants, who were caught up in the economic crisis as much as farmers, huddled together and made arrangements to distribute $1,500 worth of staples. They hoped to be reimbursed later. They also talked of helping the distressed families get highway construction work. The "England Riot" attracted nationwide publicity, much of it exaggerated; but this incident did dramatize the needs of the drought-stricken region. "Paul Revere just woke up Concord," Will Rogers quipped; "these birds woke up America."[3]

"This winter has done one good thing," Coney remarked later. "The farmers are more sociable-like . . . I think that three winters like this one would see them organized. I'll tell you that there's sure goin' to be somethin' tearin' loose 'round there someday."[4]

It was a remarkably prophetic statement. While his timing was close, Coney's words were more a cry of desperation than a prophecy. Almost anyone at the time would have found it easy to predict calamity. The stock market crash of 1929 had sent the nation's economy careening into the longest and darkest depression in American history. All major economic indexes told the same story. Gross national product: down. Industrial production: down. Income: down. The only indicators that went up were such figures as business failures and unemployment.

The natural beauty of a region like the Lower Mississippi Valley sometimes obscured the real suffering that was taking place. The landscape was abundant with variety, sweeping up from the Gulf coastal plain to the loess bluffs of Mississippi, the piney woods of Louisiana and Arkansas, and, finally, the Ozark highlands. Meandering down through the heart of the region was the rich alluvial delta of the Mississippi River itself. Within this three-state territory of over 144,296 square miles lived some eight million people in 1930. Scotch-Irish and English names predominated,

2. Little Rock *Arkansas Gazette*, 4 January 1931; *New York Times*, 5 January 1931; "Husbandry: 'Simply Got Hungry,'" *Time* 17 (12 January 1931): 13; Gail S. Murray, "Forty Years Ago: The Great Depression Comes to Arkansas," *Arkansas Historical Quarterly* 29 (Winter 1970): 296–71.

3. Roger Lambert, "Hoover and the Red Cross in the Arkansas Drought of 1930," *Arkansas Historical Quarterly* 29 (Spring 1970): 3–19; *New York Times*, 5 January 1931; Will Rogers, *The Autobiography of Will Rogers*, ed. Donald Day (Boston: Houghton Mifflin, 1949), p. 237.

4. Harris, "An Arkansas Farmer Speaks," p. 41.

but they were not a homogeneous people. Negroes made up 38 percent of the population, and the French culture of southern Louisiana was another world within itself.[5] For all of their diversity, most of the people of the region were bound by two conditions: they were rural and they were poor.

Climate, soil, and history conspired to make agriculture the basis of the region's economy. The long, warm summers and the mild winters with little freezing weather provided a growing season of over two hundred days—perfect for cotton. The pioneer farmers who fled the Carolinas and Virginia in the nineteenth century hoped to imitate the piedmont aristocrats who had been making fortunes since Eli Whitney invented his gin. Before the Civil War a few large planters settled in the river bottoms, where they took advantage of the alluvial soil and the convenience of river transportation. But the hill sections of the region were more popular with settlers than the lowlands. The hills probably reminded them of home, and the task of clearing and draining the bottoms was too onerous for people in a hurry to establish homes. They had to harvest a crop as soon as possible. The spring floods and the menaces of yellow fever and malaria—which were associated with low, swampy land even before their cause was known—also kept farmers out of the river bottoms.

The hills and basins of the interior became dotted with small farms and large plantations, all growing cotton. They were productive for a time. Once the timber had been cut and the ground cover removed, however, nothing was left to keep the topsoil from washing. The self-reliant, individualistic pioneer farmers jumped from one farm to another as they "wore out" the land. After the Civil War, logging mills cut the long-leaf pine forests and then departed, leaving highly desirable "cutover" areas where farmers cleaned out the small trees, grubbed up the stumps, and planted their crops. Only at the turn of the twentieth century was the last section of the region opened to cotton—the swampy floodplain, colloquially called the Mississippi River "delta." By then yellow fever had been stamped out and malaria was under control. The large planters organized quasi-public corporations to drain the swamps and build levees.

5. For a general overview of the region in the 1930s, see the WPA's "American Guide Series": Work Projects Administration, *Arkansas: A Guide to the State* (New York: Hastings House, 1941), pp. 58–66; *Louisiana: A Guide to the State* (New York: Hastings House, 1941), pp. 60–64; *Mississippi: A Guide to the Magnolia State* (New York: Viking, 1938), pp. 92–106. Howard W. Odum's massive *Southern Regions of the United States* (Chapel Hill: University of North Carolina Press, 1936) is an encyclopedic collection of information about the southeastern states from Texas to the Chesapeake region.

When the planters finally invaded this last frontier, they abandoned the poorer hills to small farmers, who continued to try to farm them.[6]

Despite a significant growth in urban population after 1900, the region still retained its predominately rural character. The most rural state of all was Mississippi. In 1930 two-thirds of Mississippi's people actually lived on farms, and more Mississippians were gainfully employed in agriculture than in all other occupations combined. In the fall of each year the state was white with cotton blooms. This single plant contributed from 75 to 80 percent of gross farm income, and in many parts of the state it was the only source of income. The Mississippi and Yazoo river bottoms were the most intensive cotton regions, but cotton was still grown in the hills, too. The old one-crop method of farming, however, was at last breaking down, and farmers were raising more livestock and growing more corn and hay, truck crops, and home gardens.[7]

Unlike Mississippi and Louisiana, Arkansas possessed large areas of mountainous country that was not suited for growing any type of cash crop. In addition, much of Arkansas was in forest, with lumber and wood products the state's major nonagricultural industry. Yet farm people still made up 60 percent of the population, just behind Mississippi; and cotton was the major cash crop in all but eight counties. The mountain folk of northern Arkansas engaged in a subsistence culture, but many Arkansas farmers made a living from rice, apples, peaches, dairy and beef cattle, and chickens. The families that depended entirely on growing cotton were seldom able to earn anything above the bare necessities of life.[8]

Louisiana had developed a more diversified economy than the other

6. L. C. Gray, *History of Agriculture in the Southern United States to 1860,* 2 vols. (Gloucester, Mass.: Peter Smith, 1958), 2:888–942; Rupert B. Vance, *Human Factors in Cotton Culture* (Chapel Hill: University of North Carolina Press, 1929), pp. 18–22, 41–45, 53–79; idem, *Human Geography of the South* (Chapel Hill: University of North Carolina Press, 1935), pp. 40–76; U. B. Phillips, *Life and Labor in the Old South* (Boston: Little, Brown, 1935), chap. 4, and pp. 91–111; Ladd Haystead and Gilbert C. Fite, *The Agricultural Regions of the United States* (Norman: University of Oklahoma Press, 1955), chap. 6.

7. U.S. Bureau of the Census, *Statistical Abstract of the United States, 1934* (Washington: Government Printing Office, 1934), pp. 8, 66, 67; Resettlement Administration, *Information for Prospective New Farmers in the State of Mississippi,* Resettlement Information Service Bulletin no. 10 (Washington, 1937), pp. 1–3; U.S. Bureau of the Census, *Statistical Abstract of the United States, 1939* (Washingon: Government Printing Office, 1940), p. 623.

8. Resettlement Administration, *Information for Prospective New Farmers in the State of Arkansas,* Resettlement Information Service Bulletin no. 9 (Washington, 1937), p. 7; Arkansas State Planning Board, *Progress Report* (Little Rock: Parke-Harper, 1936), pp. 28–35, 44, 45.

two states. It claimed the largest nonfarm population in the region and the only metropolitan center. In 1930 only about 40 percent of the total population lived on farms; and about a third of the total land area of Louisiana was under cultivation, compared to two-thirds of Mississippi and half of Arkansas. Outside New Orleans, however, Louisiana was still largely rural. Cotton was the state's principal cash crop, particularly in the fertile bottomlands along the Mississippi and Red rivers. Louisiana, too, had its truck farming areas, and there were sections which specialized in such crops as strawberries and peaches. The sugarcane industry centered in the south-central part of the state, and rice in the southwest.[9]

The common denominator of the three states was the broad Mississippi River delta, with its classic paradox of rich land and poor people. The alluvial soil gave it the potential to be one of the wealthiest agricultural sections of the nation. In reality it held some of the most tragic scenes of human degradation to be found anywhere.

The southern tenant farmer and sharecropper, who worked the large delta plantations, contradicted every virtue in the American yeoman ideal. They gained reputations for being lazy and shiftless, for lacking ambition and even self-respect; but these were the traits the system demanded. Sharecroppers were a class of exploited, culturally backward people who were going nowhere. Long ignored, they actually blended into the southern landscape, merely part of what one expected to see.

From 1880 to 1930 the number of southern farmers who worked somebody else's land rose from a third to more than half, and tenancy was still growing at the rate of 40,000 new tenants a year. By 1935 the South contained 1,831,475 tenant farmers and sharecroppers, the all-time high. Tenancy trapped one out of every four southerners, or more than 8 million people. What had begun as a Negro problem now included twice as many white farmers as black, but 79 percent of all Negro farmers were tenants, compared to 46 percent of white farmers.[10]

9. Resettlement Administration, *Information for Prospective New Farmers in the State of Louisiana*, Resettlement Information Bulletin no. 11 (Washington, 1937), pp. 3–5; *Statistical Abstract, 1939*, pp. 616, 619.

10. U.S. Bureau of the Census, *Historical Statistics of the United States: Colonial Times to 1957* (Washington: Government Printing Office, 1960), p. 278, ser. K-23, K-27; Charles S. Johnson, Edwin R. Embree, and Will W. Alexander, *The Collapse of Cotton Tenancy* (Chapel Hill: University of North Carolina Press, 1935), pp. 4–5; National Resources Board, *Farm Tenancy: Report of the President's Committee* (Washington: Government Printing Office, 1937), pp. 35, 39, 96; *Statistical Abstract, 1939*, p. 621; U.S. Bureau of the Census, *United States Census of Agriculture, 1935*, 3 vols. (Washington: Government Printing Office, 1936–37), 1:643, 669, 695.

Tenancy had never had a tighter hold on the Lower Mississippi Valley than in the mid-1930s. Mississippi, Louisiana, and Arkansas stood first, third, and sixth, respectively, in the national farm tenancy rankings. The region had 477,700 farm tenants, compared to 255,206 farm owners; almost two out of every three farmers did not own their own land. Over half of the tenants were sharecroppers who did not even own a plug mule to use in making a crop.[11]

After the Civil War, sharecropping replaced slavery. In the defeated South, small farmers, particularly former slaves, had no money; they needed land without having to buy it or pay cash rent. The large plantation owners had land but little else. With no banks from which to borrow money, they could not raise cash to hire workers. After trial and error, landlord and tenant together evolved a unique form of tenancy in which they substituted labor for money by sharing the crop, the only thing either of them had of marketable value. The division of the crop depended on what the landlord furnished the tenant in the way of work animals, feed, and tools. The lowest form of tenant was the sharecropper, who had to be furnished with everything, and his rent was half the crop. The more of his own needs a tenant could supply, the better deal he could command from a landlord.[12]

The tenant was at the mercy of the merchant, who took a "lien" or mortgage on the future crop in return for the supplies the tenant and his family consumed during the long, hot summer months. The lien was the key to the evils of the sharecropper system. "The seeker of credit," C. Vann Woodward has written, "usually pledged an unplanted crop to pay for a loan of unstipulated amount at a rate of interest to be determined by the creditor."[13]

The tenant was totally dependent. He was told what crop to plant, how it should be cultivated, where to process and where to market it. He just hoped that he "paid out" at the end of the year—that his share of the crop covered the cost of his "furnish." The tenant was bound to the creditor until the debt was paid, and as a rule the best he could hope for was

11. *Farm Tenancy: Report of the President's Committee*, p. 96; *Statistical Abstract, 1939*, pp. 606, 616; W. A. Turner, *A Graphic Summary of Farm Tenure*, U.S. Department of Agriculture, Misc. Pub. no. 261 (Washington: Government Printing Office, 1936), pp. 1–3.
12. On the origins of sharecropping, see William C. Harris, *Presidential Reconstruction in Mississippi* (Baton Rouge: Louisiana State University Press, 1967), pp. 182–85; C. Vann Woodward, *Origins of the New South, 1877–1913* (Baton Rouge: Louisiana State University Press, 1961), pp. 178–85; Vance, *Human Factors in Cotton Culture*, pp. 53–79.
13. Woodward, *Origins of the New South*, p. 180.

to break even. If he ever got behind he became a kind of peon, under lien to the same man year after year, trapped in the system. Interest, service charges, and artificial fees sometimes ran as high as 50 percent, and they drained off any profit which could have made the tenant into an independent farm owner.[14]

In time, many of the large plantations passed into the hands of merchants who lived in nearby towns or absentee owners whose sole concern was to extract a profit in the cheapest and quickest way possible. Whatever paternalism might have existed in the old planters was absent in men who perhaps seldom saw anything of their holdings other than the ledger books. They would risk supplies only on staples which had a ready market. Even small independent farmers had to stick with a reliable money-maker. So the South's ancient evils of absentee ownership, land monopoly, and one-crop farming were not only retained after the Civil War, but intensified. In solely economic terms, Woodward believes, the lien system may have worked more "permanent injury" on the South than slavery had.[15]

There was no paradoxical contrast of rich and poor in the upland sections. Here much of the land was as poor as the people who tried to farm it. Too many farm families were still trying to scratch a living out of hill land that was not fit for agriculture. Other families were farming acreages too small to yield a decent living. Perhaps as many as a hundred thousand families in the Lower Mississippi Valley lived on "submarginal farms" —farms which under the circumstances were not able to provide an adequate livelihood. While the mountaineers of northern Arkansas were celebrated as the region's most backward and impoverished hill farmers, submarginal agriculture was not limited to remote Ozark mountaintops. Across southern Arkansas and northern Louisiana and along the ridges of Mississippi, travelers driving the dusty country roads found farm houses at intervals of every mile or half-mile, each one overseeing its own little patches of cotton and corn. The living standard of most of these hill farmers was low, their housing run-down, and they had little hope of improvement if they stayed where they were. More and more of them were abandoning their depleted land, as the large planters had done a generation before, and moving to the delta.[16]

14. Johnson, Embree, and Alexander, *Collapse of Cotton Tenancy*, pp. 8–11, 17–20, 25–32.
15. Woodward, *Origins of the New South*, p. 180.
16. Vance, *Human Geography*, pp. 259–60; *Farm Tenancy: Report of the President's Committee*, pp. 65–68. See also National Resources Board, *A Report on National Planning and Public Works* (Washington: Government Printing Office, 1934),

The submarginal farmer had never been effectively reached through the Agricultural Extension Service, and his poor farming methods compounded his problem. Years of continuous cotton production perhaps had a detrimental effect even in the delta, but in the hills the one-crop system rapidly robbed the soil of fertility. Farmers ran their cotton rows up and down the slopes, almost challenging the next heavy rain to do its worst. But even proper terracing could not completely stop the land from washing. The thin soil of the ridges and rolling hills was badly scarred by sheet and gully erosion. At the worst places huge chasms appeared and ate their way across fields, sometimes devouring an abandoned farm house which got in the way. Of the three states, Mississippi had suffered most from erosion; four million acres of the state farm land were denuded of topsoil. In Arkansas the figure was more than three million acres; in Louisiana it was two million.[17] Thus poor land use and rural poverty were two of the major agricultural problems of the Lower Mississippi Valley.

As the Great Depression began, the South, from Virginia to Texas, was already in the grip of an agricultural crisis. The entire cotton economy was moving inexorably toward collapse.

King Cotton was a sick monarch and had been growing sicker for a long time. The United States was once the predominant producer of the world's cotton. By the 1930s some fifty countries, particularly Brazil and Egypt, were steadily crowding American cotton out of world markets. Rayon and other synthetic fabrics had also grabbed a significant share of the textile market, and they were bound to capture more. But the sickness went deeper.

Slow in adopting machinery, cotton farmers were at last on the verge of a mechanical revolution, with its anticipated lower man-hour requirements per acre and supersized farms. Some large operators had already sold their mules and bought tractors. The result was a partial shift from sharecropping to the use of day laborers, a desperate segment of the rural population lacking even the prerogatives of the poorest tenants. Sharecroppers complained of being "tractored off the land," but it was only a matter of time before the mechanical cotton picker would also make most

pp. 127, 161–89; National Resources Committee, *Regional Factors in National Planning and Development* (Washington: Government Printing Office, 1935), p. 176.

17. Odum, *Southern Regions*, p. 339; T. J. Woofter, Jr., "The Subregions of the Southeast," *Social Forces* 13 (October 1934): 43–50; Vance, *Human Geography*, pp. 99–108.

day laborers superfluous. In Mississippi the Rust cotton picker was already lumbering across cotton fields in trial runs. When perfected after World War II, it would be the most revolutionary development in cotton culture since the invention of the gin.[18]

Farmers were also losing the struggle against their oldest enemy and benefactor—the weather. Mother Nature had turned a menacing face, swinging capriciously from one extreme to the other. In rapid succession, the worst spring flooding anyone could remember was followed by a drought which broke all weather bureau records.

After a severely cold winter, the Mississippi River in April 1927 formed a vast yellow sea over 1,000 miles long and, in places, 50 miles wide, covering 25,000 square miles. The flooding hit eight states, destroyed an estimated $300 million worth of property, and took the lives of 250 people. By every standard, Arkansas was the state hardest hit. The swollen Mississippi backed up the Saint Francis and Arkansas rivers, driving 40,000 people from their homes. Flood waters covered fully 13 percent of the state, and property losses ran to $14,936,000. The farmers of the flood area watched helplessly as their young plants rotted or disappeared under the silt.[19]

Secretary of Commerce Herbert Hoover, a popular figure with a wealth of humanitarian service to his credit, was named by President Calvin Coolidge as chairman of a Special Mississippi Flood Committee. While surveying the damage, he saw an opportunity to bring about fundamental land reform, and he drew up a "resettlement plan" which he circulated among leaders in the flood-stricken area. Hoover wrote: "I felt that if we would arrange to take over foreclosed or near-foreclosed plantations, subdivide them into plots including at least 20 acres of cultivated lands, place upon them the minimum necessary housing, equipment, implements and animals, with the finance as against the first crop, it would be possible to find a great number of buyers amongst both blacks and whites." He further suggested that purchase terms extend over ten years with refinancing available.[20] His plan produced few results, but it was not idle dreaming. With the help of the United States Chamber of Commerce he created a nonprofit organization with a $10 million loan fund to assist

18. Johnson, Embree, and Alexander, *Collapse of Cotton Tenancy*, pp. 36–38, 41–45.

19. Frederick Simpish, "The Great Mississippi Flood of 1927," *National Geographic Magazine* 52 (September 1927): 243–89.

20. Bruce A. Lohof, "Herbert Hoover's Mississippi Valley Land Reform Memorandum: A Document," *Arkansas Historical Quarterly* 29 (Summer 1970): 116.

flood victims.[21] Hoover's idea was surprisingly prophetic of what the New Deal would later undertake on a larger scale.

The drought of 1930 and 1931 was a warm-up for the Dust Bowl. Across the midsection of the nation it just stopped raining. The people of Arkansas again suffered more than anyone else. Rainfall in June and July 1930 was the lowest on record, with temperatures hitting 110 degrees in August. After seventy-one rainless days, Little Rock got a sprinkle, but little more. Luckless farmers watched their crops wither.[22] The drought cut Arkansas's cotton production by more than a third, from 1,435 bales in 1929 to 874 bales in 1930.[23] This time Hoover, who had become president, appeared less anxious to help the region's suffering farmers. When he rejected all entreaties for direct federal relief, he began the destruction of his reputation as a great humanitarian. The Red Cross, at Hoover's request, took on the job of providing food to hungry drought victims.[24]

Wet or dry, nothing deterred the continuing drop in the cotton market. Cotton prices had begun a long slide in 1920, recovered in mid-decade, then fell lower. The average price was still 20.17 cents per pound in 1927. The worst was still to come. In 1929 the price slipped to 16.79 cents. The next year cotton brought 9.46 cents. In 1931 southern farmers hauled 17 million bales of cotton out of their fields, the third-largest crop to date; but with the carry-over from 1930 and foreign production, world markets were glutted. The average price fell to 5.66 cents, then strained upward to 6.52 cents in 1932. On the New Orleans Cotton Exchange the bottom was reached in June 1932 at 4.95 cents, the lowest price in almost half a century.[25] It was a disaster which crowned a decade of disasters. "Men everywhere walked in a kind of daze," W. J. Cash remembered.[26] The value of cotton produced in the Lower Mississippi Valley stood at $350,534,000 in 1929, plummeted to $144,459,000 in 1930, and reached

21. Herbert Hoover, *The Memoirs of Herbert Hoover: The Cabinet and the Presidency, 1920–1933*, 3 vols. (New York: Macmillan, 1951–52), 2:126.

22. "Arkansas's Fight for Life," *Literary Digest* 108 (28 February 1931): 5–6; Charles Morrow Wilson, "Famine in Arkansas," *Outlook and Independent* 57 (29 April 1931): 595–97; "Drought: Field Report from Five of the States Most Seriously Affected," *New Republic* 66 (25 February 1931): 40–41.

23. *Statistical Abstract, 1934*, pp. 606–7.

24. Lambert, "Hoover and the Red Cross in the Arkansas Drought of 1930," pp. 3–19.

25. *Historical Statistics of the United States*, p. 301, cols. K 302, K 303, K 309; Johnson, Embree, and Alexander, *Collapse of Cotton Tenancy*, pp. 4–5; James E. Boyle, *Cotton and the New Orleans Cotton Exchange* (Garden City, N.Y.: Doubleday, 1934), p. 188.

26. W. J. Cash, *The Mind of the South* (New York: Knopf, 1941), p. 362.

its low point of $103,647,000 in 1932. The cash income from all farm production was more than cut in half, falling from $572,900,000 to $201,700,000 in three years.[27]

Under the impact of depression prices and drought, the rural credit structure broke down. The number of failures among the region's banks was already running between fifteen and twenty a year, but in 1930 and 1931 a staggering total of 320 banks went out of business. Many merchants could no longer advance their tenants any supplies. Some tenant families stayed where they were and tried to eke out subsistence without planting a cash crop; many others, the celebrated Arkies and Okies, loaded up their rattle-trap Fords and set out for California. All over the United States, farms went on the auction block for nonpayment of taxes. On one day in April 1932 a fourth of the entire state of Mississippi was sold at sheriffs' sales. "Right here in Mississippi some people are about ready to lead a mob," Gov. Theodore G. Bilbo had earlier observed. "In fact, I'm getting a little pink myself."[28]

There were serious warnings of a coming revolution. Edward A. O'Neal, president of the American Farm Bureau Federation, told a Senate committee in January 1933: "Unless something is done for the American farmer, we will have a revolution in the countryside in less than 12 months."[29] While the England Food Riot briefly made headlines, the greatest trouble occurred in the Corn Belt. The summer of 1932 saw Iowa farmers, usually pillars of conservatism, organize the Farmers Holiday Association and block highways around Sioux City, preventing the movement of milk and livestock to market until prices went up. In Iowa and Kansas, crowds gathered at courthouses to halt mortgage foreclosures and intimidate judges.[30] Yet the surprising thing was how little violence took place.

27. U.S. Bureau of Foreign and Domestic Commerce, *Statistical Abstract of the United States, 1931* (Washington: Government Printing Office, 1931), p. 673; *Statistical Abstract, 1934*, pp. 572, 606–7.

28. "One-Fourth of a State Sold for Taxes," *Literary Digest* 112 (7 May 1932): 10; Hilton Butler, "Bilbo, the Two-Edged Sword," *North American Review* 232 (December 1931): 496.

29. U.S. Senate, Agricultural and Forestry Committee, *Hearings on the Agricultural Adjustment Relief Plan*, 72d Cong., 2d sess. (Washington: Government Printing Office, 1933), p. 15.

30. Theodore Saloutos and John D. Hicks, *Agricultural Discontent in the Middle West, 1900–1929* (Madison: University of Wisconsin Press, 1951), pp. 435–48; John L. Shover, *Cornbelt Rebellion: The Farmers' Holiday Association* (Urbana: University of Illinois Press, 1965), pp. 44–45, 47–49, 77–83.

Farmers were angry enough; but they were also beaten, their spirits broken in a hopeless struggle with forces beyond their control. Whatever revolutionary potential the depression generated soon evaporated in anticipation of Franklin D. Roosevelt's New Deal.

Part One

Back to the Land

Chapter II

"Above All, Try Something"

"The country needs . . . the country demands bold, persistent experimentation," Franklin Roosevelt said in 1932. "It is common sense to take a method and try it: If it fails, admit it frankly and try another. But above all, try something."[1]

Roosevelt's speeches leading up to the Chicago Democratic Convention seemed to hold out hope for poverty-stricken farmers, but he carefully kept his statements in vague generalities. He talked of helping the "forgotten man at the bottom of the economic pyramid," a conveniently ambiguous phrase which many groups interpreted as applying to them. He referred to the need to build "from the bottom up and not from the top down," but he did not elaborate.[2] "The millions who are in want," he warned obliquely, "will not stand by silently forever while the things to satisfy their needs are within easy reach."[3]

Once he had his party's presidential nomination, he became more cautious than ever. Roosevelt took up the familiar cry for higher farm prices and for the reduction of surpluses in staple commodities. His major campaign farm address at Topeka, Kansas, promised a national program of planned agricultural production, but he was far from explicit about how it would work. He castigated his opponent, Herbert Hoover, for pursuing a tariff policy which destroyed foreign markets. Roosevelt would work for equality between agriculture and industry, reorganize the Department of Agriculture, reduce the burden of taxation on farmers, and give them a break in their struggle with the mortgage. There was little here with which anyone could argue, and little comfort for the poorest farm families. The Democratic candidate played it safe, too, on the other

1. FDR, *Public Papers* (1928–32), 1:646.
2. Ibid., p. 625.
3. Ibid., p. 646.

issues of the campaign. It was a highly successful strategy. On 7 November 1932, Roosevelt carried all but six states. Hoover had unfairly received blame for the breadlines and unemployment, while Roosevelt, without being specific, convinced people that he would take action against the depression.[4]

As the nation waited through the interregnum, from November to March, farmers like everyone else wondered what the New Deal might mean for them. If they had followed Roosevelt's career, they knew that his solicitation for agriculture was more than a campaign posture. Of all the problems of the depression, he felt most at home with those that involved crops, cattle, and the land—problems that enabled him to draw on his personal experience.

Franklin D. Roosevelt had spent his earliest years on a large country estate near Hyde Park, New York, amid everything a boy could want. There were meadows, orchards, and woods to play in, a river to sail boats on, and horses to ride. The large house was comfortable and secure. As he matured he absorbed his father's interest in the land and its management. In fact he narrowly missed settling into the kind of life James Roosevelt lived—that of the gentleman farmer who oversaw his well-kept acres, pursued his business ventures, and attended his civic duties, while looking after the people around him with a sense of noblesse oblige. When young Franklin's career took him away from Hyde Park, he carried with him a special feeling he acquired for the land while growing up.[5]

In the eroded countryside of Meriwether County, Georgia, he learned additional lessons in farm economics. After Roosevelt was stricken with poliomyelitis, he discovered the warm mineral water which he hoped would restore his withered legs, and he built a home at Warm Springs. Between 1924 and 1928 he spent many an afternoon driving around country roads in his special hand-operated Ford roadster, stopping at

4. Roosevelt's statements on the farm problem can be followed in the *Public Papers*, vol. 1: acceptance speech at Chicago, pp. 653–56; Topeka, Kansas, pp. 693–711; Sioux City, Iowa, pp. 756–70; Springfield, Illinois, pp. 812–19. See also Frank Freidel, *Franklin D. Roosevelt: The Triumph* (Boston: Little, Brown, 1956), pp. 341–50; Gertrude Almy Slichter, "Franklin D. Roosevelt and the Farm Problem, 1929–1932," *Mississippi Valley Historical Review* 43 (September 1956): 238–58.

5. For comments on Roosevelt's sympathy for farmers and farming, see Rexford G. Tugwell, "The Preparation of a President," *Western Political Science Quarterly* 1 (June 1948): 132–33; idem, *The Democratic Roosevelt: A Biography* (Baltimore: Penguin Books, 1969), pp. 157–58, 206–7; idem, *The Brains Trust* (New York: Viking, 1968), pp. 17, 66–72; Frank Freidel, *Franklin D. Roosevelt: The Apprenticeship* (Boston: Little, Brown, 1952), p. 23; Daniel R. Fusfeld, *The Economic Thought of Franklin D. Roosevelt and the Origins of the New Deal* (New York: Columbia University Press, 1956), chap. 9.

farmers' homes and talking with them about their troubles. His new neighbors, he found, were suffering not only from the post–World War I agricultural depression, but also from the effects of continuous cotton production, poor land use, and the boll weevil.

As a private citizen, Roosevelt could do nothing about agricultural prices, but he might still make a contribution to his adopted home. He was fascinated with the accomplishments of Cason Calloway, a local textile mill operator who had made his enormous estates a showcase of purebred cattle, beautiful pastures, and experimental crops that substituted for cotton. Following Calloway's example, Roosevelt bought a farm on Pine Mountain, where he hoped to demonstrate something of practical value to his neighbors. He planted loblolly pine rather than allow his unused fields to go to brush and weeds; he established peach and apple trees, raised tomatoes, grapes, and a truck garden; and he brought in chickens, hogs, and cattle. The Pine Mountain venture was a failure; the land was too elevated and the soil too thin, and Roosevelt never found a substitute cash crop. Nor was he able to devote proper attention to the project. But the investment was not a total loss. What he learned in Georgia was not only how much poor farmers needed assistance, but that they also needed sound management advice if they were to succeed.[6]

When he became governor of New York, he pursued his interest in conservation and land use planning on the level of governmental policy. Roosevelt lost no time in appointing an agricultural advisory commission; he had at least beaten his Republican opposition to the farm relief issue. New York, despite its large urban population, was a leading farm state with serious agricultural problems. The advisory commission recommended a program of tax equalization for farmers, state aid to lift the burden of school and road construction in rural areas, the expansion of rural electrification, and more funds for agricultural research. The governor took the program to the state legislature and got it passed. He also secured $20,000 for a county-by-county soil survey, classifying land as to its most appropriate use and marking submarginal land for reforestation.[7] There was nothing drastic or radical in what Roosevelt did, nor

6. Rexford G. Tugwell, *FDR: Architect of an Era* (New York: Macmillan, 1967), pp. 141–46; Tugwell, *The Brains Trust*, pp. 88–90; Frank Freidel, *F.D.R. and the South* (Baton Rouge: Louisiana State University Press, 1965), pp. 2, 5–6, 8–18.

7. FDR, *Public Papers* (1928–32), 1:81–82, 92–93, 105–6, 116–17, 119–20; Freidel, *Roosevelt: The Triumph*, pp. 36–40; Bernard Bellush, *Franklin D. Roosevelt as Governor of New York* (New York: Columbia University Press, 1955), chap. 4.

did such a program offer much immediate help to New York's hard-pressed farmers.

In the gloomy months after the stock market crash in October 1929, Governor Roosevelt also toyed with an old dream of his—that city workers could be relocated on subsistence farms. Roosevelt, wrote Rexford G. Tugwell, "always did, and always would think people better off in the country and would regard the cities as rather hopeless."[8] The distribution of population was all wrong, Roosevelt believed. The pendulum had swung too far in the direction of the cities, and there must be a readjustment of the "economic and sociological balance" between the city and country. He saw hope in a marriage of agriculture and industry in what he called "rural industrial groups"—a broad program for decentralizing industry and giving families a chance to combine factory employment and rural living.[9]

"Suppose," Roosevelt asked, "one were to offer these [unemployed] men opportunity to go on the land, to provide a house and a few acres in the country and a little money and tools to put in a small food crop?"[10] How many would accept such a proposition? He would find out. In May 1932 the Temporary Emergency Relief Administration, New York's state relief agency, placed 244 families on subsistence farms, paying their rent and providing them with certain necessities. The number of applicants who had to be turned down was extraordinary. For Roosevelt the appeal of such a program stemmed from his interest both in land use planning and in the romantic, Jeffersonian ideal of the independent yeoman.[11]

Roosevelt, not surprisingly, had succumbed to a mild form of back-to-the-landism, one of the incongruities of the early 1930s. With rural America in the grip of drought and depression, many people despaired of the city and began to talk nostalgically of the land. Their imagination shimmered with the idealized dream of American agriculture: a trim,

8. Rexford G. Tugwell, "The Sources of New Deal Reformism," *Ethics* 64 (July 1954): 226. Tugwell, in fact, was drawn into the Brain Trust partly because of the interest he and Roosevelt shared in agriculture. See Tugwell, *The Brains Trust*, pp. 66–72.
9. Franklin D. Roosevelt, "Actualities of Agricultural Planning," in Charles A. Beard, ed., *America Faces the Future* (Cambridge, Mass.: Harvard University Press, 1932), pp. 326–47; Fusfeld, *The Economic Thought of Franklin D. Roosevelt*, pp. 123–34; Thomas H. Greer, *What Roosevelt Thought: The Social and Political Ideas of Franklin D. Roosevelt* (East Lansing: Michigan State University Press, 1958), p. 60.
10. Franklin D. Roosevelt, "Back to the Land," *Review of Reviews* 84 (October 1931): 64; see also FDR, *Public Papers* (1928–32), 1:505.
11. Freidel, *Roosevelt: The Triumph*, p. 226.

cozy cottage surrounded by green fields of plenty, sleek cattle slowly grazing in manicured pastures, and a sturdy farmer overseeing it all with homespun shrewdness.

The mystique of the small family farm stretches far back into American history. Always pushing farther west, the pioneer farmer with his independent and democratic spirit supposedly made this nation great. Proclaiming the simple yeomen to be "God's chosen people," Thomas Jefferson envisioned a vast internal empire of small farms owned by their operators. As the source of the nation's moral strength, agriculture claimed a special right to the protection of government. The Land Act of 1820, the Preemption Act of 1841, the Homestead Act of 1863, and the Federal Farm Loan Act of 1916—all of these were instances of government support of small farm ownership. As soon as large numbers of Americans began moving into towns and cities, they grew sentimental about the supposed innocence of their rural past.

The back-to-the-landers also had ideological roots in utopian colonies like Brook Farm and New Harmony and in colonization schemes which regularly appeared during industrial depressions of the late nineteenth century. The movement never really died out, and it was not strange that it reappeared with new vigor after 1929.

The Great Depression strengthened, if anything, the desire of many people to own their own farm because ownership suddenly seemed more elusive than before. Men like Bernard Baruch, Ralph Borsodi, Herbert Agar, Bernarr Macfadden, and the leaders of the Catholic Rural Life Conference were fascinated with the supposed simplicity and security of traditional farm life. They imagined an idyllic pastoral world where men and women could get away from the ugliness of modern cities and live a more fulfilling life close to the soil. A few people even envisioned a whole new social order. The world of the future, Henry Ford believed, would rest on a grand synthesis of agriculture and industry. He promoted a scheme to decentralize industry where the worker would be a part-time farmer. Yet for most people, particularly the jobless workers who drifted out of the cities, subsistence farming was only a means of temporary relief.[12]

The South itself produced the most eloquent celebration of rural vir-

12. Paul K. Conkin, *Tomorrow a New World: The New Deal Community Program* (Ithaca, N.Y.: Cornell University Press, 1969), chap. 1. See also Russell Lord, "Back to the Farm?" *Forum* 89 (February 1933): 97–103; Pascal K. Whelpton, "The Extent, Character, and Future of the New Landward Movement," *Journal of Farm Economics* (15 January 1933): 57–72.

tues. The former "Fugitive poets" at Vanderbilt University—John Crowe Ransom, Donald Davidson, Allen Tate, and Robert Penn Warren—had experienced a regional self-awakening after the Scopes Monkey Trial, metamorphosing as the Southern Agrarians. Joined by the Arkansas poet John Gould Fletcher and seven other contributors, they published the symposium *I'll Take My Stand* (1930), a revolt against the modern idea of "Progress," especially industrialism, and against the "Cult of Science," which, to them, threatened southern traditions with its philosophies of relativism and centralization.[13] The Southern Agrarians idealized the small farmer, with his qualities of independence, simplicity, and religious faith. Agriculture, Ransom wrote, was "the best and most sensitive of vocations."

If the Agrarians themselves were not ready to pick up a hoe or to plow a "south 40" somewhere, neither were they all sentimentality. They were fully aware of the evils of tenancy and absentee landlordism, and they advocated a redistribution of property and a return to subsistence farming. In essence the Agrarians believed that the best society was one in which the majority of its people owned productive property. The United States, they hoped, could once again become a nation of small proprietors and farmers—in short, return to a small-town, rural society. In the meantime, there might still be time to keep the South from following the nation down the road of centralization, urbanization, and agricultural decay.[14]

As the depression worsened, agrarian spokesmen of all stripes had seemingly won their point. The gods of industrialism and materialism had failed; "back to the land" had never before so engaged the imagination of people. A number of major cities took steps to remove unemployed men and their families to the countryside. Some corporations made garden

13. Twelve Southerners, *I'll Take My Stand: The South and the Agrarian Tradition* (New York: Harper and Brothers, 1930).

14. Edward Shapiro, "The Southern Agrarians and the Tennessee Valley Authority," *American Quarterly* 22 (Winter 1970): 792, 798–99. Frank L. Owsley claimed the Southern Agrarians had played a formative role in the introduction of farm tenancy legislation; H. C. Nixon, Donald Davidson, Lyle H. Lanier, and Owsley personally urged the passage of the Bankhead-Jones farm tenant bills in 1935. See below, Chapter VI; Frank L. Owsley, "The Agrarians Today," *Shenandoah* 3 (Summer 1952): 27; Edward Shapiro, "Decentralist Intellectuals and the New Deal," *Journal of American History* 58 (March 1972): 948–51; Sidney Baldwin, *Poverty and Politics: The Rise and Decline of the Farm Security Administration* (Chapel Hill: University of North Carolina Press, 1969), pp. 147–48. See also Frank L. Owsley, "The Pillars of Agrarianism," *American Review* 4 (March 1935): 537; Herman Clarence Nixon, *Forty Acres and Steel Mules* (Chapel Hill: University of North Carolina Press, 1936); and John Gould Fletcher, *Arkansas* (Chapel Hill: University of North Carolina Press, 1947), chap. 20.

space available to their employees. Home garden campaigns and "live at home" appeals were popular everywhere, even in rural areas. There were also the inevitable crackpot schemes, some comic and pathetic. "Buy an abandoned farm," one realtor advertised in the *Wall Street Journal*, "and live on trout and applejack until the upturn." Tragically deceived, some people poured their savings into a few worthless acres.[15]

How extensive the back-to-the-land movement was in the early depression can only be estimated. Both the jobless and the dreamers did far more talking than acting. For a brief time in 1932 the tide of migration from the farm to the city did reverse itself, giving the country a net gain of 360,000 people. In the Appalachian and Ozark regions a substantial number of people switched to farming from some other employment, but they were people who were never far from farm work anyway. The southern Cotton Belt saw large numbers of tenant farmers and sharecroppers going the other way, seeking work or relief checks in nearby cities and towns.[16]

As 4 March 1933 approached, the economic machinery of the nation seemed to grind to a halt. The bottom of the depression, after more than three years, had been reached. While the banking crisis loomed as the first challenge of the New Deal, the problem of farm relief weighed heavily on Roosevelt's mind during the Hundred Days.

The president and many of his advisers believed that the farm program would make or break the New Deal. There could be no permanent prosperity as long as the nation's farm people had lost their buying power. "One of the first things I am going to do is to take steps to restore farm prices," he promised Ed O'Neal of the American Farm Bureau Federation. "I am going to call farmers' leaders together, lock them in a room, and tell them not to come out until they have agreed on a plan."[17]

For the preceding decade agriculturists had debated various proposals

15. Lord, "Back to the Farm?" p. 98. In Baton Rouge, Louisiana, the Kiwanis Club and the Chamber of Commerce initiated back-to-the-land projects. See Sidney Tobin, "The Early New Deal in Baton Rouge as Viewed by the Daily Press," *Louisiana History* 10 (Fall 1969): 311–12.

16. Edmond deS. Brunner and Irving Lorge, *Rural Trends in Depression Years* (New York: Columbia University Press, 1937), p. 81. See also Horace G. Porter, "New Farms in the Mississippi Delta," *Louisiana Rural Economist* 2 (April 1940): 5–7.

17. Clifford V. Gregory, "The American Farm Bureau Federation and the AAA," *Annals of the American Academy of Political and Social Science* 179 (May 1935): 152; Anne O'Hare McCormick, "Roosevelt's View of the Big Job," *New York Times Magazine*, 11 September 1932, pp. 1, 2, 16.

for dealing with the high surpluses and low prices of cotton and other staples. Many of them advocated "dumping" surpluses on world markets at below cost, with the government making up the difference and guaranteeing the farmer a profit. Other experts wanted to put the burden on food processors, forcing them to pay farmers higher prices and letting the processors pass the price on to the consumer. Roosevelt's Brain Trust favored the "domestic allotment" plan, a crop control scheme which would limit farmers growing cotton, wheat, and corn to the total amount of these staples consumed in the United States during normal years. Domestic allotment aimed at the crucial problem of adjusting production with demand. The Agricultural Adjustment Act of 1933 was broad enough to embody all three of these plans, but it was the domestic allotment device which became the core of the New Deal's agricultural recovery program.[18]

In the Cotton Belt the new Agricultural Adjustment Administration (AAA) confronted a task which went against every farmer's instincts— the destruction of part of a standing crop. By the summer of 1933 the carry-over from previous years was 12.5 million bales, enough cotton to glut the market even if not a single boll were picked that fall. Roosevelt had warned Congress of the need to act before spring planting, but he lost the "race with the sun." Since farmers had already planted 40 million acres in cotton when the bill became law on 12 May, the AAA paid them to plow up about a fourth of the entire crop. The next year the government restricted production in a less heroic fashion. Every farmer signed a contract with the AAA agreeing to plant only an allotted acreage, in return for "benefit payments" which compensated for the land left idle. The AAA's goal was to insure farmers parity prices, or, in other words, the same level of purchasing power they had in the prosperous pre–World War years. In the broadest sense, parity prices were intended to equalize farm and industrial income. With production under control, it was hoped farm surpluses would gradually decline and prices stabilize.[19]

While the destruction of plenty amid want contained a cruel irony, the

---

18. Van L. Perkins, *Crisis in Agriculture: The Agricultural Adjustment Administration and the New Deal, 1933* (Berkeley and Los Angeles: University of California Press, 1969), chap. 3; Gilbert C. Fite, *George N. Peek and the Fight for Farm Parity* (Norman: University of Oklahoma Press, 1954); Russell Lord, *The Wallaces of Iowa* (Boston: Houghton Mifflin, 1947); Arthur M. Schlesinger, Jr., *The Age of Roosevelt: The Coming of the New Deal* (Boston: Houghton Mifflin, 1959), pp. 36–42; Tugwell, *The Democratic Roosevelt*, pp. 275–77.

19. 48 *US Stat.* 31; Perkins, *Crisis in Agriculture*, pp. 103–9; Slichter, "FDR and the Farm Problem," pp. 247–49.

New Deal's agricultural adjustment program did help in raising farm prices. Within six months cotton reached ten cents on the New Orleans Cotton Exchange, and better prices helped all farmers, large and small. Yet the crop reduction program ultimately hurt more than it helped the South's impoverished sharecroppers and tenants.

The Emergency Relief Act of 1933 reached the president's desk on the same day that he approved the agricultural adjustment bill. Roosevelt promptly appointed Harry L. Hopkins, his director of relief in New York, as the head of the new Federal Emergency Relief Administration (FERA). At first Hopkins's organization made grants of money to needy farm families just as it did to city unemployed. By summer more than a million farm families were drawing government relief checks. Yet direct relief, Hopkins knew, was never going to solve the problems of the poverty-stricken farmer. He wanted to shift emphasis from immediate relief to long-term rehabilitation, and he was not afraid of a little experimentation.[20]

In April 1934 Hopkins combined all FERA rural relief programs, as well as those of the Civil Works Administration, into the Division of Rural Rehabilitation and Stranded Populations, and turned the new unit over to Col. Lawrence Westbrook. Here was the beginning of a national program for coping with rural poverty. Westbrook's division loaned families money rather than giving them a dole, and it financed the purchase of tools, seed, and livestock, which they needed to earn a living. The basis of "rural rehabilitation" was a program of supervised credit in which each family was required to stick with a farm and home budget. The objective of the program was to take farm families off relief rolls, put them back on farms full-time, and help them become self-supporting. In addition, the FERA cooperated with the Land Policy Section of the Agricultural Adjustment Administration in a program to reform the land itself. The FERA's Land Program Section began buying up submarginal land, which it planned to convert to such nonagricultural uses as forest or recreation.[21]

The Federal Emergency Relief Administration undertook still another

20. Robert E. Sherwood, *Roosevelt and Hopkins* (New York: Harper and Brothers, 1948), chaps. 2, 3; Searle F. Charles, *Minister of Relief: Harry Hopkins and the Depression* (Syracuse, N.Y.: Syracuse University Press, 1963), pp. 5, 19–22; Schlesinger, *The Coming of the New Deal*, pp. 264–65, 266–68, 280; Baldwin, *Poverty and Politics*, p. 60.

21. FDR, *Public Papers* (1934), 3:108–11; Lawrence Westbrook, "The Program of the Rural Rehabilitation Division of the FERA," *Journal of Farm Economics* 17 (February 1935): 89–91.

innovation in governmental policy. An engineer, politician, and dedicated communitarian, Westbrook extended the rural rehabilitation concept to include a series of community projects which would help families on poor land acquire productive farms. While serving as director of state relief in Texas, he had taken a hundred families who were on relief and re-settled them in the Woodlake cooperative project near Houston, and he got his chance to test his community-building ideas on a national basis when Hopkins asked him to come to Washington. The FERA community program, however, never had time to get off the ground; Westbrook finished only two communities, out of about twenty-five he had planned, before the Resettlement Administration absorbed the program in 1935. One of his communities in particular caught Roosevelt's fancy: the Pine Mountain Valley project near the farm he owned in Georgia.[22]

"I really would like to get one more bill which would allow us to spend $25 million this year to put 25,000 families on farms, at an average cost of $1,000 per family. It can be done," the president wrote Sen. George Norris of Nebraska during the Hundred Days. "Also we would get most of the money back in due time. Will you talk this over with some of our fellow dreamers on the Hill?"[23]

As soon as Congress had convened on 9 March, Sen. John H. Bank-head of Alabama introduced a bill to establish a national subsistence homesteads program. Roosevelt kept his eye on its progress and tried to stir support, but even the rubber-stamp Congress of the early New Deal could be balky. When the second of two such bills died in committee, Bankhead, with the president's support, attached a subsistence home-steads section to the National Industrial Recovery Act. With virtually no debate, Roosevelt and Bankhead got what they wanted—an appropria-tion of $25 million for "aiding in the redistribution of the overbalance of population in industrial centers."[24]

Roosevelt turned the program over to Secretary of the Interior Harold L. Ickes, who set up a Division of Subsistence Homesteads within his de-partment in August 1933, and appointed Milburn L. Wilson as director.

22. Conkin, *Tomorrow a New World*, pp. 132–36; see his "It All Happened in Pine Mountain Valley," *Georgia Historical Quarterly* 47 (March 1963): 1–42.

23. Roosevelt to George Norris, 17 April 1933, FDR Papers, OF 292, quoted in Baldwin, *Poverty and Politics*, p. 70. Roosevelt's inaugural address contained a brief reference to "the over-balance of population in our industrial centers." FDR, *Public Papers* (1933), 2:13.

24. 48 *US Stat.* 195, Title 2, sec. 208; Conkin, *Tomorrow a New World*, pp. 86–89. See John H. Bankhead, "The One Way to Permanent Recovery," *Liberty Maga-zine* 10 (22 July 1933): 18.

Wilson seemingly had the academic background and practical farming experience needed to make Subsistence Homesteads a success. In the 1920s he had helped to develop Fairway Farms, an experimental farming project in his native Montana. It was another of those undertakings which anticipated the New Deal's rehabilitation and resettlement programs. Wilson had visited Hyde Park after the 1932 election to urge the adoption of the domestic allotment plan; when he broached the subject of subsistence homesteads, he found the president-elect a receptive listener. Wilson's thinking, as Paul K. Conkin has remarked, always began with crop allotments and ended with subsistence homesteads. He envisioned subsistence farming as a program for middle-class people, "not the top, not the dregs," who felt themselves to be "outcasts of the jazz-industrial age." These colonies would give such people a more secure and satisfying life.[25]

As Wilson organized his agency, suggestions began pouring in from everywhere. There were proposals for eugenics experiments, teaching modern dancing, clothing homesteaders in Greek robes, and reviving medieval craft guilds. He had some clearheaded advice, too, but not enough. Since he possessed broad authority, he built a variety of projects, ranging all the way from communities for stranded miners and homestead projects for industrial workers to full-time farm colonies.[26] The industrial homestead projects, which outnumbered all of the others, usually consisted of a cluster of twenty-five to a hundred homes located near the outskirts of a city or small town; each family raised much of their own food on a five- or ten-acre plot of land, while earning their cash income in nearby factories or in industries established within the new community itself. The most famous of the New Deal subsistence homesteads was the Arthurdale project for stranded coal miners at Reedsville, West Virginia. Eleanor Roosevelt, a back-to-the-land buff just like her husband, made it her personal pet and even invested thousands of dollars of her own money. Arthurdale, alas, proved to be a bureaucratic nightmare and an expensive failure.[27]

25. Conkin, *Tomorrow a New World*, pp. 76–77, 81–82; M. L. Wilson, "The Place of Subsistence Homesteads in Our National Economy," *Journal of Farm Economics* 16 (January 1934): 73–83. The quote is from Lord, *Wallaces of Iowa*, pp. 420–21.

26. Conkin, *Tomorrow a New World*, pp. 99–100, 103–4.

27. Millard Milburn Rice, "Footnote on Arthurdale," *Harper's Magazine* 180 (March 1940): 411–19; Joseph P. Lash, *Eleanor and Franklin: The Story of Their Relationship Based on Eleanor Roosevelt's Private Papers* (New York: Norton, 1971), chap. 37.

It was not long before the impact of these federal programs was felt at the state and local levels. If federal money was available, everybody wanted his share of it. But there were wide variations in the operation of federal agencies.

Only Arkansas, for example, among the states of the Lower Mississippi Valley, had any FERA community program. W. R. Dyess, state Emergency Relief administrator, conceived the idea of building an agricultural colony as a means of getting relief clients "back to the soil." In May 1934 he used federal funds to buy a large tract of cutover timberland and swamp near Wilson in Mississippi County and began dividing it into farm units of twenty to forty acres each. There, on the Tyronza River, Dyess built a new town complete with post office, cafe, stores, schools, hospital, and cotton gin—at its peak a bustling community of some 3,000 people.[28]

While Dyess Colony, as it was named after its founder's death, was to have been one of a series of FERA communities in Arkansas, no other project had gone beyond the planning stage by 1935. In Mississippi and Louisiana, where no communities were even planned, rural rehabilitation consisted largely of loans to families who had their own land and of submarginal land purchase projects.[29]

The Division of Subsistence Homesteads also left a spotty record in the Lower Mississippi Valley. The subsistence homesteads program in Louisiana never got off the ground. Morehouse Homesteads near Bastrop was the only Louisiana project ever to receive approval, although Bossier City was considered as a possible site.[30]

By contrast, the Arkansas program was more ambitious and seemed to have a promising future. Glenn E. Riddell, secretary of the Arkansas State Housing Board, worked closely with Bruce Melvin of the Division of Subsistence Homesteads to locate homesteads in the state. "In general," Melvin wrote Riddell in 1933, "we are trying to establish projects near

28. Arkansas Emergency Relief Administration, *Traveling Recovery Road: The Story of Relief, Work-Relief, and Rehabilitation in Arkansas, August 30, 1932, to November 15, 1936* (Little Rock: Floyd Sharp and Associates, 1936), pp. 153–57; Conkin, *Tomorrow a New World*, pp. 137–38.

29. Resettlement Administration, Arkansas Rural Rehabilitation Division, Annual Report 1936, 30 December 1936, FSA Records, NA, RG 96; Resettlement Administration, Yearly Report of the Custodian of Corporations Division (December 1936), ibid.; USHR, *FSA Hearings*, pp. 1038–49, 1071–75.

30. Resettlement Administration, *First Annual Report* (Washington: Government Printing Office, 1936), p. 144; Rep. Riley J. Wilson to Carl C. Taylor, 18 July 1935; Wilson to C. B. Baldwin, 14 October 1935; G. W. Hiatt to Rep. Newt V. Mills, 18 February 1941, all in FSA Records, NA, RG 96; Wilson to Marvin H. McIntyre, 13 August 1935, FDR Papers, OF 1568.

industrial centers where people may receive part-time employment."[31] While touring Arkansas in February 1934, Melvin showed interest in the homestead possibilities of Fort Smith, West Helena, Camden, Huttig, Warren, and Pine Bluff. In March national officials approved plans for Fort Smith, West Helena, and Camden. The Division of Subsistence Homesteads allotted $317,000 for one Louisiana project and three in Arkansas, but spent only $108 on them before transferring all four to the Resettlement Administration.[32]

Mississippi was the only state in the region where the subsistence homesteads program paid off. In December 1933 the division launched industrial projects near McComb, Laurel, Tupelo, and Meridian, plus a full-time farming project near Richton; in January 1934 Hattiesburg, too, received approval for an industrial project.[33] Construction, however, proceeded slowly as the Division of Subsistence Homesteads ran out of time. After the Resettlement Administration took over its program in 1935, Tugwell completed only Tupelo, Meridian, McComb, Hattiesburg, and Richton.[34]

Such projects were frankly experimental. Never before had the federal government undertaken a program to rehabilitate poor farm families, resettle people in rural communities, or locate city workers on subsistence plots. The Great Depression created a hospitable attitude toward experimentation, and New Dealers sought to take advantage of it. These communities, of course, offered little for the great masses of chronically poor, and this fact did not go unnoticed. But a start had been made. Only time could tell the outcome.

31. Bruce L. Melvin to Glenn E. Riddell, 17 November 1933, FSA Records, NA, RG 96.

32. Little Rock *Arkansas Gazette*, 26 February 1934; Little Rock *Arkansas Democrat*, 22 February 1934; Glenn E. Riddell to Bruce L. Melvin, 1 March 1934 (two letters), 7 March 1934, 9 April 1934; U.S. Department of the Interior, Division of Subsistence Homesteads, Monthly Project Report, 26 April 1935, all in FSA Records, NA, RG 96; Resettlement Administration, *First Annual Report*, p. 144. The abandonment of the Arkansas subsistence homesteads was reported in *Arkansas Gazette*, 7 January 1936.

33. Report of the Division of Subsistence Homesteads and Federal Subsistence Homesteads Corporation, June 1934, FSA Records, NA, RG 96.

34. "The Resettlement Administration and Its Work," 10 September 1935, FDR Papers, OF 1568; Thomas H. Hibben, memorandum to R. G. Tugwell, 29 June 1935; Tugwell, memorandum to John S. Lansill, 10 July 1935; Tugwell, memorandum to Harry L. Hopkins, 18 July 1935, all in FSA Records, NA, RG 96; Conkin, *Tomorrow a New World*, p. 111.

Chapter III

The Founding of Dyess Colony

Soon after dark on 14 January 1936, the *Southerner*, a twin-engine American Airlines DC–2, took off at Memphis, Tennessee, for Little Rock. John T. Shea, a passenger who had just left the aircraft, noticed that one of the *Southerner*'s engines did not "sound right." Flying at 3,000 feet twenty-five miles west of Memphis, the pilot, Jerry Marshall, reported scattered clouds and a fifty-five-degree temperature. That was the last radio contact with the *Southerner*, as static interfered with further efforts at communication.

Beyond Forrest City, the night fog already hung over eastern Arkansas's swamps. Two farmers near Goodwin saw the plane flying low over the woods, with an engine popping and missing. Helplessly, they watched it disappear into the trees and fog, heard a terrific crash, and then silence. George Jones, another farmer, walked to a nearby store and reported that he had heard a deafening roar to the northeast. The *Southerner* crashed of unknown causes in four or five feet of swamp water two miles from the Little Rock–Memphis highway, killing all seventeen persons aboard. At the time, it was the worst tragedy in American aviation history. Among the dead was William Reynolds Dyess.[1]

Distinguished, handsome, a trim six-footer, and, at forty-two years of age, prematurely gray, W. R. Dyess had come far in just a few years. Born near Hazelhurst, Mississippi, he finished Mississippi A & M College (later Mississippi State) and embarked on a brief military career. While a member of the regular army, he served as orderly to Gen. John J. Pershing in the Philippines. When America entered the World War, he was a cavalry captain and instructor at a small military school in Georgia. After the war he returned to Mississippi and followed in his father's footsteps

---

1. Little Rock *Arkansas Gazette*, 15–18 January 1936. Also dead in the crash was Robert H. McNair, Jr., Dyess's director of finance and reports.

as a planter and contractor specializing in levees, railroad beds, and gravel roads. He first came to Arkansas in 1926 with a contract to improve the levees on the Mississippi and White rivers. In 1930 he bought two large tracts of land in Mississippi County, in northeastern Arkansas, and made Osceola his home. Within three years his career as a public servant opened up. Dyess became president of the local farmers' organization, the Mississippi County Agricultural Committee; he was a member of the county committee on local relief; and more important for someone with an interest in politics, he was named chairman of the Mississippi County Board of Election Commissioners. Bill Dyess, "contractor, mule dealer and dreamer," as Jonathan Daniels later called him, had obviously gotten himself in with the right crowd.[2]

While Dyess was serving as liquidator of the Bank of Osceola, the national relief administrator, Harry L. Hopkins, appointed him head of the new Arkansas relief organization. Gov. J. Marion Futrell had strongly backed him for the job,[3] perhaps as a political pay-off for his support during the 1932 gubernatorial campaign. Although he had no social-work experience of any kind, Dyess made a favorable impression on Aubrey Williams, Hopkins's right-hand man. "Dyess is a young chap of thirty-eight," Williams wrote Hopkins in August 1933, "a big planter, college man, and does not have any employment . . . which I figure should make for [financial] independence."[4] That winter Dyess headed the temporary Civil Works Administration in the state. At the time of his death he was state director of the Works Progress Administration.[5]

Floyd Sharp, Dyess's successor, played a major role in the history of Arkansas relief in his own right. At thirty-seven years of age, Sharp had the difficult job of following a popular leader, and he handled it with great success, remaining director of Arkansas relief until the liquidation of the WPA during World War II.

A native of Knoxville, Tennessee, Sharp was ten when his family moved to Hot Springs, Arkansas. Over the next few years he served an

2. For brief biographies of Dyess, see *Arkansas Gazette*, 15, 16 January 1936; *Osceola Times*, 17 January 1936; Little Rock *Arkansas Democrat*, 15 January 1936, reprinted 12 July 1972. Jonathan Daniels, *A Southerner Discovers the South* (New York: Da Capo Press, 1970), p. 143.

3. J. M. Futrell to Harry L. Hopkins, 20 June 1933, FERA Records, NA, RG 69; Aubrey Williams to Hopkins, 9 August 1933, ibid.

4. Aubrey Williams to Harry [L. Hopkins], 6 August 1933, ibid. See also Williams to Hopkins, 9 August, 13 September, 13 October 1933, ibid.

5. J. M. Futrell to Harry L. Hopkins, 23 September 1933, ibid.; *Arkansas Gazette*, 15 January 1936. Dyess was one of only six state relief administrators to last through the successive stages of FERA, CWA, and WPA.

apprenticeship as a printer and worked in the composing room of the *Arkansas Gazette*, beginning a life-long association with the Little Rock Typographical Union. When the United States entered World War I, Sharp volunteered and rose to the rank of sergeant in the American Expeditionary Force. After the war he went back to his trade, winding up again in the *Gazette*'s composing room. Not content, however, he soon expanded his horizons. In quick succession he graduated from the University of Arkansas Law School, joined the Little Rock law firm of Poe and Poe, and then set out on his own. After a brief period of ill health, he took a job as attorney and statistician for the Arkansas Department of Labor, and when the depression hit, the department and Sharp found themselves deeply involved with the task of relief. His first contact with federal relief work was in the pre–New Deal State Emergency Relief Commission, which obtained its funds from the Reconstruction Finance Corporation. As Dyess's director of operations and executive secretary, he was the number-two man in the Arkansas relief organization.[6]

After his appointment, Dyess wasted no time in setting up a state relief organization. While subject to constant changes, the Arkansas Emergency Relief Administration initially included seven divisions: works, rural rehabilitation, auditing, commodities, research and statistics, transients, and education. Dyess's job was to channel federal relief funds into the hands of needy Arkansans. The Emergency Relief Administration and its successor agencies stressed work relief in preference to the "dole." In other words, Arkansas relief workers built such projects as roads, streets, airports, water plants, schools, sewers, hospitals, public buildings, recreational facilities, canning plants, utility systems, libraries, levees, and electric power plants.[7]

6. Field Men, State Emergency Relief Commission, Arkansas, n.d., ibid.; Fay Williams, *Arkansas of the Years*, 4 vols. (Little Rock: C. C. Allard, 1951–54), 2:368–83; WPA, Personal History Statements [Floyd Sharp], dated 31 January 1939, WPA Records, NA, RG 69; *Arkansas Gazette*, 18 January 1936, 20 December 1969.

7. See Arkansas Emergency Relief Administration, *A Review of Work Relief Activities in Arkansas, April 1st, 1934, to July 1st, 1935* (Little Rock: Parke-Harper, 1935); idem, *Traveling Recovery Road: The Story of Relief, Work-Relief, and Rehabilitation in Arkansas, August 30, 1932, to November 15, 1936* (Little Rock: Floyd Sharp and Associates, 1936).

See Sharp's speech favoring work relief over direct relief, arguing that the former preserved human values and skills and that work projects contributed more to local communities. Yet direct relief had its place, he conceded. Sharp, "Work Relief or Direct Relief," a speech delivered before the Arkansas Conference of

Since Arkansas was an agricultural state, one of Dyess's most important tasks was rural rehabilitation. Following the lead of other FERA state directors, Dyess set up a state rural rehabilitation corporation. Incorporated under Delaware law, the Arkansas Rural Rehabilitation Corporation was a device to facilitate the legal and financial aspects of the program. Using federal funds, the Arkansas corporation loaned money to relief clients, purchased land for rehabilitation purposes, and established a revolving trust fund to insure the corporation's existence even after the FERA was abolished.[8]

The Rural Rehabilitation Division itself supervised rural relief activities in the field. In late 1933 Dyess had recruited a professional agriculturist, E. B. Whitaker, from the Arkansas Extension Service. During the next eighteen months, Whitaker developed the same kind of rural rehabilitation program that he would later operate in the Resettlement Administration and Farm Security Administration.

In 1934, according to FERA estimates, over thirty thousand farm families in Arkansas were eligible for rural rehabilitation assistance. They included a wide variety of groups: landowners who had lost all equity in their farms, former landowners and share tenants who were unable to get credit to make a crop, sharecroppers who had been displaced from the land, and even mill workers and coal miners who had rural backgrounds and wanted to get back to the farm. The ultimate aim of the rural rehabilitation program was to help destitute families become self-supporting on small farms. Whitaker assisted some clients where they were, if the land they owned or rented was good enough. In the case of families stranded in submarginal areas, he resettled them on better land. The rehabilitation division repaired the homesteads or erected low-cost houses, mapped out a farm and home management plan for each rehabilitation client, and loaned him the necessary capital for equipment, workstock, and subsistence.[9]

Social Workers, April 1937, enclosed with D. Palmer Patterson to Aubrey Williams, 4 May 1937, WPA Records, NA, RG 69.

8. Certificate of Incorporation of the Arkansas Rural Rehabilitation Corporation, dated 30 May 1934, Secretary of State's Office, Dover, Delaware; M. J. Miller to Aubrey Williams, 10 November 1934, FERA Records, NA, RG 69; Audit Report on Arkansas Rural Rehabilitation Corporation, 28 May 1934 to 30 June 1935, ibid.; Miller, memorandum to Williams, 1 October 1934, FSA Records, NA, RG 96; see *Blytheville Courier News,* 16 October 1934; *Osceola Times,* 25 May 1934.

9. Plan of Work for Rural Rehabilitation in Arkansas, 1935, mimeographed, FERA Records, NA, RG 69.

A planter and humanitarian, Dyess was especially interested in rural relief. As the depression wore on, he apparently reacted as did many other Americans: people, the saying went, had to get "back to the land." Dyess wanted to develop a farm colony, a complete community, for relief clients.

> He conceived the idea of building an agricultural community [wrote one of Dyess's colleagues, Henry C. Baker]. A colony of five hundred homes— homes which were to be modern, liveable homes with electricity, running water, private sewage systems and other advantages usually associated only with urban communities, and which would raise the standard for farm homes to a high level. He conceived in his plan a hospital, schools, churches, in fact a new order of things for those who through no fault of their own found it impossible to make their way.[10]

It was hardly an original idea, either in American agricultural history or in the early New Deal. The depression, as previously noted, renewed the current of agrarian idealism which ran deep in American history. The Division of Subsistence Homesteads launched its own program for colonizing part-time industrial workers. In the FERA itself Lawrence Westbrook was laying plans for a series of rural projects similar to the one Dyess envisioned.

What made Dyess successful was that he had the good fortune to sell his idea to federal authorities. Dyess, too, was peculiarly suited for the job of overseeing such an enterprise. From both his military and civilian backgrounds, he knew how to handle men, mules, and construction equipment. He could also call on knowledgeable advisers like E. B. Whitaker, who looked after the agricultural end of the project.

In early 1934 Dyess personally submitted his plan to Harry Hopkins. According to Baker, "Mr. Hopkins listened attentively." More likely it was Westbrook who did the listening and urged Hopkins's approval. At any rate, the federal relief administrator did agree to Dyess's plans and released funds for the project. That was the beginning of Dyess Colony.[11]

Dyess had already picked out a location for his colony, ten miles from

10. Henry C. Baker, "Dyess Colony," in *Traveling Recovery Road*, p. 153. For descriptions of Dyess Colony, see M. C. Blackman, "Uncle Sam Waves a Wand," *Arkansas Gazette Sunday Magazine*, 22 September 1935, pp. 1, 3; Joanna C. Colcord, "Tenant into Owner: The Dyess Colony Experiment," *Survey Graphic* 26 (August 1937): 418–20; Elizabeth C. Wherry, "A Chance for the Sharecropper: Farm Colony at Dyess, Ark., Provides a New Start for Farmers Beaten by Depression," *Wallace's Farmer and Iowa Homestead* 63 (7 May 1938): 5, 16; Dan W. Pittman, "The Founding of Dyess Colony," *Arkansas Historical Quarterly* 29 (Winter 1970): 313–26.
11. Baker, "Dyess Colony," in *Traveling Recovery Road*, p. 153.

Wilson and about twenty miles from Osceola, his home town. Originally he had hoped to acquire about twenty thousand acres in separate but adjacent tracts from the Creamery Package Company, Drainage District Number 9, and Lee Wilson Company; but he was only partially success-ful.[12] In early 1934 the Arkansas Rural Rehabilitation Corporation purchased a tract of 15,144 acres of unimproved timberland and swamp, with the Tyronza River cutting through it from northeast to southwest. A lumber company had previously owned part of the land, cut the best timber, and, when the depression hit, forfeited its holdings for taxes. By any standard, Dyess made an exceptionally good bargain, but not quite as good as first reported. Newspaper accounts said only that Dyess had bought about twenty thousand acres at $2.50 per acre, without specifying the total amount paid or the total acreage. The payment of state taxes, redemptions, and purchase of state title ran up the cost somewhat. Yet an indelible impression had been created that the entire tract had been purchased for $2.50 an acre, and many colonists later reacted violently after learning they would have to pay more. When Russell Brown and Company, Certified Public Accountants, of Little Rock, audited the colony's books in 1936, they showed the total cost of the land to have been $136,994.48, making the average cost per acre $9.05.[13]

The selection of this particular land, wrote Baker, was a demonstration of "rare judgment." He doubted that "anywhere in America could land of greater potential possibilities have been chosen."[14] Until about 1900 the northeastern Arkansas delta was largely swampland and dense, almost tropical, forest. By 1920 army engineers had built levees and drained the swamps, while lumbermen had removed most of the virgin timber: white, black, and red oak, ash, elm, maple, gum of several varieties, cottonwood, and cypress. What they revealed was a fabulously rich agricultural region. The Mississippi River had spent centuries building up the alluvial soil, a black loam running from forty to several hundred feet deep. The use of fertilizer was superfluous. The climate, too, was perfect for agriculture, with a growing season of seven and a half months free from frost. After large planters moved in, Mississippi County gained

12. Blytheville *Courier News*, 19 May 1934.
13. Ibid.; *Osceola Times*, 25 May 1934; Baker, "Dyess Colony," in *Traveling Recovery Road*, pp. 153, 154; *A Review of Work Relief*, p. 130; Dyess Farms, Arkansas: The First Experiment with a New Kind of Rural Community, dated 7 May 1941; Audit Report, Dyess Colony, Inc., Dyess, Arkansas, 29 February 1936, both in FSA Records, NA, RG 96. The land lay in townships 11 and 12 north, range 8 and 9 east.
14. Baker, "Dyess Colony," in *Traveling Recovery Road*, p. 153.

a reputation for growing more cotton than any other county in the nation. In 1930 cotton was not only the dominant crop; it was virtually the only crop. Ninety percent of the farmers of the county depended almost solely on cotton for their income. But nine out of ten farmers were either tenants or sharecroppers.[15]

In May 1934 Dyess formally launched "Colonization Project No. 1," the colony's original designation. Construction crews had to hack the colony out of a veritable jungle. After the virgin timber had been removed, Baker recalled, "dense impenetrable underbrush had taken its place. Trees left at the time of the original cutting had grown to enormous size, and the whole area was almost in a wilderness."[16]

O. G. Norment was in charge of the first crew that invaded this wilderness. With a truck, tractor, and other equipment, he and his men entered the project through a winding trail that reminded him of an Indian path. "I shall never forget what a seeming[ly] unsurmountable [sic] task we had before us the first morning I arrived," he wrote later. "Practically the entire acreage consisted of cut-over hardwood timber land . . . there were a few cleared spots where old logging camps had been established, most of these grown up, however, into a mass of bushes and small saplings."[17] A few squatters lived in small log or box shacks on small patches of cleared land. Otherwise, the colony land was uninhabited, inhospitable, and forbidding.

Cone Murphy, a slender, baldish man who held the title of executive administrator, was the overall construction supervisor. After gathering an army of logging mules, wagons, and other logging equipment at the northeast corner of the project, he put several hundred unskilled men to work felling trees, while a crew of skilled laborers set up two or three sawmills. To hold costs down, Dyess's plan called for using lumber cut and sawed on the colony's own land for as much construction as possible. In a few weeks Murphy had seven sawmills in operation, one a large steam-powered mill, the others gasoline-powered. Two of the latter were portable mills. The combined daily capacity of all seven mills was about sixty-five thousand board feet of lumber.[18]

15. *A Review of Work Relief*, pp. 120–22; Dyess Farms, Arkansas: The First Experiment with a New Kind of Rural Community, FSA Records, NA, RG 96; Mabel F. Edrington, *History of Mississippi County, Arkansas* (Ocala, Fla.: Ocala Star-Banner, 1962), pp. 75–87, 91, 92, 378, 382.

16. Baker, "Dyess Colony," in *Traveling Recovery Road*, p. 154.

17. O. G. Norment, "Colonization Project No. 1," enclosed with Norment to R. G. Tugwell, 15 January 1936, FSA Records, NA, RG 96.

18. Ibid.; Report of Roland R. Pyne, Regional Engineer, Period Ending 10 November 1934, Hopkins Papers; *A Review of Work Relief*, p. 132.

By 15 June Murphy's men had completed the first structures on the project, a temporary headquarters with administrative building, barracks, kitchen, and mess halls. The barracks consisted of four screened and electrically lighted bunkhouses with accommodations for about four hundred men. Before their living quarters were finished, workmen came from Osceola by truck every day; afterward, almost the entire labor force lived a kind of camp life on the project itself. Each man slept on an iron cot, cotton mattress, and feather pillow, with clean sheets and blankets for cover. The kitchen served three mess halls, two for white workers and one for black workers. The workmen were housed and fed for about seventy-five cents a day, which was deducted from their wages. By midsummer the temporary headquarters consisted of more bunkhouses, barns, stables, blacksmith shop, supply depot, general office building, payroll building, first-aid building, dynamite building (more than a mile away), two shower bathhouses, and various storehouses.[19]

From July to September 1934 Murphy consistently had fourteen hundred workers under his supervision.[20] Most of them came from relief rolls. Dyess obtained common labor through the Mississippi County office of the National Reemployment Service and skilled labor from the agency's state office. Using the National Recovery Administration's wage scale for timber and mill workers, he paid skilled labor three to five dollars a day and unskilled labor $1.60, both roughly the prevailing rates for northeast Arkansas.[21] Dyess's wage scale, however, involved the colony in its first controversy.

When Blytheville labor union leaders protested the colony's labor practices in early July, federal officials conducted an investigation. As a result, they recommended a higher wage scale for all workers. On 7 July the National Reemployment Service ordered Dyess to begin paying common labor thirty cents an hour and skilled carpenters from seventy-five cents to a dollar an hour, while shortening the workweek from forty-eight to thirty-six hours. Dyess argued that this change would interfere with his desire to keep the investment as low as possible for families who would occupy the farm units.[22]

19. Norment, "Colonization Project No. 1," FSA Records, NA, RG 96; *A Review of Work Relief*, pp. 132, 136; *Osceola Times*, 22 June 1934; *Arkansas Gazette*, 17 June 1934.

20. Report of Roland R. Pyne, Regional Engineer, Period Ending 10 November 1934, Hopkins Papers; Norment, "Colonization Project No. 1," FSA Records, NA, RG 96; *A Review of Work Relief*, p. 138.

21. John H. Caufield to Lawrence Westbrook, 7 July 1934, FSA Records, NA, RG 96.

22. *A Review of Work Relief*, pp. 122, 132, 136. This investigation was part of

The higher wage scale both increased expenses and momentarily slowed up construction, with unexpected results. Since the men could work only six hours a day, they now had lots of leisure time on their hands. After several fights broke out at the colony, officials organized boxing matches in order to let the men work off excess energy and to accommodate those wanting to fight somebody. Boxing became a regular Saturday afternoon diversion and almost the only available form of recreation. Soon colony officials furnished material for building two boxing rings, and matches were held at night as well.

Since the colony was mostly wilderness, one of Murphy's earliest tasks was to build roads and bridges and dig drainage ditches. As soon as the sawmills began buzzing, three draglines, two Caterpillar tractors, and a pile driver went to work building new roads and repairing old county roads. Radiating out in all directions from the temporary headquarters, road crews cleared rights-of-way, graded roads, and spread gravel. When completed, the colony's road system followed the section, half-section, and sometimes quarter-section lines, forming a grill-like pattern. In all, Murphy completed about thirty-five miles of gravel roads, built twenty-four main bridges and numerous small bridges, and dug some ninety miles of drainage ditches. What made the task of road building easier was the fact that no one lived on the land the roads were traversing. The road builders, wrote O. G. Norment with obvious satisfaction, did not have "to consider what this property owner or that influential citizen had to say about it, or institute a condemnation proceeding or experience any useless delay."

Like any small town, the project also needed a railroad. The Saint Louis and San Francisco Railroad agreed to run a train to the colony, provided the colony would construct about five miles of track from the spur southeast of Wilson, Arkansas. The colony sawmills provided 24,600 oak crossties for this five miles, several sets of switch ties, and additional crossties for half a mile of switch track that served the warehouse and cotton gin. On 15 November the Frisco Railroad began running one train to the colony and back to Wilson each day.[23]

With preliminary construction out of the way, Murphy began building the farmsteads on 13 July. On the first houses he personally supervised a crew of twenty-five carpenters, and then put each of them in charge of

a larger inquiry into Dyess's operation of the colony; for more on it, see below, pp. 217–18.

23. Norment, "Colonization Project No. 1," FSA Records, NA, RG 96; *A Review of Work Relief*, pp. 132, 143.

his own crew. A Little Rock architect, Howard Eichenbaum, had drawn the blueprints for the basic three-, four-, and five-room houses, using simple designs. His three-room plan, for example, was a variation of the familiar "shotgun" house of the Cotton Belt. Turning the long side of the house to the front, Eichenbaum placed the door in the middle room, making the end rooms more accessible. The kitchen was on the left and the bedroom on the right, with the living room between. A porch on the front and a screened porch off the kitchen deceptively hid the "shotgun" look. Although Murphy's carpenters followed one basic plan for each type of house, they varied the location of rooms, porches, doors, and windows enough to avoid the monotony of "government housing." When the carpenters finished, the houses received a coat of white paint, with green, dark red, or brown trim.[24]

The three-room house would accommodate a family of three or four members. The four-roomer, for a family of five or six, had two bedrooms, while the five-room house provided three bedrooms. All of the cottages were equipped with electric wiring, but only the five-room design included indoor toilet and bath. Colony officials furnished the sample houses in order to determine the cost (it turned out to be $195 for three bedrooms, living room, and kitchen) and made them into temporary sleeping quarters for some of the carpenters. Work crews cleared about two acres of land immediately around each house and barn, but it was up to the colonists themselves to clear the remainder of their units.[25]

According to Dyess's original plan, the project was to contain five hundred three-, four-, and five-room cottages located on farm units of thirty, forty, and fifty acres, respectively. The colonists would purchase them at cost with payments amortized over a ten-year period. He estimated that the house and barn together would average $600, $800, and $1,000, depending on size. But in late August, Dyess revised the colony plan, the first of many changes. Now he intended to build 750 cottages, while limiting all farm units to twenty acres each.[26] During the summer and fall, Murphy's work crews regularly completed ten to fifteen houses each week. On 15 October Murphy had 101 houses either finished or under construction. By the end of 1934, 146 farm cottages were ready for occupancy; seven months later, the number had risen to 277 completed and

24. Pittman, "Founding of Dyess Colony," p. 318.
25. Ibid., pp. 132, 136, 138; "Rural Industrial Community Projects: Woodlake, Texas; Osceola, Arkansas; and Red House, West Virginia," *Architectural Record* 87 (January 1935): 13.
26. *A Review of Work Relief*, pp. 122–24.

16 under construction. In January 1936, Dyess Colony contained 490 completed farm homes.[27]

Near the heart of the project, Dyess set aside about 150 acres for the community center. When he first began laying plans for an agricultural colony, he knew that low-income families would be unable to provide for themselves the normal community needs of education, medical care, and recreation. With Eichenbaum's help, Dyess created not merely a community center but a veritable small-town business district. In early September Murphy assigned a crew of men the task of clearing the community center grounds and staking out the building sites, while other men laid out the streets and boulevards. In October construction crews started work on the administration complex, including the administration building itself, commissary, cafe, and various stores. In November work began on the hospital and school buildings. As the year ended, Murphy cut back sharply on farmstead work and concentrated on the community center. By early 1935 the administration building was virtually completed, with the hospital, commissary, cafe, and other commercial buildings not far behind. But bad weather and flooding slowed down construction that spring. At last in early May the administrative staff moved into their new offices, and soon afterward the commissary and cafe opened for business.[28]

The Social Service Division of the Arkansas Emergency Relief Administration supervised the selection of colonists. "The choice of Colony families is made on a very rigid selective basis," wrote Dot Kennan, division director.[29] Realizing how crucial family selection was, she was looking for people with leadership qualities, stability, and resourcefulness—people who would help make Dyess Colony a successful community of self-governing individuals. Mrs. Kennan's staff gave first consideration to former rural rehabilitation clients, especially those who had lost their homes and farm equipment during the depression. To qualify, heads of families had to have farming experience, submit references from leading citizens in their home communities, and pass a physical examination.[30]

27. Ibid., pp. 140, 143, 145; Norment, "Colonization Project No. 1," FSA Records, NA, RG 96.

28. *A Review of Work Relief*, pp. 127, 128, 140.

29. Dot Kennan, "The Procedure Followed in Selecting Applicants for Dyess Colony Project—Mississippi County, Arkansas," n.d., FSA Records, NA, RG 96.

30. John B. Holt, *An Analysis of Methods and Criteria Used in Selecting Fami-*

After a year of experience the Social Service staff tightened their selection criteria. They began requiring a physical examination of each member of the family, not just the husband, with a Wassermann test of both parents and grown children. They stressed the selection of people with special skills as well as farming experience. Most important, they explored the attitudes of applicants toward colonization and farm ownership as well as the contribution they could make to the colony. Did they want to plant deep roots in a farm, or was colonization simply a "way out" until something better opened up? The Social Service staff also paid more attention to religious affiliation: "experience has shown," one report read, "that emotional instability experienced in excessive religious fervor of certain religious sects was a disturbing element, and was interfering with work at the colony." Since a few families had come to the colony with a mistaken impression of requirements or conditions or had otherwise proved unsuited to the project, the Social Service Division began arranging for prospective colonists to visit the colony with their county relief administrator in order to make sure they thoroughly understood what they would be getting into.[31]

The Emergency Relief Administration established a definite procedure for locating and approving qualified families. At the request of the Social Service Division, each county relief caseworker and rural supervisor recommended "one or two eligible families whom they considered most likely to succeed in the colonization program." If interested, the families filled out appropriate application forms. The county administrator and his staff, along with the county agent if possible, verified the information given, studied the record of these families, and made recommendations to the state office, specifying first and second choices. A committee made up of Mrs. Kennan, W. A. Rooksbery, state director of the National Reemployment Service, Hilda K. Cornish, director of Women's Work, and E. B. Whitaker went over each application and made the final selections. When the decision came back, the county administrator gave approved clients a "twenty-four-hour preparatory notice" for removal to the colony, with the relief organization providing transportation.[32]

lies for Colonization Projects, Social Research Report no. 1 of the U.S. Department of Agriculture, Farm Security Administration, and the Bureau of Agricultural Economics (Washington, 1937), pp. 45–50.

31. *Arkansas Gazette*, 9 January 1937; Social Service Division, Report on Colonization Project No. 1, dated 25 March 1935, FSA Records, NA, RG 96; *A Review of Work Relief*, pp. 123, 127.

32. Kennan, "The Procedure Followed in Selecting Applicants for Dyess Colony

On 25 October 1934 the first colonists arrived at Dyess Colony, thirteen families from thirteen different counties. One of these families was W. H. "Harve" Smith, his wife and five children, from Bassett, Arkansas, seven miles away. A cash tenant who rented land outright, Harve Smith had been a cotton farmer all his life. The depression left him destitute. With cotton hovering around six cents a pound, he could no longer pay rent for land, nor could he find a place as a sharecropper. Forced onto relief, he and his family struggled through the winter of 1933–34. In early May he became a rural rehabilitation client and quickly demonstrated that his plight was due not to his own incompetence but to circumstances beyond his control. He grew enough food for his family, paid back his relief loan, and had money left to buy a mule. When he arrived at Dyess Colony, he also brought his own cow and calf, over a hundred chickens, enough forage to carry his stock through the coming winter, and a large supply of canned food. Before moving, the Smiths lived in a leaky three-room cabin; when it rained they had to move all the furniture out of one room. At Dyess Colony, Smith moved his family into a new five-room home, still smelling of fresh paint and located on a thirty-acre tract. He spent the first winter clearing the land and working part-time for the colony itself. In the spring of 1935 he had his unit ready for cultivation. If he stuck to it, one day he could own both the house and the land.[33] But it would not be easy.

Federal relief officials began finding fault with family selection at Dyess as early as November 1934. "Dyess Colony is troubling everyone," wrote social worker Loula Dunn. Until recently, she said, the colony had no qualified social worker, and the basis of family selection was still puzzling.[34] In 1935 there were further complaints that the pace of family selection consistently ran behind farmstead construction; available houses at the colony were simply not being filled fast enough.[35] After the first 13 families came in October, 10 families arrived in November, 18 in December, and 4 in January, bringing the total to 45 families. As a result, a large number of houses stood empty during the crop year of

Project," FSA Records, NA, RG 96; Holt, *An Analysis of Methods and Criteria*, pp. 46, 48, 49.

33. *A Review of Work Relief*, pp. 123, 126.

34. Loula Dunn, memorandum to Josephine C. Brown, 3 December 1934, FERA Records, NA, RG 69; Dunn to W. R. Dyess, 30 November 1934, ibid.

35. Social Service Division, Report on Colonization Project No. 1, dated 25 March 1935, FSA Records, NA, RG 96; Loula Dunn to Malcolm J. Miller, 20 March 1935, FERA Records, NA, RG 69.

1935 when they might have been used. By November 1935 the Social Service Division had selected a total of 161 families, 38 of whom returned home after a short stay, leaving 133 families then living on the colony.[36] In contrast, over three hundred cottages were completed and ready for occupancy.

That fall, the Resettlement Administration took over family selection. The agency's regional office at Little Rock had developed an efficient staff of family selection specialists—a staff that could possibly provide the guidance needed at Dyess. A senior selection specialist took up residence at the colony itself, while a five-man staff worked in the field visiting and interviewing rural rehabilitation clients. They approved only 2 families in December, but 13 in January 1936, 64 in February, 128 in March, 120 in April, and 22 by mid-May. Within seven months the Resettlement Administration had selected 349 families for Dyess, filling all but eighteen of the farmsteads at the colony, and these were filled soon afterward.[37]

As families arrived, colony officials assigned them to farm units according to the number of family members. A husband and wife with one or two children received a twenty-acre tract. Larger families with more manpower available settled on thirty acres. Exceptionally large families, perhaps with ten or more members, occupied the forty-acre units.

In effect, most newly arrived families went on temporary relief. If a family lacked adequate household equipment, the Emergency Relief Administration supplied them with beds, mattresses, and a stove, charging these items to their account. According to the size of the family, colonists twice a month received subsistence coupon books good for an average of twenty dollars worth of groceries and merchandise. Their subsistence, household goods, a mule (if they needed one), tools, farm implements, and seed all came under the category of capital advances, a debt repayable in the family's first three years on the colony. To further get them on their feet, colony officials offered the head of each family work on construction jobs at the colony, usually as unskilled labor. Thus they were afforded a small source of income until they could plant and harvest their first crop. They also spent much of the first winter clearing their land, and the wilderness rapidly took shape as a farming community. Only 500

36. Final Report on Selection Program, Dyess Colony, 14 May 1936, FSA Records, NA, RG 96.
37. Management Division, Region VI, News Letter, 1 July 1935 to 1 January 1936; Charles L. Gaines, Jr., to Mrs. Katherine A. Kellock, 13 November 1935; Final Report on Selection Program, Dyess Colony, 14 May 1936; T. Roy Reid to R. G. Tugwell, 9 December 1935, all in FSA Records, NA, RG 96.

acres were farmed in 1935, but the amount of land under cultivation totaled 4,875 acres the following year and some 9,000 acres by 1937.[38]

The home economist and the farm supervisor helped the colonists establish homes and farms at Dyess. Appointed on 26 October 1934, one day after the first families arrived, Mrs. Ed L. Salyers supervised home demonstration work.[39] Stressing self-sufficiency, she worked with the wives in preparing household budgets and gave instructions in canning, sewing, and other homemaking arts. To aid families with home furnishings, she converted one of the farm cottages into a home demonstration house, using furniture that carpenters could easily copy at the colony workshop. As one of their early projects, Mrs. Salyers and the Home Demonstration Club built studio couches. Many of the larger families had installed a bed in the living room; a studio couch replaced the bed and made the living area more pleasant.

While Whitaker had responsibility for the colony's overall agricultural program, J. E. "Jake" Terry was the farm supervisor on the scene. He incorporated his suggestions into "bulletins," held weekly group meetings with colonists explaining how they could best make use of their land, and moved around the project watching their progress.[40] Based on the Extension Service program of diversified farming, the colony's farm management program emphasized four basic principles: food for the family, feed for livestock, cash income, and soil improvement. Thus colonists planted not only cotton, but also corn, truck gardens, hay crops, and pastures. In addition, each farmer was expected to have a flock of chickens, a brood sow, at least one milch cow, and a mule for plowing. As farm supervisor, Terry sought to build a community of farmers who were both self-reliant and ready to act as a group when collective action would give them an advantage.[41]

After two years of construction, the Emergency Relief Administration halted work on community facilities and farmsteads. By summer of 1936 Dyess Colony had become a community of about three thousand people. At the heart of the project the community center had taken shape as a

38. Blackman, "Uncle Sam Waves a Wand," p. 5; *Arkansas Gazette*, 9 January 1938; *A Review of Work Relief*, pp. 126–67; Pittman, "Founding of Dyess Colony," pp. 319–20.

39. Ibid., p. 323; *Traveling Recovery Road*, p. 157; *A Review of Work Relief*, p. 147; *Osceola Times*, 15 February 1935.

40. *A Review of Work Relief*, pp. 126, 146, 147; Connie J. Bonslagel to Col. Lawrence Westbrook, 12 November 1934, FSA Records, NA, RG 96; *Arkansas Gazette*, 12 May 1935.

41. *A Review of Work Relief*, pp. 146, 147.

small city, with city blocks, paved streets and sidewalks, stores, offices, and residential sections.

The main administration building was a two-story brick veneer structure with smaller brick veneer buildings on either side. They formed a semicircle around a memorial plaque to the colony's founder. The building to the right contained a general store; the left one a cafe, barber shop, and post office (with rural free delivery). Two blocks away stood a combination grade school and high school, while three other grade schools were located in other sections of the project. Nearby, a woodworking and furniture factory, canning plant, sawmills, machine shops, cotton gin, and gristmill provided employment for a few colonists and vital services for all. In addition, the list of community facilities included a filling station, railroad depot, ice house, laundry, garage, and four warehouses. The community hall, a T-shaped building, held a library and movie theater–auditorium, plus space for other indoor entertainment. A baseball field and grandstand would later face the Tyronza River. Across the street would be a swimming pool, bathhouses, tennis courts, and, not far away, a city park. Besides the commercial buildings, the community center contained about forty private residences for the families of administrative personnel.[42]

Completely surrounding the community center, the colony land stretched out in every direction. When construction ended, Dyess Colony consisted of 500 farmsteads of varying sizes: 61 three-room, 233 four-room, and 206 five-room houses. Similarly, the land had been broken up into 500 farm units: 334 farms of twenty acres, 64 of thirty acres, and 102 of forty acres. The Emergency Relief Administration had invested $2,306,250 in Dyess Colony—a figure that included everything from land and construction costs to direct relief for individual colonists.[43]

The formal dedication of Dyess Colony took place on 22 May 1936, the colony's second anniversary. It was a quiet ceremony honoring the founder, dead only four months. One of the colonists had written: "I feel that W. R. Dyess loved his home and family and that is why he wanted everyone else to have a happy home. I can't tell in words how I feel the loss of that dear, fine man. We colony people, especially, will miss him terribly."[44] For many "colony people," in fact, he would quickly assume

42. Ibid., pp. 128, 129; Norment, "Colonization Project No. 1," FSA Records, NA, RG 96; Final Report on Selection Program, Dyess Colony, 14 May 1936, ibid.; *Arkansas Gazette*, 9 January 1938.
43. Audit Report, Dyess Colony, Inc., Dyess, Arkansas, 29 February 1936, FSA Records, NA, RG 96; *Traveling Recovery Road*, pp. 154, 155.
44. *Osceola Times*, 24 January 1936.

a larger-than-life image as they began blaming his successors rather than him for the colony's faults.

At the start of 1936 Dyess Colony had several serious deficiencies for a project almost two years old. Perhaps most important, no one administrative officer had ever been in charge of the entire operation. Instead, Dyess had relied on half a dozen people—Whitaker, Murphy, Terry, Mrs. Salyers, Howard Eichenbaum, and Dr. L. L. Huebner, colony physician —with each person responsible only for the specific tasks assigned to him, nothing more. Until his death Dyess himself seems to have provided the only overall direction the colony had.

Second, Dyess Colony still had no organizational structure. The Arkansas Rural Rehabilitation Corporation had launched Colonization Project No. 1 and still held title to colony property; but the project was only part of a broad program of rural rehabilitation. What Dyess Colony needed was its own organization, one that would allow the colony to achieve maturity as an independent and self-sufficient community.

Nor had another important matter been definitely worked out. Before 1936 each family signed a contract with the Arkansas Rural Rehabilitation Corporation, in reality only an agreement to enter into an agreement. If they cleared their land and otherwise accommodated themselves to the colony plan, they were promised a deed at a price to be determined by a fair appraisal of the property but not to exceed the actual cost of the land and improvements, plus interest. The colonists still did not know how much their farmsteads cost or how long they had to pay them off.[45]

After Dyess's death, the new WPA director for Arkansas, Floyd Sharp, could no longer postpone these problems as his predecessor had. The Resettlement Administration already had plans for absorbing the Arkansas Rural Rehabilitation Corporation within a few weeks. Sharp had to take immediate action if Dyess Colony was not to be absorbed along with it.[46]

45. Report of Roland R. Pyne, Regional Engineer, Period Ending 10 November 1934, Hopkins Papers.

46. See Rexford G. Tugwell to Harry L. Hopkins, n.d.; Carl C. Taylor to Hopkins, 18 September 1935; W. R. Dyess to Col. Lawrence Westbrook, 17, 22 July, 11 November 1935; Dyess, telegram to Taylor, 6 July 1935, all in WPA Records, NA, RG 69; T. Roy Reid to Taylor, 19 November 1935, FSA Records, NA, RG 69; Reid, telegram to Taylor, 11 July 1935, ibid.

Three FERA communities were not turned over to the Resettlement Administration in 1935: Pine Mountain Valley, near Columbus, Georgia; Cherry Lake Farms, near Madison, Florida; and Dyess Colony. Paul K. Conkin, *Tomorrow a New World: The New Deal Community Program* (Ithaca, N.Y.: Cornell University Press, 1959), p. 137.

At a special meeting on 17 February 1936, the board of directors of the Rural Rehabilitation Corporation formed a new organization, Dyess Colony, Incorporated, to take over the management of the colony and carry W. R. Dyess's plans to conclusion. Floyd Sharp, Henry C. Baker, and R. C. Limerick comprised both the board of directors and the stockholders of the new corporation, each holding one share of no-par-value stock. They pledged their stock to Harry Hopkins, who held it "in trust against the faithful performance of duties on the part of the Board of Directors."[47] Since all three were also stockholders in the Arkansas Rural Rehabilitation Corporation, the meeting turned into a joint conference of officers of both corporations. The Rural Rehabilitation Corporation sold for one dollar all real and personal property of Colonization Project No. 1 to Dyess Colony, Inc.[48] Then they discussed plans for the formation of a subsidiary corporation to manage the colony and community facilities and sell stock to the colony residents. "Under this plan," Sharp explained, "the residents of the colony will eventually own the land they are now purchasing and in addition will own the corporation that operates the community center."[49] At last Dyess Colony had not only the kind of organization it needed for permanence, but a new name as well. The term "Dyess Colony" had been used almost from the start, but it did not become the official designation until after Dyess's death and the creation of Dyess Colony, Inc.[50]

Less than a week after the birth of the new organization, Sharp gave E. S. Dudley a leave of absence from his job as director of the WPA's Division of Employment and appointed him colony administrator.[51] His job was to manage day-to-day operations.

That left only one unsolved problem: the terms on which colonists could get possession of their homes and farms. Again colony authorities had to reach a decision soon. Cone Murphy, who stayed on as superintendent of construction, would have the last of the five hundred farmsteads ready in June or July.[52] The Resettlement Administration planned to complete family selection by early June, and about 350 new families

47. *Arkansas Gazette*, 18 February 1936; *Osceola Times*, 21 February 1936; Extract of Minutes, Arkansas Rural Rehabilitation Corporation, dated 17 February 1936, FSA Records, NA, RG 96. See Floyd Sharp, memorandum to All Residents of the Dyess Colony, 10 February 1936, ibid.
48. Raymond O. Denham to Rexford G. Tugwell, 15 July 1936, ibid.
49. *Arkansas Gazette*, 18 February 1936.
50. *Blytheville Courier News*, 23 May 1934; Pine Bluff *Daily Graphic*, 18 January 1936.
51. *Arkansas Gazette*, 22 February 1936.
52. Ibid.

would want to know exactly where they stood in regard to future owner-ship. Equally important, as Whitaker must have stressed, a new crop year had virtually arrived, and Dyess Colony could be successful only if full use were made of its land and facilities. Within a few weeks Sharp, Baker, and Limerick, with the help of the colony's special counsel, Lawrence Westbrook, worked out what they considered to be a fair and equitable plan for home ownership. Perhaps to impress the colonists with the importance of this step, Westbrook himself visited the project and personally explained the details of the purchase plan.

Everyone would have a chance to own his own farm, Westbrook as-sured the colonists in early August. Until then, they had been merely "licensees" renting their land. But, Westbrook explained, Dyess Colony, Inc., would have each tract of land and its improvement appraised. The appraisers would consider the tax rate, replacement value, market value, and earning power of the property. Then the Dyess corporation would offer to sell each family the house and land they occupied at the appraised value, less 10 percent. "We are making this deduction to the family living there not as any special mark of favor," Westbrook explained, "but be-cause we think it would cost about that much to get someone else estab-lished there."[53]

Each colonist would receive a sales contract or a deed and mortgage, with the selling price amortized over a thirty-year period at 6 percent an-nual interest. The colonists could make monthly, quarterly, or semiannual payments as they wished; and at its discretion, the corporation could defer all or any part of a payment and extend the loan in emergency situations. No one would be permitted to resell his farm except to the colony corpo-ration. All of this was in the future for most colonists, however, since each family had to serve a two-year probationary period before becoming eligible for a purchase contract.

Westbrook did not mention the original plan to offer families a chance to buy the land and improvements at cost, but that promise was still good. The early cost estimates, however, were absurdly low, totally out of line with reality. Here was a source of misunderstanding which would rise to the surface later.

From 1936 to 1940 Dyess Colony, Inc., made other improvements, furnishing the project with all the accouterments of a well-established

53. Quoted in Lawrence Westbrook, Address to the Arkansas Farm Tenancy Commission, 21 September 1936, Hopkins Papers; Westbrook to Paul V. Maris, 10 August 1936, with enclosures, FSA Records, NA, RG 96; see *Arkansas Gazette*, 9 January 1938.

rural community. In May 1936 a weekly newspaper, the *Colony Herald,* began publication. The editor, Oden S. Williams, did a highly professional job—probably too professional and expensive, because the paper failed at the end of the year. The Arkansas Power and Light Company had run lines to the project; but after 1937 the Dyess Electric Cooperative Company, using a loan of $120,000 from the Rural Electrification Administration, furnished the colony's electric power. Dyess families also had their own bank, the Farmers Exchange and Loan Company, really a credit union. Since all available buildings in the "town" were taken, the bank moved into a portion of the cafe, which by that time was not doing well anyway. Finally, Dyess Colony organized a school district, one of many districts in Mississippi County in the era before consolidation. When school began in the fall of 1937, Dyess School District had $118,-000 worth of facilities and an enrollment of 1,021 children, about a third of the colony's total population.[54]

The colony became perhaps the most highly organized community project of Region VI; given its size, it had to be well organized. As colony administrator, Dudley was responsible for three large areas of activity: farm operations, business management, and community government.[55] He kept farm operations in the hands of his assistant administrator, Jake Terry, and a staff of farm advisers; they, in turn, worked closely with the colony's home demonstration agent and 4-H Clubs to coordinate farm and home management planning.

Dudley retained major responsibility for business, marketing, and cooperative activities, although delegating specific tasks to a business manager and accountant. After 31 October 1936, Dudley marketed all cash crops grown at the colony through Dyess Colony Cooperative Association, an Arkansas-chartered organization in which all project residents owned stock.[56] In addition, the cooperative association operated the store, gin, feed mill, cannery, commissary, lumber mill, blacksmith shop, furniture factory, and all other community facilities. " 'Cooperation' must be our watchword," Westbrook had told the colonists. "In this community here we aim to apply the principles of cooperation to all our important activities and at the same time to preserve and develop that spirit of competitive individualism which seems necessary for the highest achieve-

54. Pittman, "Founding of Dyess Colony," pp. 319, 322–23. The *Colony Herald* may be seen in the WPA Collection at the University of Arkansas, Fayetteville.
55. Azile Aaron to W. A. Rooksbery, 25 March 1936, FSA Records, NA, RG 96.
56. Articles of Incorporation of Dyess Colony Cooperative Association, dated 31 October 1936, Arkansas Secretary of State, Corporations Department, State Capitol, Little Rock, Arkansas.

ment in any line of human endeavor."[57] As time went on, the colonists themselves, through the Dyess Colony Cooperative Association, were expected to purchase the cooperative facilities and take on more and more the tasks of running their own community. As for community government, Dudley functioned as a city manager, coordinating the work of schools, utilities, public health and sanitation services, police and fire departments, plus religious, civic, and recreational activities.[58]

To some of its supporters, like Lawrence Westbrook, the development of Dyess Colony was a romantic vision of rugged, pioneer families engaged in "carving their homes out of the wilderness."[59] Undoubtedly the colony's early years did afford challenge, excitement, and a sense of blazing new trails for others to follow if the colony were successful. For the colonists, the future was to be glorious. "I predict that within ten years, this will be the most prosperous community in Arkansas or any other State," Westbrook once told the colonists. "There will be no rich people here, but everyone will be well-to-do."[60]

Westbrook's promises, however, never caught up with reality. Life at Dyess was much like life in any other rural community during the depression. It was hard. There was little romance in cutting down trees and clearing land, walking behind a mule all day long, or picking cotton from sunup to sundown.

"Any colonist with a modicum of industry," Henry Baker wrote in 1936, "can be assured of owning his own home within a reasonable time."[61] Yet in early 1938, for example, only 155 families had deeds to their homesteads, leaving about 345 families still on probationary status. A lot of people evidently did not share Westbrook's vision of paradise. There was a constant turnover of families. Between October 1934 and April 1938 a total of 649 families lived in the colony at some time; of these, 252, or 39 percent, moved away.[62]

Nor did Dyess Colony seem to be approaching the goal of becoming a self-sustaining rural community. The colony's operations lost $386,-

57. Lawrence Westbrook to Paul V. Maris, 10 August 1936, with enclosures, FSA Records, NA, RG 96.
58. Azile Aaron to W. A. Rooksbery, 25 March 1936, with enclosures, ibid.
59. *Arkansas Gazette*, 10 June 1936.
60. Lawrence Westbrook to Paul V. Maris, 10 August 1936, with enclosures, FSA Records, NA, RG 96.
61. *Traveling Recovery Road*, p. 156.
62. Charles P. Loomis and Dwight Davidson, Jr., "Sociometrics and the Study of the New Rural Communities," *Sociometry* 2 (January 1939): 57, 58.

729.02 in 1937, $221,325.70 in 1938, and $144,181.35 in 1939, though it did show constant improvement.[63]

How W. R. Dyess's death affected the colony can never be known. He died at the time the colony most needed guidance. He might have solved its problems and quelled the growing discontent, but he had done much to create those problems.

63. Audit Report, Dyess Colony, Inc., Dyess, Arkansas, 28 February 1937, 28 February 1938, 28 February 1939, all in FSA Records, NA, RG 96.

Chapter IV

McComb Homesteads: A Mississippi Idyll

"There are in one sense," M. L. Wilson once wrote, "two polar extremes of thought in respect to the direction agricultural development should follow in the future." One extreme envisioned the use of modern technology and the creation of farms of gigantic proportions, with surplus farm workers going into industry. The opposite extreme favored breaking up agriculture into small units, turning away from modern technology and specialization, and returning to "subsistence practices that were common before the industrial revolution." Wilson rejected both alternatives. As long as unemployment was high, industry could not provide jobs for surplus rural people. On the other hand, specialized, large-scale agriculture had become absolutely necessary to supply raw materials for industry and to feed the industrial population of the cities. Why go to either extreme? Why not, he asked, combine both modern, mechanized farming techniques and small subsistence farms? All agriculture need not be commercial, and subsistence farming did not necessarily mean going back to the Middle Ages; it could be as modern as any large-scale farm.[1]

As chief of the Division of Subsistence Homesteads, Wilson followed this middle course. He was enthusiastic about subsistence farming, but he did not seek to form enclaves where homesteaders could escape modern problems and retreat to a simpler life near the soil. Nor did he want to use subsistence homesteads as a defeatist attempt to reverse progress. In the South, Wilson established a few colonies for stranded workers, as at Arthurdale, West Virginia. He also built a few rural colonies for submarginal farmers, but for the most part he concentrated on homesteads

---

1. M. L. Wilson, "Beyond Economics," in *Farmers in a Changing World: The Yearbook of Agriculture, 1940* (Washington: Government Printing Office, 1940), pp. 922–37; the quote is from p. 930. Russell Lord, *The Wallaces of Iowa* (Boston: Houghton Mifflin, 1947), pp. 411, 416–17.

near industrial employment. In Mississippi alone, the Division of Subsistence Homesteads planned five industrial-type projects and one rural colony. Also taking a middle course, Mississippians saw them primarily as a means of promoting home ownership.[2]

The industrial-type projects became the best examples of what subsistence homesteads were supposed to be. A subsistence homestead, according to an official definition, was "a house and outbuildings located upon a plot of land on which can be grown a large portion of the foodstuffs required by the homestead family." The homesteader did not compete in the market with commercial farmers. He produced only for home consumption. "In that it provides for subsistence alone, it carries with it the corollary that cash income must be drawn from some outside source. The central motive of the subsistence homestead program, therefore, is to demonstrate the economic value of a livelihood which combines part-time wage work and part-time gardening or farming."[3]

Except for their small size, the Mississippi projects were typical of most industrial-type homesteads. Located near small towns, they each contained between a hundred and three hundred acres of land broken up into twenty to twenty-five units, with an average of four to seven acres per homestead. The Division of Subsistence Homesteads designed them to take up the slack of seasonal employment in cotton gins, textile mills, and other industries common in small southern towns. These projects offered opportunities both for industrial workers to practice subsistence farming and for farmers to earn cash income as part-time industrial workers.[4]

The Division of Subsistence Homesteads drew up plans for industrial-type projects at McComb, Laurel, Tupelo, Meridian, and Hattiesburg.[5] None of these towns was an urban center, but they all possessed economic potential. In 1935 Meridian had the largest population (31,954), with Hattiesburg (18,601) and Laurel (18,017) almost equal; McComb (10,057) and Tupelo (6,361) were considerably smaller.

Meridian, Mississippi's second-largest city, was located in the east-central part of the state, a region famous for yellow pine, hardwood, cot-

2. See Clarksdale *Daily Register*, 1 May 1934.
3. U.S. Department of the Interior, Division of Subsistence Homesteads, *Bulletin 1* (Washington, 1934), p. 4, quoted in Paul K. Conkin, *Tomorrow a New World: The New Deal Community Program* (Ithaca, N.Y.: Cornell University Press, 1959), pp. 110, 111.
4. Conkin, *Tomorrow a New World*, pp. 105, 106, 110, 111.
5. Report of the Division of Subsistence Homesteads and Federal Subsistence Homesteads Corporation, June 1934, FSA Records, NA, RG 96; U.S. Department of the Interior, Division of Subsistence Homesteads, Monthly Project Report, 26 April 1935, ibid.

ton, livestock, and dairy farms. Timber was practically the only natural resource of this region, but lumber companies had already stripped the best virgin forests. The most important railroad center in eastern Mississippi, Meridian was the junction of the Mobile and Ohio Railroad, the New Orleans and North Eastern, the Saint Louis and San Francisco, and several smaller lines. Meridian's cotton mills produced more cotton oil for sale in Europe than did any other city in Mississippi; a shirt factory and three hosiery mills made the city an important textile town as well. In the northeastern part of the state, Tupelo was one of the first TVA cities and perhaps Mississippi's best example of the "New South." Like many other southern towns, Tupelo took its first step away from the land with a cotton mill; but three garment factories soon became the city's major industry.[6]

McComb, Hattiesburg, and Laurel all lay within the coastal plain. At one time this region had consisted of thick forests of long-leaf yellow pine, but in the 1930s it too was largely cutover land with little marketable timber left. In addition, southern Mississippi was a truck farming area specializing in corn, sweet potatoes, oats, tobacco, sugarcane, garden vegetables, pecans, and peanuts.

For both industry and truck farming, McComb occupied a favorable geographical position as the largest town along the Illinois Central Railroad between New Orleans and Jackson. McCombians found industrial opportunities in Illinois Central repair shops, sawmills, textile mills, and a woodworking plant. Once a mere sawmill camp, Hattiesburg had become an important manufacturer of naval stores, a railroad center, and a college town. Twenty-five miles north, Laurel was still primarily a lumber town on the extreme northeastern edge of the yellow pine forest.[7]

Since the only function of the Division of Subsistence Homesteads was to build homestead projects, it had no need for an elaborate regional or state-by-state organization to mediate between the national and local offices. Wilson was a strong advocate of "grassroots democracy" and administrative decentralization. At the top he created the Federal Subsistence Homesteads Corporation, with subsidiary corporations planned for individual projects. Except for a few field representatives, the Division of Subsistence Homesteads operated its entire program through these local corporations.

6. Federal Writers' Project of the Works Progress Administration, *Mississippi: A Guide to the Magnolia State* (New York: Viking, 1938), pp. 227–31, 261–65.
7. Ibid., pp. 396, 417, 222–27.

The Mississippi industrial-type homesteads followed the same basic stages of development; they were also virtually identical as completed projects. First, the Federal Subsistence Homesteads Corporation incorporated the five projects, assigned each one a general manager, and released an allotment to cover development and management costs. Subsistence Homesteads officials worked closely with chambers of commerce and other local "sponsors" in selecting the actual project sites. Next, the general manager began clearing and surveying the land into individual subsistence plots. At the same time, he opened bidding on the homesteads, outbuildings, and roads. As originally planned, each homestead would cost between $2,500 and $2,800, including land and all improvements.[8] Since the projects were all close to towns, the Division of Subsistence Homesteads planned no major community facilities for project residents. The general manager also supervised the work of selecting the future homesteaders.[9]

At first, McComb set the pace for the subsistence homesteads program in Mississippi. During a visit to McComb on 26 and 27 December 1933, I. R. Bradshaw, Mississippi's field representative, and N. A. Keller, land-clearing specialist of the Department of Agriculture, revealed unofficially that the city had won approval for a subsistence homesteads project.[10] The people of the city responded with enthusiasm. In fact, a special committee of the McComb Chamber of Commerce had already been lobbying for a project.[11] To businessmen, a homestead project meant more than homes for twenty or twenty-five families; it meant employment for laborers, carpenters, plumbers, electricians, and other workers who would build the homesteads.

Within a week after Bradshaw and Keller left, a group of McComb people decided to ask Mrs. Franklin D. Roosevelt to dedicate the project; knowing her interest in the subsistence community idea, they also wanted to name the project the Eleanor Roosevelt Homesteads. Edgar G. Wil-

8. Report of the Division of Subsistence Homesteads and Federal Subsistence Homesteads Corporation, June 1934, FSA Records, NA, RG 96.
9. Conkin, *Tomorrow a New World*, pp. 106, 107. Besides the industrial projects, the Division of Subsistence Homesteads announced a full-time farm colony at Richton, Mississippi, purchased 7,753 acres of farm land for $36,753.24, and made plans to divide it into about 310 farm units. But the Resettlement Administration inherited Richton in 1935 before any development work was done on it. U.S. Department of the Interior, Division of Subsistence Homesteads, Monthly Project Report, 26 April 1935, FSA Records, NA, RG 96.
10. *McComb Enterprise*, 29 December 1933.
11. W. M. Webb (for McComb Chamber of Commerce) to Rexford G. Tugwell, 6 April 1935, FSA Records, NA, RG 96.

liams, chairman of the Mississippi State Democratic Committee, agreed to present their invitation to the First Lady at the White House; and Sen. Pat Harrison set up the appointment with Mrs. Roosevelt. Harrison asked her if she knew Edgar G. Williams. "Oh, I remember him," she said. "He's the gentleman from way down in South Mississippi who wore a silk suit and a red necktie to the inauguration."

When Williams called at the White House, he found her well posted on plans for McComb. She was pleased with the invitation, he reported, but she could not give a definite answer since Wilson had not officially approved McComb for a project.[12]

On 29 December 1933 the Federal Subsistence Homesteads Corporation formed McComb Homesteads of Mississippi, Inc.[13] Organized under Delaware law, McComb Homesteads was responsible for developing and operating the McComb project. A legal device, McComb Homesteads of Mississippi would borrow money from the parent corporation; hold title to the land, buildings, and other property; enter into contracts with architects, contractors, and building supply companies; make all expenditures; and issue purchase contracts to individual families. Once construction work was over, McComb Homesteads would manage the project. As on all subsistence homesteads, the corporation officers were prominent citizens of the local community. In early 1934 Williams became president of the corporation. J. O. Emmerich, editor of the *McComb Enterprise*, took over as general manager, while Mayor Xavier A. Kramer and businessmen W. M. Webb and J. C. Flowers rounded out the board of directors.[14]

Senator Harrison and two congressmen, H. D. Stephens and Russell Ellzey, wired Emmerich on 18 January: "MC COMB HAS BEEN SELECTED A SUBSISTENCE HOMESTEAD SITE [STOP] ANNOUNCEMENT BY DIRECTOR OF SUBSISTENCE HOMESTEADS TO BE MADE TODAY."[15] A few days later M. L. Wilson officially gave the board of directors full authority to go ahead with plans for developing a project. The board soon announced the

12. *McComb Enterprise*, 5, 19 January 1934.
13. McComb Homestead Project SH-MS-4, Report of Examination, dated 22 June 1937, HHFA Records, NA, RG 207; Conkin, *Tomorrow a New World*, pp. 106, 107.
14. *McComb Enterprise*, 5 January, 2 February 1934. In May 1934, however, Secretary of the Interior Harold L. Ickes federalized all subsistence homesteads projects, abolished the control of the subsidiary corporations, and placed the entire program directly under the Federal Subsistence Homesteads Corporation. See Conkin, *Tomorrow a New World*, pp. 120–23.
15. *McComb Enterprise*, 19 January 1934.

purchase of a 364-acre tract of land three miles southeast of the city. McComb Homesteads of Mississippi paid John O. Lanier, a local farmer, $2,200 for the undeveloped land.[16] Emmerich was impatient to get started. Almost as soon as the purchase was made, he had an engineer, Jimmie Barnes, and two crews of men on the project drawing contour maps of elevations, streams, and other landmarks, while a third crew under Walter Fitzgerald marked the property boundaries. In the meantime, the board of directors began working on plans for the project with agricultural engineers, horticulturists, and the state extension service.[17]

Within a few weeks homestead officials had drawn up building plans for an initial group of twenty-five homes, with more homes planned for future development. On 5 March a capacity crowd of prospective homesteaders and other interested people jammed the McComb City Hall auditorium, where Emmerich outlined the corporation's plans for "Eleanor Roosevelt Homesteads." Since the engineering work had been completed, he explained, actual construction awaited Washington's approval of final building plans. Emmerich had already submitted these plans to Bradshaw; he in turn had approved them and sent them on to Washington. "The program," Emmerich wrote later, "will carry out a dream of President and Mrs. Roosevelt to provide modern homes in ideal surroundings near a city for part-time industrial workers."[18]

On 24 April, McComb Homesteads held a ground-breaking ceremony, an event that put it ahead of all other subsistence homesteads projects in Mississippi. A. B. McKay, state horticulturist, and J. T. Copeland, state agricultural engineer, had both participated in planning the project; now they turned over the first spade of earth on the site of the first homestead.[19]

This ceremony did not actually launch the building program at McComb. Emmerich had already started construction on three homesteads; he added five more within a week and planned to keep enlarging the construction program until all twenty-five houses were under way at once. Between April and September 1934 Emmerich completed twenty homesteads. The McComb houses were all frame clapboard structures except for two of frame shingle construction; eight had four rooms; ten, five

16. Ibid., 2 February 1934; A. T. McCurdie, memorandum to J. Lloyd Taylor, 15 January 1946, HHFA Records, NA, RG 207.
17. *McComb Enterprise*, 9 February 1934.
18. Ibid., 9 March 1934.
19. Ibid., 27 April 1934.

rooms; and one, six rooms. The original project plan called for equipping them with running water, indoor toilets, electric lights, gas for cooking and heating, and telephone service; but electricity, gas, and telephones were later dropped because of high installation costs. Emmerich's engineers divided the land into different-sized plots. Nineteen homesteads ranged from four to fourteen acres each, and one had a twenty-four-acre plot. In addition to the dwelling, each unit contained a garage and wellhouse and a combination cow stall, chicken house, and storeroom. All of the homesteaders had some wooded land, a truck garden, and an orchard, as well as the use of a thirty-seven-acre community pasture. Emmerich let contracts for drilling a well on each unit and for installing individual septic tanks. Each homesteader would have his own sow, milch cow, mare, twenty-five to fifty hens, and essential farm equipment. Relief labor built dirt roads through the project, connecting the homesteads with each other and with existing roads. For recreation, homesteaders had a park and lake, but no other community facilities were provided.[20]

As early as January 1934 Emmerich called for applicants, even though he had not yet received the proper application forms. He invited all interested persons to leave their names and addresses with the McComb Chamber of Commerce.[21] When the forms arrived, they could fill them out and make formal application. Within two weeks, 232 people had applied for homesteads; by April the number had risen to 518.[22] To handle family selection, the Division of Subsistence Homesteads set up a series of four committees from local to national levels. First, a committee of McComb citizens interviewed each applicant and drew up a list of the most promising families. Then the board of directors of McComb Homesteads formed a selection committee of its own membership, reviewed the citizen committee's list, and made their own recommendations to a state committee. The state committee served as a clearinghouse for family selection on all Mississippi subsistence homesteads; its members, Ann Jordan of Mississippi State College and I. R. Bradshaw, went over the choices and passed the revised list on to Washington. Charlotte Smith of the Division of Subsistence Homesteads headed the national committee, which made the final selection for all projects in the nation. The Division

20. For the floor plans, see ibid., 15 March 1935; Resettlement Administration, "Project Description Book," March–December 1936, Project Registers Box, FSA Records, NA, RG 96; see also *McComb Enterprise*, 18 January 1935.

21. Ibid., 5 January 1934.

22. Ibid., 19 January, 6 April 1934.

of Subsistence Homesteads was looking for thrifty, industrious, honest people who had already proven themselves reliable. The most preferred families were those who earned part of their income in local industrial work. Heads of families had to be under fifty years of age, possess a reputation for good character, and show ability to pay for the homestead.[23]

By April the Division of Subsistence Homesteads had approved nine McComb applicants: a linotype operator, railroad switchman, brakeman, truck driver, cotton mill worker, blacksmith, restaurant cook, printer, and mechanic.[24] Their average annual income was between $1,000 and $1,200. These people were probably attracted by the McComb project because of the security and stability they believed it would afford. Most homestead families were interested above all in home ownership. In the division's plan, each client occupied his homestead under a "temporary licensing agreement," a contract calling for monthly rental payments based on the unit's size and cost. The homestead corporation would later offer each family a sales contract with payments amortized over a thirty-year period at 3 percent interest. What each family had paid as licensees would apply to the final purchase price of their homestead unit. As permanent residents, they would continue making monthly payments.[25]

Emmerich planned for families to occupy the homesteads as they were completed. In early June 1934 Guy A. Betz, a mechanic and night watchman, took the first homestead.[26] Two other families, those of J. R. Butler and M. T. Rhodes, soon followed. Emmerich initially advised them that the homesteads would each cost $2,500, more or less; he could not determine the exact price until construction was further advanced. But somewhat later, he presented the three families with licensing agreements based on a purchase cost of $3,200. Betz refused to sign, and Butler and Rhodes followed his lead, objecting that the price was unreasonably high. On instructions from Washington, Emmerich ordered them to vacate their homesteads. For the time being, the Division of Subsistence Homesteads decided not to move any more families into the project. The Betz episode may have contributed to the decision, but it was not the only reason. Emmerich had wired the finished houses for electricity, but then decided

23. Ibid., 6 April 1934; John B. Holt, *An Analysis of Methods and Criteria Used in Selecting Families for Colonization Projects*, Social Research Report no. 1 of the U.S. Department of Agriculture, Farm Security Administration, and the Bureau of Agricultural Economics (Washington, 1937), pp. 36, 37.
24. *McComb Enterprise*, 6 April 1934.
25. Conkin, *Tomorrow a New World*, p. 127.
26. *McComb Enterprise*, 8 June 1934.

the cost of extending power lines to the project was too high. Thus the McComb homesteads were without lights; and since the well pumps were electric, they were also without water.[27]

The reception of McComb Homesteads had been enthusiastic; and until early summer, the project had developed almost too smoothly. Emmerich and Mayor Kramer had proudly presented Betz with the keys to his homestead, the first one in the state to be occupied. McComb Homesteads even received national publicity. The *New York Times* carried photographs of Betz and his new home, prompting a high official of Western Union Telegraph Corporation to request the blueprints; he wanted to use them for the construction of a summer home. When the first three homesteaders moved in, Emmerich talked about having a "housewarming," but it never came off. All of a sudden nothing seemed to work.[28]

In early 1935 the Division of Subsistence Homesteads came up with a plan for reorganizing McComb. After a restudy of the project, Charles E. Pynchon, Wilson's successor as head of the Federal Subsistence Homesteads Corporation, proposed the construction of ten more houses, bringing the total to thirty-five and reducing the size of the larger homestead plots. Although he contemplated spending an additional $26,000 at McComb, Pynchon pointed out that these changes would lower the average cost of each homestead from about $3,800 to $2,865—a price that he hoped would attract settlers to the project. Secretary of the Interior Harold L. Ickes gave approval, but then the old curmudgeon apparently changed his mind. After February 1935 the Division of Subsistence Homesteads suspended all activity at McComb except for such work as planting trees along project roads. Since no permanent residents were on the project and no effort was being made to find any, McComb Homesteads went into a kind of limbo until the Resettlement Administration took it over three months later.[29]

Soon after construction started at McComb, the Division of Subsistence Homesteads launched building programs at Tupelo, Hattiesburg,

27. Project Analysis Questionnaire, McComb, Mississippi, Project No. 27, n.d., HHFA Records, NA, RG 207; McComb Homestead Project SH-MS-4, Report of Examination, dated 22 June 1937, ibid. This was not the J. R. Butler associated with the Southern Tenant Farmers' Union.
28. *McComb Enterprise*, 8 June, 20 July, 24 August 1934.
29. Charles E. Pynchon, memorandum to Secretary of the Interior, 5 February 1935, File no. 1-277, Ickes Papers, NA, RG 48; *McComb Enterprise*, 18 January 1935.

and Meridian. As was the case at McComb, the agency itself did not exist long enough to see the work completed.

Tupelo Homesteads of Mississippi purchased a 171-acre tract for $6,259.37, built twenty-five clapboard homes of English and colonial American design, and leased them primarily to low-income families employed in the textile industry. Tupelo had three parks and a lake with a community pavilion. The Wilson Dam power plant of the Tennessee Valley Authority supplied electricity for the project, and all occupants had one-party telephone service.[30] Magnolia Homesteads, near Meridian, consisted of 233 acres of land in three tracts, costing a total of $5,325. Mrs. L. C. Gray, general manager of Magnolia, was the only woman in the nation to manage a subsistence homesteads project. The homes at Magnolia were bungalow-type frame structures, with electric lights but no gas or telephone service. Like McComb and Tupelo, Magnolia had a park and lake for recreational purposes.[31] Hattiesburg Homesteads invested $2,379.20 in a mere 129-acre tract, the smallest project in the state. The Hattiesburg project had twenty-four frame clapboard houses, a park but no lake or other community facilities, and no utilities at all.[32] At Laurel a 183-acre tract was purchased for $2,010.33, but the project never got as far as construction.[33]

With a minimum of prior experience, Subsistence Homesteads launched a rather ambitious program in Mississippi. Like many of the agency's projects, they possessed an amateurish quality; and in the long run, they were among the most unsuccessful of all New Deal community projects in Region VI. For the perceptive observer, they gave a hint of the difficulties similar efforts might later encounter.

While the Division of Subsistence Homesteads had left a disappointing record, the Mississippi projects, like Dyess Colony, would have a second chance. On 30 April, Roosevelt abolished the twenty-one-month-old

30. Resettlement Administration, "Project Description Book"; Mississippi Projects, 1 June 1935, FSA Records, NA, RG 96.
31. Project Analysis Questionnaire, Magnolia Gardens, Meridian, Mississippi, HHFA Records, NA, RG 207; Thomas K. Shuff, memorandum to Lee Pressman, 15 July 1935, ibid.
32. Rexford G. Tugwell to Rep. William M. Colmer, 20 May 1936, FSA Records, NA, RG 96; Report on Examination, Hattiesburg Homestead Association, dated 20 September 1943, ibid.; A. T. McCurdie to H. V. Rouse, 20 June 1935, HHFA Records, NA, RG 207.
33. Mississippi Projects, 1 June 1935, FSA Records, NA, RG 96; Report of the Division of Subsistence Homesteads and Federal Subsistence Homesteads Corporation, June 1934, ibid.

agency. Since Subsistence Homesteads and the FERA's Rural Rehabilitation Division were pursuing similar problems on a roughly parallel course, he combined both of them, together with the FERA Land Program and the Land Policy Section of the AAA, into a new agency, the Resettlement Administration, under one of his Brain Trusters, Rexford G. Tugwell. The creation of the Resettlement Administration at last signaled the beginning of a concentrated attack against the evils of rural poverty.

Part Two

A War against Poverty

Chapter V

Summer of '35:
The Resettlement Administration's Region VI

The grim days of 1933 soon passed, along with the sense of despair. In its first two years the New Deal had established a record of genuine accomplishment, but the depression stubbornly refused to go away. With the immediate crisis over, Roosevelt's critics found their voices.

While the American Liberty League spoke for conservative business opinion, the New Deal was most seriously imperiled by a rising chorus of abuse from the left. Once a friend of the administration, Father Charles E. Coughlin, the radio priest from Detroit, was on the air every Sunday evening blasting Roosevelt. The old-folks' crusader, Dr. Francis E. Townsend, had formed a political organization which cut into Roosevelt's support, an unsettling threat with a presidential election coming up. Sen. Huey P. Long, the Louisiana Kingfish, dreamed of riding his "Share Our Wealth" plan into the presidency.[1] Long's popularity was particularly high in neighboring states. Arkansas and Mississippi trailed only Louisiana itself in the number of Share Our Wealth clubs. In 1932 he had invaded Arkansas with a whirlwind campaign for Sen. Hattie W. Caraway, and she came from behind to win.

The Lower Mississippi Valley was the source of still another, though politically less threatening, disturbance. The Agricultural Adjustment Administration had worsened the plight of tenant farmers and sharecrop-

---

1. See David H. Bennett, *Demagogues in the Depression: American Radicals and the Union Party, 1932–1936* (New Brunswick, N.J.: Rutgers University Press, 1969); Donald R. McCoy, *Angry Voices: Left of Center Politics in the New Deal Era* (Lawrence: University of Kansas Press, 1958); Arthur M. Schlesinger, Jr., *The Age of Roosevelt: The Politics of Upheaval* (Boston: Houghton Mifflin, 1960), pp. 15–68.

pers; and their outrage, expressed in the form of a new tenant farmers' union, was slowly building into a crescendo.

Even Congress, though heavily Democratic in both houses, began defying the president and getting away with it. But the old master soon reasserted command. The summer months of 1935 were filled with excitement, beginning what historians have called the Second New Deal. Never before had a single session of Congress churned out so much legislation of major importance: a $5 million emergency relief appropriation, social security, holding-company regulation, banking and tax reform, and labor legislation. Besides the Resettlement Administration, Roosevelt created by executive order the Works Progress Administration, National Youth Administration, and Rural Electrification Administration.[2] Before the end of August, he was back on top. Roosevelt had stolen the thunder of the left.

Most of the new programs served in part a political purpose. The Resettlement Administration (RA) would calm the rural discontent which fed the ambitions of Huey Long, Roosevelt's most worrisome problem. One of Tugwell's aides, Laurence Hewes, later put it this way: "if Resettlement effectively met health, food, shelter needs in the deep South, it would in time bolster the fortunes of [Joseph T.] Robinson of Arkansas, [Pat] Harrison of Mississippi, [Richard] Russell of Georgia, and the Bankheads [John H. and Will] of Alabama."[3] Whatever the RA's political value, the primary concern of the leaders of the agency was to improve rural living conditions simply because these conditions were detrimental.

Rexford Tugwell himself had persuaded Roosevelt to bring together all federal rural poverty programs into one independent agency. With his Ivy League credentials, Tugwell was the personification of the New Deal liberal. Above all, he had gained a reputation as an iconoclast— skeptical of tradition, individualism, and laissez faire economics. His hope for the future rested on economic planning through governmental action, and he aroused the fears of conservatives everywhere. Tugwell had first provoked the suspicion of businessmen with his sponsorship of pure food and drug legislation. After his appointment as assistant secretary of agriculture, he became well known as a spokesman for the small farmer, but he showed little respect for the dogmas of agrarian orthodoxy. He had no faith in mere ownership as a panacea for distressed farm families,

2. Ibid., pp. 1–11; William E. Leuchtenburg, *Franklin D. Roosevelt and the New Deal* (New York: Harper and Row, 1963), pp. 150–66.
3. Laurence Hewes, *Boxcar in the Sand* (New York: Knopf, 1957), p. 75.

and he dismissed the subsistence homesteads approach as sentimental escapism.[4]

His goal, as Hewes has recalled, "was a permanent reconstruction of American rural life."[5] Tugwell talked about land reform. He favored the government purchase of submarginal land in vast amounts, the retirement of land unfit for agriculture, and the resettlement of uprooted families. Land reform and resettlement, he believed, would attack the fundamental and long-range causes of rural poverty. He did not kid himself about what such a plan meant if carried to its logical conclusion. "We must study and classify American soil," he said in 1933, "taking out of production not just one part of a field or farm, but whole farms, whole ridges, perhaps whole regions. . . . It has been estimated that when lands now unfit to till are removed from cultivation, something around two million persons who now farm will have to be absorbed by other occupations."[6] In his youth Tugwell had dreamed of "making America over," and now he had a chance to try some of his ideas.

In the Resettlement Administration he launched a dual attack on the erosion of human resources and natural resources. The RA's Land Utilization Division sought to improve submarginal land through soil conservation, reforestation, and flood control; such land was converted to nonagricultural uses. The Resettlement Division completed most of the old subsistence homesteads and FERA projects, and initiated its own community program. Tugwell's real love was the suburban greenbelt towns, but most of the new projects were rural communities for low-income families. Absorbed from FERA, Rural Rehabilitation was the emergency phase of the program, and though secondary at first, it even-

4. See Bernard Sternsher, *Rexford Tugwell and the New Deal* (New Brunswick, N.J.: Rutgers University Press, 1964), pp. 9–10, chap. 17; Arthur M. Schlesinger, Jr., *The Age of Roosevelt: The Coming of the New Deal* (Boston: Houghton Mifflin, 1959), pp. 354–61, 369–70; Rexford G. Tugwell, "The Future of National Planning," *New Republic* 89 (9 December 1936): 162–64. "A farm," Tugwell once wrote, "is an area of vicious, ill-tempered soil with a not very good house, inadequate barns, makeshift machinery, happenstance stock, tired, over-worked men and women—and all the pests and bucolic plagues that nature has evolved . . . a place where ugly, brooding monotony, that haunts by day and night, unseats the mind." Quoted in Sidney Baldwin, *Poverty and Politics: The Rise and Decline of the Farm Security Administration* (Chapel Hill: University of North Carolina Press, 1968), p. 88.

5. Hewes, *Boxcar in the Sand*, p. 61.

6. Quoted in Webster Powell and Addison T. Culter, "Tightening the Cotton Belt," *Harper's Magazine* 168 (February 1934): 308; Sternsher, *Rexford Tugwell*, p. 5; Rexford G. Tugwell, *The Brains Trust* (New York: Viking, 1968), pp. 69–70; Tugwell Diary Notes, 23 January–2 May 1935, Tugwell Papers.

tually involved more money and more people than the better-known community projects. The Rural Rehabilitation Division made loans and grants to individual farm families to help them become self-supporting farm owners, sponsored rural cooperatives for purchasing farm machinery, and helped work out satisfactory debt adjustments between creditors and distressed farmers who were about to lose everything.[7]

In the frantic summer months of 1935, Tugwell put together his Washington staff and set up a decentralized administrative structure, with eleven (later twelve) regional offices and a chain of command that reached down through dozens of state, district, and county offices. Arkansas, Louisiana, and Mississippi made up Region VI, a natural unit which dominated the Lower Mississippi Valley.

Tugwell originally planned to have two directors in each region, each with complete authority over his respective sphere but together constituting the regional leadership. For Region VI, T. Roy Reid would direct rural rehabilitation and resettlement, and Bueford M. Gile the land utilization program.[8] Reid also assumed responsibility for the rural relief work of the FERA, the subsistence homesteads program, and in time the three state rural rehabilitation corporations.[9] Gile, who currently was a regional director in the Land Policy Section of the AAA's Division of Planning,[10] merely transferred his activities into the Resettlement Administration. But Tugwell dropped this dual arrangement in November 1935, and designated one man, Reid, as regional director. From the beginning, Reid had the primary task of setting up the entire administrative organization of Region VI from the regional office on down.[11]

B. M. Gile's career stretched back before World War I. After gradu-

7. Resettlement Administration, *First Annual Report* (Washington: Government Printing Office, 1936); Rexford G. Tugwell, "Changing Acres," *Current History* 44 (September 1936): 57–63; idem, "Cooperation and Resettlement," ibid. 45 (February 1937): 71–76; Baldwin, *Poverty and Politics,* chap. 7.

8. Rexford G. Tugwell to the President, 10 July 1935, FSA Records, NA, RG 96; Little Rock *Arkansas Gazette,* 29 June, 2 July 1935.

9. In almost every state the board of directors of the state rural rehabilitation corporation agreed to turn over their assets to the Resettlement Administration. See above, Chapter III, n. 46.

10. L. C. Gray, memorandum to Rexford G. Tugwell, 22 May 1935, FSA Records, NA, RG 96. Gile's region of the Land Policy Section covered Arkansas, Louisiana, Mississippi, Oklahoma, and Texas. See also Julian N. Friant, memorandum to Laurence I. Hewes, Jr., 14 June 1935, ibid.

11. Rexford G. Tugwell, telegram to B. M. Gile, 15 November 1935, ibid.; Carl C. Taylor to Harry Wise, 26 July 1935, ibid.

ating from the University of Wisconsin in 1913, he went into agricultural extension work and vocational education. In the 1920s he completed his education at the University of Minnesota, earning a master's degree in agricultural economics in 1925 and a doctorate in 1927. Next he joined the faculty at the University of Arkansas's College of Agriculture. With the coming of the New Deal, he went into federal service, joining first the Farm Credit Administration and then the Land Policy Section of the AAA. Over the years he had authored numerous experimentation bulletins and highly technical articles.[12]

T. Roy Reid also possessed a broad background of educational and agricultural experience. He was a farm boy, born in 1889 near Gowensville, South Carolina. He got his undergraduate education at Clemson College and later went to the University of Wisconsin for a master's in agriculture. Since he had occupied rural classrooms before and during his college work, he decided to make a career in education. He taught science and economics at Clinton College in Kentucky, and, moving to Arkansas, spent two years teaching agriculture in the Fourth District Agricultural School at Monticello.

In 1917 Reid left the classroom and took the local county agent's job. A year later he joined the new state Agricultural Extension Service in Little Rock and became a livestock and marketing specialist. By the time of his appointment as regional director of the Resettlement Administration, he had worked his way up to the number-two position in the Arkansas Extension Service. He had previously taken an active part in New Deal programs by serving on the board of directors of the Arkansas Rural Rehabilitation Corporation and as state director of agricultural adjustment programs. He also sat on various drought and flood committees.[13]

A conservative man, Reid was not one to stir up trouble for himself by rocking the boat. Yet he sympathized with the need of small farmers for public assistance. Too often, he felt, government aid for agriculture had not reached those who needed it most, largely because they did not have the means to make improvements or try new methods. Reid saw the Resettlement Administration as a way to take the Extension Service's

12. Rexford G. Tugwell to the President, 10 July 1935, ibid.
13. Ibid.; T. Roy Reid to W. W. Alexander, 26 October 1937, ibid.; *Arkansas Gazette*, 29 June 1935, 13 December 1936; C. B. Baldwin to Sen. John E. Miller, 13 February 1941, FSA Records, NA, RG 96. See Inez Hale MacDuff, "27 Years in Rural Arkansas," *Arkansas Gazette Sunday Magazine*, 30 March 1941, p. 3.

farm and home management program for the first time to low-income families.[14]

When the new appointment came through, he canceled a much-needed vacation that he had coming. He was already a nonstop worker, but now he was going to be busier than ever. He spent a few days attending conferences in Washington with other regional directors, heard a presidential address, and returned to Little Rock.[15] "You know," he told reporters wistfully, "I did think for a while that Mrs. Reid and I would go off in the country somewhere and rest and loaf a couple of weeks this summer. But I guess now we won't." He thought of his job with Resettlement as temporary, and assumed he would go back to the Extension Service when it was over.[16] The new regional director officially stepped into his job on 1 July 1935.

When announcing Reid's appointment, Washington officials said nothing about the location of the regional office. The *Arkansas Gazette* expected Fayetteville to be chosen.[17] Fayetteville, after all, already claimed the state Extension Service, the College of Agriculture, and the regional office of the AAA's Land Policy Section. The town was in fact the early choice of Washington officials. But on 17 July, Carl C. Taylor, national chief of the Resettlement Division, wired Reid to establish his headquarters at Little Rock. The decision set off some shock waves. The Senate majority leader, Joseph T. Robinson of Arkansas, summoned Laurence Hewes to the Senate Office Building and subjected him to "a terrifying tongue lashing." Robinson was enraged because he had not been consulted on the decision to move the regional office.[18]

Fayetteville partisans also put in their objection. Leslie S. Read, editor of the Fayetteville *Daily Democrat* ("an original Roosevelt and pro-administration anti-Long newspaper"), warned Tugwell that this decision

14. T. Roy Reid, "Public Assistance to Low-Income Farmers of the South," *Journal of Farm Economics* 21 (February 1939): 188–94; idem, "The Problem of Farm Tenancy," *Richland Beacon-News* (Rayville, La.), 7 November 1936.

15. *Arkansas Gazette*, 29 June 1935; FDR, *Public Papers* (1935), 4:277–79; Hewes, *Boxcar in the Sand*, pp. 66–67.

16. *Arkansas Gazette*, 29 June 1935.

17. Ibid., 2, 3 July 1935.

18. Carl C. Taylor, telegrams to T. Roy Reid, 17, 19 July 1935, FSA Records, NA, RG 96; *Arkansas Gazette*, 20, 22 July 1935; Hewes, *Boxcar in the Sand*, pp. 68–69. In the early stages of locating regional headquarters, Washington officials considered and rejected two other land grant college towns, Starkville, Mississippi, and Baton Rouge, Louisiana. Baton Rouge also had the disadvantage of being Huey Long's capital. Michael H. Mehlman, "The Resettlement Administration and the Problems of Tenant Farmers in Arkansas, 1935–1936" (Ph.D. diss., New York University, 1970), p. 69.

would lose support for the Roosevelt administration, since it came at a time when W. H. "Coin" Harvey of Free Silver fame was opening a Huey Long headquarters near Fayetteville. Dan T. Gray, dean of the College of Agriculture at the University of Arkansas and director of the Extension Service, also regretted the move to Little Rock; he wanted the regional office at his own institution and perhaps under his wing.[19]

Probably the Resettlement Administration turned down Fayetteville because northwestern Arkansas was rather inaccessible to the rest of the region; Little Rock would be closer to most resettlement projects and other activities. Another matter which possibly influenced the decision was that Reid made his home in Little Rock. Beyond reasons of convenience, Resettlement officials may have been thinking politically. Tugwell—who did not have, as he once said, a "damn bit of confidence" in the Extension Service—probably used Little Rock to keep his new agency away from its influence.

The Little Rock office was an organizational kaleidoscope. Following instructions from national headquarters, Reid first divided his staff into a series of coordinate divisions: rural resettlement, land utilization, management, construction, finance, personnel, information, business management, legal, and labor relations. The "action" divisions, which conducted the agency's programs in the field, were land utilization, rural resettlement, and management. B. M. Gile's Land Utilization Division consisted of project planning, land acquisition, farm development, and project development sections.[20] For regional chief of rural resettlement, Reid chose E. B. Whitaker, who came with the FERA's Rural Rehabilitation Division in Arkansas. Whitaker's division, the largest in the region, was the one about which the general public heard most. Besides the resettlement program itself, the Rural Resettlement Division originally included all rural rehabilitation work, a community and cooperative staff, and a farm debt adjustment section. The Management Division chief was James B. Lawson, a transfer from the Mississippi subsistence homesteads program, where he had developed the Tupelo project.[21]

19. Lessie S. Read, telegram to Rexford Tugwell, 16 July 1935, FSA Records, NA, RG 96; Dan T. Gray to C. C. Taylor, 22 July 1935, ibid.; Horace Thompson, project manager at Lake Dick and one-time head of the regional Tenant Purchase Division, interview with the author, 19 January 1968.

20. Warren Bruner to James H. Wells, 30 October 1935, FSA Records, NA, RG 96.

21. E. E. Agger, memorandum to Will W. Alexander, 18 October 1935, ibid.; Resettlement Administration, Annual Report, Region VI, as of 31 December 1936, ibid.

After a year had passed, Reid created three assistant directorships to take charge of the growing resettlement, rehabilitation, and management programs. He gave rural rehabilitation full divisional status in recognition of its growing importance, naming another agriculturist, Thomas P. Lee, as division chief. Rehabilitation now embodied all types of loans, farm debt adjustment, and farm management work. Whitaker's Resettlement Division supervised all projects, both land use and rural resettlement, and handled most of its own development work, including architecture and engineering, land analysis, surveying, purchasing, and project construction. In Management, Lawson was responsible to the regional director for managing the completed projects, collecting rent, maintaining the property, and social service functions such as family selection.[22]

Next to Reid, Whitaker became the most important man in the regional office. He was a native of Mississippi, and like Dyess, a graduate of Mississippi A & M College at Starkville. He did graduate work in agriculture at the University of Wisconsin, but never earned a graduate degree. Like Reid, he was with the Arkansas Extension Service when he went into federal employment. In 1934 W. R. Dyess had made him director of rural relief. In the Resettlement Administration, Whitaker started out as state director of rural resettlement for Arkansas, and in rapid order became regional chief of the Rural Resettlement Division and assistant regional director in charge of resettlement.[23]

As the process of expansion, consolidation, and musical chairs continued in the regional office, Reid tended to rely more and more on Whitaker. In 1937 he combined the resettlement and management divisions under him; in 1938 Reid ended the experimentation in his office, and returned to Whitaker most of the responsibilities he had in his original Rural Resettlement Division.[24] The purpose of these moves seems to have been for Whitaker to take control of all phases of the regional resettlement program. In May 1940 Whitaker became assistant regional director, without special designation but in direct charge of resettlement, farm management, home management, cooperative services, and com-

22. Ibid.; Region Organization Chart, n.d., ibid.; George S. Mitchell to T. Roy Reid, 9 May 1939, ibid.
23. E. B. Whitaker, interview with the author, 19 January 1968; James H. Wells to Warren Bruner, 9 October 1935, FSA Records, NA, RG 96.
24. Whitaker interview; T. Roy Reid to Will W. Alexander, 17 February 1937, 31 March 1938, FSA Records, NA, RG 96; Lewis E. Long to E. R. Henson, 7 August 1937, ibid.

munity and family services.[25] More than any other one man, he *was* the resettlement program in Region VI.

In addition to the regional headquarters at Little Rock, the Resettlement Administration maintained three state offices. When Carl Taylor notified Reid of the Little Rock decision, he included instructions for "completely regionalizing the three states of region 6."[26] In other words, Reid should arrange office space at Little Rock not only for his staff but also for that of the state directors of Louisiana and Mississippi as well as Arkansas. Normally, state offices were domiciled in the state they served. In another departure from usual practice, Tugwell went out of the region to pick Robert W. "Pete" Hudgens as Louisiana's state director. Hudgens was a Greenville, South Carolina, investment broker who had done some experimenting of his own in rural resettlement. When a reporter asked Reid why the state offices were established at Little Rock, he refused comment. But the political implications were obvious. "RRA Kept Out of Long's Clutches," headlined the *Arkansas Gazette*.[27]

Huey Long was a charter member of the FRBC group (For Roosevelt before Chicago), but he had broken with the national administration during the Hundred Days. Long's attacks on the New Deal grew more and more vociferous until Roosevelt resolved to freeze out the Louisiana Kingfish, particularly where patronage was concerned. On 5 February the Louisiana situation came up at a meeting of the National Emergency Council with the vice-president and secretary of state present. Roosevelt exclaimed: "Don't put anybody in and don't keep anybody that is working for Huey Long or his crowd! That is a hundred percent!"

JOHN NANCE GARNER: That goes for everybody!
ROOSEVELT: Everybody and every agency. Anybody working for Huey Long is not working for us.
CORDELL HULL: It can't be corrected too soon.
ROOSEVELT: You will get a definite ruling any time you want it.[28]

Throughout the summer of 1935 Senator Long engaged in a running battle with the Roosevelt administration, particularly with Secretary of

25. T. Roy Reid to Will W. Alexander, 25 May 1940, ibid.; Farm Security Administration, Region VI, Quarterly Report, July–September 1940, ibid.
26. Carl C. Taylor, telegrams to T. Roy Reid, 17, 19 July 1935, ibid.
27. *Arkansas Gazette*, 22 July 1935.
28. Lester G. Seligman and Elmer E. Cornwell, Jr., eds., *New Deal Mosaic: Roosevelt Confers with His National Emergency Council* (Eugene: University of Oregon Press, 1965), p. 437.

the Interior Harold L. Ickes. Long wanted to control all federal money spent in Louisiana, and he rammed bills through the Baton Rouge legislature in an attempt to accomplish this purpose. In response, Ickes threatened to halt all Public Works Administration projects in the state; and in July, about the time Taylor informed Reid of the location of Region VI headquarters, Ickes did stop PWA work, ruling out any future projects unless state laws regulating the expenditure of federal funds were repealed. Now Tugwell had the task of setting up a field organization in Louisiana, an organization that would have to reach into every rural parish in the state.[29]

Pete Hudgens did not relish the Louisiana job, but he had taken a close look at what he was getting into. After touring the state in early July, Hudgens and George M. Reynolds, head of the RA's Labor Relations Division, submitted a report to Tugwell outlining three options for a field organization in Huey Long's fiefdom.[30]

First, they said, the Louisiana organization could cooperate with the Long machine, an unthinkable choice since Long opposed New Deal programs at practically every turn. Second, it could be set up in alliance with the anti-Long forces of Louisiana. This was what the Louisiana Emergency Relief Administration had done, reported Hudgens and Reynolds, and it had cost the relief organization much independence and efficiency, besides diverting it from its primary work. The Resettlement Administration should not, they advised, allow itself to be used as part of an anti-Long machine, especially if this would defeat the purpose for which the RA existed. Third, the Resettlement Administration could form a nonpolitical organization, keeping it independent of any faction. The latter was the best, most practical course, they argued; this approach was not expected to incur the wrath of the Huey Long machine. (Reynolds and Hudgens believed that the most for which Long hoped was to neutralize the political effect of federal spending in Louisiana, not to dominate it.) But they anticipated opposition from the anti-Long faction since the latter believed the RA's purpose should be to help them build up their organization. Ironically, the report ended: "to follow the third course and do an excellent piece of work is . . . in the long run the most effective opposition to Senator Long."[31]

29. *Arkansas Gazette*, 6, 19, 20 July 1935.
30. Robert W. Hudgens and George M. Reynolds, memorandum to R. G. Tugwell, 15 July 1935, FSA Records, NA, RG 96.
31. Ibid. The next year Reynolds published a book on Louisiana entitled *Machine Politics in New Orleans, 1897–1926* (New York: Columbia University Press, 1936).

Hudgens's independence would presumably enable him to stand up to the Kingfish, especially in the task of filling some four hundred jobs that the agency expected to create in the state. But the first real trouble, as he and Reynolds had predicted, came from Long's enemies rather than from Huey himself. The anti-Longs were promoting candidates in the Democratic primaries that summer, and they wanted Hudgens to back them. When he said no, one congressman blurted out: "My God! Here he sits with the most powerful patronage weapon in Louisiana, and he's not going to do a Goddam thing about it." During the next few weeks, the anti-Long leaders continued nagging him with their demands for patronage.[32]

Long was perfectly aware that Hudgens was supposed to keep him from taking over the Resettlement Administration's field organization, and the senator was watching the state director for any indication that he had thrown in with the anti-Long faction. "All I'm concerned about is that you help these poor people," the Kingfish told him. "As long as you stick to that job, I'll never bother you." Then he added, "The first time I catch you appointing somebody because one of those sons of bitches tells you to I'll drive you out of Louisiana."[33]

Long's death in September relieved the Resettlement Administration of its dilemma. In May 1936 Reynolds wrote: "The Long faction has made peace in Washington—they evidently are taking the attitude they will vote in accordance with the wish of FDR on any measure." He further reported that Gov. Richard W. Leche was favorably inclined toward the RA, as was Rose Long, Huey's widow.[34] Soon Reid moved the Louisiana office out of Little Rock, first to New Orleans and later to Alexandria. The Mississippi state office went to Jackson.

The Resettlement Administration's thorough field organization existed mainly to conduct the rural rehabilitation program, which involved extensive supervision of loan clients and educational work in over two hundred counties in the region. Each state office contained a rural rehabilitation director and his staff, a state farm debt adjustment committee, and a loan advisory committee composed of important state leaders. The state directors and their offices were under close supervision from Little Rock and possessed no authority to take any initiative in policy matters.

In each state four district offices covered a number of counties or par-

32. Quoted in Baldwin, *Poverty and Politics*, p. 101.
33. Quoted in T. Harry Williams, *Huey Long* (New York: Knopf, 1969), pp. 854, 855.
34. George M. Reynolds to W. W. Alexander, 22 May 1936, FSA Records, NA, RG 96.

ishes; the typical district office comprised a rehabilitation supervisor, a home management supervisor, and their staffs. The county officials consisted of rehabilitation and home management supervisors, a county farm debt adjustment committee, a county rural rehabilitation committee, and later a county tenant purchase committee. Committees were composed of local citizens who helped make decisions about who should get loans or whose debts should be scaled down and by how much. Thus the agency insured a sense of local support and participation.

A separate group of officials handled the resettlement projects. The community or project manager reported directly to the regional office, skipping the county, district, and state offices.[35]

"The men placed at the head of these Resettlement Programs," wrote Mississippi state senator James C. Rice in 1939, "are broken down Ford dealers, junk men, or airplane builders—or just anybody but someone who has actually made a living out of farming."[36] He was complaining because too many employees of the Farm Security Administration, the RA's successor, were, in his view, book farmers with college degrees. This much, at least, was true. The most essential qualification for all supervisory personnel was a degree in agriculture. From first to last the men who ran the programs formed a kind of fraternity which preceded their coming to the agency. Many had attended college together, almost always a land grant college. Curiously, Mississippi State furnished a large number of the region's administrative employees. Many members of this fraternity had previously worked together, and some of them had gotten their jobs through personal contacts. They knew each other well, and they naturally called on one another when filling jobs. Only a few positions, however, were occupied by outright political appointees.

With few exceptions, top officials were not only trained agriculturists, but they also had regional connections. Reid recruited his division and section chiefs either from the state extension services or from local offices of other federal agencies. In 1935 and 1936, as a matter of fact, the administrative personnel of the regional office, including the regional director himself, consisted largely of people on leaves of absence from the Arkansas Extension Service and the University of Arkansas's College

35. Baldwin, *Poverty and Politics*, pp. 244–55; Stanley W. Brown and Virgil E. Baugh, comps., *Preliminary Inventory of the Records of the Farmers Home Administration*, National Archives and Records Service Pub. no. 118 (Washington: National Archives, 1959), pp. 10, 11, 28–30.
36. James C. Rice to Sen. Theodore G. Bilbo, 7 April 1939, FSA Records, NA, RG 96.

of Agriculture.[37] Many others came to the Resettlement Administration with the AAA's Land Policy Section, the FERA's state rural rehabilitation programs, or the Division of Subsistence Homesteads.

The field personnel also came out of the region's agricultural colleges. They were young men just beginning a lifetime of federal service; many of them later succeeded to important posts in the Farmers Home Administration. The project manager and county supervisor positions could not be filled by just anyone. These positions required the ability to work with people; and technical competence in agriculture—knowledge of livestock, soils, and markets—was absolutely essential. As time went on, the quality of field personnel became a major difficulty. Civil service status was denied most RA and, later, FSA employees, and salary schedules were low. Consequently, qualified men often could not be recruited.

Regional information chief George Wolf wrote in 1939, "We now have in the region 1,879 employees, making us by far the largest agricultural agency in the three states." Located on the fourth floor of Little Rock's Donaghey Trust Building, the regional office alone held a third of the agency's total employees in the region. At first the *Arkansas Gazette* reported plans for the office to employ between 75 and 80 persons. At the end of 1937 the Little Rock office contained 216 employees; by 1941 it had expanded to 559.[38]

Resettlement and Farm Security personnel also went into every nook and cranny of the three states. By 1937 the FSA had 185 employees stationed in Louisiana, 285 in Mississippi, and 308 in Arkansas—all based on the proportion of farms in each state as compared to the entire region. Two years later there were 12 district offices and 201 county offices with a combined total of 1,102 employees; among these grass-roots workers were 709 rehabilitation and home management supervisors and 393 clerks.[39]

In 1937 a rumor circulated that Mississippi and Arkansas had taken the lion's share of the available Farm Security jobs while Louisiana got the short shift. Cong. Overton Brooks made an inquiry. It was true, said assistant administrator C. B. Baldwin, that Louisiana had only 23.7 percent of all employees headquartered outside Little Rock, but the state

37. Dan T. Gray to Raymond A. Pearson, 20 April 1936, ibid.; *Arkansas Gazette*, 20 November 1936. Reid did not resign from his Extension Service job until 1937.
38. *Arkansas Gazette*, 20 July 1935; Personnel Report, Region VI, 31 December 1939; George Wolf to John Fischer, 10 April 1939; A. D. Stewart to C. B. Baldwin, 20 August 1941, all in FSA Records, NA, RG 96.
39. C. B. Baldwin to Rep. Overton Brooks, 2 December 1937, ibid.; A. D. Stewart to Baldwin, 20 August 1941, ibid.

had only 23 percent of the total farms in the region.[40] Brooks was presumably satisfied. Yet evidence did exist to indicate discrimination at least in the resettlement program. When all community building stopped in 1941, Louisiana had only four resettlement projects, compared to ten for Mississippi (including five subsistence homesteads) and sixteen for Arkansas. The amount of funds spent in Louisiana was similarly disproportionate.[41]

Reid ran a large and complex bureaucratic structure in Region VI, and he contended with the problems that plague any such organization. Some of his problems were mundane: acquiring more office space as his regional staff grew, keeping new employees supplied with appropriate government procedure manuals, and setting up a badly needed stenographic pool to handle the flood of paper work.[42] A more serious problem was that of defining the authority of the regional office vis-à-vis the state, district, and county offices, and welding every part of the three-state organization into a smooth and efficient operation.

Although the regional organization was dominated by the "agri fraternity," a couple of outsiders originally held state directorships. Besides R. W. Hudgens in Louisiana, George Reynolds took responsibility for Mississippi. When Reynolds showed up with instructions to take charge, Reid wired national headquarters: "I feel that it is essential that we have a strong agricultural man in charge."[43] He clearly did not want Reynolds. Soon friction developed, since Reynolds was not one to withhold his criticisms. "There is a lack of coordination," he wrote, "both in the region and the state offices, which is due to the fact that there is no centralization of authority over the entire program, either in the region or the state [of Mississippi]." His solution was to abolish the dual regional directorship and to put the entire resettlement program under one general regional director—a change that was made; however, he also favored giving state directors, like himself, the same power in their states as the regional di-

40. Rep. Overton Brooks to Will W. Alexander, 5 October 1937; C. B. Baldwin to Brooks, 2 December 1937; see Brooks to Alexander, 5 October 1937; A. D. Stewart to Baldwin, 24 October 1941, all ibid.
41. A. D. Stewart to C. B. Baldwin, 20 August 1941, ibid.; FSA, "Resettlement Projects." No fewer than fifty-two resettlement projects were originally considered for Arkansas alone. E. B. Whitaker to T. Roy Reid, 14 August 1935, FSA Records, NA, RG 96; see Rexford G. Tugwell to Rep. William J. Driver, 15 June 1936, ibid.
42. T. Roy Reid to Division Heads and Section Chiefs, 30 April 1940, ibid.; James H. Wells to Warren Bruner, 20 August 1935, ibid.
43. T. Roy Reid to Carl C. Taylor, 5 September 1935, ibid.

rector possessed in the region. Region VI's early difficulties, wrote two Washington officials, were "attributable in no small degree to the strong attitudes of state directors who desired to operate programs with little control from the regional office."[44]

Before long, Hudgens and, more important, Reynolds left the region for other assignments. E. C. McInnis took over the Louisiana state office; Marvin T. Aldrich followed Reynolds in Mississippi. Arkansas had been safe all along with Whitaker himself in charge, although he soon turned the job over to A. M. Rogers. McInnis, Aldrich, and Rogers, all natives of the respective states, were the kind of men Reid wanted.

From 1936 to 1939 Reid further strengthened regional control. For example, he took the authority to approve loans and grants out of the state offices and placed it in the regional office. At the same time, he reduced state office functions to directing the work of district and county supervisors and managing the work of the state rural rehabilitation corporations (the new office of regional Custodian of Corporations soon took away the latter function). In addition, he concentrated in his assistant regional director, Whitaker, almost every activity related to resettlement, again preempting the authority of the state directors.[45]

As a result, there were complaints of too much centralization. In 1939 George S. Mitchell, troubleshooter for the national office, wrote Reid that "the extreme concentration of functions in your Assistant Regional Director is thought unwise." More authority, he said, should be delegated to community managers. Mercer G. Evans, another Washington representative, criticized "a tendency on the part of the regional office not to delegate authority and responsibility to subordinate field offices." This criticism applied especially "to the programs under Whitaker." John Fischer, national information director, complained about the resettlement program in Region VI: "there is little written material available for reference in the regional office and . . . Mr. Whitaker keeps most of the pertinent facts in his head."[46]

These difficulties were never completely resolved. A certain tension always existed between Washington officials who gave advice and field

44. George M. Reynolds to Will W. Alexander, 15 November 1935, ibid.; C. B. Baldwin and Robert W. Hudgens to Will W. Alexander, 18 November 1939, ibid.
45. Resettlement Administration, Annual Report, Region VI, as of 31 December 1936, ibid. See A. D. Stewart to C. B. Baldwin, 18 August 1941, ibid.
46. George S. Mitchell to T. Roy Reid, 9 May 1939, ibid.; Mercer G. Evans, memorandum to Mitchell, 15 April 1939, ibid.; John Fischer, memorandum to Mitchell, 6 April 1939, ibid.

personnel who thought they were doing the best local circumstances would allow. When years later Whitaker read the criticism of him, he commented that neither Reynolds, Mitchell, nor Evans had "any training, connection or understanding of professional agriculture." "All three," he said, "were jealous of land grant college graduates." To him, such men possessed an unrealistic conception of how to deal with many of the problems arising in the down-to-earth administration of the program.[47]

The Resettlement Administration had an impressive repertoire of antipoverty weapons, and Reid as quickly as possible threw them into action. During the eighteen months from 1 July 1935 to 31 December 1936, rural rehabilitation and land utilization activities made the largest impact on the region. By July 1936 Region VI was leading all other eleven regions in rehabilitation loans, with 45,497 low-income farm families borrowing $6,186,442. The Land Utilization Division had optioned 590,630 acres of land unfit for agriculture at a total purchase cost of $3,248,268, and had employed about forty-three hundred men to develop the land as forests, pasture, and game refuges. This effort also led the nation.[48]

During the same period, Whitaker launched the resettlement program. By December 1936 he had drawn up plans for eighteen resettlement projects, sixteen of them active and two on which activity had previously been suspended. According to early estimates, these projects would ultimately resettle 2,574 farm families and cost about $4 million.[49] The resettlement program involved months and months of detailed planning on the part of most of the divisions and sections in the regional office.

The Land Acquisition Unit of the Land Utilization Division appraised 419,226 acres for resettlement purposes. Once the purchases had been made, the architectural and engineering staff's field survey teams began marking out boundaries and subdivisions at project sites and locating future roads, bridges, and drainage ditches. Their job also included preparation of all blueprints and sketches, building specifications, and cost estimates for forwarding to Washington. As 1936 closed, the Construc-

---

47. E. B. Whitaker, memorandum to the author, 1 April 1970. This division between agriculturists and nonagriculturists was similar to the split within the AAA. See pp. 84–85.

48. New Orleans *Times-Picayune*, 23 June 1937; *Madison Journal* (Tallulah, La.), 3 July 1936; Rexford G. Tugwell to T. Roy Reid, 2 February 1937, FSA Records, NA, RG 96.

49. Resettlement Administration, Annual Report of Assistant Regional Director in Charge of Rural Resettlement [E. B. Whitaker], ibid.

tion Division was just beginning work on the first resettlement project in the region.[50]

The Management Division took over the unfinished work of the Division of Subsistence Homesteads and began preparations for transferring four Mississippi projects to local homestead associations (Richton had to be developed almost from scratch). The management staff also began investigating and selecting families for occupancy on both inherited and new community projects.

After a short delay, each of the state rural rehabilitation corporations transferred its stock in trust to Tugwell and turned over its assets.[51] With one major exception, they continued their activities much as in the past. Since the regional office had already assumed the task of family selection at Dyess Colony, it was rumored that the Resettlement Administration might take over the entire project once construction was out of the way. But the Arkansas Rural Rehabilitation Corporation sold the project to the new organization, Dyess Colony, Inc., keeping it under WPA control for another three years.

In just a few weeks Tugwell had built a truly national agency. The Resettlement Administration's decentralized structure ran from Washington down to the most remote rural counties of the nation. In size and scope of operations, the Resettlement Administration and its successor, the Farm Security Administration, joined the ranks of the major federal agricultural agencies—the Agricultural Extension Service, the Forest Service, and New Deal creations like the Agricultural Adjustment Administration, Soil Conservation Service, Rural Electrification Administration, Farm Credit Administration, and Civilian Conservation Corps.

Tugwell, however, had taken on a big job—one so immense that he knew he could not possibly do it well. The explosion of the southern tenant problem dramatized the task which lay ahead.

50. Management Division, Region VI, News Letter, 1 July 1935 to 1 January 1937; Region VI, Progress Report, Land Utilization Division, Period Ending 31 December 1936; Report of the Architectural and Engineering Staff, Region VI, 1 July 1935–31 December 1936; Resettlement Administration, Construction Division, Progress Report for Projects in Development and Planning, 1 July 1936 to 1 August 1936; Resettlement Administration, Annual Report, Region VI, as of 31 December 1936; Rexford G. Tugwell to T. Roy Reid, 2 February 1937, all ibid.

51. When the Resettlement Administration joined the Department of Agriculture, the stock of state rural rehabilitation corporations was pledged to the secretary of agriculture.

Chapter VI

Arkansas Sharecroppers and the New Deal

On a hot July evening in 1934 a small group of sharecroppers—eleven whites and seven blacks—met at a run-down schoolhouse near Tyronza, Arkansas, and formed a union. Some of the white men were former members of the Ku Klux Klan; one aged Negro had been a member of a union broken up in the wake of the Elaine Massacre in 1919. Knowing how the planters had always played white and Negro tenants against each other, they laid aside racial animosities to form one union for both races. They turned for leadership to H. L. Mitchell, a former sharecropper and current owner of a small dry-cleaning shop, and Henry Clay East, the service station operator next door. Mitchell and East made up the core of a Socialist group around Tyronza. During the next few years, the Southern Tenant Farmers' Union (STFU), as it was soon known, placed Arkansas in the middle of a controversy which stirred the nation's conscience.[1]

What had aroused these croppers was the injustice of the Agricultural Adjustment Administration. Not only did the philosophy behind agricultural adjustment overlook the problem of rural poverty, but also the operation of the program simply did not fit the South's unique sharecropper-lien system. All benefit payments went to the landowner, who dominated the local administration of the program. Tenant farmers and sharecroppers were not represented on the AAA county committees, nor

---

1. See Donald H. Grubbs, *Cry from the Cotton: The Southern Tenant Farmers' Union and the New Deal* (Chapel Hill: University of North Carolina Press, 1971); David Eugene Conrad, *The Forgotten Farmers: The Story of Sharecroppers in the New Deal* (Urbana: University of Illinois Press, 1965), chap. 5; M. S. Venkataramani, "Norman Thomas, Arkansas Sharecroppers, and the Roosevelt Agricultural Policies, 1933–1937," *Mississippi Valley Historical Review* 47 (September 1960): 225–46; Jerold Auerbach, "Southern Tenant Farmers: Socialist Critics of the New Deal," *Labor History* 7 (Winter 1966): 3–18.

did AAA cotton contracts safeguard their interests. As a result, many landlords accepted government checks for taking acreage out of production and either cheated croppers out of their share of the subsidy or evicted families whose labor they no longer needed. Many sharecroppers slipped to the status of wage laborer, others became migrant workers who followed the seasons, and some drifted into the cities looking for work.[2]

The AAA's tenant troubles crept into the headlines in early 1934, when Socialist Norman Thomas paid his first visit to the Arkansas delta. Under the AAA, he found, "hundreds of thousands [of sharecroppers] . . . are either being driven out on the roads without hope of absorption into industry or exist without land to cultivate by grace of the landlord in shacks scarcely fit for pigs." He added: "No satirist ever penned such an indictment of a cruel and lunatic order of society as was written by the author of the Agricultural Adjustment Act."[3]

For the Tyronza croppers, one planter, Hiram Norcross, embodied every evil of the AAA. An absentee landlord from Saint Louis, Norcross owned the forty-five-hundred-acre Fairway Farms plantation in Poinsett County. He was determined to make his plantation pay, and exploited his tenants to do so. In 1932 Norcross had evicted about forty families who exceeded their credit at the plantation commissary. When two years later he allegedly deprived his tenants of their share of the AAA parity payment, they sought the help of two local businessmen who had a reputation for fairness among local croppers.

Organizing an "Unemployed League," Mitchell and East had successfully appealed to the Civil Works Administration for more federal relief in Tyronza and vicinity; and they had invited Norman Thomas to examine conditions in eastern Arkansas. Thomas addressed a large crowd in the Tyronza High School auditorium. The audience had never heard anyone speak so critically of the plantation system or the AAA, which was per-

---

2. Van L. Perkins, *Crisis in Agriculture: The Agricultural Adjustment Administration and the New Deal, 1933* (Berkeley and Los Angeles: University of California Press, 1969), pp. 99, 114–16; Fred C. Frey and T. Lynn Smith, "The Influence of the AAA Cotton Program upon the Tenant, Cropper, and Laborer," *Rural Sociology* 1 (December 1936): 497–500; Harold Hoffsommer, "The AAA and the Cropper," *Social Forces* 13 (May 1935): 494–502. See also Edwin G. Nourse, Joseph S. Davis, and John D. Black, *Three Years of the Agricultural Adjustment Administration* (Washington: Brookings Institution, 1937), pp. 342–49; and Henry I. Richards, *Cotton and the AAA* (Washington: Brookings Institution, 1936), pp. 138–62.

3. Oklahoma City *American Guardian*, 2 March 1934, quoted in Richards, *Cotton and the AAA*, p. 149n.; Norman Thomas, *The Choice before Us: Mankind at the Crossroads* (New York: Macmillan, 1934), p. 7.

petuating it. What was needed in the delta, Thomas told Mitchell and East privately, was an organization—a sharecroppers' union. With a union, sharecroppers could hope to stop evictions and chiseling under AAA contracts and to gain some bargaining power with their landlords. At first the fledgling STFU remained in obscurity, but union growth was rapid. At the end of its first year the STFU had about fourteen hundred members in four or five northeastern Arkansas counties; at the end of 1935 about thirty thousand members were scattered in Arkansas, Oklahoma, Texas, Missouri, Mississippi, and Tennessee.[4]

Within the hierarchy of the AAA the sharecropper issue became entangled in a power struggle between two rival factions. The practical, professional agriculturists who actually ran the AAA were not only reconciled to the rural status quo; the "agrarians," as they were sometimes called, were part of it. Like many regional officials of the Resettlement Administration, they were men who came up through the land grant colleges and state extension services; and they were "extraordinarily landlord-minded," as Russell Lord has remarked. The first AAA director, George Peek, and his successor, Chester C. Davis, did not want the crop reduction program to operate to the disadvantage of the tenant and sharecropper; at the same time, they did not favor using the AAA as an instrument of social reform. To them, such a purpose was outside the AAA's purview.[5]

The cotton contract for 1934–35 contained some protection for sharecroppers in paragraph 7, a provision which required landlords to keep the same *number* of tenants as they had the previous year. That was as far as the "agrarians," who dominated the AAA's powerful Cotton Section, were willing to go. But another group, Jerome Frank and the "urban liberals," urged more than minimum protection. They were mostly young lawyers rather than agriculturists, very protective and sympathetic toward tenant farmers, and viewed by the other faction as impractical idealists.

With supreme irony, it was the Norcross case which precipitated the

4. H. L. Mitchell, Columbia University Oral History Project interview, mimeographed, STFU Papers; idem, "Organizing Southern Share-croppers," *New Republic* 80 (3 October 1934): 217–18; Conrad, *Forgotten Farmers*, pp. 84–85.
    5. Russell Lord, *The Wallaces of Iowa* (Boston: Houghton Mifflin, 1947), p. 359; Perkins, *Crisis in Agriculture*, pp. 97–99; Conrad, *Forgotten Farmers*, chap. 6; Grubbs, *Cry from the Cotton*, chap. 3. On Peek, see Gilbert C. Fite, *George N. Peek and the Fight for Farm Parity* (Norman: University of Oklahoma Press, 1945), pp. 253–55.

showdown within the AAA. From a letter Norcross had written explaining his recent actions, Frank learned that the Cotton Section was placing its own interpretation on paragraph 7. In February 1935, while Davis was away on a western field trip, Frank circulated a directive which interpreted the controversial paragraph to require that planters retain not only the same number of tenants but also the same *individuals* as tenants. When Davis returned to his desk, he found his agency in an uproar over the unexpected change. He canceled the directive, and with the backing of President Roosevelt and Secretary of Agriculture Henry A. Wallace, fired Frank and most of his allies.[6]

The controversy placed Wallace in a difficult position. While he disapproved of Frank's proposed interpretation of the cotton contract, he was sympathetic with the plight of landless farmers in the South. But he could not afford to do anything which might jeopardize the AAA's support among the large landowners. Farm tenancy had existed long before the AAA, Wallace reasoned, and the low standard of living of croppers was not due to the new crop reduction program. In fact the AAA was not responsible for all of the tenant displacement, much of it being normal and only aggravated by the general depression.

While turmoil gripped the AAA, the nation began getting an education in the realities of Arkansas rural life. The catalyst was Ward Rogers—a young FERA employee, Methodist minister, and STFU organizer. There had been threats against the lives of union members, he reminded a large audience of tenants and sharecroppers at Marked Tree, Arkansas, in January 1935. "Well, that is a game two can play," he said. "If necessary I could lead the sharecroppers to lynch every planter in Poinsett County." The county prosecuting attorney arrested him just as he left the platform, charging him with anarchy, attempting to overthrow and usurp the government of Arkansas, blasphemy, and barratry. The conviction of Rogers a month later brought the STFU its first national publicity.[7]

The eastern Arkansas planters had at first joked about the union (the

6. Lord, *Wallaces of Iowa*, pp. 393–409; Conrad, *Forgotten Farmers*, chap. 8; Arthur M. Schlesinger, Jr., *The Age of Roosevelt: The Coming of the New Deal* (Boston: Houghton Mifflin, 1959), pp. 77–80; Howard Kester, *Revolt among the Sharecroppers* (New York: Covici, Friede, 1936), pp. 20–30.

7. Grubbs, *Cry from the Cotton*, pp. 70–71; Conrad, *Forgotten Farmers*, pp. 154–60; "Farmers: 'Bootleg Slavery,'" *Time* 25 (4 March 1935): 13–14. Kester, *Revolt among the Sharecroppers*, p. 68, quotes Rogers as saying, "If necessary I could lead the sharecroppers to lynch every planter in Poinsett County, but I have no intention of doing so."

Socialists and the Republicans were getting together, they chuckled), but when it began making headlines they struck back with a "reign of terror." Deputies and riding bosses harassed, beat, and jailed union members; they broke up meetings by shooting into homes and churches. A few known union meeting-places were burned down. When union members moved their meetings outdoors, they sometimes listened to bullets whistling overhead.

"I don't know, though, but what it would have been better to have a few no-account shiftless people killed at the start than to have had all this fuss raised up," commented Abner Sage, one of Marked Tree's religious leaders. "We have had a pretty serious situation here, what with the 'mistering' of the niggers and stirring them up to think the Government was going to give them forty acres."[8]

Norman Thomas returned to northeastern Arkansas that spring, to Trumann, Gilmore, Marked Tree, Lepanto. He encountered hostility but no violence. At Birdsong his luck ran out. A group of riding bosses barged into a meeting and dragged him off the platform. "Ladies and gentlemen—" began Howard Kester, a union leader; but he got no further with Thomas's introduction. "There ain't no ladies in the audience and there ain't no gentlemen on the platform," a voice boomed out. Thomas was run out of town and some of his companions beaten. "We don't need no Gawddamn Yankee bastard to tell us what to do with our niggers," they explained.[9]

When Thomas called at the White House after the Birdsong incident, Roosevelt advised restraint: "I know the South, and there is arising a new generation of leaders in the South and we've got to be patient."[10] It was poor consolation. The STFU had no chance against a campaign of quasi-official violence. They adopted a policy of passive resistance, anticipating Martin Luther King's nonviolent philosophy, and moved their headquarters to Memphis.

The news reports out of Arkansas formed only part of the unrest rumbling across the Cotton Belt in the early 1930s. Besides the STFU, the Share Croppers' Union had gained a foothold in Alabama amid violence far worse than that in Arkansas. The STFU had its Socialist supporters,

8. *New York Times*, 6 April 1935.
9. Kester, *Revolt among the Sharecroppers*, pp. 80–81; John Herling, "Field Notes from Arkansas," *Nation* 140 (10 April 1935): 419–20; H. L. Mitchell and J. R. Butler, "The Cropper Learns His Fate," ibid. 141 (18 September 1935): 328–29.
10. Quoted in Schlesinger, *Coming of the New Deal*, p. 378.

but the Share Croppers' Union was Communist-led, a fact reinforcing the specter of political upheaval.[11]

When Secretary of Agriculture Wallace went to Capitol Hill in early March to testify at hearings on tenancy legislation, it was evident that he had been reading the papers:

> The present conditions, particularly in the South [he told the Senate Committee on Agriculture and Forestry], provide soil for Communist and Socialist agitators. I do not like the bitterness that is aroused by this sort of agitation, but I realize that the cure is not violence or oppressive legislation to curb these activities but rather to give these dispossessed people a stake in the social system. The American way to preserve the traditional order is to provide these refugees of the economic system with an opportunity to build and develop their own homes and to live on the land which they may call their own and on which they can make a modest living year after year.[12]

Alabama senator John H. Bankhead, who had sponsored subsistence homesteads legislation two years before, was the author of the bill before the committee. He proposed a federal program to assist tenant farmers and sharecroppers toward farm ownership; Cong. Marvin Jones of Texas, chairman of the Committee on Agriculture, had introduced a similar measure in the House of Representatives. In principle, Wallace endorsed this type of legislation. The Bankhead bill, Wallace said, was based on the traditional American ideal of "trying to get the good farm land of America into the hands of owner-operators who live on family-sized farms, but with proper safeguards to prevent [land] . . . speculation."[13]

The spring of 1935 was not an auspicious time for a tenancy bill. Congress was jammed with New Deal legislation carrying a higher priority, and in April the Senate was tied up in a filibuster against an antilynching bill. Despite these difficulties, Majority Leader Joseph T. Robinson succeeded in getting the Bankhead bill passed, but Jones's bill died in committee.

Huey Long was in his best form that spring and summer, only months before his death. Many of the people who crowded into the Senate galleries came solely to watch his antics, and he seldom disappointed them.

---

11. John Beecher, "The Share Croppers' Union in Alabama," *Social Forces* 13 (October 1934): 124–32.

12. U.S. Senate, Committee on Agriculture and Forestry, *Hearings on the Bill to Create a Farm Tenant Homes Corporation*, 74th Cong., 1st sess., 1935, quoted in Sidney Baldwin, *Poverty and Politics: The Rise and Decline of the Farm Security Administration* (Chapel Hill: University of North Carolina Press, 1968), p. 135.

13. Ibid.

On one occasion during the debate over the Bankhead bill the senator from Louisiana amused the galleries with his own farming experience. "I was raised on a farm, Mr. President. I am one of the world's most successful farmers. [Laughter.] I left the farm as early as I could possibly get away, and I have never gone back since, demonstrating long in advance a keen knowledge of farming."[14] The galleries roared; but his point was that no one could make a living on a farm anymore, so it made no sense to put more people under more mortgages.

He liked to ridicule federal agricultural policy for its inconsistencies. "We have two agencies of farm relief, one to hire a man not to raise, and the other to hire him to buy land on which to raise. Where in the hell are we going?" He elaborated: "Are we going to sign up a farmer in 1935, this very year, not to plant cotton, and put him on the relief rolls, and then loan him money to go back and plant cotton after we have moved him off his farm, and go back next year and pay him again not to raise cotton?" He also pointed out the contradiction in plowing up crops when people did not have enough to eat.[15]

There was some good in the Bankhead bill, he admitted, but there was more harm. Long doubted that such a program would be administered honestly—or that it would really be administered nonpolitically. He also thought that landlords wanted the bill in order to sell land to the government.

If Long had his eye on the political aspects of the Bankhead bill, he had good reason. Sen. Theodore G. Bilbo of Mississippi saw it as a way to take a cut at his neighbor. "THE BANKHEAD SHARE CROPPER BILL," he wired Roosevelt and Robinson, "IS NOT ONLY ONE OF THE MOST CONSTRUCTIVE BILLS THAT HAS BEEN BEFORE CONGRESS THIS SESSION BUT WITH IT WE CAN DRIVE HUEY LONG OUT OF THE SOUTH." On the final roll call, Senators Robinson and Hattie Caraway of Arkansas, Bilbo and Pat Harrison of Mississippi, and John Overton of Louisiana voted yea. Long was one of the few southern senators voting nay.[16]

The president did not exert any pressure on the House to pass the Jones bill. Nor would he get involved with the sticky mess in Arkansas. The union was no more than a small cloud on the horizon, not posing anything like Long's threat. Except for work relief, there was little fed-

14. *Congressional Record*, vol. 79, 74th Cong., 1st sess., 18 April 1935, p. 6279.
15. Ibid., pp. 6137, 9939.
16. Theodore G. Bilbo to Franklin D. Roosevelt and Joseph T. Robinson, 8 August 1935, FDR Papers, OF 1650; *Congressional Record*, vol. 79, 74th Cong., 1st sess., 24 June 1935, p. 9958.

eral help in sight for the long-suffering sharecropper. The new Resettlement Administration was gearing up its broad-ranged attack on rural poverty, but the RA's impact in the Cotton Belt or anywhere else was still months away.

After the cotton was picked that fall, trouble flared up again in eastern Arkansas, building toward a climax in 1936, a presidential election year. Many landlords evicted families for union activity, throwing them out along the roadsides in the dead of winter, and circulated blacklists of union members. In January the Southern Tenant Farmers' Union set up a tent colony near Parkin to shelter a group of tenant families (about a hundred people), all recently evicted from a Cross County plantation. When someone threw a dynamite stick among their tents, Arkansas governor J. Marion Futrell visited Parkin, heard the complaints of harassment, and declared it was all "much ado about a very little."[17]

In May and June the STFU organized a cotton chopper's strike which idled five thousand sharecroppers in eastern Arkansas, and violence again broke out. Some strikers were beaten, arrested on vagrancy charges, and forced at gunpoint to return to work in the fields. A "March of Time" newsfeature flashed the story of the strike across theater screens. When five or six unidentified men seized Rev. Claude Williams, a union organizer, and Miss Willie Sue Blagden, and flogged them on a lonely country road, the story appeared in national publications. This was "true Arkansas hospitality," *Time* magazine declared. "More than any other single event," the union's historian has written, the Williams-Blagden beating "made the nation demand action on behalf of sharecroppers."[18]

For half a century southern tenancy had been a regional scandal. Agricultural economists had explored every aspect of the subject, but their work remained inside a small circle of experts.[19] Suddenly the Agricul-

17. Little Rock *Arkansas Gazette*, 29 February 1936.

18. Grubbs, *Cry from the Cotton*, p. 113; "Farmers: 'True Arkansas Hospitality,'" *Time* 27 (29 June 1936): 12–14; Willie Sue Blagden, "Arkansas Flogging," *New Republic* 87 (1 July 1936): 236–37.

19. For a comprehensive bibliography on the subject, see U.S. Department of Agriculture, Bureau of Agricultural Economics, *Farm Tenancy in the United States, 1918–1936: A Selected List of References*, Agricultural Economic Bibliography no. 70 (Washington: Government Printing Office, 1937). Among the best scholarly studies are T. J. Woofter et al., *Landlord and Tenant on the Cotton Plantation*, Works Progress Administration, Research Monograph no. 5 (Washington: Government Printing Office, 1936); and Carl C. Taylor, Helen W. Wheeler, and E. B. Kirkpatrick, *Disadvantaged Classes in American Agriculture*, Farm Security Administration, Social Research Report no. 8 (Washington: Government Printing Office, 1938).

tural Adjustment Administration and its nemesis, the Southern Tenant Farmers' Union, put the tenant farmer and sharecropper in the headlines for all to see, creating a national cause célèbre. Newspaper reporters such as Frazier Hunt of the New York *World-Telegram* conducted personal investigations of tenant conditions, and such magazines as *Nation, New Republic, Survey Graphic,* and *Time* began taking notice of sharecropper troubles. Even one travel account, Jonathan Daniels's *A Southerner Discovers the South,* included Tyronza in its itinerary.

Yet the new interest in the lowly sharecropper derived from other sources, too. The literature of the 1930s contained a sharecropper vogue. Erskine Caldwell's *Tobacco Road* (1932) and *God's Little Acre* (1933), originally popular because of their frank treatment of sex, were forerunners of the "proletarian" novels of the depression. John Steinbeck's *Grapes of Wrath* (1939), perhaps the great American novel, told the story of the refugees of the Arkansas-Oklahoma border; the ill-starred Joad family, sharecroppers who lost out to drought and low crop prices, headed for California, where they did not find conditions any better for migrant workers. One could really learn how tenants lived from an unheralded and overlooked book, *Let Us Now Praise Famous Men* (1940), by James Agee and photographer Walker Evans, who spent six weeks with three sharecropper families in Alabama.

Even scholarly studies of tenancy had a new quality about them; they read as if something were going to be done about the problem. The regionalist school at the University of North Carolina virtually began with the tenancy problem. As early as 1929 Rupert B. Vance had published *Human Factors in Cotton Culture,* a sociological rather than agricultural treatment of the subject. Vance's *Human Geography of the South* (1935) and Howard W. Odum's magnum opus, *Southern Regions of the United States* (1936), placed tenancy within a larger context of southern problems. In *Shadow of the Plantation* (1934), Charles S. Johnson of Fisk University focused on Negro life in Alabama. Johnson collaborated with Edwin R. Embree, president of the Rosenwall Fund, and Will W. Alexander, later head of the Farm Security Administration, in a hard-hitting little book entitled *The Collapse of Cotton Tenancy* (1935), summarizing the investigations at Fisk and at Chapel Hill for a popular audience; the answer for the thousands of families no longer needed as cotton tenants, they stressed, was a federal program of small farm ownership. Arthur F. Raper, a sociologist with the Commission on Interracial Cooperation, wrote about Georgia sharecroppers in *Preface to Peasantry* (1936) and in its sequel, *Tenants of the Almighty* (1943).

What these books described was shocking, even in the Great Depression. Croppers occupied rickety, weather-beaten cabins, sometimes teetering to one side, with cotton planted right up to the back door. Children, parents, and grandparents all crowded into two or three rooms, without privacy, under a leaky roof. Inside the cabin one could see daylight in almost any direction. The windows and doors were unscreened against flies and mosquitoes. Since the tenant's occupancy was uncertain at best, he had little incentive to improve the property.[20]

One of the persistent myths of American agrarianism is that farm life is healthy. Even a casual observer in the Cotton Belt could see plenty of evidence to the contrary. A distressingly large number of croppers and their families were sick, often with malnutrition. The monotony of their basic diet—salt pork, cornmeal, and molasses—explained the high incidence of pellagra among them; malaria, hookworm, and bad teeth were also common. Croppers and tenants had no vegetable gardens, either because they could not be bothered or because the landlord would not spare them any land for the purpose. Indoor plumbing was unknown; tenant families had open surface outhouses or nothing. "After all, Miss," one Arkansas landlord instructed a newcomer into local customs, "all that a sharecropper needs is a cotton patch and a corn cob."[21]

Whole families worked in the fields from "can to can't"—from dawn to dusk. It was literally back-breaking work with plenty of bending and stooping, and it wore people out. Men and women aged prematurely, the hard work and inadequate diet turning the men rail-thin and the women thin or often fat. For such work they earned only enough to get by. In the lower delta, according to one study, the average cropper made $154 a year—less than half of the $312 croppers got in the South as a whole.[22]

When not working, a cropper family had little to do. They might be found sitting on the front porch to escape the heat in the summer—men

20. The FSA Photographic Section left a fabulous collection of photographs, which was deposited in the Library of Congress. See Erskine Caldwell and Margaret Bourke-White, *You Have Seen Their Faces* (New York: Modern Age Books, 1937), and Rupert B. Vance, *How the Other Half Is Housed: A Pictorial Record of Sub-Minimum Farm Housing in the South* (Chapel Hill: University of North Carolina Press, 1936); F. Jack Hurley, *Portrait of a Decade: Roy Stryker and the Development of Documentary Photography in the Thirties* (Baton Rouge: Louisiana State University Press, 1972).

21. Kester, *Revolt among the Sharecroppers*, p. 41.

22. Woofter et al., *Landlord and Tenant*, pp. 83, 220; see also Charles S. Johnson, Edwin R. Embree, and Will W. Alexander, *The Collapse of Cotton Tenancy* (Chapel Hill: University of North Carolina Press, 1935), pp. 11-13.

in ragged, filthy overalls, women in faded gingham dresses, a scrubby gang of boys and girls in the small, bare yard. Their eyes showed fear and desperation. The drudgery of such an existence was enlivened by religious emotionalism, corn liquor, and perhaps an occasional lynching.

Croppers lived in such extreme poverty that many observers sensed something un-American about their plight. On a trip through the South, Frazier Hunt saw groups of pickers working their way across cotton fields. "In some strange way, they reminded me," he said, "of Chinese coolies working in the soya beans along the Southern Manchurian Railroad." "They seemed to belong to another land than the America I knew and loved." "We have conditions in America," Herbert Agar wrote, "that are not being tolerated today anywhere in Europe, unless the Russians tolerate them as a form of Asiatic punishment to be inflicted on the enemies of the State." Living conditions among Arkansas sharecroppers made the worst impression on many travelers. "It is in Arkansas that one finds the situation of the sharecropper really tragic," wrote free-lance author Fred Kelly. "I have never seen living conditions on lower standards, even in backward sections of Europe." Naomi Mitchinson, an English novelist, made a visit to Arkansas in 1935. "I have traveled over most of Europe and part of Africa," she said after emerging from the delta, "but I have never seen such terrible sights as I saw yesterday among the sharecroppers of Arkansas."[23]

Many Arkansans, too, grew increasingly concerned with what they were reading in the papers. "The latest trouble," the Pine Bluff *Daily Graphic* commented of the STFU strike in 1936, "should be a lesson to the leaders of this state that unless they . . . take some remedial steps, a dangerous situation may arise." Equally distasteful for the *Graphic* was the bad publicity Arkansas was getting in national publications.[24]

On 15 August 1936, Governor Futrell revealed that he would appoint a special commission of impartial and fair-minded citizens to investigate

23. New York *World-Telegram*, 30 July 1935; Herbert Agar, in Louisville *Courier-Journal*, 30 March 1936, quoted in Grubbs, *Cry from the Cotton*, p. 5; Fred Kelly, in *Today*, 30 March 1935; Mitchinson, quoted in STFU, Statement to Futrell Farm Tenancy Commission, STFU Papers. See n. 28.

24. Pine Bluff *Daily Graphic*, 11 June 1936. For other reactions, see *Arkansas Gazette*, 22 October 1936; M. C. Blackman, "Farm Tenancy in Arkansas," *Arkansas Gazette Sunday Magazine*, 11 April 1937; Little Rock *Arkansas Democrat*, 24 September 1936; and Arkansas State Policy Committee, *Agricultural Labor Problems in Arkansas*, Published Paper no. 1 (31 October 1936). For a view from Mississippi, see William Alexander Percy, *Lanterns on the Levee: Recollection of a Planter's Son* (New York: Knopf, 1941), pp. 280–84.

all aspects of the tenancy problem and to recommend a solution. With his retirement from office just five months away, he had "decided to devote the rest of his term to the sharecropper problem"—at least that was the way he put it to the press. But since, just three days before, United States Attorney General Homer Cummings had announced a federal grand jury probe into possible violations of peonage laws in eastern Arkansas, Futrell's critics quickly accused him of having ulterior motives. Of course he did. He naturally wanted to avoid any investigation, and he hoped to improve Arkansas's image. But he also seemed to be genuinely concerned with tenancy as a roadblock to economic progress in the South. When he made his announcement he declared that farm tenancy was "eating at the vitals of the South's economic structure and, whether exaggerated or not, is of such serious character as to call for immediate and exhaustive study and examination with a view to its definite settlement."[25] The Arkansas Tenancy Commission was the first such body in the nation, and Futrell even envisioned his commission's becoming a model for other states. Clyde E. Palmer, a Texarkana newspaper publisher and owner of a chain of papers in south Arkansas, got the job as chairman; for commissioners Futrell picked mostly businessmen, planters, professional people, and government officials.[26]

On 21 September 1936 the commission members assembled at the Arlington Hotel in Hot Springs. As they began their formal introductions, several trucks drove up and out jumped a group of dusty, overalled share-

25. *Arkansas Gazette*, 13, 16 August 1936; Grubbs, *Cry from the Cotton*, pp. 118–19. See Pete Daniel, *The Shadow of Slavery: Peonage in the South, 1901–1969* (Urbana: University of Illinois Press, 1972), pp. 172–74.

26. *Arkansas Gazette*, 27 August 1936; Memphis *Press-Scimitar*, 27 August 1936; Memphis *Commercial Appeal*, 28 August 1936; Grubbs, *Cry from the Cotton*, p. 119.
Here is the list of original members: C. E. Palmer, publisher, Texarkana; Dean Dan T. Gray, University of Arkansas, College of Agriculture; Dr. A. C. Millar, editor, *Arkansas Methodist*; J. B. Watson, president, Arkansas A M & N College, Pine Bluff; C. C. Randall, director, Arkansas Extension Service; Floyd Sharp, state director, WPA; James Hammond, publisher, Memphis; B. C. Morton, Heber Springs; Donald Murray, publisher, Jonesboro; Joe Knight, Paragould; Paul N. Pfeifer, Piggott; Horace Sloan, Jonesboro; T. Roy Reid, regional director, RA; James W. Sargent, regional director, Soil Conservation Service; James Crane, Wilson; J. O. D. Beck, Hughes; A. Carlson, Trumann; John Mitchell, Havana; Clyde Byrd, El Dorado; Miss Connie Bonslagel, Little Rock; V. C. Kays, president, Arkansas State College, Jonesboro; J. K. Mahoney, El Dorado; T. J. Gaughan, Camden; Rev. Ray L. Davis, Wynne; Carl Hollis, banker, Warren; M. L. Sigman, Monticello; Charles Evans, Pine Bluff; M. E. Melton, Texarkana; Bob Hall, El Dorado; Mrs. E. W. Frost, Texarkana; Mrs. Scott Wood, Hot Springs; Mrs. Winifred Pope; Col. T. H. Barton, oil man, El Dorado; C. T. Carpenter, Marked Tree; C. E. Dungan, Augusta; W. G. Padgett, Marion; Harry Williamson, Hughes; Charles Goslee, publisher, Hot Springs.

croppers, STFU president J. R. Butler, and the infamous minister Claude Williams, all uninvited. When the opportunity came, Butler and Williams introduced themselves to the assembly, making a point of the fact that they represented the nation's largest organization of farm tenants, but had no representation on the governor's commission. "I won't be pressured!" Futrell fumed in a whisper to friends, but he quickly collected himself and invited them to join the commission. The governor later made the invitation official, but he substituted W. L. Blackstone, an attorney from Wynne, for Williams.[27]

As the commission got down to business, Howard Kester submitted a statement on the evils of tenancy and the union's view of how to eliminate them. The document covered a broad spectrum of reforms, ranging from free speech and assembly to the abolition of private prison farms, usury, and the poll tax. Other demands included the end of plantation commissaries, enforcement of child labor laws, and compensation to tenants for improvements on the land.

Kester went on to criticize the Resettlement Administration. The agency's decentralized structure, he argued, enabled local officials to block the efforts of top administrators to carry out genuine reforms. The document also attacked the Bankhead-Jones farm tenant bills, currently under reconsideration in Congress, as throwbacks to the day of "forty acres and a mule." The philosophy of small family farms would lead to a "subsidized peasantry." Instead, the government should encourage large cooperative farms as the replacement for plantations. "Through cooperative farming," Kester wrote, "a new and altogether high type of rural life may be developed in the South."[28]

The Palmer commission also had more conservative sources supplying it with ideas. Edward J. Meeman, editor of the Memphis *Press-Scimitar*, addressed the commission in an open letter. To him, the solution was to replace the present sharecropper economy, square mile by square mile, with a "new and sound one of independent farmers"; and he pictured the ideal farm community as he conceived it:

> Let us take a great circle of land. It need not be an exact circle, of course; a square or an irregularly shaped tract, not too narrow, would do as well. We say circle because that suggests best the idea. Divide this into pieces as you would a pie, except that you reserve a tract at the head of the project

27. Grubbs, *Cry from the Cotton*, pp. 120–21.
28. Southern Tenant Farmers' Union, Executive Council, "A Statement Concerning Farm Tenancy Submitted to the Governor's Commission on Farm Tenancy," STFU Papers; *Press-Scimitar*, 19 September 1936.

for common purposes, such as forest, pasture and the like. Each of these "slices" represents the homestead of a farm family. His house lies somewhere toward the center of the tract. Near it are his garden, his small crops, his chickens, his hogs, or whatever little side crop he might care to raise.
The outer portion of his land would be clear of buildings. Here he would raise his major crop. Thus the major crop land of all the small farmers would lie together. This would permit the efficient co-operative use of all existing labor-saving machinery such as an airplane cotton duster, and any [other machinery] that the future may bring.

Each farmer would be independent, but he would not be at a disadvantage in competing with the great plantation which might lie next door or with the great cotton ranches of Argentina and Brazil.

Let a government agency, Meeman suggested, encourage the establishment of such communities by buying up large tracts of land, dividing them into slices, and leasing the slices to good farmers. That agency, he added, should be the Resettlement Administration: it had already been working somewhat on these lines; it had made mistakes, but acquired valuable experience; and T. Roy Reid, the regional director, "had shown himself to be a practical man."[29]

The Resettlement Administration, in fact, had its own representatives on the Palmer commission—no less than Reid himself, and a social worker, Connie Bonslagel. Just before Thanksgiving the commission released its report, and it sounded remarkably similar to what the Resettlement Administration was already doing. Rather than the whitewash STFU leaders expected, the commission pulled no punches in depicting tenancy as an evil. "A majority of tenants are unable without assistance to extricate themselves from tenantry," the report observed. "Tenancy has become a serious menace to American institutions, and threatens the fertility of the soil and the character of the people."

To reverse and eventually eliminate the problem, the commission recommended a new "homestead policy" which offered those who cultivated the soil the opportunity of owning their own farms. The federal and state governments, they suggested, should cooperate in making suitable farm lands available for purchase by tenant farmers and sharecroppers over a period of years at low interest rates. The necessary financing should come from a federal farm purchase act; according to their estimates, $40 million a year would be required to reduce the number of tenants. (A majority of commission members would presumably have been satisfied with the Bankhead-Jones bills.) They further recommended not only a program

29. "An Open Letter: How the South Can Build a Wholesome Enduring Rural Prosperity," *Press-Scimitar*, 18 September 1936.

of supervised credit like the Resettlement Administration's farm and home budgets, but also the practice of requiring contracts between landlord and tenant, which was already a feature of the rural rehabilitation program.[30]

The commission was also concerned with the improvement of rural living conditions. They had suggestions for education, particularly adult education, and health care; illiteracy and poor health, they noted, were two important reasons why families became trapped in the vicious cycles of tenancy and poverty. Finally, they reaffirmed their support for the constitutional rights of assembly and petition for redress of grievances.

The commission had based its recommendations on the time-honored tradition of small farm-home ownership. "Farming is a way of life all its own," the report declared; the farmer produced the necessities of life for everyone, but he did more than that. The ownership of a small farm, it said, was a source of social stability, of good character and patriotism—perhaps a backhanded slap at the Socialist-minded STFU. The farm also supplied the nation with "healthy and strong citizens." "The cities can no longer keep themselves alive," the report echoed William Jennings Bryan and a thousand other agrarian spokesmen; "they must be steadily replenished by the country."

Yet not all the commission said had a traditional ring. So enamored were the majority with the mystique of the small farm that they endorsed legislation to "discourage the ownership of farm lands in large tracts necessitating cultivation through tenancy or day labor," a proposal not likely to win many friends among eastern Arkansas planters.[31]

Palmer described the report as "sane, comprehensive, feasible." If action were taken promptly, he pointedly observed, it would "end all danger from socialist and communist activities in rural sections." The commission seemed to have plenty of support behind its recommendations. In December a Gallup poll showed that Arkansans, by an 89 percent majority, favored government loans to enable tenant farmers to buy farms of their own.[32]

The approaching presidential election at last produced Roosevelt's personal involvement in the sharecropper issue. The Arkansas terrorism came up in a cabinet meeting on 6 March 1936, according to Drew Pear-

30. Farm Tenancy Commission of Arkansas, Findings and Recommendations, Hot Springs Meeting, 24 November 1936, copy in STFU Papers.
31. Ibid.; *Arkansas Gazette*, 15 November 1936; *Daily Graphic*, 8 November 1936.
32. *Birmingham* (Ala.) *News*, 13 December 1936.

son and Robert S. Allen's "Washington Merry-Go-Round" column. Secretary of Labor Frances Perkins proposed sending a federal arbitrator to work out the differences between the planters and the union. Roosevelt liked the idea, as did other members of the cabinet. But Vice-President John Nance Garner was alert to the political amenities of such a step. "It would embarrass Joe Robinson," he cautioned. "We ought not to do anything without taking it up with him. He's up for reelection this fall, and that's a very delicate situation in Arkansas." Roosevelt agreed, and privately asked the Senate majority leader to intercede with Futrell in stopping the violence. But the terrorism could not be stopped so easily, and the sharecropper problem remained an open sore for the New Deal.[33]

While Roosevelt was moved by the injustice of the sharecropper's plight, he could not come to the aid of the STFU without dumping the conservative southern leadership in Congress and risking much of his legislative program. The southern conservatives had the power; sharecroppers were usually voteless. He asked for patience while waiting until something could be done safely. He had not lent his support to the farm tenancy legislation before Congress in 1935. As he made ready to throw his weight into the battle in early 1936, the United States Supreme Court declared the AAA unconstitutional; and no tenancy bill passed that year, either. When the president paid a visit to Little Rock on 10 June during the state's centennial celebration, he made no public mention of the current sharecroppers' strike, and refused to accept a petition from a delegation of union members. But Roosevelt had definitely made up his mind to press for action.[34]

During the campaign he wrote Senator Bankhead and Congressman Jones, asking them to meet with him in December to complete recommendations to Congress for new legislation. At Omaha, Nebraska, while on his "nonpolitical" tour of the drought-ridden Great Plains, he reaffirmed his determination to attack the evils of farm tenancy. "We cannot, as a Nation, be content until we have reached the ultimate objective of every farm family owning its own farm." His speech made a strong appeal to the mystique of land ownership. "In all our plans we are guided . . . by the fundamental belief that the American farmer, living on his own land, remains our ideal of self-reliance and of spiritual balance—the source from which the reservoirs of the Nation's strength are constantly re-

33. Drew Pearson and Robert S. Allen, "The Washington Merry-Go-Round," 17, 18 March 1936, cited in Grubbs, *Cry from the Cotton*, p. 99.
34. Baldwin, *Poverty and Politics*, pp. 160–61; for his speech, see FDR, *Public Papers* (1936), 5:195–202.

newed." Then on 16 November, a few days before Palmer issued his findings, Roosevelt created a special Committee on Farm Tenancy. "The rapid increase of tenant farmers during the past half century," he wrote Henry Wallace in a letter asking him to serve as chairman of the committee, "is significant evidence that we have fallen far short of achieving the traditional American ideal of owner-operated farms."[35]

Secretary Wallace had kept in touch with the sharecropper controversy and with the Resettlement Administration. He had even taken part in the discussions leading up to the agency's establishment, although it was outside his official responsibility. Like Tugwell, the secretary of agriculture believed that the government should get at the root causes of rural poverty rather than administer a form of stopgap relief. In late 1936 he had a chance to bring the agency into his department.

Tugwell, long rumored to be leaving government service, had indeed submitted his resignation. What would become of his agency and the ambitious programs he had undertaken? Tugwell hoped it would be transferred from its independent status to the Department of Agriculture. Wallace may have already favored the transfer, but he soon had any doubts removed. Tugwell talked him into taking a tour of the South to see tenant conditions and RA activities. Tugwell himself had taken such a tour earlier in the year and knew firsthand what Wallace would find. It was also highly recommended travel for a man just appointed the chairman of a farm tenancy commission.[36]

Wallace spoke in Little Rock on 17 November at the annual convention of the Arkansas Farm Bureau Federation; then in the company of Reid and a group of RA officials he went to Memphis and joined Tugwell, who arrived by plane from Washington. The Wallace and Tugwell entourage spent the next two days on an inspection tour of resettlement activities. They visited a Tennessee park project near Memphis, went on to Dyess Colony, saw a land utilization project between Forrest City and Marianna, and toured the Lakeview resettlement project near Helena. Back in Little Rock on 19 November, Tugwell confirmed reports of his resignation. At a press conference the next day Wallace admitted for the first time that the Resettlement Administration would probably be transferred to the Department of Agriculture sometime the following year.

35. Franklin D. Roosevelt to William B. Bankhead and Marvin H. Jones, 21 September 1936, pp. 373–74; Omaha speech, pp. 431–39; Roosevelt to Henry A. Wallace, 16 November 1936, pp. 591–92, all ibid.
36. Baldwin, *Poverty and Politics*, pp. 120–22, 164; Edward L. Schapsmeier and Frederick H. Schapsmeier, *Henry A. Wallace of Iowa: The Agrarian Years, 1910–1940* (Ames: Iowa State University Press, 1968), p. 206.

That afternoon the Wallace and Tugwell party drove down along the Arkansas River to England for the dedication of the Plum Bayou resettlement project before continuing their tour into Mississippi, Alabama, and Georgia.[37]

The sight of haggard farmers, run-down shacks, and eroded fields shook the secretary of agriculture. Wallace returned to his office ready to make the Resettlement Administration a permanent part of his department. "I have never seen among the peasantry of Europe poverty so abject as that which exists in this favorable cotton year in the great cotton states from Arkansas on to the East Coast," he wrote in the *New York Times.* The president signed an executive order on 31 December making the transfer official; and Wallace named Will W. Alexander as Tugwell's successor. In a radio talk over the "Farm and Home Hour" two weeks later, Wallace discussed the resettlement program: "The government is definitely going to the bottom of the heap, and trying by supervision and encouragement to get them started on the road upward." He showed far more interest in the rehabilitation loan program than in the community projects.[38]

In mid-December the presidential committee's full membership of thirty-three distinguished citizens, including Arkansas's new governor, Carl E. Bailey, met at Washington and heard Wallace urge them to consider the broader problem of rural poverty rather than limit themselves to tenancy. A working subcommittee conducted public hearings in several cities and did the actual task of gathering technical data and drafting the recommendations.

The President's Committee on Farm Tenancy submitted its findings to the White House on 11 February 1937. Its report was an endorsement of what the Resettlement Administration was already doing, and its recommendations even paraphrased sections of the Resettlement Administration's *First Annual Report.* Yet since the underlying objective of the report was the concept of "farm security" and since the Resettlement Administration bore the stigma of a temporary agency concerned with emergency relief measures, the committee recommended a Farm Security Administration as its replacement, with a new "tenant purchase" program to enable families that had the prerequisite ability and experience to buy

37. *Arkansas Gazette,* 15, 18, 19, 20 November 1936.
38. Henry A. Wallace, "Wallace Maps a Farm Program," *New York Times Magazine,* 3 January 1937, p. 1; idem, "The Rural Resettlement Administration of the Department of Agriculture," radio talk, "Farm and Home Hour," 12 January 1937, mimeographed, FSA Records, NA, RG 96.

farms on easy terms. The new agency should also cooperate with state and local governments in assisting tenants with lease arrangements, preferential tax policies, and improvements in rural health and education. The committee's report envisioned a situation where all farmers lived on privately owned family farms.[39]

Not surprisingly, there was some dissent on the committee. Edward O'Neal of the American Farm Bureau Federation objected to a statement in the final report recommending that states guarantee tenants, croppers, and migratory laborers "the rights of peaceful assembly and of organization to achieve legitimate objectives." On the other hand, W. L. Blackstone, again representing the Southern Tenant Farmers' Union viewpoint, argued that the report did not do enough in the area of civil rights. He filed a minority report urging that the federal government also stress cooperative farming communities as a realistic alternative to small homesteads. Although the committee was sufficiently impressed to suggest the initiation of such communities "on an experimental scale," this approach lay well outside the framework of agrarian orthodoxy.[40]

Senator Bankhead and Congressman Jones now introduced two new bills which roughly followed the committee's recommendations. For the first time the Roosevelt administration put its full weight behind farm tenancy legislation. The House of Representatives acted first, but it was no rubber stamp. Jones's bill ran into determined opposition in his own Committee on Agriculture, and it was rewritten twice. When the revised bill reached the House floor, it prompted an outpouring of sentimentality about the virtues of rural living. No one dared oppose the sacrosanct family farm itself, but in the floor debate several congressmen, including some from Region VI, did echo the criticism which had dogged the bill in committee.[41]

John E. Miller of Arkansas, for example, shared many congressmen's fear of large-scale government land purchases and government supervision over such land. These features of the Bankhead-Jones program represented a "dangerous socialization of land and regimentation of farmers." "The loan," Miller remarked, "should be given him [the farmer] as a free man and not as an indentured workman." He added,

39. National Resources Board, *Farm Tenancy: Report of the President's Committee* (Washington: Government Printing Office, 1937).

40. Ibid., pp. 20–24.

41. Baldwin, *Poverty and Politics,* p. 184; *Congressional Record,* vol. 81, 75th Cong., 1st sess., 28 June 1936, p. 6434.

"Just as far as I can I want to take out of our agricultural program supervision by the bureaucrats [of Washington]," identifying them as "book farmers and theorists . . . living in musty libraries."[42]

Wall Doxey of Mississippi was a member of Jones's Committee on Agriculture. He claimed to have proposed a plan which was used as a basis for Title I, the new tenant purchase program. Like Miller, Doxey objected to the government's going into the land purchase business. Instead, why not loan money to the farmer and let him buy his own farm? But he was willing, he said, to leave the program up to the discretion of the secretary of agriculture. Another critic was Doxey's colleague John E. Rankin. Congressman Rankin favored making it possible for every farmer who wished to do so to be able to own his own home. The program under consideration was too small, he acknowledged, but it was meant to be only a beginning. He, too, opposed the idea of government supervision. This aspect of the program underestimated the intelligence of the average tenant farmer. When white tenant farmers become landowners, Rankin said, they "do not need guardians to tell them what to do, when to sow and when to reap, or how to plow or hoe."[43]

Two congressmen from Region VI offered amendments which were incorporated into the final version of the bill. William M. Colmer of Mississippi inserted a provision limiting administrative expenses in the tenant purchase program to not more than 5 percent of the total amount of its appropriation in any fiscal year—rather than a fixed amount of $400,000. Newt V. Mills of Louisiana proposed that the program be extended specifically to include farmers who had moved to town but who wished to return to the farm. This type of legislation, he added, was "nothing new, as it was advocated by the early philosophers, also the Pilgrims and Puritan forefathers, as well as the Bible itself." The Jones bill would go a long way toward redistributing the wealth, he said, pointing out that he was elected on a Share Our Wealth platform.[44]

"I do not believe there is anyone in this House who has a keener sympathy for or deeper interest in the class of people for whose benefit we are undertaking to legislate today than I have," Arkansas congressman John L. McClellan said as he rose to speak. Ahead lay his long career in the United States Senate and his relentless pursuit of labor racketeers. He reminded his listeners that he was reared as the son of a tenant farmer.

42. Ibid., pp. 6434–35.
43. Ibid., pp. 3994–95, 6553.
44. Ibid., pp. 6569, 6548.

This bill was only a start, but if successful, he said, Congress could then broaden it.[45]

With William J. Driver of Osceola presiding, the House passed the bill on 29 June by an overwhelming vote of 308 to 25. Every congressman from Region VI voted for it except four who were recorded as not voting.[46]

The Bankhead bill also changed in committee, but less drastically than the Jones bill had; and when it reached the Senate floor on 1 July, its passage was assured. The Senate had passed a similar bill in 1935, when the House let the matter die. There was little debate, all of it perfunctory, and the bill passed by voice vote the next day. A Senate-House conference committee reconciled the two bills. Robinson, who worked hard to see the Bankhead bill enacted, died just as the committee submitted its report closely conforming to the House version. The president signed it into law on 22 July.[47]

The Bankhead-Jones Farm Tenant Act of 1937 provided for tenant purchase loans repayable over a forty-year period at 3 percent interest. They were to be financed by a $10 million appropriation for the first year, $25 million the second, and $50 million thereafter. A rural rehabilitation program was authorized but not given a specific appropriation; the money would come out of funds for work relief. As for the resettlement program, Congress permitted only the completion and administration of projects already in existence. At last, however, the Bankhead-Jones Act stamped the Resettlement Administration's major programs with legislative authorization.[48]

On 1 September, pursuing the recommendations of the President's Committee on Farm Tenancy, Secretary Wallace abolished the Resettlement Administration, created the Farm Security Administration in its place, and assigned it the functions provided for in the new law.[49] In a purely administrative sense the Farm Security Administration was Tugwell's old agency under a new name with the same personnel, including his successor, Will Alexander, as administrator.

Dr. Will, as he was known, had lobbied for the passage of the Bankhead-Jones bills, but he was a political amateur and a novice in the field of large-scale public administration. Nor was he well qualified by agri-

45. Ibid., p. 6550.
46. Ibid., pp. 6582–83.
47. Ibid., pp. 7133–37; Baldwin, *Poverty and Politics*, pp. 186–87.
48. 50 *US Stat.* 522; *Arkansas Gazette*, 2 September 1937.
49. Secretary of Agriculture, Memorandum no. 732, 1 September 1937, FSA Records, NA, RG 96; Will W. Alexander, night letter to All Regional Directors, 1 September 1937, ibid.; Baldwin, *Poverty and Politics*, p. 188.

cultural training, yet he did bring with him an outstanding reputation. For twenty-five years Alexander had headed the Commission on Interracial Cooperation at Atlanta, an organization working for justice and harmony in southern race relations. He was founder and first president of Dillard University in New Orleans. After the AAA began uprooting tenants, he became interested in the relationship of rural poverty, farm tenancy, and race. In 1935 he co-authored *The Collapse of Cotton Tenancy*, a major embarrassment to the AAA.[50]

Alexander's FSA was the depository for a diversified collection of rural welfare programs accumulated over the previous five years. While he lost the land use program to the Bureau of Agricultural Economics of the Department of Agriculture, he still had his hands full. He continued the RA's resettlement and rural rehabilitation activities, and administered the new Bankhead-Jones tenant purchase loans. With the resettlement projects obviously low in congressional favor, rural rehabilitation was Alexander's chief concern.[51]

The FSA was not the grand vision with which Tugwell began—the transfer of the land program abruptly ended all talk of land reforms; nor did the FSA signal an all-out attack on rural poverty. Its programs were in fact less ambitious than the recommendations of the President's Committee on Farm Tenancy. Obviously the heady enthusiasm of earlier years had not worn well. Yet the agency retained a large share of the RA's idealistic leadership. Among the most prominent holdovers was C. B. "Beanie" Baldwin, a liberal Virginian who in 1940 succeeded Alexander as FSA chief.

At Little Rock the change from RA to FSA occurred without missing a beat. The regional organization remained essentially the same. The turnover in personnel which the departure of Tugwell prompted in the national office made little impact in Region VI. Still regional director, T. Roy Reid added a Tenant Purchase Division, which complemented the old divisions of rehabilitation, resettlement, and management; and he knew whom he wanted to run it. T. B. Fatherree had served briefly as chief of Community and Cooperative Services while on leave from Mississippi State College. Reid asked him to rejoin his staff as regional chief of tenant purchase.[52] The regional director also took care of a few

50. See Wilma Dykeman and James Stokely, *Seeds of Southern Change: The Life of Will Alexander* (Chicago: University of Chicago Press, 1962).
51. Will W. Alexander, "Rural Resettlement," *Southern Review* 1 (Winter 1936): 528–39.
52. T. B. Fatherree to the author, 28 November 1972; *Daily Graphic*, 21 November 1937.

housekeeping chores. A sign painter changed names on the third-floor doors of the Donaghey Building; the secretarial pool started x-ing through the words "Resettlement Administration" and typing in "Farm Security Administration" until the old stationery was used up and new letterheads arrived.

More than three years had elapsed between the formation of the Southern Tenant Farmers' Union and the creation of the Farm Security Administration. While many forces helped fashion the Bankhead-Jones Farm Tenant Act and the Farm Security Administration, the sharecroppers' union that began in Arkansas played a key role in changing the course of the New Deal. Mitchell had reason to congratulate himself, but he probably took little comfort in the FSA. The agency stood philosophically opposite the union, and it was incapable of scratching below the surface of the immense problem of rural poverty. Mitchell and his friends had found it easier to elicit movement from the cumbersome federal bureaucracy than to determine the direction that movement would take. For the union, only one of the FSA's major activities aroused any genuine enthusiasm: the resettlement communities.

Chapter VII

Little White Houses

For sheer daring and imagination, the community projects surpassed everything else the Resettlement Administration did. They were unmatched, too, for controversy and misunderstanding. When the Farm Security Administration came under fire during World War II, the community program was an easy mark for critics. The charges of "Communistic communities" and "un-American social experiments," however inaccurate, created doubt about the nature of the agency's entire program. Many people had always suspected the worst about "Rex the Red" Tugwell, anyway; and although he had left government service in 1936, they detected his sinister influence in the FSA. The suspicion of heresy received apparent confirmation when Congress stripped the FSA of its controversial functions and subsequently abolished it outright.

Historians perpetuated the radical image of the New Deal communities. In an outstanding study, Paul K. Conkin wrote that the development of the community program was "one of the most open breaks with individualistic tradition in American history." The term "community," he said, "became a synonym for a form of collectivism and an antonym of individualism. These communities were to be examples of a new, organic society, with new values and institutions."[1] The wartime critics might have agreed, but Conkin wrote with approval, not criticism.

The Resettlement Administration engaged in just enough experimentation to lend credibility to the charge of radicalism. A critic of competition and individualism in American economic life, Tugwell questioned the agrarian devotion to the family farm. As Resettlement chief, he approached the problem of rural poverty with the conviction that security

1. Paul K. Conkin, *Tomorrow a New World: The New Deal Community Program* (Ithaca, N.Y.: Cornell University Press, 1959), p. 6.

offered a better goal for tenants than ownership did. Anxious to attack poverty at its sources, he argued that ownership could be just as bad as tenancy. "One trouble with tenancy is landlordism," wrote Tugwell in 1937; "one trouble with ownership is the mortgage."[2] Small owners were no better off than tenants, he contended, if they carried the weight of mortgages and faced the specter of foreclosure. What they needed more than immediate ownership was health care, better diets, clothes, livestock, seed, fertilizer, and specialized assistance.

In an economy based on large-scale units, he argued, the small family farm was an anachronism. The rise of commercial agriculture employing modern technology on hundreds of acres had outdated the forty-acre, one-horse farm. He believed that rural resettlement would work best on large community-type projects stressing mechanized farming and cooperative organization. Tugwell carried this idea to its logical conclusion on projects where farmers worked the land in common and shared the returns of their labor without any hope of ownership.[3]

Tugwell was not alone in his enthusiasm for cooperative farming. Many individuals and groups, particularly the Southern Tenant Farmers' Union, observed the same trends in agriculture. The STFU, in fact, became involved with one cooperative experiment. After the 1936 cotton choppers' strike, some of the tenants evicted for union membership took refuge in Delta Cooperative Farm at Hillhouse, Mississippi. Sherwood Eddy—the famed social worker, writer, and lecturer—raised the money and publicized the project. Former sharecroppers worked the land in common and experimented with the new Rust cotton picker, trying to combine technological efficiency and cooperative organization. For union leaders Hillhouse typified the way of the future. Yet a poll of union members taken in late 1935 indicated a strong majority favored home ownership or long-term leases, while cooperative farming proved decisively unpopular.[4]

2. Rexford G. Tugwell, "Behind the Farm Problem: Rural Poverty," *New York Times Magazine*, 10 January 1937, p. 5.
3. Conkin, *Tomorrow a New World*, pp. 149, 159–60; Arthur M. Schlesinger, Jr., *The Age of Roosevelt: The Coming of the New Deal* (Boston: Houghton Mifflin, 1959), pp. 369–71; Richard S. Kirkendall, *Social Scientists and Farm Politics in the Age of Roosevelt* (Columbia: University of Missouri Press, 1966), pp. 112–13; Bernard Sternsher, *Rexford Tugwell and the New Deal* (New Brunswick, N.J.: Rutgers University Press, 1964), pp. 265–68.
4. On Delta Cooperative Farm, see "Self-Help for Sharecroppers," *Literary Digest* 121 (11 April 1936): 16; A. W. Taylor, "Sherwood Eddy Launches a New Enterprise," *Christian Century* 53 (22 April 1936): 607–8; Sherwood Eddy, "Delta

What should be emphasized about the New Deal community program, however, is its debt to traditional agrarian values. The Farm Security Administration had responsibility for almost two hundred resettlement projects, but only a handful of them operated as actual collective farms or otherwise attempted to form a new society with collectivist values and institutions. The overall program drew its inspiration from the individualism of the family-sized farm.

How many resettlement projects practiced cooperative farming? The number varied according to the definition of the term "cooperative," but the overall picture was clear. In 1943 Joseph W. Eaton, head of the Rural Settlement Institute of Chicago, published a study of the FSA's "cooperative group farms," which he defined as "an association of members of farm families who operate jointly a large scale farming enterprise and who equitably share the returns of their group effort." According to Eaton, twenty-seven such communities existed; "the traditional family farm pattern" predominated on the remaining projects. The same year, Farm Security administrator C. B. Baldwin, testifying before the Senate Committee on Appropriations, stated that while his agency at one time or another had managed 195 projects of all types, only thirteen were cooperative farm communities. "Over 97 per cent of the project units," he said, "are operated on an individual, family-farm basis." A. Whitney Griswold, in a 1948 study, counted fifteen "cooperative cooperation farms." "The great majority of the projects," he wrote, "consisted of groups of small, individually leased and operated family farms on government-owned tracts of land."[5]

However anachronistic the family farm might have become, most leaders of the Roosevelt administration invoked it instinctively when dis-

Cooperative's First Year," ibid. 54 (3 February 1937): 139–40; Jonathan Daniels, *A Southerner Discovers the South* (New York: Da Capo Press, 1970), pp. 148–55. J. R. Butler and Ward Rogers, Questionaire [*sic*] to Members, 30 December 1935 (?), STFU Papers. Only 20 percent of the union membership, by Mitchell's later estimate, actually favored cooperative farming. H. L. Mitchell, Columbia Oral History Project interview, mimeographed, STFU Papers.

5. Joseph W. Eaton, *Exploring Tomorrow's Agriculture* (New York: Harper and Brothers, 1943), pp. 62, 66–67. Eaton wrote: "All except about 750 full-time farm families resettled by the FSA are on family farm units. The 750, or 2 per cent, who do not conform to this traditional pattern are settled on cooperative farms," p. 42. USS, *USDA Approp. Hearings, 1944*, 78th Cong., 1st sess., pp. 614, 630; A. Whitney Griswold, *Farming and Democracy* (New York: Harcourt, 1948), p. 167. See also Kirkendall, *Social Scientists and Farm Politics*, p. 129; Sidney Baldwin, *Poverty and Politics: The Rise and Decline of the Farm Security Administration* (Chapel Hill: University of North Carolina Press, 1968), p. 268.

cussing tenancy. Besides Roosevelt himself, a strong voice for the family farm within the top echelons of the New Deal came from the secretary of agriculture. "I know of no better means of reconstructing our agriculture on a thoroughly sound and permanently desirable basis," wrote Henry Wallace, "than to make as its foundation the family-sized, owner-operated farm." M. L. Wilson, who went from Subsistence Homesteads to assistant secretary of agriculture, described himself as a "deep believer in farm ownership by the family who operates the farm." The report of the President's Committee on Farm Tenancy and the enactment of the Bankhead-Jones Farm Tenant Act reaffirmed the small, privately owned farm as the ideal setting of American agriculture.[6]

The family farm concept naturally embodied considerable flexibility. On the Great Plains, for example, it might range from a few hundred to several thousand acres. The majority of farms in the Lower Mississippi Valley averaged under a hundred acres, even with the presence of the large delta plantations. Whatever its size, the family farm had to be small enough that one family, usually without hired help, could do all the work, but still large enough to produce an adequate income.[7]

The community program fit easily into the region's predominantly small-farm economy as well as into its philosophical orientation. Despite Tugwell's convictions about the future of agriculture, he never tried to operate a program which went beyond public opinion; every undertaking stayed close to regional and local norms or at least had solid local support. Even so, he retained considerable room to maneuver. The resettlement program operated on the assumption that society, rather than the individual, was primarily responsible for rural poverty. While relief of distress was indeed a goal, the RA and FSA placed major emphasis on getting at the fundamental causes of distress—an objective with revolutionary potential. The tension, however, between potential and reality was quickly resolved. In the hands of local officials the character of the resettlement program became, if anything, too cautious and traditional.

6. See above, Chapter V; FDR, *Public Papers* (1936), 5:591; Henry A. Wallace, "Wallace Points to the Danger of Tenancy," *New York Times Magazine*, 31 March 1935, p. 21; M. L. Wilson, "The Problems of Poverty in Agriculture," *Journal of Farm Economics* 22 (February 1940): 12.

7. U.S. Bureau of the Census, *Statistical Abstract of the United States, 1938* (Washington: Government Printing Office, 1939), p. 591. Since a tract of land under the direction of a single operator, whether a sharecropper or owner, is a farm according to the census definition, it is difficult to make precise comparisons of the size of farms on a regional basis.

Between November 1935 and February 1936 regional officials obtained approval for all but one of their resettlement projects.[8] Construction continued through 1940 as funds became available.

At one time or another E. B. Whitaker had charge of thirty resettlement projects, new and inherited. While possessing basic similarities, these projects represented several major types. Some were complete communities formed by breaking up one or more large plantations into small farms; others consisted of single, isolated farms or clusters of farms scattered throughout several counties. Some were Negro projects, but most contained whites only. Most projects subleased land to clients for individual operation. Only two communities and part of another broke with tradition and experimented with communal farming.[9]

Plum Bayou, near England, Arkansas, became the earliest test of the practicality of government community-building. In 1931 tenant farmers of the area had participated in the England Food Riot. Four years later Whitaker purchased 9,854 acres of bottomland along the Arkansas River and resettled 180 families, including perhaps some former rioters, on farm units averaging 42 acres each.[10]

Lakeview, the first of several black resettlement communities in the region, was located near another famous Arkansas site, that of the bloody Elaine Massacre. After the depression hit, this heavily black area witnessed a sharp drop in the number of sharecroppers and a sharp rise in the number of farm laborers. Acquiring 8,163 acres in Phillips and Lee counties, Whitaker divided the land into 142 units.[11] The defunct Camden and nearby West Helena subsistence homesteads were intended as Negro projects; however, the Resettlement Administration became the first community-building agency to show effective concern for the region's black population.

8. Resettlement Administration, Construction Division, Progress Report for Projects in Development and Planning, 1 July 1936 to 1 August 1936; Resettlement Administration, Annual Report, Region VI, as of 31 December 1936; Rexford G. Tugwell to T. Roy Reid, 2 February 1937; Resettlement Administration, Annual Report of Assistant Regional Director in Charge of Rural Resettlement, 1 July 1935 to 31 December 1936, all in FSA records, NA, RG 96.

9. For factual data on almost all resettlement projects, see RA, "Project Description Book," ibid.; and USHR, *FSA Hearings*, pt. 3. Assembled by the regional office, FSA, "Resettlement Projects, Region VI," FSA Records, NA, RG 96, is the most convenient source of basic information on resettlement projects in the region. See also M. C. Blackman, "Arkansas's Largest Landlord," Little Rock *Arkansas Gazette Sunday Magazine*, 13 October 1935, pp. 5, 14.

10. *Arkansas Gazette*, 20 November 1936. See below, Chapter IX.

11. Ibid., 15 February 1936.

Subsistence Homesteads   ▲
FERA Community   ✚
RA & FSA Communities   ●
Region VI: Major New Deal Resettlement Communities

Another early project, Lake Dick, ran counter to the family farm pattern. Near Altheimer, Arkansas, not far from Plum Bayou, Lake Dick covered 4,529 acres of sandy loam and buckshot soil. Under the prodding of national officials, Whitaker initiated a pattern common in European agriculture where farmers lived in villages and went out to work in surrounding fields. The homes and community buildings formed a tiny village of eighty families around the banks of a horseshoe-shaped lake. The project families collectively "owned" the land, their homes, the community center, school, store, dairy, cotton gin, and barns. As individuals, they liked to say, they owned only their "children and chickens." They worked as day laborers for wages paid at the end of each week and shared annually in the association's profits, if any. Homes and garden plots came rent-free.[12]

Whether white or black, collectively or individually operated, these were community projects, the type best adapted to the delta regions, where large tracts of rich land could be purchased cheaply. Another type of project avoided the idea of setting up separate colonies apart from other farmers by placing families on units scattered or "infiltrated"—a favorite word—into existing farm districts. The agency's infiltration projects were a more versatile type of resettlement (if less glamorous) that could be better used in hill country, where land was neither rich nor available in large contiguous tracts.

Infiltration projects complemented other resettlement activities. The regional office sought to coordinate submarginal land purchases with the development of projects where uprooted families might find new homes and better land. Any family could elect to move to one of the community-type projects in the delta, but Whitaker also located infiltration projects as close as possible to submarginal purchase areas. As a rule, families moved no more than fifty miles from their former home. Northwest Arkansas Farms in Benton and Washington counties provided farms for families displaced in the Ozarks. Northeast Mississippi Farms—a project covering Choctaw, Clay, Kemper, Lowndes, Noxubee, Oktibbeha, and Winston counties—offered opportunity for similar families in the northern Mississippi hills.[13]

The Resettlement Administration undertook a series of "farm tenant security" projects, one in each of ten southern states. They, too, were infiltration projects, although some contained tracts large enough to exist as separate communities. The Louisiana Farm Tenant Security project, for example, consisted of nineteen tracts of land totaling 7,165 acres; fourteen tracts contained eight units or less; but one tract, the Millsaps plantation at Crew Lake in Richland Parish, contained 2,947 acres. Crew Lake closely resembled Plum Bayou or Lakeview, while the development

12. Conkin, *Tomorrow a New World*, pp. 168–70; Eaton, *Exploring Tomorrow's Agriculture*, pp. 66–67; Oren Stephens, "FSA Fights for Its Life," *Harper's Magazine* 186 (April 1943): 482; "These Arkansas Sharecroppers Are 'Tractored Onto' the Land," Little Rock *Arkansas Democrat Sunday Magazine*, 11 August 1940.

13. National Emergency Council, "Report of the Proceedings of the Statewide Coordination Meeting of Federal Agencies Operating in Arkansas . . . April 24, 1936," Little Rock, Arkansas, mimeographed, pp. 18E-G, Sharp Papers.

of most other units did not differ essentially from other infiltration projects.[14]

In early 1936, after a southern tour which included a week in Arkansas and two days in Mississippi, Rexford G. Tugwell set aside additional money for the purchase of resettlement land in Region VI. "How much money is there unallocated in the resettlement fund?" he asked his assistant administrator, C. B. Baldwin. A little over $2 million, he was told. "Give it to Region VI," Tugwell said. "They've got the land down there and they can make better use of it than any other region."[15]

Combining the new grant with rural rehabilitation trust funds, the regional office created a conglomerate project known as Arkansas Delta Farms, which evolved into five separate projects. Biscoe, Clover Bend, and Lonoke accepted white families; Desha and Townes accepted blacks. These projects were essentially infiltration-type, but they differed from the farm tenant security projects by utilizing larger tracts of land. They actually included many plantations of a thousand or more acres scattered up and down the delta. The total project acreage usually ran from three thousand to five thousand acres and contained between fifty and a hundred units. They often lacked the variety of community facilities characteristic of other projects.[16]

Until about 1937 Arkansas virtually monopolized the community program. Then the regional office dusted off old project plans and launched a new round of construction, giving Louisiana and Mississippi special attention.[17]

Transylvania Farms, north of Tallulah, Louisiana, was one of the region's most ambitious community-type projects. Acquiring two plantations which totaled 10,725 acres, Whitaker divided the land into 160 units. Controversy dogged Transylvania from the start. When protests arose because the Transylvania purchase displaced many Negro families who farmed the land as croppers, the nearby Mounds project became a

14. See "Fine Project in Richland Area," *Monroe Morning World*, 6 May 1938; "Farmers Pioneer New Deal Experiment in Louisiana," New Orleans *Morning Tribune*, 30 May 1937. Donald Holley, "Old and New Worlds in the New Deal Resettlement Program: Two Louisiana Projects," *Louisiana History* 11 (Spring 1970): 142–49, discusses Crew Lake in detail.
15. *Arkansas Gazette*, 11, 12 January, 4 February 1936.
16. T. Roy Reid to Will W. Alexander, 17 May 1939, FSA Records, NA, RG 96; FSA, "Resettlement Projects, Region VI," ibid.; USHR, *FSA Hearings*, pp. 1038–49, 1074–75; see, for example, "Proud Families to Greet Visitors Who Attend Clover Bend Project Dedication," Memphis *Press-Scimitar*, 29 March 1938.
17. T. Roy Reid to Employees of the Farm Security Administration in Region VI, 6 July 1938, FSA Records, NA, RG 96.

safety valve. There, a few miles east of Tallulah on an 11,896-acre plantation, 145 black families found resettlement farms.[18]

In southern Louisiana, Whitaker merged four Terrebonne Parish plantations totaling 5,960 acres into a single collective farm of seventy families. The Terrebonne project benefited from Lake Dick's experience, and its operation was somewhat more successful. Farmers were allowed more private land to do with as they pleased. Despite plans for cooperative ownership, Whitaker split the land into forty-acre units—an indication of growing doubts about the practicality of cooperative farming.[19]

Less well known than either Lake Dick or Terrebonne, the Marcella project was a 2,686-acre collective farm in Holmes County, Mississippi. Regional officials almost shunted Marcella out of sight; it was part of Mileston Farms, the only project in Region VI that the FSA was solely responsible for initiating, planning, and developing. Constructed in 1939 and 1940, Mileston consisted of 9,350 acres and 106 farm units, only 36 of which operated collectively.[20]

On Mississippi's coastal plain, Whitaker purchased 5,744 acres of cutover bottomland near Lucedale, built a community center, and developed ninety-three farm units. Unlike those at most other resettlement projects, Lucedale clients derived income primarily from truck crops, grains, and livestock rather than cotton.[21]

With the Bankhead-Jones Act prohibiting the creation of any new resettlement communities, T. Roy Reid made a proposal which resulted in a series of land-leasing associations, and Region VI pioneered the program. Using all their accumulated experience, regional officials perhaps showed Washington how they thought rural resettlement and rehabilitation ought to be handled. In 1938 Reid arranged for 827 tenant families in various combinations to lease seventeen cotton plantations. Within a year the program doubled in size: 1,699 families leasing thirty-one plantations. When it reached its peak in 1943, fifty-two such groups existed in eight states.[22]

18. USHR, *FSA Hearings*, p. 1064. See below, Chapter XI.
19. J. T. Armstrong, "A New Kind of Life and Farming in Thibodaux Cooperative," New Orleans *Item-Tribune*, 25 June 1939; see below, Chapter X.
20. Eaton, *Exploring Tomorrow's Agriculture*, pp. 142, 151; USHR, *FSA Hearings*, pp. 1072, 1073; FSA, "Resettlement Projects, Region VI," FSA Records, NA, RG 96.
21. Ibid.
22. R. W. Hudgens, "The Plantation South Tries a New Way," *Land Policy Review* 3 (November 1940): 26–29; see *Item-Tribune*, 5 February 1939; Albert Proctor, "Huge Cooperative Project Launched by 50 Farmers on Allen Parish Tract," *The Progress* (Hammond, La.), 17 October 1939.

The plan was eminently practical. With the agency's help, a group of families leased a large tract of land which they divided into family-sized units. Beyond that, the land-leasing projects functioned very much like resettlement communities, except, of course, the land was not purchased outright, nor were funds available for the construction of community facilities. The program sought to remedy the insecure land tenure so endemic in the Cotton Belt, where most land-leasing projects were located.

Inadvertently, the land-leasing associations became one of the FSA's most controversial programs. While the President's Committee on Farm Tenancy had recommended such enterprises, the Bankhead-Jones Act contained no specific authorization for them. To Farm Security critics, they looked suspiciously like an effort to evade the will of Congress by expanding resettlement activities. Perhaps, it was whispered, they were even a sinister government effort to gain control of vast amounts of land.

Besides their own activities, regional officials administered the old FERA and Subsistence Homesteads projects. When the Resettlement Administration inherited the FERA's rural rehabilitation program in 1935, the regional office assumed responsibility for land which the state rural rehabilitation corporations held options on or had purchased outright. (Dyess Colony, of course, was an exception to this.) Using state corporation trust funds, Whitaker completed the FERA's most feasible plans; he had, most likely, originated most of them.

Arkansas claimed all but one of these rural rehabilitation projects, again taking the lion's share of available funds. Two sister projects, Trumann Farms and Saint Francis River Farms, were both located in Poinsett County, the stamping ground of the Southern Tenant Farmers' Union. The two projects together consisted of 6,195 acres of land divided into 143 units. The Arkansas Rural Rehabilitation Corporation also financed two projects in the southeastern part of the state, Chicot Farms in Chicot and Drew counties and Kelso Farms in Desha County, both later leased to the War Relocation Authority (WRA) for use as Japanese relocation centers during World War II. Chicot Farms, the second-largest community project in Arkansas, covered 13,781 acres broken up into 241 units, and included the entire town of Jerome. Kelso was still undeveloped as a farm project when leased to the WRA. Central and Western Arkansas Valley Farms, originally two separate projects, consisted of 85 farm units widely scattered throughout Conway, Crawford, Faulkner, Franklin, Johnson, Logan, Pope, Sebastian, and Yell counties. Here were homes for families living in submarginal purchase areas of the Boston Mountains and on Magazine Mountain.[23]

Near Terry, Mississippi, Whitaker used rural rehabilitation trust funds to buy a 5,404-acre tract of gently rolling sandy loam. Here he build Hinds Farms, a community project for eighty-one families.[24] The fact that Louisiana had not one rural rehabilitation project might be attributable in part to Huey Long's intransigence. The Mississippi FERA, perhaps because of lack of state leadership, simply never developed a strong rural rehabilitation program.

The regional organization gained its first actual experience with community building in the unfinished business of the subsistence homesteads program. Reid inherited a troublesome legacy in Mississippi. Subsistence Homesteads officials had located the projects on rather poor soil, did not always insure sufficient employment opportunities for occupants, and sometimes furnished rather haphazard management.

After examining the status of each project, Reid dropped Laurel, since it was so far from completion; but he went ahead with McComb, Tupelo, Hattiesburg, and Magnolia (or Meridian).[25] With one exception, no construction was undertaken on any of the projects beyond finishing what had already been started. The Construction Division built ten additional houses at Tupelo, bringing the total number of units to thirty-five and making it the largest of the Mississippi projects. James B. Lawson, regional chief of the Management Division, made repairs at Hattiesburg and Meridian, as some of the homes had badly deteriorated. At McComb, Lawson enlarged some of the homestead tracts by redividing the land, erected more outbuildings, and installed gasoline well pumps. In addition, the Management Division investigated and selected families for all twenty units, while filling the vacancies at Tupelo, Hattiesburg, and Meridian.[26]

23. Resettlement Administration, Arkansas Rural Rehabilitation Division, Annual Report 1936, 30 December 1936; Resettlement Administration, Yearly Report of the Custodian of Corporations Division (December 1936); FSA, "Resettlement Projects, Region VI," all in FSA Records, NA, RG 96; USHR, *FSA Hearings*, pp. 1038–49, 1071–75. On Trumann Farms, see Eugene Rutland, "For the Poor Farmer, a New Lease on Life," Memphis *Commercial Appeal*, 9 April 1939.

24. USHR, *FSA Hearings*, pp. 1071–72. The Resettlement Administration originally planned to build a project at Tupelo, Mississippi, known as Tupelo Suburban Gardens. The agency invested $29,047.32 before dropping the project. Resettlement Administration, *First Annual Report* (Washington: Government Printing Office, 1936), p. 145; USHR, *FSA Hearings*, p. 1118.

25. See above, Chapter IV.

26. Management Division, News Letter, Region VI, 1 July 1935 to 1 January 1936; Rexford G. Tugwell to T. Roy Reid, 2 February 1937; "Subsistence Home-

Beyond this point the Resettlement Administration followed the original intention of the Division of Subsistence Homesteads. Once each project reached full capacity, the regional office organized the families into a local homestead association, the same kind of organization used in all of its own community projects. At first, both old homesteaders and new families remained under the terms of the Division of Subsistence Homesteads' licensing agreements. When the new homestead association took over, officials offered every family a chance, after a one-year trial period, to enter into a Tenure Form A contract, a long-term purchase agreement. Those not wanting to purchase their homesteads could take a Tenure B contract, a monthly lease based on the unit's selling price. The occupants were required to follow a live-at-home program of home management in order to help them reduce living expenses.[27]

But it was not quite so simple. For the next five years, 1935 to 1940, the Resettlement Administration and then the Farm Security Administration struggled unsuccessfully with the problems of the Mississippi subsistence homesteads.

At McComb, Lawson quickly ran up against the project's old nemesis. "The selection of families and the filling of the houses on the McComb project are progressing in accordance with our anticipation," he wrote in November 1935, "that is, we are having trouble in getting the houses filled." Families who could qualify, he reported, refused to accept the properties under the terms of the old licensing agreements.[28] By June 1936, however, Lawson had filled nineteen of the twenty homesteads, using basically the family selection criteria devised by the Division of Subsistence Homesteads.[29]

On 12 January 1937, when the probation period ended, the regional office incorporated McComb Homesteads Association under Mississippi law. The association had authority to issue 250 shares of common stock with a par value of three dollars per share. According to the charter of incorporation, McComb Homesteads Association was to "participate in the establishment, maintenance, and development of a community at Mc-

steads," April 1935; "Mississippi Projects," 1 June 1935; see Leon Shirman, memorandum to Mrs. L. M. Walker, 9 February 1937; Edward Stone, memorandum to Walker, 14 December 1936, all in FSA Records, NA, RG 96.

27. Conkin, *Tomorrow a New World*, pp. 215, 216.

28. J. B. Lawson to Robert K. Straus, 6 November 1935; see T. Roy Reid to Rexford G. Tugwell, 9 December 1935; Wendell Lund, memorandum to Mrs. Loretta M. Walker, 10 March 1937; John O. Walker to Reid, 17 April 1937, 17 May 1939, all in FSA Records, NA, RG 96.

29. Rexford G. Tugwell to Rep. Dan R. McGehee, 30 June 1936, ibid.

Comb Homesteads . . . for the mutual benefit of the members of such community; to engage in activities designed to rehabilitate such members and make them self supporting; and to do and perform all acts and things necessary, convenient, useful or incidental to the accomplishment of these purposes."[30] The regional office next drew up plans for selling the project property and assets to the association for $44,360, less credits of $2,250.17 for rent paid, leaving a new price of $42,109.83. In contrast, the total estimated cost of the McComb project was $110,088. Homesteaders would pay an average of $2,218 per unit in monthly installments over a forty-year period at 3 percent interest.[31]

Despite the $65,728 write-off, the Resettlement Administration's plans for a homestead association at McComb failed miserably. The new project manager, John S. Grant, offered each family the option of signing a Tenure A contract with the association or staying for a reasonable length of time under the present agreement while looking for a new home. Most of them took the latter course. In July 1938 only five families remained, all still on temporary status. The McComb project experienced difficulty keeping occupants because of its distance from the corporate limits of McComb, its lack of utilities, and its generally poor soil. Like all subsistence homesteads in Mississippi, McComb also suffered from the shortage of employment opportunities.[32]

After conferring with citizens of McComb, regional officials decided to scrap the plan for a homestead association. If the units were simply offered at an average price of $1,200 each at 6 percent interest with a twenty-year term, McComb citizens contended, enough clients could be drummed up to fill the project. Although such an arrangement would come close to eliminating government control, regional officials went ahead. That feature may have been the best part of the deal. In July 1938 they made an outright sale to individual clients, giving each homesteader a deed and taking a mortgage and promissory note. Homesteaders agreed to repay the purchase price in equal monthly installments amortized over twenty years at 5 percent (another concession), with average monthly

30. Charter of Incorporation of McComb Homesteads Association, dated 12 January 1937, HHFA Records, NA, RG 207. The charter was published in *McComb Enterprise*, 11 February 1937.
31. Edward Stone, memorandum to Donald MacGuiness, 17 March 1937, HHFA Records, NA, RG 207; Mastin G. White, memorandum to the Secretary of Agriculture, 18 July 1938, Wallace Papers, NA, RG 16.
32. Milo Perkins, memorandum to the Secretary of Agriculture, 14 July 1938, ibid.; J. O. Walker, memorandum to the Solicitor [Mastin G. White], 15 April 1938, HHFA Records, NA, RG 207.

payments of $14.25. At $1,200, the government lost $3,114 per unit, or an additional $52,292. At long last the Farm Security Administration had little trouble finding occupants for the project.[33]

Hattiesburg and Meridian were the only two subsistence homesteads projects in the nation that defaulted after being organized into associations. On 30 September 1936, the Resettlement Administration sold the Meridian project to Meridian Homesteads Association for $60,000, less $2,424.67 in credits for rent paid.[34] Hattiesburg Homesteads Association acquired the Hattiesburg property and assets on 1 October 1936 for $49,720, minus credits of $3,473.61.[35] Meridian had cost $92,488.20, Hattiesburg $91,035.36. The Meridian homesteaders bought their units for an average price of $2,400 with an average monthly payment of $18.64, while at Hattiesburg the units sold for an average of $2,075 with an $18.08 monthly payment. At both Hattiesburg and Meridian, regional officials and interested local citizens agreed that the price not only represented the fair market value of the homesteads, but was also in line with real estate values in the area and imposed no undue burden on the homesteaders.[36] Yet plans again went awry.

The Resettlement Administration found it difficult to attract families at either project and almost impossible to keep them once they came. For one reason, the regional office built up a heritage of misunderstanding when it sought to purge both projects of undesirable occupants before offering purchase contracts. After the cooperative associations were organized, other residents withdrew voluntarily, feeling they were unable to make the monthly payments. At Hattiesburg, especially, the homesteaders were dissatisfied with the terms and conditions of the Tenure A contracts. "The chief reason," Reid reported, "probably is that the total monthly outlay under Tenure Form 'A' is a few dollars more than it was under the Temporary Licensing Agreement."[37] They also objected to the

33. Mastin G. White, memorandum to the Secretary of Agriculture, 18 July 1938, Wallace Papers, NA, RG 16; T. Roy Reid to Rexford G. Tugwell, 4 September 1936, FSA Records, NA, RG 96; Leon Shirman, memorandum to Edward Stone, 11 September 1936, ibid.
34. Ibid.; Milo Perkins, memorandum to the Secretary of Agriculture, 18 July 1938, Wallace Papers, NA, RG 16.
35. Milo Perkins, memorandum to the Secretary of Agriculture, 14 July 1938, ibid.; E. E. Agger to T. Roy Reid, 22 January 1937, FSA Records, NA, RG 96. See Hattiesburg American, 9 December 1936.
36. Milo Perkins, memorandum to the Secretary of Agriculture, 14, 18 July 1938, Wallace Papers, NA, RG 16.
37. T. Roy Reid to Rexford G. Tugwell, 4 November 1936, FSA Records, NA, RG 96.

cooperative association; "some of the individuals," Reid wrote, "feel that they should be allowed to purchase directly from the Government and not through the association, thereby relieving them of any responsibility in connection with the balance of the property." In addition, they felt they should not bear any management expenses; and some were worried about the forty-year clause, though none could make a substantial down payment. "I believe," Reid wrote, "that all of the above reasons are due primarily to the lack of business experience of a group of people such as we have on the project."[38] He had only his own family selection staff to blame.

From 1934 to 1938 Hattiesburg experienced a 92 percent turnover. By July 1938 only six families remained in occupancy.[39] Meridian's record was similar. Neither association could make the first payment, which came due on 31 October 1937, nor could they meet any subsequent payment on their obligations. In 1938, after reappraising Meridian, the regional office lowered monthly charges to $16.24, an amount based on an average selling price of $1,840 per unit; at Hattiesburg, the new figures were $14.74 per month and $1,578.42 per unit.[40] This reduction made the projects more attractive, but it was not a permanent solution. In March 1941, acting as regional director, T. B. Fatherree wrote: "The affairs of the Magnolia and Hattiesburg Homestead Associations are so badly involved as to be considered insolvent, and to all purposes are looked upon as such by those of us responsible for their operation."[41]

Tupelo was the last project to be transferred to a homestead association. Regional officials formed Tupelo Homesteads Association on 17 May 1937, and approved its purchase of the $149,290 project for $110,000.[42] The Tupelo homesteaders did not wait any longer before starting to voice complaints. When the new board of directors put the question of sale to a vote, the homesteaders turned it down cold. The regional office failed to take into consideration recent changes in Tupelo real estate values. In

38. Ibid.
39. John O. Walker, memorandum to Will W. Alexander, 9 July 1938, ibid.
40. John O. Walker to T. Roy Reid, 28 July 1938, 30 July 1940, ibid; Milo Perkins, memorandum to the Secretary of Agriculture, 18 July 1938, Wallace Papers, NA, RG 16.
41. T. B. Fatherree to C. B. Baldwin, 22 March 1941, FSA Records, NA, RG 96. See Washington, D.C., *Times-Herald*, 26 May 1942. Fatherree probably meant "insolvable," but "insolvent" was correct, too.
42. Will W. Alexander, memorandum to the Secretary of Agriculture, 15 April, 2 October 1937, Wallace Papers, NA, RG 16; Charter of Incorporation of Tupelo Homesteads Association, dated 17 May 1937, FSA Records, NA, RG 96. A copy was published in *Tupelo Daily News*, 31 May 1937.

April 1936 a tornado had ripped through the city, killing 201 people, injuring more than a thousand others, and causing considerable property damage. As a result, building activity increased sharply and peaked in early 1937. By May more rental apartments and homes were available in Tupelo than before the tornado, and the new buildings were superior to the ones lost. The Land Utilization Division, with the assistance of local citizens, reappraised the project and recommended that the price be dropped to $95,557.50, making a new loss of $53,732.50. The board of directors favored the offer, but the homesteaders still objected strongly. After the regional office reappraised the project a second time, the association finally agreed on 1 October 1938 to purchase the project for $73,182. Tupelo still faced an unstable future. Since a large number of the families were Tennessee Valley Authority employees, not Tupelo natives, they were still not interested in purchasing their homes.[43]

In Region VI the Farm Security Administration started its liquidation program with the Mississippi subsistence homesteads. For practical purposes, McComb had been in a state of liquidation since the project was opened for sale to homesteaders in 1938. On 31 October 1940, according to a memorandum of understanding with the secretary of the interior, the National Park Service took over the Tupelo project and made it part of the Natchez Trace Parkway system.[44] In December 1941 both Hattiesburg and Meridian homestead associations transferred all assets, real and personal property, to the United States government, and then voluntarily dissolved.[45] The Bureau of Plant Industry had already taken over five units at Meridian for its Horticulture Field Station.[46] But now the regional office sold the remaining homes to individual purchasers, either current homesteaders or new families who filled the unoccupied units. As World War II stimulated employment, it was less difficult to obtain occupants than ever before, especially since in terms of wartime inflation these units were ridiculously cheap.

On 1 October 1942, the Farm Security Administration transferred to the Federal Public Housing Authority all resettlement projects on which

43. Mastin G. White to Brooks Hays, 21 September 1938, HHFA Records, NA, RG 207; Hays to White, 29 September 1938, ibid.; Report of Examination, Tupelo Homesteads Association, for the Period 15 November 1934 to 10 October 1940, FSA Records, NA, RG 96; Deed of Trust Note, dated 1 October 1938, ibid.
44. Frank W. Hancock to Rep. John E. Rankin, 4 December 1944, ibid.; John O. Walker to T. Roy Reid, 5 October 1940, ibid.
45. C. B. Baldwin, memorandum to the Secretary of Agriculture, 8 March 1942, ibid.; D. L. Hopkins to E. G. Benser, 20 July 1943, ibid.
46. John O. Walker to T. Roy Reid, 30 July 1940, ibid.

clients did not earn their principal income from agriculture.[47] The Mississippi subsistence homesteads came under this classification. Alexander T. McCurdie opened an office for the Federal Public Housing Authority at Hattiesburg and operated the three remaining projects—McComb, Hattiesburg, and Meridian—throughout World War II. McCurdie, who had been one of the Division of Subsistence Homesteads' project managers in Mississippi, functioned chiefly as a rent collector. After the end of the war he handled their liquidation. Under the Federal Public Housing Authority, occupants could receive quit-claim deeds to their homesteads when they paid 20 percent of the purchase price, signing a note and mortgage as security for the balance.[48] By June 1946 McCurdie had sold all units on the three projects and issued homesteaders their deeds. On June 28 he closed his Hattiesburg office.[49] The government must have given up the Mississippi subsistence homesteads with a sigh of relief.

Whatever the flaws of the subsistence homesteads concept, Reid's organization made its own mistakes in Mississippi. Yet if the Division of Subsistence Homesteads had not pointed up some of the hazards of community building, or if the Mississippi projects had not provided an opportunity for "practice," perhaps he would have made greater mistakes in developing his own projects.

47. Mason Barr to A. D. Stewart, 30 September 1942, ibid.
48. Conkin, *Tomorrow a New World*, pp. 231, 232.
49. Oliver C. Winston, memorandum to John P. Broome, 1 May 1946, HHFA Records, NA, RG 207; A. T. McCurdie, memorandum to Arthur Taylor, 5 June 1946, ibid.

Chapter VIII

If You Want to Build a Community . . .

The Resettlement Administration and later the Farm Security Administration followed one basic pattern in building their resettlement projects.[1] As the first task, regional directors selected land for resettlement purposes and recommended specific projects to Washington.

T. Roy Reid drew on every available resource, both inside and outside his organization, for help in locating suitable land. He and E. B. Whitaker themselves possessed a vast knowledge of agriculture and land values in Region VI. A regional land use committee and similar state committees approved possible resettlement areas and insured the involvement of local citizens. To help with the selection of land, Reid also sought the advice of the land grant colleges, agricultural extension services, and experiment stations of the respective states.

He received many unsolicited suggestions from individuals with land for sale and from groups wanting federal money spent in their communities. Oscar Ameringer, Socialist editor of the Oklahoma City *American Guardian*, tried to sell the agency a 5,500-acre plantation in Louisiana that he described as "my personally conducted resettlement project."[2] In 1936 a group of citizens of Attala County, Mississippi, complained to Sen. Pat Harrison that the RA had not bought any land in their county for some time; they wanted to sell the government more land. At the same time, other people warned of fraudulent schemes for selling worthless land to the government. In early 1936 Mississippi's Theodore G. Bilbo cautioned Tugwell that "a lot of high powered real estate agents,

1. Establishment of Community Organizations, Memorandum Approved by the President, 24 December 1936, FSA Records, NA, RG 96.
2. T. Roy Reid to C. B. Baldwin, 14 September 1937, ibid.; Oscar Ameringer to Will W. Alexander, 14 January 1937, ibid.; Oscar Ameringer, "No Thoroughfare to Utopia," *Reader's Digest* 37 (July 1940): 13–16.

racketeers, and lawyers bought from the state a lot of land [which had been forfeited for taxes] . . . all for the purpose of unloading this on the Federal Government."[3]

Once a general resettlement area received approval, Whitaker sent out someone with a knowledge of land values to canvass the area. This person, perhaps a county agent or the man designated as project manager, located and took options on likely tracts of land owned by people wanting to sell. In some instances Whitaker also issued a press release inviting tenders on farm land, an announcement that both urban and smalltown newspapers would carry.[4]

The Resettlement Administration did not engage in land speculation. Whitaker was anxious to buy land on a strictly competitive basis—the best land available for the lowest possible price. After the initial options were taken, B. M. Gile's Land Utilization Division undertook a thorough appraisal of the land and made a recommendation to the regional office, which then passed it on to Washington. The Resettlement Administration demanded that land meet certain standards of price, market value, and productivity. Whitaker wanted to buy land that was under cultivation, free from flooding, and containing little timber. Ideally, he preferred land located near improved roads and power lines and accessible to schools, churches, towns, and markets. After Gile submitted his appraisals, Whitaker usually took new options at the appraised value, or less if possible. Finally, the federal government actually paid for land only if the vendor could furnish a title acceptable to the Department of Justice.[5]

Although Region VI contained some of the richest farm land in the United States, the high rate of tenancy resulted in part from a lack of ownership opportunities. Large planters and absentee landlords held much of the most fertile land, and they were rarely willing to break their large holdings into small tracts for sale to individual farmers. Nor did the presence of millions of acres of land unused for agriculture suggest many opportunities for new farmers. In Region VI most of the vast acreage of

3. Sen. Pat Harrison to E. B. Whitaker, 21 August 1936; see T. Roy Reid to Will W. Alexander, 31 March 1938; Sen. Theodore G. Bilbo to Rexford G. Tugwell, 12 June 1936, all in FSA Records, NA, RG 96.
4. Resettlement Administration, Annual Report of Assistant Regional Director in Charge of Rural Resettlement, 1 July 1935 to 31 December 1936, FSA Records, NA, RG 96. See, for example, *Madison Journal* (Tallulah, La.), 14, 21 February 1936.
5. Resettlement Administration, Annual Report of Assistant Regional Director in Charge of Rural Resettlement, 1 July 1935 to 31 December 1936, FSA Records, NA, RG 96. E. B. Whitaker to Rep. Will M. Whittington, 25 February 1937, ibid.; *Madison Journal*, 14 February, 21 August 1936.

undeveloped land was not suitable for growing crops, because of unproductive soil, rough topography, erosion, poor drainage, or flooding. About 22 million acres in Mississippi and two-thirds of Louisiana were in cutover land, forest, pasture, and swamp; and in Arkansas much of the land area consisted of dense forest or mountainous terrain.[6]

In 1937 the Resettlement Administration published bulletins for "prospective new farmers" in Arkansas, Louisiana, and Mississippi, stressing that ownership was becoming more difficult for farmers of limited means. According to the Resettlement Administration's farm management studies, sixty acres constituted the minimum size which could be considered for a family farm in the cotton areas of Region VI. During the mid-1930s the selling price for improved farm land averaged between $45 and $70 per acre in Mississippi and between $35 and $50 in Arkansas and Louisiana. So for land alone, a sixty-acre farm meant an investment of $3,000 to $4,000 in Mississippi and $2,500 to $3,000 in Arkansas and Louisiana, depending upon location, productivity, and number of cleared acres. In southern Louisiana, sugarcane land sold for $40 to $75 per acre; and since about thirty-five acres of cane land was needed to support a family, no substantial difference in cost existed between farms in sugarcane and cotton areas. (A small farmer could buy undeveloped land for $12 to $15 per acre, but it was usually less productive; and the cost of clearing the land drove the price back up to around $50 per acre.) To build a small cottage and the minimum of farm buildings and to buy the necessary livestock and equipment meant an additional investment of $1,500 to $2,000, and probably more. Thus Resettlement experts estimated that the total investment for a family farm would run between $4,000 and $5,000. This price, of course, was far beyond the means of croppers and share tenants or even most cash tenants.[7]

While almost any large tract of land would contain poor, buckshot soil, Whitaker was under no compulsion to settle for anything but the best, since the depression had knocked the bottom out of land values. "Almost without exception," he wrote in 1936, "the land selected for resettlement

6. Resettlement Administration, Annual Report, Region VI, as of 31 December 1936, FSA Records, NA, RG 96.
7. Resettlement Administration, *Information for Prospective New Farmers in the State of Louisiana*, Resettlement Information Service Bulletin no. 11 (Washington, 1937), pp. 8, 9, 18–21; idem, *Information for Prospective New Farmers in the State of Mississippi*, Resettlement Information Service Bulletin no. 10 (Washington, 1937), pp. 6, 7; idem, *Information for Prospective New Farmers in the State of Arkansas*, Resettlement Information Service Bulletin no. 9 (Washington, 1937), pp. 24–26.

purposes has an average yield higher than the average yield of the basic crops in the community where the land is located."[8] At the same time, his policy was not to take advantage of any landowner in distress. Whitaker refused to pressure anyone to sell his property; he purchased land only from those who really wanted to sell.[9] But he did take advantage of certain conditions created by the depression. As he explained:

> It was the exception, rather than the rule, if such land was not owned by an absentee landowner. A number of larger tracts were bought from banks or insurance companies in the process of liquidation, and the fact that the national government was in a position to pay one hundred per cent cash made the Resettlement Administration a very desirable purchaser of the tracts in question. This enabled us to buy land at a much lower cash price than the same land would have sold for to a private concern where from fifty to seventy-five per cent of the purchase price would have been deferred.[10]

In Region VI the Resettlement Administration purchased 194,482 acres of resettlement land at a cost of $4,823,927.92. Overall, Whitaker paid an average of $24.80 per acre. The cheapest land was in Arkansas ($21.55 per acre), while land in Louisiana ($28.00) and Mississippi ($28.57) was somewhat higher.[11]

Each resettlement project involved painstaking planning and months of work from conception to authorization, construction, and completion. After locating land for a possible resettlement project, Whitaker and Reid submitted a preliminary proposal to Washington showing that the project had enough merit to warrant the expenditure of time and money on the preparation of a "project plan." Tugwell's staff checked the proposal and, if they approved, authorized a detailed study made of the project and released allotments for that purpose. Only then did Whitaker begin taking options on the necessary land.

In the project plan, Whitaker presented a justification of the project, including full details on everything involved in its development: Would it need a cooperative store, a gin, or a school? What crops could be grown

8. Resettlement Administration, Annual Report of Assistant Regional Director in Charge of Rural Resettlement, 1 July 1935 to 31 December 1936, FSA Records, NA, RG 96.

9. *Madison Journal*, 21 August 1936.

10. Resettlement Administration, Annual Report of Assistant Regional Director in Charge of Rural Resettlement, 1 July 1935 to 31 December 1936, FSA Records, NA, RG 96.

11. Computed from FSA, "Resettlement Projects, Region VI," ibid.

profitably? What were the estimated costs of land, of construction, and of administering the project? Did local landowners and businessmen favor the idea of a project? Then Reid submitted the project plan to Tugwell, who checked it for feasibility, soundness, legality, and availability of funds. If satisfied, he authorized the construction of the project. The regional office then proceeded to purchase the land and draw up construction plans, specifications, and plots for a final check by the Washington office. Tugwell reviewed the plans a last time to compare them with budget estimates. After receiving word of final approval, Whitaker immediately began building the homesteads, dividing the land into individual farm units, and selecting families.[12]

At first the Resettlement Administration did all of its own construction work, using WPA labor and occasionally some of its own clients. But the Construction Division's building costs ran far beyond what low-income farmers could ever hope to repay.[13] After 1937 the Farm Security Administration fought to hold construction costs to an absolute minimum. Will Alexander placed a cost limitation of $1,300 on houses built in the South and, because of the harsher climate, $2,100 on houses built in the North.[14] In 1938 the FSA turned all construction over to private contractors, who built houses more cheaply than could the Construction Division. On community-type projects in Region VI, private construction firms negotiated a single contract for building all necessary structures, with the FSA acting as consultant and architect.[15] On projects where units were scattered, contractors had to make separate contracts for the construction of each homestead.[16]

Still fighting high costs, Whitaker engaged in a small amount of experimentation with precutting and prefabrication building methods. Pre-

12. Resettlement Administration, Administrative Order 162 (Revision 1), 8 July 1936, ibid.
13. Henry A. Wallace to the President, 19 March 1937, FDR Papers, OF 1568; Rep. Will M. Whittington to Will W. Alexander, 26 July 1938, FSA Records, NA, RG 96.
14. Nathan W. Robertson to Paul Wooton, 1 March 1939, ibid.; Paul K. Conkin, *Tomorrow a New World: The New Deal Community Program* (Ithaca, N.Y.: Cornell University Press, 1959), p. 171.
15. C. B. Baldwin to Rep. Will M. Whittington, 19 August 1938, FSA Records, NA, RG 96; R. B. Lord to T. Roy Reid, 5 April 1939, ibid. See Resettlement Administration, Construction Division, Progress Report for Projects in Development and Planning, 1 July 1936 to 1 August 1936, ibid.
16. "FHA [FSA] Helps Construction," *Construction News* 5 (28 September 1938): 5, 6; C. B. Baldwin to Rep. A. Leonard Allen, 24 November 1937, FSA Records, NA, RG 96.

fab construction proved most successful where fifty or more houses were erected within a radius of about twenty-five miles. Setting up a small portable sawmill on the project and using a limited number of house plans, a construction crew cut lumber to exact specifications and assembled as many parts as possible in this central shop. They completed entire sections: wall panels, gables, window and door casings, and floor frames. Then the components were trucked to the building sites and nailed together. Whitaker first tried prefabrication in Arkansas and later Mississippi, but he never used it on a large scale.[17]

The resettlement projects of Region VI included about fifteen types of houses. Like those at Dyess Colony, resettlement homes were conventional wood-frame structures stressing utility and economy. Architects eliminated all purely decorative features as well as every unnecessary gable, beam, and rafter; they also standardized house plans as much as possible without making the various types look too much alike. Built on concrete piers, the typical resettlement home contained three to five bedrooms, living room, kitchen, built-in sink, pantry, shelving, and screened porch. Newspaper reporters generally described project houses as modern, comfortable, and convenient; but the structures did not measure up to all of these standards. For example, they had no indoor plumbing, although each one had a storeroom designed for conversion into a bath when the family could afford it. The exteriors were usually white, the interiors finished in natural pine, with the kitchen painted enamel. In addition to the dwelling, the typical homestead unit included a barn, chicken house, outhouse, all necessary fencing, several acres of pasture, and about forty acres of farm land.[18]

Resettlement housing was undoubtedly better than the dilapidated shacks most tenants and croppers inhabited. It was clean, if not luxurious. There were even protests—both from jealous neighbors who perhaps resented someone else's getting a break, and from congressional conservatives who disliked "coddling"—that housing on resettlement projects was

17. Nathan W. Robertson to Paul Wooton, 1 March 1939, ibid.; Farm Security Administration, *Report of the Administrator of the Farm Security Administration, 1938* (Washington: Government Printing Office, 1938), pp. 18, 19; idem, *Report of the Administrator of the Farm Security Administration, 1940* (Washington: Government Printing Office, 1940), pp. 17–19; C. B. Baldwin to Sen. Pat Harrison, 16 February 1938, FSA Records, NA, RG 96.

18. "FHA [FSA] Helps Construction," pp. 5, 6; FSA, *Report of the Administrator of the Farm Security Administration, 1938*, p. 18; idem, *Report of the Administrator of the Farm Security Administration, 1940*, p. 19; Conkin, *Tomorrow a New World*, pp. 170–73.

too good for people living "on the government"; such criticisms were usually accompanied by stories of how clients allegedly abused their new homes.

While construction crews were at work, the Community and Family Services Section of the Management Division started looking for families to occupy the homestead units. Kate Fulton (later Mrs. T. Roy Reid), regional chief of this section until 1941, sought families who could measure up to rather high standards.[19]

The family selection staff's criteria were similar to those laid down by the Bankhead-Jones Act. Families qualified for resettlement if they were low-income farm owners, farm tenants, sharecroppers, or farm laborers. No one without farming experience was even considered, nor was anyone who could obtain credit on reasonable terms from other federal or private lending agencies. Candidates for resettlement had to show evidence of initiative and ambition, have a reputation for paying their debts, and show promise of being able to repay the cost of their units. They had to be free from disease or other physical disabilities and pass a medical examination before final acceptance. The selection staff preferred married couples with no more than five or six children, a limitation imposed by the size of the homesteads. The head of each family had to be at least twenty-one years of age and under fifty. There was no discrimination on the basis of nationality, race, or creed, although officials did demand homogeneity, especially on community-type projects, in order to insure smooth relations among families living as neighbors.[20]

The regional family services section and the community managers worked together to select qualified families. Applications started pouring in as soon as Whitaker announced the purchase of resettlement land; only in a few cases did a shortage of qualified families develop.[21] By 31 December 1940, the regional office had received over eleven thousand applications for some twenty-eight hundred farm units on its resettlement projects.[22] County extension agents, home demonstration agents, and

19. *Madison Journal*, 26 February 1937.

20. Resettlement Administration, Administrative Order 105 (Revision 3), 25 September 1936, mimeographed, FSA Records, NA, RG 96; Joseph W. Eaton, *Exploring Tomorrow's Agriculture* (New York: Harper and Brothers, 1943), pp. 94–99; John B. Holt, *An Analysis of Methods and Criteria Used in Selecting Families for Colonization Projects*, Social Research Report no. 1 of the U.S. Department of Agriculture, Farm Security Administration, and the Bureau of Agricultural Economics (Washington, 1937), pp. 6–15.

21. The most notable exceptions were Terrebonne and the subsistence homesteads program in Mississippi. See pp. 116–17, 118, 161.

22. Community and Family Services Section, Annual Report, 1 January 1940 to

district and county rural rehabilitation supervisors recommended most of these families.

On each resettlement project the community manager organized a family selection committee, consisting of himself as chairman, the regional chief of the family services section, a project family selection specialist, and usually the home economist and the farm management specialists assigned to his project. The committee gave preliminary approval to families which seemed most qualified and enthusiastic about resettlement. The family selection specialist interviewed them and visited their neighbors, their landlord, the merchants they patronized, and the family physician, seeking opinions as to the family's chances for successful home ownership. After consulting with the family selection committee, the project manager submitted a list of names to Kate Fulton, who then reviewed each case and made the final decision. The committee arranged for the approved families to visit the project while it was under construction. The community manager made sure every family understood all responsibilities and obligations incumbent upon members of the project. The family had one week after returning home to reach their final decision and to notify the community manager. If they said yes, he took care of moving their household goods to the project.[23]

At Dyess Colony the FERA had taken families off relief rolls on a more or less wholesale basis; the Resettlement and Farm Security administrations tried to be more careful. Family selection was a crucial step. A project's future might be jeopardized even before it began operation if many poor choices were made. The selection process contained another danger which might frustrate the intent of the entire program. It was always too easy to pick only families who seemed likely to succeed and thus make the project "look good," and reject families who were in greater need. The family selection staff had to steer carefully between the horns of this dilemma.

The Community and Cooperative Services staff, headed after 1936 by Claude Woolsey, handled the problems of legal organization for the Resettlement Division in Region VI. Woolsey formed the typical resettle-

31 December 1940, FSA Records, NA, RG 96; Farm Security Administration, Report of Family Selection Applications, Acceptances, and Occupancies for Units on Projects as of 1 July 1942, dated 20 August 1942, ibid.

23. Resettlement Administration, Administrative Order 105 (Revision 3), 25 September 1936, ibid.; Eaton, *Exploring Tomorrow's Agriculture*, pp. 94, 95; *Madison Journal*, 26 February 1936; Conkin, *Tomorrow a New World*, pp. 186–88.

ment project into a cooperative association.[24] Each association included a president and board of directors, sold its members capital stock, and possessed authority to engage in all activities related to agricultural production. The articles of incorporation of Terrebonne Association, Inc., for example, authorized its members:

> To engage in any activity in connection with the producing, marketing, selling, harvesting, dairying, preserving, drying, processing, canning, packing, milling, ginning, compressing, storing, handling, or the utilization of any agricultural products produced by it or produced or delivered to it by its members; or the manufacturing or marketing of the by-products thereof; or in connection with the purchase, hiring or use by it or its members of supplies, machinery, or equipment; or the construction or maintenance of houses, barns, sheds, or facilities for its use or the use of its members; or in connection with performing or purchasing services of an economic or educational nature to its members.[25]

Arkansas and Mississippi already had suitable laws regulating the formation of such cooperatives; but in Louisiana, Woolsey used a statute governing business corporations until the state legislature passed an agricultural cooperative law in 1939.[26]

The cooperative association was primarily intended to simplify certain administrative problems on resettlement projects. The regional office leased the association all project land, houses, community buildings, schools, stores, gins, and other community facilities. This move allowed the project residents themselves, rather than the government, to collect rent, maintain and repair buildings, and perform other routine tasks. In addition, the association received a cooperative loan to finance construction of homestead units and to purchase necessary farm equipment. By granting the association a loan, officials insured that development and operating funds would be available at all times; otherwise, it would be necessary to reapply to Washington every time money was needed.[27]

24. Claude Woolsey, interview with the author, 19 January 1968; Eaton, *Exploring Tomorrow's Agriculture*, pp. 105–12; Conkin, *Tomorrow a New World*, pp. 202–10.

25. "Articles of Association of Terrebonne Association, Inc.," dated 8 November 1938, Corporation Division, Secretary of State's Office, State Capitol, Baton Rouge, Louisiana.

26. Woolsey interview; Mastin G. White, memorandum to Will W. Alexander, 26 September 1938, FSA Records, NA, RG 96; see Conkin, *Tomorrow a New World*, pp. 202–13, 215. See below, Chapter X, n. 18.

27. Establishment of Community Organizations, Memorandum Approved by the President, 24 December 1936, FSA Records, NA, RG 96; Walter E. Packard to All Regional Directors, n.d., ibid.

The federal agencies also dealt with clients through the cooperative association. The head of each family was entitled to membership in the association and to one vote in all decisions. The president of the association was a project client, and so were members of the board of directors. On most projects the families subleased individual farm units from the association, not the government. After a five-year trial period, each family entered into a sales contract with the association for purchasing their unit at 3 percent interest over forty years. On cooperative projects like Terrebonne and Lake Dick, of course, farmers had no promise of future ownership of individual farms.[28]

Ultimately, the cooperative associations served as the instrument through which projects could become self-governing. Under the articles of incorporation, the board of directors possessed broad authority to conduct the project's business activities. Subject to approval by the general membership, the board of directors could employ a farm manager, determine management policies, authorize budgets, set membership requirements, admit new families, and control the terms of their contracts.

Yet a group of former sharecroppers predictably would not possess the necessary experience to operate a business enterprise. At the beginning most clients even had to learn parliamentary procedure. They attended "night classes" at the community center, where the project manager explained over and over the basic principles of cooperatives.

The ideal of democratic control obviously came into conflict with the need for safeguarding the government's investment. Thus the regional office, under the provisions of its loan agreement with each association, retained the government's complete power of control and veto.

The project manager exercised effective control over the association and the entire project, and he often served on the board of directors. He approved all operating budgets and controlled every expenditure made by the association, from wages to dividend payments. He also supervised the work of the project staff. Since the government paid the salaries of the farm manager, who directed daily farm operations, and the project accountant, they were for all practical purposes federal employees, although both remained responsible to the association under the terms of the articles of incorporation. No change in the articles of incorporation could be made without prior permission of the regional office, nor could

28. Woolsey interview; E. B. Whitaker, interview with the author, 19 January 1968.

any member be expelled from the project unless the government agreed that such action was justified.[29]

Besides the cooperative associations, the regional office usually formed subsidiary cooperatives to carry on certain specialized tasks. The Resettlement Administration, wrote Whitaker, encouraged each farmer "to cooperate with his neighbors in owning grain binders, grain separators, tractors, grist mills, blacksmith shops, sweet potato curing houses, cooperative stores, cooperative gins . . . and other such cooperative activities where the participation of the whole community is desirable for the success of the undertaking."[30] The typical community-type project would also have a livestock-breeding association and several kinds of marketing associations. The regional office did not wish to force local merchants into bankruptcy, but it would not completely avoid competition with private businesses. Ideally, a project would be justified in operating a cooperative store or gin if these services were not available nearby. Yet the greatest value of local purchasing and marketing cooperatives existed in freeing families from any dependence on the pernicious "furnish system."[31]

Since poor health was one of the major handicaps of many low-income farm families, clients also enjoyed medical care cooperatives, which afforded them a kind of health insurance. Each family made a fixed annual payment, usually about twenty-five dollars, to a trustee who divided the money into twelve parts, one for each month of the year. In case of illness the family could go to any local physician participating in the program; the physicians sent their bills each month to the trustee. If the amount on hand was not enough to pay all bills in full (which often proved the case), each physician received his pro rata share. Even so, they received more money than they might have otherwise.[32]

Critics easily confused such cooperative organizations with Soviet-style "communist collectives," since, after all, the resettlement agencies

29. Stanley W. Rhodes, interview with the author, 6 December 1972; Eaton, *Exploring Tomorrow's Agriculture*, pp. 105–13.

30. Resettlement Administration, Annual Report of Assistant Regional Director in Charge of Rural Resettlement, 1 July 1935 to 31 December 1936, FSA Records, NA, RG 96.

31. See FSA, "Resettlement Projects, Region VI"; J. T. Holliday to G. E. Lukas, 30 April 1940; Shelby Thompson to Frank J. Welch, 10 February 1942; Rexford G. Tugwell to T. Roy Reid, 8 May 1936, all ibid.; Raub Snyder, "Small Farmers Discover Rural Cooperation," *Land Policy Review* 6 (Fall 1943): 22–26.

32. *Report of the Administrator of the Farm Security Administration, 1940*, pp. 21–24; Richard Hellman, "The Farmers Try Group Medicine," *Harper's Magazine* 182 (December 1940): 72–80.

sponsored cooperative farming experiments also. Cooperatives existed primarily to give small farmers the advantages that size conferred on large-scale operators. Their use represented neither a loss of faith in individualism and private property nor an attempt to rebuild society with collectivist values. On the contrary, the Resettlement and Farm Security administrations worked hard to encourage individual effort in the resettlement program. Farmers owned their own cows, chickens, workstock, and all farm implements that a family-sized farm justified them in owning. Above all, they had a chance to own their farms and homes. Yet cooperative enterprises played an important role on every resettlement project. According to the FSA annual report of 1938, "Large-sale farms that can use highly mechanized operation methods have, in some areas, become a serious threat to the small, family-sized farm enterprise. The small farm, for example, may not be large enough to justify the use of a tractor or other heavy machinery. If a number of small farmers band together, however, they can take advantage of these modern, large-scale methods, and at the same time preserve the traditional values of independent farm ownership."[33] Since this banding together took the form of cooperative organization, no contradiction existed in pursuing individualistic ends with cooperative means.

The use of cooperative enterprises hardly represented a sudden or spectacular change in American agriculture. More than half a century before the New Deal, the Grangers had experimented with cooperative shipping associations, cooperative fire insurance companies, and, especially, cooperative stores patterned after those of the English Rochdale societies. Following World War I, many farm leaders saw cooperative action as a means of alleviating the effects of the agricultural depression without involving direct government action. In 1920 the American Farm Bureau Federation launched a campaign to encourage cooperative handling and selling of farm products. The Capper-Volstead Act of 1922 defined the legal status of farm cooperatives and exempted them from antitrust laws. In 1929 President Hoover sponsored the Agricultural Marketing Act, which, among other things, set up a Federal Farm Board to administer a revolving fund for the encouragement of agricultural cooperatives. Essentially, cooperatives were a businesslike approach to increase the farmer's bargaining power in the competitive marketplace.[34]

33. FSA, *Report of the Administrator of the Farm Security Administration, 1939* (Washington: Government Printing Office, 1939), p. 17.
34. See Murray R. Benedict, *Farm Policies of the United States, 1790–1950* (New York: Twentieth Century Fund, 1953), pp. 135, 136, 184, 237, 238, 240,

The farm and home management program lay at the heart of the concept of rural resettlement. Every project was provided with a staff of farm supervisors and home economists to teach low-income families the basic tools of successful farm living. With many settlers having less than a grade school education, resettlement projects took on the appearance of an adult education program. Through expert supervision, it was believed, families could achieve a satisfactory standard of living and pay for their farms.

Since most clients came to the program with few possessions, each family got a standard rural rehabilitation loan. These loans, ranging as high as $500 or $600, were used to buy livestock, fertilizer, seed, and equipment as needed. A typical tenant family also needed new clothing, medical care, and food to eat while putting in a crop. Every nickel and dime of the loan was budgeted for specific purposes, and deposited in a joint bank account under the family's name and the project manager's name. He countersigned every check.

Early each year the supervisory staff worked with client families in preparing a twelve-month budget, which provided the basis of any new rehabilitation loan. The farm management plan called for a diversified farm program rather than a continuation of the South's one-crop system of agriculture. Cotton remained the major cash crop of most projects; but every farmer also planted corn, truck crops, perhaps soybeans, and raised livestock. Like all other farmers, of course, they followed AAA regulations and practiced soil conservation.[35]

The wives pursued a "live at home" program designed to produce as much as possible of the family's needs on the farm and reduce store purchases to a minimum. Since most farm tenants could not (or would not) cultivate gardens, their diets lacked essential foods. But in helping housewives plan the home budget for the year, home management supervisors insisted that each family plant a garden and can vegetables for the winter months. The key to the home management program was the pressure cooker, and the RA and FSA were responsible for distributing thousands of them throughout the rural South. When government officials made inspection tours of resettlement homes, the women often seemed proudest

241; George B. Tindall, *The Emergence of the New South, 1913–1945* (Baton Rouge: Louisiana State University Press, 1967), pp. 116–21, 132, 133. See also Robert H. Montgomery, *The Cooperative Pattern in Cotton* (New York: Macmillan, 1929).

35. Milo Perkins to T. Roy Reid, 19 October, 15 November 1938, FSA Records, NA, RG 96.

of their canned goods neatly lined up on the pantry shelves. Farm wives also received instruction in sewing, sanitation, personal hygiene, and landscaping.[36]

"Ideally," Sidney Baldwin has written, "the county supervisor played the role of teacher, banker, farm and home expert, family case worker, and community organizer."[37] The same thing could be said for the project manager. The relationship between the project manager and the client family was a delicate one. He spent considerable time on their farm, giving advice, watching their bank account, "checking up" on them, while the home management supervisor spent time in their home, poking around in the kitchen and pantry. Sometimes a project manager tended to play the role of riding boss; perhaps some of them lacked patience and basic sympathy for the people they were trying to help. On the other hand, the family consisted of two adults who had always made their own way, and they sometimes resented any interference.

The client families could pose the most frustrating obstacles in the resettlement program. The New Dealers began to learn a hard lesson: the difficulty of helping people. It was one thing to provide families with new homes, farm equipment, and services, but it was another matter entirely to bring about fundamental changes in old attitudes. On the retraining of poor, uneducated families, however, hung the success of the entire program.

Many clients stubbornly resisted new ideas. Cooperatives were unfamiliar, perhaps never really understood by some, and therefore suspect. Crop diversification would "tie them down," they often complained. A straight furrow was a mark of distinction, and damn the notion that contour plowing prevented soil erosion.

Across the South's plantation country, "settlement day" came at the end of the year when landlords figured the year's earnings. If tenants escaped the "crooked pencil," they enjoyed buying something frivolous or having a good time. Government clients, too, could not be ascetics. After a hard year, they wanted to relax, enjoy themselves, and perhaps return home during the winter, paying for the trip out of their feed money. The farm and home budgets did not take such expenditures into account.

36. Joyce Mullins, "Some Facts about Resettlement," *Caldwell Watchman* (Columbia, La.), 21 May 1937; Rena B. Maycock, "Home Economic Work in the Resettlement Administration," *Journal of Home Economics* 28 (October 1936): 560–62.
37. Sidney Baldwin, *Poverty and Politics: The Rise and Decline of the Farm Security Administration* (Chapel Hill: University of North Carolina Press, 1968), p. 252.

Even if from the family's viewpoint the money went for a worthwhile purpose, the project manger tended to feel that the client violated his agreement. Thus the family might pick up the "uncooperative" label.[38]

The Resettlement and Farm Security administration made bitter enemies when officials encouraged clients to vote and take part in local community affairs, intruded into their personal affairs, supervised what they
grew, and regulated how they spent their money. Here was the specter
of "paternalism" and "regimentation." Yet the farm and home program
was not as new as critics charged. The original purpose of the Agricultural Extension Service was to promote better farm and home practices
through practical training and demonstration. In reality, the resettlement
program amounted to a new application of the techniques developed by
the Extension Service's force of county agents and home economists;
for the first time, low-income families were receiving such assistance.

The farm and home management program attracted friends as well as
enemies. The Arkansas Farm Tenancy Commission endorsed the idea of
credit supervision, leaving little doubt where they found their model. The
agency's educational program was indeed paternalistic, admitted the
Helena Record, "but paternalism is . . . required to bring the nation's less
privileged citizens into new and better conditions."[39]

New conditions, however favorable in the long run, were often difficult.
Most families were strangers, having moved from their home communities. Aware of the need to ease such adjustments, regional officials tried
to create a genuine sense of community life. All community- and many
infiltration-type projects contained a community center, which provided
the focus for social and educational activities. Stressing the need for
recreation, the project managers encouraged the use of community centers for dances, plays, musical programs, and occasional movies. The
Community and Family Services staff conducted a broad educational program for resettlement clients. Where necessary, the government built
schools for local school districts to operate. Vocational teachers arranged
regular classwork for adults in scientific agriculture, farm management,
and cooperative organization. Counselors furnished vocational guidance
for school dropouts, helping them get into Civilian Conservation Corps
camps, National Youth Administration projects, or trade schools. Religious denominations held services on many resettlement projects. At
Dyess the major denominations leased lots in the community center and

38. Ibid., pp. 273–78.
39. *Helena* (Ark.) *Record*, 20 June 1938.

erected church buildings; but on most community projects, Protestant groups formed a union church that clients could attend if they wished. Moreover, officials encouraged the observance of certain special days of project activity. One of the most widely used in Region VI was Settlers' Day, an annual open house for an entire project. Clients invited friends from outside the project, the community manager invited prominent people from nearby towns, and both clients and manager put the project on public display. Some projects sponsored a similar program of Neighborhood Training Days lasting two or three days. If the county or parish had no established fair, resettlement families substituted a similar event known as Achievement Days. Such activities were an effective means of building good public relations while contributing to the educational and social progress of project families.[40]

From the beginning, the Resettlement Administration designated the resettlement program to be self-liquidating. In other words, the cooperative associations were eventually to pay back their development loans and take sole responsibility for managing the projects. No resettlement project was to remain permanently in government hands. But during World War II, before this process could run its normal course, Congress ordered the liquidation of the entire resettlement program. The later projects had barely reached completion. The Farm Security Administration canceled its leases with all cooperative associations and gave individual farm families a mortgage to their land and homestead.

They were then on their own.

40. George Wolf to John Fischer, 18 November 1939; A. D. Stewart to C. B. Baldwin, 10 November 1941; Community and Family Services Section, Annual Report, 1 January 1940 to 31 December 1940, all in FSA Records, NA, RG 96.

Chapter IX

Plum Bayou: Forty Acres and a Mule

On the afternoon of 20 November 1936 a solid line of cars jammed the main road leading through the new resettlement community of Plum Bayou, Arkansas. The Resettlement Administration had invited the public to the project's official dedication, the first such ceremony held by the agency. After working all summer and into the fall, the regional office had five homesteads ready for occupancy and over ninety other homes under construction.

At project headquarters about three thousand people milled around and found seats in front of a temporary stage made of unpainted lumber. T. Roy Reid, acting as master of ceremonies, introduced the project's special guests—a roster which left out few names of importance in New Deal agricultural circles or in Arkansas politics. Secretary of Agriculture Henry A. Wallace was there, and so was the chief of the Resettlement Administration, Rexford G. Tugwell, his deputy administrator Will W. Alexander, and the new director of the Agricultural Adjustment Administration, Howard R. Tolley. Arkansas was represented by Senate Majority Leader Joseph T. Robinson, Sen. Hattie W. Caraway, Cong. John L. McClellan, Gov. J. Marion Futrell, and Governor-elect Carl E. Bailey.

Most of the guests made brief speeches. "I want businessmen to see this experiment in farmstead operation," Wallace said, indicating the nearest homestead, so that they will be "convinced that thousands of houses like this one can be built and thousands of farms like this sold on a business basis as a paying proposition." "People who live in the country," Tugwell remarked, "have a right to security of possession that is beyond question, to an income sufficient for a decent standard of living, to rear healthy families." The first three families selected for Plum Bayou were present to accept the keys to their homes. "These are not keys to houses—they are keys to the future," Tugwell told them. Each farmer, alone or with his family, crossed the stage and accepted his key: "I sure do thank you."[1]

The Arkansas A & M College band, from Monticello, regaled the crowd with music. Once the speech-making was over, visitors ate doughnuts and drank coffee, courtesy of the England Kiwanis Club, then filed through the new homes.

The Resettlement Administration had made an impressive start with its community program. Plum Bayou's dedication afforded exposure through the local and national news media. Little Rock and Memphis newspapers, which entered large numbers of Region VI homes, sent reporters. The Associated Press and United Press also covered the event. A large, interested crowd capped a big day for Plum Bayou and a milestone for the Resettlement Administration.

While Dyess Colony typifies the FERA's rural rehabilitation program and McComb the industrial-type subsistence homesteads, Plum Bayou serves as an illustration of the Resettlement Administration's activities. Plum Bayou also offers an excellent example of the resettlement program's stress on the family farm, in contrast to cooperative farming. Although Plum Bayou was a community project, the term "community" did not in any way imply collective operation. Clients farmed their own units individually and looked forward eventually to owning them free and clear.

The Resettlement Administration launched Plum Bayou at a time of growing unrest among sharecroppers and tenants in eastern Arkansas and of growing desire among Arkansans to see something done about tenancy. For Arkansas, in fact, 1936 was the year of the sharecropper—the tent colony at Parkin in January, Governor Futrell's "much ado about a very little" statement after his visit there in February, the cotton choppers' strike beginning in May, the flogging of Mr. Williams and Miss Blagden in June, and, finally, Futrell's appointment of the Arkansas Farm Tenancy Commission in August. The commission began work in September, held session throughout October, and turned out a report just before Thanksgiving.[2]

The members of the commission watched with interest the Resettlement Administration's work at Plum Bayou. In November, chairman Clyde Palmer postponed a meeting for three days so that members could attend

1. Little Rock *Arkansas Gazette*, 21 November 1936; Pine Bluff *Daily Graphic*, 21 November 1936. For the publicity leading up to 20 November, see *Arkansas Gazette*, 8, 15, 20 November; *Daily Graphic*, 8, 12, 20 November.

2. See above, pp. 89, 92–96.

the dedication ceremony.[3] Soon afterward the commission released its conclusions, and they were remarkably similar to policies which project officials had already put in action. It seems certain that Plum Bayou made a positive contribution to the commission's work.

Plum Bayou embraced some of the most desirable farming land in the state. The Arkansas River had carried the first settlers into the territory's interior over a century before. When its fertile bottomlands at last opened to agriculture, wealthy planters staked out large tracts of land as far up the river as Little Rock and brought in cotton and slaves. In the early twentieth century one of their successors, Earl Wright, put together a large plantation on the northeastern side of the river near England. Beginning about 1910 he acquired the first tract of land and added more tracts as time went on. But his luck did not hold out. Wright, heavily mortgaged, lost everything in the post–World War agricultural depression. His plantation changed hands several times. For a few years the Arkansas State Penitentiary cultivated about thirty-six hundred acres of it with convict labor. The rest of the land suffered from spring floods, but it was suitable for future drainage and development.[4]

In late 1935 the Arkansas Rural Rehabilitation Corporation began negotiations with the current owner, W. W. Bowman, for the purchase of the property. Then in March 1936 the Resettlement Administration's Little Rock office completed the purchase, paying $198,000 for 5,644 acres of land. According to regional officials, the Wright plantation "was the first tract of resettlement land in the United States bought and paid for by the RA."[5]

In May, E. B. Whitaker purchased more land in the same vicinity with a view to expanding the Wright project. He acquired the Ferda plantation (1,880 acres) for $97,500 and the Morrow plantation (1,240 acres) for $54,000, both in Jefferson County.[6] At the same time, Whitaker purchased several scattered tracts in Pulaski and Lonoke counties: a 120–acre tract for $5,100, a 260-acre tract for $10,100, a 320-acre tract for $8,500, and

3. *Arkansas Gazette,* 15 November 1936; *Daily Graphic,* 8 November 1936.
4. Records in office of Jefferson Abstract Company, Pine Bluff, Arkansas; George E. Cherry to the author, 9 January 1973. Mr. Cherry worked as a farm manager for Earl Wright from 1917 to 1920.
5. *Arkansas Gazette,* 15 February 1936; *Daily Graphic,* 15 February, 21 November 1936; Wright Community Resettlement Project, n.d., mimeographed, FSA Records, NA, RG 96; Albert Maverick, Jr., to John O. Walker, 11 October 1937, ibid.
6. FSA, "Resettlement Projects, Region VI," ibid.; Carl C. Taylor to T. Roy Reid, 18 February 1936, ibid.

a 390-acre tract for $12,800. This made a total of 9,854 acres purchased at a total cost of $386,000. After being enlarged, the Wright Community Resettlement project took the name of a lake left by an old channel of the Arkansas River—Plum Bayou.[7]

The regional office began making plans for developing the Wright plantation while the Arkansas Rural Rehabilitation Corporation still held it under option. As both regional resettlement director and secretary-treasurer of the rural rehabilitation corporation, Whitaker occupied a perfect position to coordinate the activities of both agencies. Between October 1935 and January 1936, Tugwell released two allotments totaling $205,000 to cover the cost of land and preparation of project plans. On 23 December 1935 Whitaker's preliminary plans for the Wright plantation won approval from Tugwell; and on 12 February 1936 Tugwell approved the final project plan at an estimated cost of $845,750 (the cost of community facilities, however, was not included at this time).[8] Whitaker proposed to establish a hundred farmsteads averaging thirty-six acres each. The regional office began constructing the hundred homesteads without delay; work crews also started draining and clearing two thousand acres of low, wet land where about fifty or more families could be resettled at a later date. As for community and cooperative facilities, Whitaker planned a cotton gin, community center, cooperative store, and other facilities; but FSA assistant administrator Carl C. Taylor recommended further study of their operation before granting authorization. Since construction was to start that spring, there was no chance the project could begin full operations during the current (1936) crop year. Rather than let the land lie fallow and become infested with weeds or lose the plantation's cotton base of two thousand acres, the regional office proposed to operate thirty-six hundred acres with relief labor until regular clients could take over in 1937.[9]

By the time Reid made his first annual report at the end of 1936, his organization had already put more than a year's work into Plum Bayou. First, the regional architectural and engineering staff dispatched a field survey party to the project. By May the surveyors finished locating all boundaries, roads, bridges, drainage ditches, wells, and septic tanks, and staked out the final unit subdivisions and all building foundations. Work-

7. FSA, "Resettlement Projects, Region VI," ibid.
8. *Arkansas Gazette*, 15 February 1936; *Daily Graphic*, 15 February 1936; Carl C. Taylor, memorandum to Rexford G. Tugwell, 12 February 1936; Taylor to T. Roy Reid, 18 February 1936; see F. P. Bartlett to W. E. Packard, 3 July 1936, all in FSA Records, NA, RG 96.
9. Carl C. Taylor to T. Roy Reid, 18 February 1936, ibid.

ing with the Resettlement Division, the architects and engineers also drew up both the preliminary and final project plan books, which Reid sent to Washington; here was assembled information on the surrounding area (average annual rainfall, nearby towns and markets, and so on) as well as detailed maps, specifications, sketches, and cost estimates of all proposed work.[10] The Management Division made a study of social, economic, education, health, and recreational phases of the project, worked out an agreement with local school officials for the project's use of their facilities, and formulated criteria for the selection of families. The family selection unit investigated 252 applicants, rejected 136, and approved 47, with 79 still pending.[11] In April the Construction Division moved its crews to the plantation and began work on the homesteads themselves. According to a report made before they started, it would cost an estimated $358,000 to build a hundred units on the Wright plantation, and require 214,800 man-hours of work (or an average monthly employment of 215 men.)[12]

As construction got underway, Plum Bayou acquired a project manager. Stanley W. Rhodes possessed the familiar credentials of the professional agriculturist. A Mississippian by birth, he went from Mississippi A & M to Crowley, Louisiana, as county agent of Acadia Parish. In 1935 he joined the Resettlement Administration's state office at Jackson, where he assumed the task of buying land for resettlement purposes. He served as project manager at Plum Bayou until the bitter end during World War II.[13]

The dedication of Plum Bayou on 20 November gave the public its first chance to see what the Resettlement Administration was doing. After the formal ceremony, the chief construction engineer, George Barton, took the visitors on an inspection tour of the new farmsteads. "Come over and see the houses we're living in," one man gushed proudly. "Come over and see the new farm we have."[14]

A newspaper reporter described the homes as "tasteful, simple, and

10. Report of Architectural and Engineering Staff, Region VI, Little Rock, 1 July 1935 to 31 December 1936, ibid.
11. Management Division, News Letter, Region VI, 1 July 1935 to 1 January 1936, ibid.
12. Employment on Resettlement Administration Projects, 18 February 1936, ibid.; Resettlement Administration, Annual Report, Region VI, 31 December 1936, ibid.
13. Stanley W. Rhodes, interview with the author, 15 April 1971.
14. *Arkansas Gazette*, 21 November 1936; *Daily Graphic*, 21 November 1936.

distinctive." Each farmstead came equipped with electrical wiring, plumbing, running water, and outdoor toilets, at least until septic tanks could be installed later. As yet no grass or shrubbery grew around the houses, although plans called for them to be landscaped with shrubs and trees. Each farmstead, Barton told the visitors, would include a barn, other outbuildings, and fencing. For water, Plum Bayou families would rely on individual wells equipped with gasoline pumps. Each farmer would have an orchard and a small pasture for stock. When construction crews finished in early 1937, thirty-nine four-room, fifty five-room, and eleven six-room houses would stand on the former Wright plantation. At Plum Bayou the Resettlement Administration's authorized farmstead cost (planning, land purchase, and construction) totaled $739,151, or an expensive $7,392 per farmstead unit. The net annual income from each unit was estimated to be $300 or more, theoretically enough income to justify the purchase of a $7,000 unit.[15]

"These five homesteads that you see here are not for everyone," Tugwell stressed in his speech. "They are only for the farm families who have proved their good intentions and have shown definite ability to succeed."[16] Plum Bayou offered opportunities specifically to young farm families; the age limit for heads of families was thirty-five, or younger preferably, not the standard age of fifty at most community-type projects. To qualify, farmers also needed a background of 4-H Club, Smith-Hughes, or similar training in farm operation and management. The regional office chose settlers from families on rural rehabilitation rolls all over the state of Arkansas.[17]

Only three families moved into their new homes at Plum Bayou before the formal dedication, but they represented the kind of people the Resettlement Administration wanted.[18] At thirty-four, Joe F. Lackey was almost too old to qualify for Plum Bayou. But he "just kept after the Resettlement folks until they gave us a chance," he said. During the 1920's he and his family spent seven lean years on a farm in Faulkner

15. *Arkansas Gazette*, 15, 21 November 1936; *Daily Graphic*, 21 November 1936; Wright Community Resettlement Project, n.d., mimeographed, FSA Records, NA, RG 96; Facts about Plum Bayou Farms, n.d., Wallace Papers, NA, RG 16; RA, "Project Description Book," FSA Records, NA, RG 96; Carl C. Taylor to Rexford G. Tugwell, 12 February 1936, ibid.
16. *Arkansas Gazette*, 21 November 1936.
17. Wright Community Resettlement Project, n.d., mimeographed, FSA Records, NA, RG 96; *Daily Graphic*, 8, 21 November 1936; *Arkansas Gazette*, 8 November 1936.
18. Ibid., 21 November 1936.

County, Arkansas, before giving up. He then worked in a rice mill at DeWitt and later as a carpenter in Little Rock; but when his three children were old enough to help with the chores, he turned back to the farm. Prior to coming to Plum Bayou, the Lackeys lived on the Case plantation, a rural rehabilitation project north of Little Rock, and farmed fifty acres on a share-rent basis. There they accumulated livestock, enough feed to carry them through a winter, and 650 cans of fruits and vegetables.

La Vaughn York, age twenty-seven, his wife, twenty, and their seven-month-old daughter also served an apprenticeship on the Case project, where they rented a twenty-four-acre tract. They borrowed $461 to make a crop, paid it back, and raised enough food and foodstuffs to make the next year's crop. As rehabilitation clients, they acquired livestock and farm implements, and canned 175 quarts of fruits and vegetables. Born on an Indiana farm, York struggled to get a high school education and one year of technical agricultural training. Ira W. Counts was twenty-five, his wife twenty-two, and Wilbur, Jr., about three. Counts was born and reared on a Lonoke County farm. He moved to a nearby town early in the depression, but soon decided to go back to farming. He struggled for several years as a sharecropper before joining the Plum Bayou project, where conditions for success were far more favorable.

When a family moved into Plum Bayou, they brought with them their personal property, including furniture and household goods, farm implements, and livestock. But project officials knew that the first task was to put these families back on their feet. Every farmer received a standard rehabilitation loan to put in a crop and take care of his family's food and clothing needs during the long summer months before his crop was harvested. The family, of course, obligated themselves to stick to a farm and home budget. A new client might also receive small, emergency grants to help his family over the initial difficulties. He might also borrow money from the agency to buy a mule, a rather large investment in relation to a tenant farmer's income.

At first each family occupied their unit on an annual rental contract, and, ironically, worked their land on a share-crop basis: one-fourth of the cotton and cottonseed and one-third of the corn and feed crops. At the end of the year a farmer made the rental payment, paid off his other obligations, and (hopefully) had something left over. Many farmers kept themselves relatively free of debt, but others carried debts over from one year to the next. Under the terms of the RA's flexible lease agreement, the actual annual payments might be lower in case of a poor crop year. After a five-year trial period farmers who proved their mettle became eligible to enter into a lease-and-purchase contract. Then they had forty years in which to pay the association for their farms.[19]

Having made a favorable impression on dedication day, Plum Bayou won the endorsement of the leading newspapers in Arkansas. "All who realize the purpose of the Plum Bayou homesteads project," the *Arkansas Gazette* commented editorially," . . . must hope for its complete success." As the *Gazette* put it, that purpose was "to demonstrate the feasibility of land ownership by young farmers and young farm wives following a 'live at home' program."[20] But was it all too good to be true? Each separate farm, the editorial said, will make a pretty picture with its modern, comfortable house and outbuildings,

> . . . with its landscaping of native shrubs and trees, its orchard, its trim barn and cotton house and hog house and poultry house, and its flat fertile crop land stretching out beyond. Too pretty to last, might be the criticism of conservatives familiar with many unfortunately typical sections of rural Arkansas and the rural South. Wait, such a pessimist might say, until ranging stock has had its way with young shade trees and shrubbery, until hogs have rooted in that young orchard and insect pests taken their toll, until needed repairs to buildings have gone unmade for a year to two, and then see how pretty things will look.

The *Gazette* saw the hope of Plum Bayou in the kind of people who could meet the membership qualifications. "The RA is giving its Plum Bayou clients high standards to live up to," the paper said. "But it is selecting them shrewdly." These farmers were "the best equipped in character, training, and outlook." What the *Gazette* wanted for Arkansas was "more small farms whose owners can be proud of the attractive and comfortable homes those farms support."

The editor of the Pine Bluff *Daily Graphic* was another booster for Plum Bayou. "According to our way of thinking," he wrote, "projects of this kind will do more for the country than any other effort put forth by the Roosevelt Administration." Such projects, he believed, should be encouraged because they will "eventually get us away from so-called relief projects." "This is one plan of the New Deal wherein the government will get back some of the money it is putting out."[21]

With full operations beginning in the spring of 1937, the next major step was to create a legal organization. Plum Bayou had two cooperative

19. E. B. Whitaker to C. B. Baldwin, 7 August 1940, FSA Records, NA, RG 96.
20. *Arkansas Gazette*, 20 November 1936.
21. *Daily Graphic*, 12 November 1936.

associations, not one as did most later projects.[22] On 2 March 1937 the regional office incorporated the Plum Bayou Cooperative Association under the laws of Arkansas for a period of fifty years. According to its articles of incorporation, the Plum Bayou Cooperative Association could issue up to $500 worth of capital stock with a par value of a dollar per share. The stockholders consisted of individual family heads at Plum Bayou, each buying five shares of stock but having only one vote. No stockholder was allowed to own more than 5 percent of the capital stock of the association. The president of the first board of directors was Stanley Rhodes. With one of their own employees in charge, regional officials could easily influence the board's decisions as well as guarantee the experience necessary for successful operation.[23]

On 9 April 1937 regional officials set up a second cooperative association, the Plum Bayou Homestead Association, this one for a period of perpetual existence. The Plum Bayou Homestead Association was organized as a benevolent corporation, rather than a business corporation as in the case of its sister association. Under this form of organization, it could operate without issuing capital stock or paying dividends.[24]

If Plum Bayou had followed the regional office's original intention, the function of the homestead association would have been to borrow funds for development work, construct the individual farm units and all cooperative facilities, lease the land and the improvements, and then manage the project, while the cooperative association would operate the community and cooperative services. Plum Bayou, however, reversed this pattern. The cooperative association started doing business before the homestead association officially acquired title to the land.[25] Perhaps the mix-up resulted from an oversight, or it may have been due to impatience to get the project under way.

Since the Construction Division erected the homesteads, the Plum Bayou Homestead Association took no part in the development of the

22. Acting Regional Cooperative Specialist [?] to Assistant Regional Director [E. B. Whitaker], n.d.; T. Roy Reid to Rexford G. Tugwell, n.d.; Edward Stone to J. O. Walker, 27 May 1937; Plum Bayou Cooperative Association, Economic Justification, n.d., all in FSA Records, NA, RG 96.

23. By-laws of the Plum Bayou Cooperative Association, n.d.; Audit Report, Plum Bayou Cooperative Association, Near England, Arkansas, for the Period 2 March 1937 to 30 June 1938; Petition for the Incorporation of the Plum Bayou Homestead Association, 16 April 1937, all ibid.

24. Audit Report, Plum Bayou Homestead Association, Wright, Jefferson County, Arkansas, for the Period 9 April 1937 to 30 June 1939, ibid.; Petition for the Incorporation of the Plum Bayou Homestead Association, 16 April 1937, ibid.

25. Stanley W. Rhodes, interview with the author, 6 December 1972.

Wright plantation. Instead, officials simply transferred the completed units to the homestead association, which became the "landlord organization" for the entire project. For example, the association's board of directors assumed responsibility for paying taxes, insurance premiums, repair and maintenance bills, and repaying all obligations due the government.

The homestead association, in addition, had the task of managing the entire project, with the advice of the project manager. The association leased the farm units to individual clients and collected rent. The association also appointed a farm manager, who supervised agricultural operations. Plum Bayou's farm management plan called for each farmer to plant thirteen acres of cotton, ten of corn, and three of alfalfa, with five acres devoted to the farmstead itself, five to pasture, and the remaining acreage to truck and minor crops.[26]

The two associations played separate but complementary roles in providing cooperative services. On 21 June 1937 the Resettlement Administration made a $65,966 loan to the Plum Bayou Homestead Association and a $32,095 loan to the Plum Bayou Cooperative Association.[27] The homestead association's loan went for construction of a store, warehouse, gin and cottonseed house, personnel house, feed and grist mills, repair shop, and breeding barns. Then the association leased these facilities from the government and, in turn, subleased them to the Plum Bayou Cooperative Association. The cooperative association used its loan to operate these facilities. In reality, however, this association used the store, equipment, and other buildings for two years without signing a lease or paying any rent for their use. At Plum Bayou such leases were sometimes rather informal; the regional office held the project so tightly in its grip that an unwritten understanding was satisfactory. But sooner or later a formal arrangement had to supersede the informal one. On 1 April 1939 the cooperative association signed a five-year lease with an option to purchase.[28]

The community and cooperative services existed for obvious purposes: to furnish members with facilities they could not own individually and to provide the benefits of bulk purchasing of certain items. Only in this

26. E. B. Whitaker to C. B. Baldwin, 7 August 1940, FSA Records, NA, RG 96.
27. Acting Regional Cooperative Specialist [?] to Assistant Regional Director [E. B. Whitaker], n.d.; T. Roy Reid to Rexford G. Tugwell, n.d.; Edward Stone to J. O. Walker, 27 May 1937, all ibid.
28. Plum Bayou Cooperative Association, Economic Justification, n.d., ibid.; Audit Report, Plum Bayou Homestead Association, Wright, Jefferson County, Arkansas, for the Period 9 April 1937 to 30 June 1939, ibid.

way could the farm and home management programs actually succeed in making Plum Bayou self-sufficient. The Plum Bayou farmers ginned their cotton in their own gin and bought farm supplies at a store in which they owned an interest—all at cheaper prices than they could get if they acted individually. They also hoped for a partial return on the money they spent in the form of patronage dividends. Rather than depend on outsiders, they operated for themselves such cooperative enterprises as a livestock-breeding service, feed and grist mills, and a syrup mill; and they cooperatively marketed all farm produce, from cotton to livestock. Eventually the cooperative association added a meat-curing plant and a potato-curing house. An established farm community would already have such facilities; but in the work of community building, there was no time to wait on natural growth.

Plum Bayou farmers enjoyed one of the most elaborate community centers in Region VI, second only perhaps to the center at Dyess Colony. Costing $85,000, the community center complex included a gymnasium that doubled as an auditorium, a three-room home, economics building, and a school building. The latter contained a library, conference rooms, and a vocational shop. After construction, the Plum Bayou Homestead Association turned the school over to Plum Bayou School District Number 16. The school served all white children from the fourth to twelfth grades in the district, whether or not their parents lived on the project. The first three grades attended another school nearby.[29]

In 1938 the regional office expanded Plum Bayou with the development of the so-called Ferda Addition, consisting mainly of the Ferda and Morrow plantations. Once part of a defunct project, Arkansas Delta Farms, the Ferda Addition consisted of 3,700 acres of bottomland with about 2,920 acres in cultivation, all located adjacent to the Plum Bayou project. Besides the land, the original investment included a store building, an old cotton gin, a livestock barn, a usable residence, and several other usable buildings, although the tenant houses were valuable chiefly as salvage material. When Plum Bayou took over, FSA rural rehabilitation clients were farming the land under temporary arrangements until definite plans could be implemented.[30]

29. Ibid.; FSA, "Resettlement Projects, Region VI," FSA Records, NA, RG 96; *Arkansas Gazette*, 16, 22 January 1938; *Daily Graphic*, 16, 22 January 1938.
    30. *Arkansas Gazette*, 22 January 1938; *Daily Graphic*, 16, 22 January 1938; J. O. Walker, memorandum to Milo Perkins, 29 June 1938, FSA Records, NA, RG 96; Proposal for Development of Ferda Addition to Plum Bayou Project, n.d., ibid.

The Ferda Addition took advantage of Plum Bayou's existing legal machinery. With a $256,272 loan, the Plum Bayou Homestead Association erected the necessary housing units, improved the land, constructed or repaired the necessary cooperative facilities, and leased the Ferda property from the government. Finally, the homestead association subleased certain land, buildings, and equipment to the Plum Bayou Cooperative Association, and the individual farm units to the clients. The cooperative association borrowed an additional $10,436 from the government in order to operate several cooperative services on the Ferda Addition. As construction started, project manager Stanley Rhodes supervised the task of subdividing 3,111 acres into sixty-six units averaging 47.1 acres each. This left 589 acres, which included a community pasture and woodland and another area scheduled for later development. Rhodes filled all of these units in time for the 1939 crop season. With the Ferda and Morrow units, Plum Bayou contained room for 180 families, with twenty units undeveloped.[31]

When the editor of the *Daily Graphic* visited Plum Bayou in 1939, he found a trim, neat community, its homes and farm buildings a pleasant contrast to the ugly tenant housing of the area. After a talk with Dr. J. D. Niven, a local landowner and "one of Jefferson county's best known citizens," he was even more convinced that his earlier support of Plum Bayou had been correct. The good doctor took his New Deal with a dash of Abraham Lincoln:

> Dr. Niven pointed out that the project [Plum Bayou] was yielding an influence for good. He related how a little girl came to his store a few weeks ago to buy some goods. She lacked 41 cents having enough to pay the bill. He told the child he would credit her with the 41 cents but reminded her that her father [a resettlement client] owed him a bill of several years' standing. A few days later the child returned to the store, paid the 41 cents and part of the old bill. Since that time the father has paid the old account in full.
>
> "That has shown me," Dr. Niven said, "the value of these resettlement projects. They are making men feel different. They are giving them renewed ambitions, creating a desire to deal honestly with their fellow men and pointing a way to success and prosperity."

The editor put in the last word: "If the government through these resettlement projects will . . . inculcate in the minds of the residents the principles of the Golden Rule . . . the effort will stand for years to come as a me-

31. Ibid.

morial to the present administration."[32] Regional officials would have preferred results which looked better on a balance sheet.

Henry Wallace also took a later look at Plum Bayou. The project gave every appearance of success. Plodding through a steady rain, he inspected the community building, home economics department, and administrative offices. In the gym, with a photograph of President Roosevelt on the wall behind him, Wallace praised the progress he saw. "If this project proves as successful as it now appears to be," he said, "we may expect to have others in Arkansas and the South." He predicted that Congress would be willing to expand the program. Wallace also greeted the three original settlers. Joe Lackey reminisced that he had entered the project "with two bits, a little load of furniture and a house full of kids." The future at the moment looked bright, but ahead lay only disillusionment.[33]

If any resettlement project should have been successful, it was Plum Bayou. While Terrebonne and Lake Dick departed from traditional land tenure policy, Plum Bayou matched local requirements right down the line. The project was launched under the approving smiles of the state's political leadership. Regional officials made it their pet project, lavishing on it time and money no other project of the region would enjoy. Yet after seven years Plum Bayou was obviously in trouble, beset by debt, controversy, and insecurity.[34]

The developers of Plum Bayou handicapped the project with mistakes. The Wright plantation had a long history of flooding, going back before the time the state prison tried to farm it. The flooding continued after it became a government project. Plum Bayou contained areas which had been under water one or more times each spring since the project started, and the results showed up in low repayment records and discouragement.

> How can they expect a man to pay his debt when his alfalfa is drowned on the ground? [one farmer complained]. Everybody knows that high water kills alfalfa quick. My neighbor has had high water on his land every year. It got in one man's house, and another man had his car stranded on the bridge across the ditch. We planted cotton three times one year. I had a right good garden that year, too, cabbage and everything up high, but it got drowned. They were going to ditch the water out, but somehow they just ditched it in instead.[35]

32. *Daily Graphic*, 22 February 1939.
33. *Arkansas Gazette*, 27 May 1939.
34. Inez Hale MacDuff, "Mr. Wallace's Rosy Prophecy Proves a Bust: Plum Bayou Not a Promised Land," *Arkansas Gazette*, 18 April 1943.
35. Inez Hale MacDuff, "New Deal Experiment Placed on Land That Floods Every Year," *Arkansas Gazette*, 2 May 1943.

Moreover, many of the farmers at Plum Bayou were burdened with too much debt. Some of them owed as much as $2,000 in old rehabilitation loans, and regional officials had no authority to cancel these obligations.

Stanley Rhodes and three assistants—a storekeeper, bookkeeper, and home economist—saw that everything moved properly on an everyday basis. But the success of a venture like Plum Bayou involved far more than the technicalities of operation. Rhodes dealt with some 180 families with varying aspirations and temperaments.

Small problems inevitably arose, nameless, unremembered headaches, often petty matters, but capable of breaking the morale of families accustomed to failure as a way of life. If left unattended, minor matters could grow into miniature revolts. In such moments of small crises, the project manager sometimes turned for help to the family selection agent who had brought the family to the project. Or perhaps the home management supervisor could play the role of sympathetic friend when a family just needed someone to listen. Rhodes conducted weekly meetings where he tried to iron out most of the problems that arose, but occasionally family squabbles forced him to pin on his deputy sheriff's badge.[36]

One of the most common problems of project officials involved "uncooperative" clients. Plum Bayou had its share of families with that dubious distinction, right or wrong. Here and elsewhere were men who would not submit themselves to direction; they were unprepared to learn. Many families also lacked the discipline to stick to their prepared budgets. A few clients at Plum Bayou took employment outside the project and refused to keep their land under full cultivation.

On the clients' side were frequent complaints of being "regulated to death" and lack of privacy. "Your entire life down here," one client commented, "is controlled by regulation and everything you do must be done by rule and rote. Which is all right during a period when you're 'proving yourself,' but there comes a day when the very spirit of Americanism reels against the constant invasions upon family life you're subjected to." He complained of demands to have his home on exhibition, with visitors "sticking their noses into every room, closet, nook and cranny at all hours."[37]

The turnover of families at Plum Bayou was large. By 1943 Joe Lackey, La Vaughn York, and Wilbur Counts were gone; in fact, only 22 of the

36. Rhodes interviews; Jack Bryan, "There Are Few Troubles on Farm Homesteads That a Little 'Talking To' Won't Heal Perfectly," Memphis *Press-Scimitar*, 17 February 1939.

37. Quoted in Helene Ward, "Model Farmer Perplexed by Eviction Order," Little Rock *Arkansas Democrat*, 26 March 1943.

original 95 families remained. In all, 293 families lived on the project at one time or another.

Many Plum Bayou families felt that the government failed to live up to its part of the bargain. The original plan called for a five-year probationary period, after which each family would be given a deed to their farm. But no one at Plum Bayou possessed a deed. Other families were guilty only of having been placed on poorly planned and unproductive units, and they simply could not make a living. In one accounting, the FSA offered this breakdown of Plum Bayou dropouts:

41 went into war work, many of them taking jobs at the Pine Bluff Arsenal

37 left the project to become rehabilitation borrowers, renting privately owned land

3 went into military service

3 bought farms on their own

2 were stricken with bad health

17 were asked to leave

26 left for miscellaneous reasons of no particular significance

4 were in the process of eviction[38]

If Plum Bayou had its unhappy families, at least the project had no organized dissension movement to keep it constantly in the newspapers, as in the case of Dyess Colony. Those who were dissatisfied, it seems, left. Only in the project's last years did any significant controversy make the newspapers, when an outside critic dragged Plum Bayou into congressional hearings as an example of the FSA's injustice and mismanagement.

Resettlement officials knew that the community projects must succeed financially. Plum Bayou, however, left an uneven, disappointing record. The Plum Bayou Homestead Association, of course, lost money from the start and never broke out of the red.[39] Since it received no income from sales or patronage, the homestead association's income consisted solely of rental payments; and the rents collected were not enough to cover the cost of maintaining and managing the project.[40] The homestead association leased a considerable portion of its assets to the Plum Bayou Cooperative Association, but failed to collect any rent on this property until

38. USHR, *USDA Approp. Hearings, 1944*, 78th Cong., 1st sess., pp. 1653–55; see below, Chapter XV.
39. Plum Bayou Homestead Association, Annual Financial Report, for the Fiscal Year Ended 31 December 1943, FSA Records, NA, RG 96.
40. T. Roy Reid to Will W. Alexander, 9 May 1939, ibid.

1939. Even afterward, little financial improvement took place. After making arrangements to liquidate its assets, the Plum Bayou Homestead Association ceased operations on 31 December 1943.[41]

On the other hand, the Plum Bayou Cooperative Association built a reputation for profitable operation. At the end of 1939, for example, the board of directors disbursed a patronage dividend totaling $4,445; and other dividend payments followed.[42] From 1937 to 1944 the cooperative association made a profit every year except 1940, when the project suffered general crop failures. On 15 December 1944 it actually made the final payment on its FSA loan, a milestone not many associations in Region VI reached.[43] But certain weaknesses soon caught up with it.

In essence, the association's cooperative enterprises had long been deadweight. By 1943 livestock improvement and heavy equipment programs, repair shop, syrup mill, feed and seed mill, and sweet potato plant were operating in the red, while only the store and cotton gin turned a profit. As a result, the association liquidated most of these activities, retaining only three "departments"—store, gin, and repair shop.[44] The move strengthened the association financially but failed to solve its basic problem: not all members used the facilities to the fullest extent possible. In 1942, for example, eight tenants did not gin any of their cotton at the cooperative gin; the board of directors took a firm stand and refused to renew their leases.[45] Soon the store was also in trouble. Rhodes had dif-

41. Audit Report, Plum Bayou Homestead Association, Wright, Jefferson County, Arkansas, for the Period 9 April 1937 to 30 June 1939, ibid; Plum Bayou Homestead Association, Wright, Arkansas, Annual Financial Report, for the Fiscal Period Ended 20 March 1945, ibid.

42. T. Roy Reid to the Board of Directors, Plum Bayou Cooperative Association, 9 November 1939; J. T. Holliday to Ben Ash, 10 November 1939; Claude Woolsey to Stanley W. Rhodes, 10 November 1939; Will W. Alexander to Reid, 21 September 1939. See Rhodes to A. M. Rogers, 4 December 1942; Woolsey, memorandum to E. B. Whitaker, 16 March 1942, all ibid.

43. Audit Report, Plum Bayou Cooperative Association, Wright, Jefferson County, Arkansas, for the Six Months Ended 31 December 1938 and the Calendar Year 1939; Plum Bayou Cooperative Association, Annual Financial Report, for the Fiscal Year Ended 31 December 1944. See Financial Condition of Plum Bayou Cooperative Association, Inc., as of 30 November 1944, all ibid. In 1939 the board of directors increased its authorized capital from $500 to $1,000 so that clients on the Ferda and Morrow tracts could become members.

44. Stanley W. Rhodes to Claude Woolsey, 6 July 1942, ibid.; Audit Report, Plum Bayou Cooperative Association, Wright, Jefferson County, Arkansas, for the Period 1 January 1940 to 31 December 1943, ibid.

45. Ibid.; Plum Bayou Cooperative Association, Annual Financial Report, for the Fiscal Year Ended 31 December 1943, ibid.; Plum Bayou Cooperative Association, Annual Financial Report, for the Fiscal Year Ended 31 December 1942, ibid.

ficulty finding and keeping an experienced manager; in one year (1943) the store had three different managers, and profits sagged. The sales volume was hurt also because two-fifths of the membership of the association lived over five miles from the store, and almost half the members lived nearer outside stores (and cotton gins) and patronized them to save time.[46] Without a hundred percent participation, the savings the association could provide were reduced for everyone, good customers and bad.

In August 1945 the board of directors went ahead with a move they had been contemplating for the past year or more. For $27,000, they purchased from the government the cooperative facilities held under lease—store, gin, feed mill, repair shop, and several dwellings—plus the land these facilities occupied.[47] Trying to raise a $6,600 cash downpayment, the association amended its by-laws to provide for a capitalization of $50,000 (1,000 shares of common stock at $1 each, and 4,900 shares of preferred stock at $10 each).[48] The hope was that members would willingly invest more money in the association in order to purchase outright the facilities they used, but in fact they proved to be quite unwilling. The board made the downpayment, but could not meet the first annual payment due on 31 December 1945.

What was wrong? First, the investment was sound but ill-timed. When World War II ended in August, the demand for cotton plummeted—just before harvest. Taking a heavy loss, the cooperative ginned only 426 bales of cotton instead of the 1,500 or more common in previous years. At the end of the year, more than 50 percent of the cotton grown on the project and in its vicinity remained in the fields, with no prospect for picking.[49]

Second, an older problem became worse than ever. The members of the association no longer backed their cooperative; "lack of membership participation," explained regional cooperative specialist Claude Woolsey, "is the contributing factor to the unsuccessful operations in 1945."[50] In early 1946 the Plum Bayou Cooperative Association's financial condi-

46. Plum Bayou Cooperative Association, Annual Financial Report, for the Fiscal Year Ended 31 December 1944, ibid.

47. Minutes of the Special Meeting of the Board of Directors of Plum Bayou Cooperative Association, Inc., Wright, Arkansas, held 9 August 1944, ibid.

48. J. V. Highfill, memorandum to Elstner D. Beall, 27 July 1945, ibid.

49. Plum Bayou Cooperative Association, Wright, Arkansas, Annual Financial Report, for the Fiscal Year Ended 31 December 1945, ibid.

50. Ibid.; J. V. Highfill, memorandum to Elstner D. Beall, 19 February 1946, ibid.

tion reached "an alarming stage."[51] It was unable to carry on operations for another year.

In 1942 the Farm Security Administration had begun planning the sale of individual units and community facilities at Plum Bayou.[52] Some three years passed before the process reached completion.

Over a ten-year period the resettlement agencies poured $386,000 into land and $1,203,893.44 into homestead development, while the cost of community facilities amounted to $373,919.49. Each homestead represented an average investment of $8,052.80, the highest unit cost in Region VI, by $2,000. Plum Bayou was, in fact, the second most expensive resettlement project in the region. By June 1945 regional officials had sold 141 out of 151 reorganized units for a total of $636,333. To that point Plum Bayou had lost $495,541.94 in the sale of units; the project had also fallen behind $135,957.74 in operating expenses. Its deficit totaled $631,499.58. No other FSA-built project, either community- or infiltration-type, came within $300,000 of Plum Bayou's sorry record.[53]

When liquidating a resettlement project, the Farm Security Administration appraised each unit separately, using an impartial committee which based its recommendations on the fair market value of the land and buildings. The results of this final appraisal explained a large part of Plum Bayou's deficit. Although the average investment was $8,052.80 per unit, Plum Bayou settlers paid an average price of only $4,214.12, a difference of $3,838.58.[54] At Plum Bayou regional officials fell into the deadliest trap of the resettlement program: overcapitalizing the project families. Perhaps since it was the first project in the region, they ambitiously—and foolishly—invested more money in the farmsteads than the clients could ever hope to repay, raising the cost of the units far beyond their true value. In other words, families were provided with a standard of living beyond the earning capacity of their small farms.

Plum Bayou taught a valuable but expensive lesson. The regional office never again made this mistake—at least not on this scale.

51. Ibid.
52. A. D. Stewart to C. B. Baldwin, 1 October 1942, ibid.
53. USHR, *USDA Approp. Hearings, 1947*, 79th Cong., 2d sess., pp. 1392, 1404, 1412.
54. Ibid.

Chapter X

Terrebonne: Esprit de Co-op

Terrebonne Parish had every characteristic of southern Louisiana. The Creole and Cajun population, the French and Spanish names, the old plantation homes, the lazy bayous, the great live oaks heavy with Spanish moss—all suggested strong ties with the past, a country rich in traditions. Thirty years ago, as today, Houma, the parish seat, was famed for shrimp, oysters, and, above all, sugarcane. Terrebonne's rich, black soil—the "good earth" for which the parish was named—made it one of the largest sugarcane-producing parishes in Louisiana.

Even in the depression, its citizens liked to think of Terrebonne as a "modern garden of Eden."[1] Yet southern Louisiana was hardly a paradise for farmers, especially small owners and tenants. In 1935 slightly more than half of all Terrebonne Parish farmers did not own their own land.[2] Young families found it difficult to get a start in farming. Low sugarcane prices forced many small operators to fall back on mere subsistence agriculture, while large numbers of farmers completely lost their hold on the land.

In this almost timeless land, the New Deal tried an approach to rural relief and rehabilitation that made old and new, traditional and experimental, stand out in sharp contrast. The Farm Security Administration's project near Schriever, a little town three miles south of Thibodaux, experimented with collective farming.[3]

---

1. *Houma Courier*, 26 August 1938.
2. U.S. Bureau of the Census, *United States Census of Agriculture: 1935, General Report, III* (Washington: Government Printing Office, 1937), p. 161.
3. Except for the new Delta Cooperative Farm at Hillhouse, Mississippi, Louisiana was the only state in the region with any history of cooperative farming. The New Llano Colony, near Leesville in Vernon Parish, operated from 1917 to 1937. See Henry Edward Wilson, "The History of the Llano Cooperative Colony" (M.A. thesis, Louisiana State University, 1951).

The Terrebonne project, Lake Dick, and Marcella were the only resettlement projects in Region VI which ran counter to the traditional pattern of individually owned family farms. The strongest promoters of such projects considered large-scale cooperative farming to be a viable social and economic pattern, one that would become the wave of the future.[4] The family farm, they believed, could not compete with newer, larger-scale commercial agriculture. Farms were not only getting larger; machinery and hired labor were replacing sharecroppers, tenants, and even small owners. Perhaps the cooperative farm could help farmers readjust to the agricultural revolution without sacrificing economic democracy.

In Region VI, however, most resettlement officials were not enthusiastic about cooperative farming, since it called for fundamental changes in agricultural structure and social values. The land grant college graduates and former county agents of the regional organization always took for granted the traditional values associated with individual land ownership. They believed that the family farm had a place even in a world of large-scale mechanized agriculture. Regional officials went along with such experiments as Terrebonne, but they twisted the philosophy of cooperative farming enough to make it more palatable. E. B. Whitaker, for example, saw Terrebonne primarily as a training school for low-income farm families that could not as yet measure up to the responsibilities of individual ownership or even of tenancy. Here such families could gain practical experience, under trained supervision, in running a farm. After a few years they could probably "graduate" to individual farming.[5] These two points of view were basically incompatible, but did not clash in the short run.

In June 1937, state director E. C. McInnis announced the purchase of three adjacent Terrebonne plantations—Waubun, Saint George, and Julia. In August he added the Isle of Cuba plantation, located away from Schriever toward Houma.[6] Altogether the Resettlement Administration paid $147,346.60 for 5,960 acres of gummy sugarcane land.[7] The Farm

4. Joseph W. Eaton, *Exploring Tomorrow's Agriculture* (New York: Harper and Brothers, 1943), pp. 80–85.

5. E. B. Whitaker, interview with the author, 19 April 1968.

6. New Orleans *Times-Picayune*, 23 June 1937; New Orleans *Morning Tribune*, 6 August 1937; see *Times-Picayune*, 9 October 1938; *Caldwell Watchman* (Columbia, La.), 29 January 1937; Louis J. Rodriguez, "The Terrebonne Project: Ideological Revolution or Economic Expediency?" *Louisiana Studies* 6 (Fall 1967): 267–77.

7. FSA, "Resettlement Projects, Region VI," FSA Records, NA, RG 96.

Security Administration inherited the Terrebonne project in September 1937, and made plans to put it into operation. George S. Harmount, community manager, built a village of farm homes near Schriever, developed the land with new roads, fences, and drainage ditches, and organized the project into a collective farm large enough to support eighty families.

The Terrebonne colony had a history of controversy, disappointment, and delay. The regional office began planning the project in 1935, but Terrebonne did not officially open as a resettlement project until 1939.[8] Soon after concluding the purchase, the FSA leased its land in Terrebonne Parish to the Louisiana Rural Rehabilitation Corporation, and relief labor operated the property as a sugarcane plantation for the next two years. After a freeze destroyed the project's cane crop in 1937, the corporation was unable to meet the terms of its lease; by the end of 1938 its losses amounted to $24,276—perhaps an ill omen.[9]

The work of the Louisiana Rural Rehabilitation Corporation kept alive interest in a resettlement project at Schriever, but local business and civic leaders from Terrebonne and Lafourche parishes were anxious to see it developed on a permanent basis. For months the Schriever project, according to the *Houma Courier*, was "a hot and cold proposition."[10] In November 1937 the presence of an FSA engineering crew at Schriever raised the hopes of the Thibodaux Rotary Club, which made inquiries about the project's future.[11] But at that time no further work was done. The following spring, the regional office began preliminary work on Terrebonne. In April 1938 Harmount announced a meeting in Thibodaux for anyone interested in the Schriever resettlement project.[12] Before launching any resettlement community, officials routinely secured the backing not only of local civic leaders but even of adjacent property owners. Those who met in Thibodaux supported the project, but they wished primarily to see federal money spent in their parish.

At the meeting T. Roy Reid, who made a special trip from Little Rock, explained why the Schriever project had been delayed. The time required to investigate the titles to the land purchased for the project, Reid said, threw Terrebonne far behind schedule. When the land was finally transferred to the government, the end of the fiscal year (30 June 1937) arrived; and the funds appropriated for developing the project had to be

8. RA, "Project Description Book," ibid.
9. Henry A. Wallace to Sen. Allen J. Ellender, 1 February 1940, Wallace Papers, NA, RG 16.
10. *Houma Courier*, 6 April 1938.
11. Ibid., 19 November 1937.
12. Ibid., 8 April 1938.

returned to the United States treasury. Consequently no improvements could be made. This was the practice, he said, at the end of each fiscal year with money appropriated but not yet used for any project. But now, according to Reid, money was again available, and the project was going to be carried out as planned.[13]

What Reid did not discuss was the indecision within the Farm Security Administration itself during 1937 and 1938 over how to organize Terrebonne. "The Terrebonne project," wrote J. O. Walker, national director of the Resettlement Division, "has been the subject of considerable difference of opinion."[14] The central issue was whether the ultimate aim should be to operate Terrebonne as a cooperative farm or "to have each homesteader own and operate a family size farm."[15] Reid's Little Rock staff appeared anxious not to have a project that critics could compare to a Soviet collective farm; nor did they want another Lake Dick, the Arkansas cooperative project which gave them headaches.[16] But as they knew, cane production was a type of agriculture requiring a large outlay for heavy power equipment. It had always been carried on more successfully by large-scale operators than by family-size farmers.

About the same time officials decided in favor of cooperative farming, the regional office assigned George Harmount to Terrebonne as project manager. He had been FSA parish supervisor before his promotion and identified with the diversified farming movement at Houma. But he hardly fit the pattern of other resettlement personnel in Region VI. "We had the craziest fellow down there," Whitaker remarked years later. Although a graduate of Yale University, Harmount possessed no formal agricultural training.[17] Since most FSA personnel in Louisiana preferred individual farm ownership, Harmount's enthusiasm for trying a cooperative farm in the state more than qualified him for his job as Terrebonne project manager. He was the man most responsible for developing the Terrebonne colony.

Claude Woolsey, regional chief of the Cooperative Section, formed the project into a cooperative association known as Terrebonne Association, Inc., filing its papers with the Louisiana secretary of state's office on 8 November 1938. Conrad M. LeBlanc, Sr., one of the project members,

13. Ibid.
14. J. O. Walker, memorandum to Edwin G. Arnold, 30 March 1938, FSA Records, NA, RG 96; see E. B. Whitaker to C. B. Baldwin, 1 August 1941, ibid.
15. Mastin G. White, memorandum to Will W. Alexander, 26 March 1938, ibid.
16. Whitaker interview; Horace E. Thompson, interview with the author, 19 January 1968; Little Rock *Arkansas Gazette*, 3 January 1939.
17. Whitaker interview; *Times-Picayune*, 9 April 1939.

served as president, and Harmount himself was a member of the four-man board of directors. Every Terrebonne family head paid fifty dollars for one share of capital stock, making him a member of the association, and he had a vote in its business meetings.[18]

The Farm Security Administration gave Terrebonne Association a ninety-nine-year lease on all project land and financed its activities with an initial loan of $415,619. Of this sum, the association used $280,549 in constructing the homes, barns, poultry houses, fences, and roads, and in renovating the community center. The balance, $134,980, was invested in farm implements, mules, and equipment used in the production of sugarcane. Under its lease with the government, Terrebonne Association's annual rent for the use of FSA land was a fifth share of the sugarcane and a fourth share of all other crops. The association relied upon subsidiary cooperatives to carry on special tasks such as marketing produce and purchasing heavy machinery. It also became part owner of the Magnolia Sugar Refinery for use by the colonists.[19]

The qualifications for membership in the Terrebonne colony differed somewhat from those of most community projects. A. D. Roberts, family selection specialist, stressed that applicants should be enthusiastic about the cooperative idea, because a person with strong individualistic tendencies would not fit into the program. Even in the face of a shortage of project families, Roberts's office refused some applicants because they showed signs of being "rugged individualists."[20] "The plan for the development of this project," a news release said, "is something new and

18. "Articles of Association of Terrebonne Association, Inc.," Secretary of State's Office, State Capitol, Baton Rouge, Louisiana; Claude Woolsey, interview with the author, 19 January 1968. Since Louisiana law did not authorize cooperative associations to engage in agricultural production, Terrebonne had originally been incorporated under a 1922 law regulating business corporations. Organized on 10 May 1938, Terrebonne Farm, Inc., issued eighty shares of capital stock worth $50 each. On 13 June the Louisiana legislature approved Act No. 40 of the 1938 session, permitting the organization of cooperative associations without capital stock but with all the powers possessed by Terrebonne Farm, Inc., as well as substantial tax advantages. As a result, Terrebonne Farm was reorganized as Terrebonne Association. T. Roy Reid to Will W. Alexander, 13 April 1938; Mastin G. White, memorandum to Alexander, 26 March, 26 September 1938, all in FSA Records, NA, RG 96; *Louisiana Revised Statutes of 1950*, vol. 1, title 3, chap. 2, pp. 42–62. If families selected for the project could not afford to buy their own share (most could not), the FSA included $50 in their farm and home management plan to meet this initial expense.

19. Economic Justification, Proposal for Development of Terrebonne Project, RR-LA 12, n.d., FSA Records, NA, RG 96; *Times-Picayune*, 9 October 1938; New Orleans *Item-Tribune*, 25 June 1939.

20. *Times-Picayune*, 9 April 1939; *Item-Tribune*, 25 January 1939.

it will be up to those families who first enter [Terrebonne] to make it a success; therefore, it is necessary that families be capable of understanding and adapting to these new conditions."[21]

At Terrebonne special preference was given to young married couples with reasonable education who had reached adulthood since the beginning of the depression, although heads of families between twenty-one and fifty years of age could qualify. As always, the family selection staff looked for families in good financial condition, with reputations for sobriety, honesty, and diligence.[22] Experience with sugarcane production was essential. "Our clients must be either a tenant farmer or a farm laborer," Roberts said. "He must not be burdened with debts and we prefer that he have subsistence livestock."[23]

When the selection process began in April 1938, Harmount planned to settle eighty families, the optimum number Terebonne's size could support with a satisfactory standard of living.[24] Paul N. Mayeau, FSA supervisor in Terrebonne Parish, advised those interested in settling on the project to make application at his office in Houma.[25] On 8 April, Mayeau organized a meeting to discuss the project with interested families in Houma; a second one followed in Thibodaux the next day.[26] He scheduled trips to the project site at Schriever for those wanting to go. Soon he had about three hundred family applicants on file, yet he was never able to get enough qualified families to fill all the project units.[27] By 5 August 1938, the *Houma Courier* announced, the "final selection" of all tenant families for the project was under way. But on 19 August the *Courier* reported that "additional applications" were being sought. On 9 September "complete final arrangements" were again being made at Schriever, but more families for the project were needed.[28] After a year's operation, in July 1940, only sixty families occupied the project—twenty short of the planned number—and since construction stopped with seventy-one units, eleven new houses still stood empty.[29]

One of the new colonists was Robert Thibodaux, the great-grandson

21. *Houma Courier*, 19 August 1938.
22. *Times-Picayune*, 9 October 1938; *Item-Tribune*, 25 January 1939; *Houma Courier*, 5, 19 August 1938.
23. *Times-Picayune*, 9 April 1939.
24. RA, "Project Description Book," FSA Records, NA, RG 96; *Houma Courier*, 19 August, 6 September 1938.
25. Ibid., 5 August, 22 July 1938.
26. Ibid., 8 April 1938.
27. *Times-Picayune*, 9 April 1939.
28. *Houma Courier*, 5, 19 August, 9 September 1938.
29. *Times-Picayune*, 15 July 1940.

of a Louisiana governor. A century before, his grandfather had owned a nearby plantation, but lost it during the Civil War. Robert Thibodaux, unlike his wealthy ancestors, never owned a farm. A tall, thin, weatherbeaten man, he had always been a tenant farmer and farm worker, doing a little house-painting on the side. Having read of the plight of migrant workers in California, he was content to stay at Terrebonne. The Thibodaux family seemed to fit right in. He and his four sons were quite musical, and they organized a band to play in the "community night club," an institution which did not grace most projects in the region.

Conrad LeBlanc was probably more typical of most farmers at Terrebonne. He was born and reared on a sugarcane plantation. For many years he worked for sugarcane companies, sometimes as a foreman; but he returned to farming in 1936. He was enthusiastic about Terrebonne. "In union there is strength," he said, "and I think there is strength in co-operation."[30]

On Saturday, 13 January 1939, Mrs. Allen J. Ellender, wife of the Louisiana senator, came to Schriever to attend the ceremony officially opening the Terrebonne project. The general public was invited; and scores of interested spectators, including many of the families already selected to become colonists, flocked to the community center. Acting as master of ceremonies, Harmount presided over a series of nine speeches given by both FSA officials and civic leaders from Houma and Thibodaux. E. C. McInnis outlined the organization and operation of the Schriever project, recounted its history, and gave details of other FSA activities in Louisiana. Whitaker, representing the regional office, stated that the success of the Schriever experiment would lead to the application of private capital to similar projects.

That the project attracted much local suport seems evident. Among other speakers, for example, Col. Julius Dupont, president of the Houma-Terrebonne Chamber of Commerce, discussed the educational benefits of the project; and R. L. Caldwell, president of the Lafourche Parish Police Jury, said, "The people of Lafourche parish are behind the project 100 per cent and expect to do everything in their power to assist." After the speeches, Mrs. Ellender turned over the first shovelful of earth to begin construction work at Terrebonne.[31]

Once under way, the development of Terrebonne progressed rapidly. In September 1938 Harmount asked for bids on the construction of

30. *Item-Tribune*, 25 June 1939.
31. *Times-Picayune*, 15 January 1939; *Houma Courier*, 17 January 1939. A police jury is the administrative body of a parish.

seventy-three homestead units (219 separate structures); four months later the contractor with the lowest bid began work.[32] The homes were light frame structures built according to FSA specifications. They had two or three bedrooms, living room, kitchen, dining room, and screened side porch. The house plans did not include indoor plumbing, but did include the ubiquitous storeroom that could be converted into a bathroom later. Although erecting the structures on a mass-production basis, the FSA sought to avoid a monotonous "tenement" atmosphere by building several different types of houses, ranging in cost from $1,495 to $1,732. Newspaper stories said that the cost of each homestead, complete with auxiliary buildings, would average about $2,600, a typically low estimate. By July 1939 the project had reached completion.[33]

Even before construction crews left, Terrebonne Association began cooperative operations on 3,140 acres of crop land and 640 acres of pasture land leased from the government. The Terrebonne cooperative association entered into "work and occupancy agreements" with its members, furnishing them, rent-free, two acres of land, their house, barn, poultry house, toilet, water cistern, and livestock. In return, the head of each family worked on the cooperative acreage as a day laborer. Farm experts estimated that work would be available at Terrebonne during most of the year for all family heads. At harvest time the association employed additional laborers from outside sources. During the development stage at Terrebonne, clients previously chosen took construction jobs as much as possible.[34]

Under Harmount's supervision, the president and board of directors laid out a farm program for each year and appointed a foreman to take charge of farming operations. He, in turn, assigned the men work for which they were best suited. Some worked as tractor drivers, others as plow hands, and still others took care of the stock. The association paid each family head for his work at the same rate he could get from private sugarcane planters. In 1939, for example, the current rate was $1.20 a day for cultivating cane and $1.50 a day for harvesting, plus overtime. At the end of the year the association paid its expenses—overhead costs, installment on FSA loan, lease payment, and reserve fund—and divided the balance, if any, among the members according to the number of

32. Ibid., 6, 27 September 1938, 13 January 1939; for additional delay in awarding bids, see ibid., 25, 28 October, 4 November 1938; J. O. Walker, memorandum to Edwin G. Arnold, 12 December 1938, FSA Records, NA, RG 96.

33. *Item-Tribune*, 25 June 1939; *Houma Courier*, 6 September 1938.

34. Economic Justification, Proposal for Development of Terrebonne Project, RR-LA 12, n.d., FSA Records, NA, RG 96.

hours of work each had put in during the year. The project families, there-fore, relied on two major sources of income: their daily wage, which should have covered day-to-day living expenses, and a year-end dividend paid out of profits on the cane and other cash crops.[35] In reality, how-ever, the Terrebonne Association was never successful enough to pay a dividend. So project families depended on their income as day laborers on the project, rather than on dividends as part owners in the cooperative association.

Harmount subdivided 480 acres of project land into homestead units of 6 acres each, 2 acres of which served as a homestead site, with the other 4 devoted to garden vegetables, poultry, and livestock. Although project members occupied their individual homestead units rent-free, each family paid $30 rent a year on the 4-acre tract; they could either keep its produce for their own use or sell it and keep the profit as a source of income. Terrebonne's remaining 2,148 acres included space for roads, ditches, community center, community pasture, and uncleared land.[36]

Since the Terrebonne project was located in the heart of the sugar bowl of southern Louisiana, the major portion of its arable acreage was planted in sugarcane. I. C. Borland, farm management supervisor, de-signed the project's farm program to comply with recommendations made by the Louisiana Experiment Station; so, besides cane, the FSA program included corn, soybeans, Irish potatoes, truck crops, and livestock.[37]

At Terrebonne the Resettlement Administration originally planned to imitate the so-called European village style of agriculture. The home-steads were to be grouped together to form a village in the center of the project, with the fields stretching out in the distance. But when develop-ing the project, Harmount scattered the homesteads and, despite plans for communal farming, broke up the arable land into individual units of forty acres each. The most important reason for this change was the fear on the part of Little Rock officials that plans for operating Terre-bonne as a collective farm would not be practical. Whitaker, for example, wanted to be prepared to split the community into individual family units if collective operations should fail.[38] Thus the Schriever land was divided into separate units, which at first seemed to serve no real purpose. At the

35. *Item-Tribune*, 25 June 1939; *Houma Courier*, 13 September 1938.
36. Economic Justification, Proposal for Development of Terrebonne Project, RR-LA 12, n.d., FSA Records, NA, RG 96; *Item-Tribune*, 25 June 1938.
37. Ibid.; *Times-Picayune*, 9 April 1939.
38. Whitaker interview.

same time, Harmount found it expedient to group dwellings together in twos and threes so that more than one family could use the same well, thus cutting costs and encouraging informal cooperation.[39]

The communal organization at Terrebonne was the source of local controversy. One outspoken critic was Edward A. Ford, Presbyterian minister at Thibodaux. Addressing the Houma Rotary Club on 20 September 1939, Mr. Ford offered several objections to the project's operation. As planned by the FSA, he asserted, Terrebonne was in grave danger of failing. The spirit of the resettlement program was to permit people to own land of their own. But at Schriever tenants could never own the land as individuals. Since ownership was impossible, he contended that personal initiative would be destroyed and a less desirable type of farmer would be drawn to the project.[40]

The following week Harmount and John Lynch, one of his colleagues, appeared before the Rotary Club to answer Ford's criticisms. Did the project fail to provide incentive for families since it did not anticipate eventual ownership? The answer, Harmount explained, was not as simple as Ford believed. Harmount argued that it was difficult to find people who were capable of operating their own farms, and that the cooperative plantation provided a means of discovering people with the qualities for farm ownership. He argued that if a man must buy livestock, equipment, and other needs for a modern farm, it would require several thousand dollars, while at Terrebonne a man could get started for fifty dollars. The fact that the land had been divided into forty-acre tracts indicated, Harmount said, that the FSA may have in mind actual tenant ownership at a future date. Lynch argued that from a practical standpoint sugarcane lent itself better to large-scale cooperative farming than to small family farms.[41]

On an earlier occasion, Harmount made an interesting defense of the operation of the Schriever project. The farmers there were not merely clients on another government project; they were, he said, stockholders in a business proposition. What of the charges of radicalism that were sometimes made? "Socialized farming? Communistic? Radical?" mused Harmount. "I don't like those words. They do not apply here. We are operating a business. Strictly business."[42] In Louisiana and other southern states, the FSA could also present its cooperative plantation projects

39. Eaton, *Exploring Tomorrow's Agriculture*, p. 79.
40. *Houma Courier*, 23 September 1938.
41. Ibid., 30 September 1938.
42. *Times-Picayune*, 9 April 1939.

like Terrebonne as a continuation of the South's plantation system.[43]

Community facilities constituted an integral part of every resettlement project, whether based on individual or cooperative ownership. At Schriever, Harmount converted the old Waubun plantation mansion into a community center containing his office and space for social and educational activities; an athletic field was laid out near the building. The government built a school on the project and turned it over to the Terrebonne Parish School Board. Local physicians and the parish health unit worked through the association's medical cooperative to provide medical attention and health education for project residents.[44]

One of the idealistic arguments for Terrebonne was that it afforded farm families a full community life. Living and working together as members of a close-knit community, the Terrebonne settlers and their families derived special benefits from their cooperative effort toward social and economic security—benefits they would miss if every man competed as an individual farmer. Such community fellowship supposedly appealed to young farm families and kept them from drifting into the cities.[45] While Harmount encouraged them to be "cooperatively minded" and the dramatics club staged skits with titles like "Esprit de Co-op," most of the clients were unable to readjust their values and work together as a team.[46] Many settlers eagerly worked their own plots on good days, but wanted to work the association's land only on rainy or otherwise bad days.[47] While the cooperative system did not suffer a complete breakdown, it was not the success that Harmount expected. Most Terrebonne farmers were probably still unconvinced that community property rather than private ownership was the answer to their problems. "I guess every man would like to own land," Robert Thibodaux observed. "But it's pretty hard to raise a family and acquire land as a farm worker or tenant. I think this project gives my family more security. I know we'll eat better."[48] Like that of most others, his attitude rested on economic expediency; he stayed because Terrebonne meant steady work and perhaps a chance to save enough money to buy a farm of his own.

The Farm Security Administration wanted every resettlement project to stand on its own feet financially and repay the government's invest-

43. Ibid., 9 October 1938.
44. *Houma Courier*, 20 September 1938.
45. Ibid.
46. *Item-Tribune*, 25 June 1939.
47. F. L. Spencer, farm management supervisor in Region VI and project manager at Mounds, interview with the author, 2 December 1963.
48. *Item-Tribune*, 25 June 1939.

ment. Few of its communities proved immediately successful in a business way, however, and the FSA found itself having to carry projects operating in the red. Terrebonne was one of the agency's most unsuccessful cooperative plantations. In 1940 the project suffered a net loss of $42,684. In 1941 Harmount cut the loss to $16,582—a clear indication of financial improvement. Terrebonne's total income in 1942 totaled about $15,000 more than in 1941, but it still fell $24,700 short of the project budget. Brice M. Mace, Jr., national chief of the FSA's Farm Management Division, estimated that Terrebonne could operate profitably by 1944; even then, it would still be a year behind any other cooperative farm project. Mace would not venture a guess as to when Terrebonne would be able to wipe out its deficit. The future of Terrebonne, Mace said, was "highly problematic."[49]

In 1943 C. Stott Noble, FSA assistant administrator, took charge of liquidating the Schriever project.[50] He first canceled Terrebonne Association's ninety-nine-year lease by mutual agreement with its membership. Under incessant congressional prodding, Noble quickly made plans to sell the land. Making use of the fact that Terrebonne was already broken up into individual farms, Noble offered project residents a chance to buy the units they occupied; he also agreed to sell units to eligible farm families who were not Terrebonne residents. By June 1945 he had sold fifty-two of fifty-five units currently in use at an average price of $4,312; this included all but 214 acres of the project's land. The FSA recovered $224,200 through sales of individual units, whereas it had invested $300,389.67 to purchase the land and develop the homesteads. In land and development costs the Terrebonne project lost $59,804.78. In addition, Terrebonne had invested $205,270.25 in community facilities; and after five years its accumulated operating expenses amounted to $47,769.47 more than its income. Since neither amount was recoverable, the deficit totaled $307,871.50, less than half that of Plum Bayou.[51]

Terrebonne's losses were due in part to handicaps over which it had little control. While one agency of the federal government sought to help these families produce more, another agency placed limits on the number of acres they could farm. Terrebonne was crippled by restrictions on the

49. Eaton, *Exploring Tomorrow's Agriculture*, pp. 163, 154; USS, *USDA Approp. Hearings, 1943*, 77th Cong., 2d sess., pp. 656–59.
50. USS, *USDA Approp. Hearings, 1946*, 79th Cong., 1st sess., p. 287.
51. USHR, *USDA Approp. Hearings, 1947*, 79th Cong., 2d sess., pp. 1393, 1413; see A. D. Stewart, memorandum to Frank Hancock, 27 October 1944, FSA Records, NA, RG 96. The Terrebonne Association discontinued operations as of 31 December 1943. Stewart, memorandum to Hancock, 14 January 1944, ibid.

amount of cane and other crops that could be produced under AAA regulations. Harmount originally intended to divide his arable land into 700 acres of cane, 1,000 of corn, 100 of potatoes and vegetables, and 640 of pasture land. But AAA quotas limited Terrebonne to 398 acres of sugarcane, 90 of potatoes, and 60 of truck vegetables—a total of 548, or about 9 acres for each of the sixty families living on the project.[52] The AAA initially based Terrebonne's sugarcane allotment on the fact that the project operated as a single plantation; in order to increase the acreage, Harmount asked for cane quotas for seventy-two individual family farm units rather than for one large plantation operated by seventy-two day laborers. As a result, Terrebonne received permission to cultivate a maximum of 10 acres of cane per family, thus increasing the entire cane acreage to 710. The AAA did not revise its allotments for other crops at Terrebonne until unprecedented wartime demand for farm products and sharp rises in agricultural prices weakened the crop control program.[53] If allowed to cultivate half of its arable acreage (about 2,700 acres), as Harmount wished, Terrebonne would still have provided only 22.5 acres per family.[54]

Harmount offered a steady stream of apologies for Terrebonne's record in his annual financial reports. Despite growing losses, he never wavered from his claim that project operations showed consistent improvement. After Terrebonne received orders to liquidate, he wrote: "The Association [in 1939] took over this property, which was then made up of four old run down plantations, [with] poor drainage, insufficient cane, potato or vegetable quotas . . . and for the last five years, at great sacrifice to themselves, fought their way upward, overcoming handicaps of floods, freezes, droughts, crop diseases, failures and faulty farm planning forced upon them."[55] By 1943, Harmount claimed, the members of the association "felt they were achieving their goals and could see success in the future." Claude Woolsey believed Harmount was overly optimistic. He

52. *Times-Picayune*, 15 July 1940.
53. John J. Riggle, memorandum to Brice Mace, Jr., 15 April 1940; see E. B. Whitaker to Will W. Alexander, 24 June 1939; C. B. Baldwin to Joshua Bernhardt, 28 May 1940; T. Roy Reid to Alexander, 6 April, 29 May 1940; J. O. Walker to Reid, 6 May 1940, all in FSA Records, NA, RG 96. See Little Rock *Arkansas Democrat*, 2 March 1943.
54. *Times-Picayune*, 15 July 1940.
55. Comments by the Community Manager on the 1943 Financial Statement and Operation of Terrebonne Association, Inc., with Annual Report for the Fiscal Year Ended 31 December 1945, FSA Records, NA, RG 96. See also Association Manager's Comments, Annual Financial Report, Terrebonne Association, Inc., for the Fiscal Year Ended 31 December 1942, ibid.

blamed weak management for Terrebonne's failure to work out its problems.[56]

In making a wide departure from traditional farm practice, Terrebonne illustrated the radical side of the rural resettlement program. Bad weather, faulty planning, and mismanagement doomed Terrebonne to failure, despite the optimism of Harmount and some of the project members. "I think we are going to put it over," said one settler soon after the project opened. "I think everybody will get together and work hard and put it across."[57] But everybody would not get together and work hard in a community effort. Most still had not given up hope of owning their own land.

56. Comments by Regional Chief, Cooperative Section [Claude Woolsey], Annual Financial Report, Terrebonne Association, Inc., for the Fiscal Year Ended 31 December 1942, ibid.

57. *Times-Picayune*, 9 April 1939.

Part Three

Conflict and Controversy

Chapter XI

Disturber of the Peace?
Or Keeper of the Peace?

When a New Deal agency opened a field office in a region like the Lower Mississippi Valley, it ventured a long way from the Washington Mall. Every federal agency brought its innovations and spent its money, often without dramatic results; but the local environment had a more predictable effect. Local values went to work on the agency's representatives, guiding their activities within the broad limits of community tolerance; and perhaps local people took a piece of the action. Special interest groups always sought to influence, if not control, any new federal program. In time a curious transformation took place. To some degree, the agency merged with its environment, duplicating the local patterns of leadership and social outlook.

The local success of any federal agency depended on the interplay of several forces: the people who represented it in cities, small towns, and rural districts; the program they administered and the flexibility they exercised in adapting it to local conditions; and finally the social, economic, and political environment. The welter of local pressures could help the agency—and hinder it. Almost certainly it adapted to its environment if it survived.[1]

Local influence in the Resettlement Administration's Region VI began with the appointment of T. Roy Reid as regional director. He and other top officials were products of the region's agricultural establishment, and they consciously and unconsciously channeled many of the values of the region into their official actions. Regional officials, however, were never disloyal to the program. Given the nature of resettlement work, dis-

1. See Michael S. Holmes, "The New Deal in Georgia: An Administrative History" (Ph.D. diss., University of Wisconsin, 1969).

loyalty was hardly an issue. Reid always sought to carry out the resettle-ment program as the national office wanted. What moral struggles or misgivings he harbored, if any, can be only a matter of conjecture. At the very least he probably wished he did not have cooperative projects like Terrebonne hung around his neck.

Reid took on a difficult assignment. He often found himself in the middle of conflicting, even irreconcilable, viewpoints; and his role as opinion broker became more untenable as time passed. Perhaps his great-est challenge was to exert personal control over a large staff of rural southerners and maintain organizational discipline, and he carried it off with considerable success.[2]

The field personnel, like Stanley Rhodes and George Harmount, lived on the firing line where the agency met the community in daily contact; they operated under the most direct influence of local pressures. In the intimacy of community relationships, they came face to face with their clients, with their clients' neighbors and friends, and with civic leaders. The project managers and county supervisors could not function in an atmosphere of hostility; and they hardly wanted, given their own pro-fessional training, to undertake any course of action antithetical to local customs. For advice and assistance they looked to the county agent and home demonstration agent, the local 4-H Club, the superintendent of schools, perhaps the county health unit, and other local institutions; on the other hand, many local citizens participated in the agency's programs by serving on advisory committees.

While the Farm Security Administration engaged in some experimen-tation, the agency based its program on the oldest tradition in American agriculture. What the resettlement agencies tried to accomplish in the field of farm and home management was already familiar to farmers through the state extension services. Even in the South, perhaps the most static region of the nation, the Great Depression and the difficult years which preceded it largely swept aside the prejudice against direct govern-ment aid; southerners were not only ready, but eager, for federal assis-tance.

Nevertheless, the resettlement program contained elements which challenged the status quo, creating the image of the agency, in Sidney Baldwin's phrase, as a "disturber of the peace."[3] Complaints that large-

2. Laurence I. Hewes to the author, 16 February 1973; Brooks Hays to the author, 6 August 1973; J. L. Henderson to the author, 9 January 1974.
3. Sidney Baldwin, *Poverty and Politics: The Rise and Decline of the Farm Security Administration* (Chapel Hill: University of North Carolina Press, 1968), chap. 9.

scale government land purchases were "un-American" or that a con-spiracy existed to nationalize the land and socialize agriculture were palpably ridiculous. Yet any change, no matter how modest, threatened somebody; and the fear the agency aroused was real enough. Some of the FSA's national leaders made no secret of their dislike of fee-simple owner-ship, the hallowed concept of American agrarians. They attacked com-fortable myths, and refused to sweep unpleasantries under the carpet. The leaders of the agency assumed society, rather than the individual, was responsible for poverty; but it was the individual they hoped to change. The revolutionary potential of the agency lay not in a bogey such as cooperative farming, but in the attempt to replace traditional atti-tudes, to teach people things they evidently did not want to learn or did not know they needed to learn. If such reforms could arouse anxieties, what might have been the outcry if some federal agency had attempted fundamental changes which boldly challenged local values?

When the Resettlement Administration set up a regional office in Little Rock and its agents fanned out over the three states, they came at a most auspicious time. The people of the region, particularly of Arkan-sas, were very much aware of rural poverty; the subject had become front-page news, and they were ready to see something done. In December 1936, according to a Gallup poll, public opinion in the South overwhelm-ingly favored government help for low-income farmers. Gallup's question was, "Would you favor government loans, on a long-time and easy basis, to enable farm tenants to buy the farms they now rent?" In Arkansas 89 percent of those polled answered yes, as did 88 percent in Mississippi and 84 percent in Louisiana.[4] Without strong support, there would have been little use in the federal government's proceeding further.

In his first annual report Reid stressed the good relations enjoyed be-tween the Resettlement Administration and the general public in Region VI. "The press," he wrote, "has been favorable and generally anxious to carry information about Resettlement." Such local groups as civic clubs, farmers organizations, and home demonstration councils gave their sup-port. "There have been no opposing organizations, and the public, gen-erally, seems to be very favorable to the work which Resettlement is doing. There is, occasionally," he admitted, "criticism of procedures or of delays in activities, but the general objectives of the work seem to be meeting with strong public favor." Almost a year later John Fischer, national information director, reported: "Newspapers continue to be ex-

4. *Birmingham* (Ala.) *News*, 13 December 1936.

tremely friendly both to work undertaken by RA and the new work of
FSA. The opening of projects in Arkansas and completed projects in
Mississippi received wide and laudatory comment."[5]

The enthusiastic newspaper reaction at the opening of Plum Bayou pre-
saged similar receptions elsewhere; even cooperative projects like Terrebonne and Lake Dick were gratefully received. "The RA was thought
of by God Himself," a farm wife in West Carroll Parish, Louisiana, told
a home demonstration supervisor.[6]

The Information Division of the regional office served as Reid's liaison
between the action divisions (like Resettlement and Rehabilitation) and
the general public. O. E. Jones was the first information advisor, followed
by George Wolf and J. Lewis Henderson, all professional newspapermen.
The information adviser became in effect the press secretary for the
regional office. His most important service was to establish and maintain
cordial relations with the public in Region VI. To do this, he commanded
an organization that included radio, photographic, correspondence, and
editorial sections. The emphasis of the public relations effort, however,
centered on dispensing information about resettlement activities rather
than on propaganda as such. On the other hand, the Information Division's Press Clipping Unit kept its finger on the regional pulse with its
weekly "editorial reaction reports."

The best and friendliest medium for conveying information to the
public proved to be daily and weekly newspapers. The Information Division staff wrote everything from simple press releases to feature stories
for Sunday magazine sections, distributing them through a network of 450
newspapers on a regular mailing list. They supplied the public with
pamphlets on resettlement in Region VI, worked up exhibits for county
and state fairs, and handled arrangements for dedicatory ceremonies at
resettlement projects. Where possible, the division worked through civic
clubs, churches, fraternal groups, chambers of commerce, labor unions,
farm organizations, public schools, and colleges. For example, Wolf estimated that from January to August 1939, local personnel gave 884
luncheon club talks, regional and state personnel 150 talks.[7]

5. Resettlement Administration, Annual Report, Region VI, as of 31 December 1936, FSA Records, NA, RG 96; John Fischer, memorandum to W. W. Alexander, 20 November 1937, ibid.
6. Martha D. Dinwiddle to R. G. Tugwell, 23 July 1936, ibid.; see, for example,
New Orleans *Item-Tribune*, 25 June 1939; Little Rock *Arkansas Democrat*, 11
August 1940.
7. Report of Activities of Information Division, from 1 July 1935 to 31 December 1936; John Fischer, memorandum to All Information Advisers, 10 December
1940; George Wolf to Fischer, 16 August 1939, all in FSA Records, NA, RG 96.

As long as the depression hung over the countryside, the resettlement agencies enjoyed widespread popularity. While criticism always existed, it was sporadic, unorganized, and without any real consequence. Once the need for relief lessened, opposition increased. The New Deal itself ran into more and more trouble after 1937; the latent forces of opposition which had been poised all along began showing their strength.

About 1940, according to a story of unknown origin, a sociologist visiting Pine Bluff, Arkansas, stopped someone on a street corner and asked him, apparently right out of the blue, what he thought of the Farm Security Administration. "Well, it's this way," the man said.

The government spends a million dollars or so to buy a forty-acre farm for a down-and-out sharecropper. They give him a mule, a bathtub, and an electric shoelacer. They lay a railroad track to his house to carry the tons of forms he has to fill in. A bunch of experts figure his milking I.Q. Lo and behold, they teach his wife how to hook rugs and can beef and spinach, and they show the feller how to plant soybeans and prune an orchard—and by darn, Luke, them government people can actually do it! After we poke fun at their red tape for a year or two, they ups and proves their experiment is self-liquidatin'—that the feller is makin' his payments and raisin' a family, too. And I don't know who's more surprised, me or the 'cropper.[8]

This statement correctly summarized the basic arguments, pro and con, over resettlement; but most critics were less open-minded.

When Lakeview, a Negro project in Phillips County, Arkansas, was announced, the *Helena World* expressed skepticism: "We want to see how many families will succeed in becoming independent when the means to do so come handed out on a platter from a bountiful government."[9] In 1937 an El Dorado, Arkansas, man complained that government assistance to low-income farmers was an unfair disadvantage to hard-working citizens, presumably like himself. "I believe we have too many farmers already," he wrote Secretary of Agriculture Wallace. "You or our National Congress want to buy land and place more farmers to farm against each other." "The old pioneer citizen and taxpayer of the country [is] trying to live, and pulling himself up by his boot straps, while his neighbor [is] supported by the Government."[10]

When the resettlement agencies aroused fears and resentment among special interest groups, posing a threat to their economic and political

8. Work Projects Administration, *Arkansas: A Guide to the State* (New York: Hastings House, 1941), p. 65; also quoted in Oren Stephens, "FSA Fights for Its Life," *Harper's Magazine* 186 (April 1943): 479.
9. *Helena* (Ark.) *World*, 11 November 1935.
10. B. Justiss to Henry Wallace, 26 December 1937, FSA Records, NA, RG 96.

power, the reaction could be swift and sure. Governors, legislatures, and business spokesmen of several northern states raised a storm of protest over the presence of a few small hosiery factories on FSA projects. Similarly, southern cotton planters feared that resettlement programs would upset the stability of their labor supply. The land-leasing and cooperative associations could be construed as threats to plantation owners, "furnish" merchants, and rural banks.

In early 1939 the Arkansas General Assembly sent President Roosevelt a petition signed by thirty-six of its members (not, of course, a majority), protesting the FSA's policy of operating farms in "direct competition with private farmers." Upset by the new land-leasing program, they declared that "the leasing and operating of such competing farms is causing wide-spread unrest and panic and might even create a riot." The FSA "cooperative" program, they added, "strikes viciously at the heart of the great system upon which economic security and the very life of the South depends."[11]

The United States Department of Agriculture never let such a protest pass without trying to correct any misapprehensions it might contain. Wallace rebutted each complaint in a draft of a letter for the president's signature. The Farm Security Administration had not leased any land nor was it operating farms, Wallace asserted, taking refuge in a little hair-splitting; the farm families who actually held the leases had been farming in the area for years. "The Government," wrote Wallace, "is merely giving them assistance similar to that given to many other low-income farmers in this and other areas." The program, he asserted, helped to stabilize rather than disrupt the farm labor supply; and it would help such people assume their responsibilities as citizens. And Reid visited the legislators in an attempt to clarify the program's purposes.[12]

Meeting at Biloxi in May 1939, the Mississippi Bankers Association passed a resolution condemning FSA credit policies. The bankers association criticized government lending agencies for making loans in competition with private bankers. The FSA responded by sounding out the extent and nature of opposition among Mississippi bankers and by attempting to clear up any misunderstanding about FSA programs.

Mississippi state director Marvin T. Aldrich and his staff contacted several bankers; with some of them they ran up against solid opposition.

11. Petition of thirty-six members of the Arkansas General Assembly, enclosed with John E. Miller to Franklin D. Roosevelt, 3 February 1939, FDR Papers, OF 1568.
12. Henry A. Wallace to Marvin H. McIntyre, 2 March 1939, ibid.

Frank Allen of Canton, one of the leaders behind the resolution, "was not in favor of any of the New Deal governmental agencies," an FSA official reported. "In his opinion the Farm Security Administration was not making any loans that the bank[s] cared to make but [it] interfered with the banks' loans to the landlords, who were to furnish the tenants."[13] But Aldrich found the banking community badly split over the resolution, with some of its members anxious to make excuses for their association.

A. L. Rogers, president of the bankers association, had not been behind the move to name the FSA specifically in the resolution. The bankers, Rogers told Aldrich, directed their resolution primarily at such agencies as the Home Owners' Loan Corporation, the Federal Housing Administration, the Farm Credit Administration, and the Farm Labor Board. They included the FSA because of the fear on the part of some bankers that it *might* later encroach on the lending functions of private bankers, not because of any of its current activities.[14] Information adviser George Wolf also found that the resolution did not represent the feelings of rural bankers in Mississippi; he reported the existence of "a sharp division— the city bankers voting for the resolution and the country and small-town bankers voting against it."[15]

R. L. Goodwin, vice-president of the Farmers and Merchants Bank of Forest, wrote that the FSA in his country handled a large volume of loan and long-term credit "which was not available from any local bank." "You have helped a great many farmers who could not have received this kind of help from any other source," he wrote Will Alexander. "I consider the Farm Security Administration the finest New Deal project established by President Roosevelt."[16] With opinion divided, the FSA could count on support from at least some Mississippi bankers for its credit programs.

The pocketbook was not the only sensitive area. The quickest way to overstep the boundaries of regional tolerance was to violate its racial mores. And in much of what Resettlement and Farm Security did lay an implied rejection of Jim Crow. "At the risk of its political life," William E. Leuchtenburg has written, "the FSA was scrupulously fair in its treat-

13. T. Roy Reid to Will W. Alexander, 18 May 1939, FSA Records, NA, RG 96; Sidney J. Johnson to Marvin T. Aldrich, 17 June 1939, ibid.
14. M. T. Aldrich to T. Roy Reid, 31 May 1939, ibid.; Reid to Will W. Alexander, 7 June 1939, ibid.
15. George Wolf to John Fischer, 27 May 1939, ibid.
16. R. L. Goodwin to Will W. Alexander, 12 May 1939, ibid.

ment of Negroes."[17] Rexford Tugwell was not primarily known for his commitment to the cause of Negro rights, but as Resettlement chief he sought to include black farmers fully in the agency's programs. Significantly, too, he picked Will W. Alexander as his deputy administrator.

Alexander always thought in terms of people. He abhorred any impersonal condition, such as racial prejudice, which held people back. His work at the Commission on Interracial Cooperation and Dillard University earned him a national reputation. Along with other New Dealers, he courageously took steps to break out of a racially discriminatory system. As Tugwell's successor in the Resettlement Administration and first head of the Farm Security Administration, Will Alexander did more than any other one man to insure the black farmer his share of New Deal benefits.[18]

One out of every four families on resettlement projects across the South was black—about the proportion of Negro farmers among all southern farm operators. The raw totals, however, were not impressive. By 1940 only 1,393 Negro families had found homes in FSA communities, and over half of these families were located in Region VI alone. The Little Rock office developed 791 units for Negroes—a substantial 32 percent of its available space. Although no other region could match this percentage, it still fell short of the proportion of black farmers in the Lower Mississippi Valley. The resettlement projects of Region VI should have had a black population of 42 percent if the proportional test were to be met.[19]

In racial terms the Resettlement Administration built three types of projects: those for whites only, those for blacks only, and those for both white and black families. But the agency never dared challenge the Jim

17. William E. Leuchtenburg, *Franklin D. Roosevelt and the New Deal, 1932–1940* (New York: Harper and Row, 1963), p. 141. See also Allen Francis Kifer, "The Negro under the New Deal, 1933–1941" (Ph.D. diss., University of Wisconsin, 1961), pp. 190–209; Raymond Wolters, *Negroes and the Great Depression: The Problem of Economic Recovery* (Westport, Conn.: Greenwood, 1970), pp. 60–73; Donald Holley, "The Negro in the New Deal Resettlement Program," *Agricultural History* 45 (July 1971): 179–93.

18. See Statement of Dr. Will W. Alexander, Second National Conference on Problems of the Negro and Negro Youth, 13 January 1939, mimeographed, FSA Records, NA, RG 96; idem, "Our Conflicting Racial Policies," *Harper's Magazine* 190 (January 1945): 172–79; and Wilma Dykeman and James Stokely, *Seeds of Southern Change: The Life of Will Alexander* (Chicago: University of Chicago Press, 1962), chap. 19.

19. Richard Sterner, *The Negro's Share: A Study of Income, Consumption, Housing and Public Assistance* (New York: Harper and Brothers, 1943), pp. 306–9, 423. According to Sterner, 1,761 resettlement farms were available for Negro families in June 1940, but not all were occupied.

Crow system overtly. Arkansas had three of the region's five all-Negro projects: Desha Farms (88 units), in Desha and Drew counties; Lakeview (142 units), a farm community in Phillips County, near Helena; and Townes Farms (37 units), in Crittenden County, near West Memphis. The other two were Mounds Farms (176 units), located in Madison and East Carroll parishes, near Tallulah, Louisiana; and Mileston Farms (136 units), near Mileston, in Holmes County, Mississippi. In addition, some two hundred Negro families were members of predominately white projects where the two races lived apart.[20]

Although the black communities were dramatic, it was the rehabilitation and tenant purchase programs which provided Negroes the greatest benefits. From 1936 through 1939, standard rehabilitation loans went to 34,248 white families and 13,039 black families in Region VI, meaning that 28 percent of all rehabilitation clients were Negro. Compared with the FSA's other southern regions, Region VI was the only one in which the number of black rehabilitation clients fell short of the proportion of Negro farm operators. At the same time, black tenant purchase borrowers were below the percentage of Negro tenants in every Deep South state, and Reid's record was little worse than that of any other regional director. In the tenant purchase program's first three years, regional officials approved 668 Negro families, 25.4 percent of all borrowers. As for the land-leasing program, not only was Region VI's achievement outstanding, but other regions had little or nothing to compare with it. The program was only a couple of years old in 1940, but Negro families made up about half of the 1,100 participating families.[21]

Looking across the South, Alexander could see many gratifying accomplishments, but he must have also agonized over the agency's performance. He could do no more than scratch the surface of the great mass of poverty-stricken farmers, black or white. Not even counting the rest of the South, the states of Region VI alone held some 477,000 tenants, plus other farmers who were eligible for assistance, a total far larger than it was humanly possible to reach. Yet a mere numbers game does not tell the whole story. On one hand, it is dangerous to apply contemporary standards in a situation that was quite unlike present circumstances. After all, a beginning was made in helping all poor farmers. On the other hand,

20. FSA, "Resettlement Projects, Region VI," FSA Records, NA, RG 96; Sterner, *Negro's Share*, p. 424.
21. Ibid., pp. 298–307, 424; "The Southern Negro on the Farm: His Problems and What the FSA Is Doing about Them," n.d., mimeographed, FSA Records, NA, RG 96; Rural Rehabilitation Division, Program Analysis Report no. 15, Racial Aspects of Rural Rehabilitation Family Progress, December 1940, ibid.

racial discrimination did exist, whether deliberate or incidental. Negro families appeared in larger proportions than did whites among that class of farmers the program was designed to assist. They were likely to be worse off than white farmers; and when blacks did receive assistance, their loans tended to be for smaller amounts.

The resettlement agencies never intended to operate a program for the most down-and-out sharecroppers and tenants. The selection of clients and the size of loans did not depend on need alone. Since clients paid for their farms, they had to be good risks, with good credit-ratings and reputations for hard work and honesty. The poverty-stricken condition of most Negro applicants automatically disqualified many of them as resettlement clients and tenant purchase borrowers. They could more easily qualify for rehabilitation loans, but still Negro farmers were at a disadvantage since they had few assets, little experience as independent operators, and little education.

In addition, FSA officials were sometimes overly concerned that the loan programs make a good showing. Instead of digging down into the lower levels of poverty, they tended to "skim the cream"; that is, they often selected borrowers most likely to succeed and rejected applicants needing special assistance. Finally, the Farm Security Administration, like the Agricultural Adjustment Administration, worked through committees of local citizens in awarding both the rehabilitation and tenant purchase loans. Such committees paved the way for local acceptance and involvement; they were only advisory, but since Negroes held no committee memberships, committee decisions could reflect local racial attitudes.[22]

To win approval and avoid controversy, the agency conformed to the local pattern of race relations; regional and local officials were not great liberals on the subject of racial justice, and they really could not afford to be. They wanted to help black people, but they did so largely in the context of traditional southern paternalism, and federal influence could do little to change such attitudes.

The regional office had to be acutely sensitive to the danger of alienating whites. When they planned Negro projects, they sometimes effectively used reverse psychology by holding out the bait of federal money and letting local business and civic leaders apply pressure to obtain a project,

22. Gunnar Myrdal, *An American Dilemma: The Negro Problem and Modern Democracy* (New York: Harper and Brothers, 1944), pp. 273–76; Baldwin, *Poverty and Politics*, pp. 196–97. See Will W. Alexander to Charles H. Houston, 12 February 1937, FSA Records, NA, RG 96.

even an all-black project. In any case, officials never went ahead with proposals for Negro resettlement without first having the solid support of the white majority. On the Louisiana Farm Tenant Security project, for example, community manager Lee O. Sumrall not only sounded out local opinion on plans for resettling Negroes on some of the units, but also asked reputable citizens and landowners to write letters expressing their approval of the idea.[23] Farm Security officials never selected any location for resettlement, particularly a black project, without first obtaining the support of local community leaders. Every adjoining landowner had to request the project. The local board of aldermen, the sheriff, and other officials had to make a personal appeal. The FSA scarcely wanted to place a group of families in a hostile environment.

The Farm Security Administration's policy of nondiscrimination meant trouble from blacks as well as whites, with the regional office caught in the middle. Some blacks were quick to object when they believed racial discrimination existed in the resettlement program. Regional officials, for example, ran into protests over their handling of the Transylvania project in East Carroll Parish, Louisiana. When they made the Transylvania purchase, about 250 Negro families farmed the land under private ownership. But they developed Transylvania as a white project, meaning that every Negro family moved off and white families took their places. The American Negro Press (ANP)—a wire service for such papers as the Pittsburgh *Courier*, the Kansas City *Call*, and the New Orleans *Louisiana Weekly*—challenged this action on the ground of racial discrimination.[24]

The regional office appeared anxious to keep the confidence of the Negro press. In early February 1939 E. B. Whitaker, O. E. Jones, and E. C. McInnis spent two hours in New Orleans with Leon Lewis, Pittsburgh *Courier* reporter. Specifically, Whitaker and McInnis presented a plan to ensure fair treatment for Negro farmers. The Mounds project, Lewis learned, would take care of qualified Negro families displaced at Transylvania. Lewis "was not only satisfied—he was enthusiastic," Jones reported of the meeting; Lewis's personal investigation convinced him that his race "was, if anything, getting the best of the bargain there."[25]

In reality he remained as skeptical as ever. There was no discrimination in the incident, he reported to his paper. "The same thing that is

23. Lee O. Sumrall to E. B. Whitaker, 31 August 1936, ibid.; T. Roy Reid to Will W. Alexander, 11 December 1937, ibid.; Whitaker to the author, 30 October 1970.

24. Nathan W. Robertson, memorandum to Will W. Alexander, n.d., FSA Records, NA, RG 96; George Fischer, memorandum to C. B. Baldwin, n.d., ibid.

25. O. E. Jones to Nathan Robertson, 8 February 1939, ibid.

being done to Negroes is being done to whites, and they are complaining [just] as much." The Information Division afterward made a conscious effort to keep the ANP informed of progress at Mounds. When the construction contract was awarded, Jones wired full details of building plans. As a result, the wire service let up on its criticism.[26]

One proof of the Resettlement Administration's interest in the Negro was its personnel policy. Within a few days of becoming Resettlement chief, Tugwell ordered the personnel department to accept Negro job applicants on the same basis as whites. He wanted to place a "suitable proportion" of Negroes in office jobs, on resettlement projects, and in the rehabilitation program. Since Resettlement would reach a segment of the rural population with a large proportion of black families, Negro personnel, he thought, could make the agency more effective in reaching their own people.[27]

While Tugwell's deputy administrator, Alexander employed Joseph H. B. Evans in the Washington office with the title of race relations specialist. Evans followed the work of all programs, sought to prevent discrimination against black families, and tried to place more black personnel at every level where Negroes were involved.[28] Whatever Tugwell's "suitable proportion" originally meant, it turned out to be meager. Negro workers were used only when their work would bring them into contact exclusively with other blacks. A white person filled any job requiring contact with clients of both races.

Negro workers were employed throughout the regional organization, beginning at the top. Osie Lee Smith, Sr., was a Negro administrative assistant to the regional director, a position paralleling the one Evans held in the Washington office. But he, too, achieved little where Negro employment was concerned. Most black employees were women serving as home management supervisors on Negro projects, with a few in charge of home management work for an entire project. A few black men worked

26. Leon Lewis to Claude Barnett, 4 February 1939, ibid.; Division of Information, Farm Security Administration, telegram to Associated Negro Press, 7 February 1939, ibid.

27. Will W. Alexander to Joseph H. B. Evans, 12 July 1935, ibid.; R. G. Tugwell to T. Roy Reid, 16 March 1936, ibid.

28. For examples of Evans's work, see Evans, memorandum to John O. Walker, 15 September 1937, ibid.; Evans, memorandum to Will W. Alexander, 1 November 1937, ibid. See also John Hope Franklin, *From Slavery to Freedom: A History of Negro Americans*, 3d ed. (New York: Knopf, 1967), pp. 530–34; Department of the Interior, Appointment of Joseph H. B. Evans, 19 September 1934, FSA Records, NA, RG 96. Evans was an employee in the Division of Subsistence Homesteads before transferring to the RA.

as farm management advisers and field representatives in the rural rehabilitation or tenant purchase programs. Given the large black population
of the region, the actual number of Negro personnel was absurdly low.
In 1939 the agency employed eleven Negroes in Arkansas, seven in
Louisiana, and fourteen in Mississippi.[29]

Tugwell originally intended to have a Negro staff wholly responsible
for projects in which clients were black. But no Negro ever ran a rural
resettlement project without white supervision. When T. Arnold Hill of
the National Urban League inquired if Negro projects would have Negro
managers, Alexander promised him that would indeed be the case. "The
matter of putting white people in charge of Negro projects has never at
any time been considered by the [Resettlement] Administration," he wrote
Hill. But Alexander did place whites in charge of Negro projects, although the managers of most such projects had a black assistant. Besides
the community manager's regular responsibilities, this position was a
public relations job, a consideration which supposedly ruled out Negro
leadership at the top of any project.[30]

Negro protests generally contained less potential danger to resettlement work than did the aroused wrath of the white majority over racial
matters. Despite all precautions and the limited use of Negro personnel,
racism was a nagging problem. Concerning Negro participation in FSA
programs, a Mississippi woman wrote: "I know that the aim of this Administration is to force racial equality on us here in the South, and the
farm program is the biggest weapon they have. Government lending
without security and wastefulness in general," she said, "is killing what
little thrift and initiative our Negroes had to start with."[31]

In 1938 a group of Adams County, Mississippi, citizens decided that
the FSA had gone too far. They drew up a resolution protesting the employment of a Negro in the county office at Natchez. He served as
assistant rural rehabilitation supervisor for Adams County. They called
attention to the fact that the FSA office was in the courthouse, that "young
white ladies" were employed in the office and came into contact with the

29. E. B. Whitaker to the author, 30 October 1970; William F. Littlejohn, memorandum to George S. Mitchell, 14 November 1940, FSA Records, NA, RG 96; T.
Roy Reid to Will W. Alexander, 26 April 1940, ibid.; Roy Hendrickson, memorandum to Mitchell, 24 May 1940, ibid.
30. There was a black manager in the subsistence homesteads program: William
Walker ran Aberdeen Gardens, a project at Newport News, Virginia. See Kifer,
"The Negro under the New Deal," pp. 156–78. T. Arnold Hill to Will W. Alexander,
9 June 1936, FSA Records, NA, RG 96; Alexander to Hill, 13 June 1936, ibid.
31. Ruby (Mrs. J. J.) Pugh to George Mitchell, 9 September 1941, ibid.

Negro employee. Sen. Theodore G. Bilbo also strongly protested this "outrage." "You," he wrote M. T. Aldrich, "as a good Mississippian, should clean out this situation at once." "Mississippi is still a white man's country," he said, "and we do not want Negroes bumping up against our white girls in the official life of the state."[32]

The FSA quickly yielded to prejudice. Adams County had 133 Negro clients, Reid explained to Bilbo; "it is necessary for someone to contact them and go into homes and work intimately with them in the home and farm planning operations." The Negro employee "does not have an office with white people," Reid added. "It is not the desire of this office to place a Negro worker where it is objectionable to the people."

Assistant administrator Milo Perkins thought that officials had acted in accordance with a "well established principle throughout the South" —that of letting Negroes work with Negroes. In addition, Perkins noted, the black assistant supervisor "was to operate entirely under the immediate supervision of the white rural rehabilitation supervisor and was to spend all his time in the field. Consequently, he would have had no occasion to enter into office relationships with the other employees of the county unit." The unfortunate man was transferred out of Adams County, presumably to a more congenial location. A standard excuse was that officials would "employ Negro personnel when it can be done without creating a situation that would injure rather than improve the advancement of the colored people."[33]

The FSA did not in every case yield to such protests, but its representatives were very circumspect in the sensitive area of race relations, always anxious to avoid any unnecessary disturbance of southern prejudice. In truth, they had all the problems they could handle without getting involved with a crusade for racial equality.

The resettlement agencies did not operate as if in a political vacuum, going about nobly uplifting the rural poor and blithely ignoring the realities of power. Rexford Tugwell automatically consulted congressional leaders when appointing men to top positions. In 1935 he wrote President Roosevelt that Reid was "a democrat and acceptable to Senator [Joseph T.] Robinson." After six years Reid left Little Rock for a Washington post, and a Mississippian, A. D. Stewart, took his place. Before Stewart

32. Rep. Dan R. McGehee to C. B. Baldwin, 31 October 1938, ibid.; Sen. Theodore G. Bilbo to M. T. Aldrich, 29 October 1938, ibid.
33. T. Roy Reid to Sen. Theodore G. Bilbo, 4 November 1938; Milo Perkins to Sen. Pat Harrison, 18 November 1938; A. D. Stewart to C. B. Baldwin, 10 December 1941, all ibid.

was formally offered the job, Farm Security administrator C. B. Baldwin cleared the appointment with Senators Pat Harrison and Theodore G. Bilbo of Stewart's home state.[34] Men like Robinson, Harrison, and Bilbo were extensions of the region's influence in a greatly magnified form.

While the congressional delegations from Region VI were as conservative as their constituents, they supplied votes time after time for New Deal legislation. They voted almost unanimously for the Bankhead-Jones Act in 1937, and in the heyday of Farm Security they backed its appropriations. They often tried to secure resettlement projects for their district or state, they appeared at project dedications, and occasionally they became involved in disputes with the agency.

The name Joseph Taylor Robinson properly dominates any discussion of Arkansas and the New Deal. It was in part because of the Southern Tenant Farmers' Union that the Senate majority leader so strongly favored federal tenancy legislation. Eastern Arkansas, he remarked in the course of Senate debates in 1935, was fallow ground for "seeds of discontent, professional agitators, representatives of communistic and socialistic organizations and schools," and his inference was clear.[35] He defended the right of tenants to organize, but he believed agitators in eastern Arkansas wanted to create trouble rather than help tenants. As proof he alluded to Ward Rogers's speech at Marked Tree.

Yet Robinson was full of surprises. At a meeting with H. L. Mitchell and other STFU leaders during the Democratic National Convention the following year, he stunned them by agreeing to fight for a platform plank endorsing the extension of the Wagner Labor Relations Act to agricultural workers. If enacted, this change would have given farm labor the same guarantees that industrial workers enjoyed to organize and bargain collectively for better hours, wages, and working conditions.[36]

Robinson claimed to have been working on a draft of a tenancy bill when Sen. John H. Bankhead introduced his measure, and in order to facilitate passage he abandoned his own plans.[37] In 1935 Joe Robinson drove the Bankhead bill through the Senate, speaking for it time after time and opposing any crippling amendments; and he repeated the per-

34. Rexford G. Tugwell to the President, 10 July 1935, ibid.; C. B. Baldwin, telegram to R. W. Hudgens, 7 February 1941, ibid.

35. *Congressional Record*, vol. 79, 74th Cong., 1st sess., 18 April 1935, pp. 5927–28.

36. Donald H. Grubbs, *Cry from the Cotton: The Southern Tenant Farmers' Union and the New Deal* (Chapel Hill: University of North Carolina Press, 1971), p. 137.

37. *Congressional Record*, vol. 79, 74th Cong., 1st sess., 18 April 1935, p. 5923.

formance in 1937. No doubt he saw the political value in a program to help relieve the national administration of an embarrassment; but his motivation probably went beyond mere party regularity, the standard explanation of why Robinson supported New Deal legislation with which he presumably did not agree. The Bankhead-Jones concept of the family farm was quite compatible even with Robinson's conservative views, and it was also a possible way to defuse the growing social discontent of eastern Arkansas.

Senator Robinson and the Resettlement Administration got off to a minor disagreement when Tugwell switched the regional headquarters from Fayetteville to Little Rock without consulting the Arkansas senator. As majority leader, Robinson presumably could have exercised a powerful veto over resettlement activities in his home state if he so wished; instead, he approved of RA programs, and not reluctantly. He attended the dedication of Plum Bayou. "Nothing, in my judgment," he said in his speech, "is better calculated to sustain the fundamental institutions upon which society and government in the United States rests, than the effective encouragement of home ownership." He supported the Resettlement Administration in the agency's budget fights; and it was chiefly through his efforts, according to his biographer, Nevin Eugene Neal, that RA funds were not cut. For his efforts, Neal writes, Resettlement officials showed little appreciation.[38]

Yet Reid remained on friendly terms with Arkansas's senior senator. After a conference with Robinson in late 1936, Reid reported that he held a favorable attitude toward resettlement work; "he seems," Reid wrote, "to be pleased that he helped push the passage of the Bankhead-Jones Bill through the Senate."[39] With Robinson's death in the summer of 1937, FSA leaders lost a friend whom they could not replace.

The RA and FSA received support from other members of the congressional delegations of the three states. Pat Harrison, chairman of the Senate Finance Committee, had helped attach the subsistence homesteads section to the National Industrial Recovery Act, and his state became one of the program's major beneficiaries. He later favored tenancy legislation. In 1936 the Mississippi senior senator wrote Tugwell that he "followed the Resettlement Administration one hundred per cent." His colleague, Theodore G. Bilbo, was enthusiastic about the Bankhead-Jones bill, but

38. Quoted in Nevin Eugene Neal, "A Biography of Joseph T. Robinson" (Ph.D. diss., University of Oklahoma, 1958), p. 398.
39. T. Roy Reid to Will W. Alexander, 23 December 1936, FSA Records, NA, RG 96.

largely as a means of undercutting his neighbor, Huey Long. He knew full well that the bill would not solve his state's tenancy problem. Yet he was, he declared on the Senate floor, in sympathy with the work being done by the Resettlement Administration.[40]

Arkansas congressman Wilbur D. Mills was "very much interested in our program," wrote C. B. Baldwin in 1939, "and was to a large extent responsible for the fact that our part of the program did not strike any snag in [the House Banking and Currency] committee." The same year, Cong. A. Leonard Allen of Louisiana told a constituent: "I think I have often said that I was as much interested, or perhaps more, in the work this department [FSA] is doing, than any other agency created by the Roosevelt Administration. . . . This is one New Deal agency that I would like to see continued and I have no hesitancy in voting funds for it."[41]

Congressional relations turned sour during World War II, but even before then everything was not always sweetness and light. In December 1937 Sen. John E. Miller, who took Robinson's seat, protested against "federal jobs not being given to administration supporters in Arkansas." The context of Miller's complaint was obviously political. He had just won election in a special primary in which a coalition of most federal agencies was alleged to have been arrayed against a faction known as the statehouse crowd. Although Reid personally stayed out of politics, some of his county supervisors and other local employees evidently had sided with Miller's opponent. Now Miller told Secretary of Agriculture Wallace that the "economic slant" and "social views" of some of the out-of-state persons appointed to FSA jobs in Arkansas were not in accord with the American form of government.[42]

Of all the political problems the Resettlement Administration faced in Region VI, none had more explosive potential than that of Sen. Huey P. Long and his political machine. As discussed earlier, regional officials got their politically independent organization in Louisiana, but Long died while the organization was still in an embryonic stage, its operation never tested. They luckily escaped a situation that could have been disastrous.[43]

40. Sen. Pat Harrison to R. G. Tugwell, 16 July 1936, ibid.; Baldwin, *Poverty and Politics*, p. 70; *Congressional Record*, vol. 81, 75th Cong., 1st sess., 28 June 1937, pp. 6758–60.
41. C. B. Baldwin to T. Roy Reid, 25 August 1939, FSA Records, NA, RG 96; Rep. A. Leonard Allen to Col. A. L. Smith, 13 May 1939, ibid. Reid often met with congressional delegations from Region VI. See Reid to Will W. Alexander, 14 March 1939, ibid.
42. R. M. Allison, interview with the author, 11 April 1973; Little Rock *Arkansas Gazette*, 16, 18 December 1937.
43. See above, Chapter V.

Reid wanted to build up support among state political leaders, but he met widely different attitudes toward the plight of farm tenants and share-croppers. Arkansas's J. M. Futrell apparently recognized the seriousness of the sharecropping situation, and he hoped that other states in the South would follow his example by setting up their own tenancy commissions. Gov. Richard W. Leche of Louisiana commented only that "it never hurts to discuss a situation." Gov. Hugh White, whose state had the highest tenancy rate in the nation, declared, "we have no sharecropping problem in Mississippi that I know anything about."[44] Neither Louisiana nor Mississippi ever showed as much official concern for tenancy as did Arkansas. If Governors Futrell, Leche, and White accurately reflected public opinion in their respective states, one should not be surprised to find Arkansas most receptive to New Deal resettlement activities.

Ernest Whitworth Marland of Oklahoma was the only governor to follow Futrell's suggestion, while Arkansas went on to see a second farm tenancy commission. Gov. Carl Bailey reappointed the old commission in 1937, keeping many original members but adding Brooks Hays, who was then with the FSA, state labor commissioner Edward I. McKinley, Sr., and a few state legislators. Following the commission's recommendations, the Arkansas General Assembly passed the Land Policy Act of 1939, implementing a program of cooperation between the state land commission and federal agencies to dispose of forfeited state lands by sale in family-sized tracts. This had been one of the original commission's key proposals. Arkansas, a state usually reviled for its backwardness, proved for once to be a leader.[45]

Taking advantage of the new law, the Farm Security Administration, the Bureau of Agricultural Economics, and the State Land Office combined their resources to purchase 500,000 acres of tax-forfeited lands in eastern Arkansas. The regional office planned to divide the land into 5,000 homesteads for low-income farmers, but the program came too late to accomplish much.[46]

The New Deal resettlement agencies ran into their most serious opposition, both political and ideological, from farm organizations. All major

44. *Arkansas Gazette*, 16 August 1936.
45. Ibid., 13 November 1937; Grubbs, *Cry from the Cotton*, pp. 124–25; Arkansas Land Policy Act (Act 331), approved 16 March 1939, *Acts . . . of the Fifty-second General Assembly of the State of Arkansas . . .* (Little Rock: Arkansas Printing and Lithographing, 1939), pp. 863–71.
46. For the implementation of the new program, see *Arkansas Gazette*, 2, 3 May 1941.

organized farm groups operated in one or more of the three states.[47] In Arkansas the Southern Tenant Farmers' Union, the American Farm Bureau Federation, and the National Farmers Union were active, as was the National Grange to a lesser degree. Louisiana farmers had to choose either the Farm Bureau or the Farmers Union, while Mississippians had only the Farm Bureau. Since both the STFU and the Farmers Union were dealing with roughly the same class of people, they reached an agreement in 1941: neither would set up an organization in territory where the other was already organized.[48]

For Region VI this arrangement meant that the STFU would continue unchallenged in most of eastern Arkansas, but left the rest of the state and all of Louisiana to the Farmers Union. Since the STFU tended to expand toward the newer cotton regions of the southwest rather than to the older lands of the east, the union never attempted to organize in Mississippi.[49] The Farmers Union limited its efforts to Arkansas and Louisiana. The Farm Bureau was, then, the only farm organization to function in all three states of Region VI.

Following national policy, regional officials tried to work with all major farm groups. They encouraged membership in farm organizations without becoming active partisans for any one group. Nor did they attempt to hinder the development of any organization.[50] Many resettlement projects had their own "farm bureaus," and STFU membership was not uncommon among resettlement clients in eastern Arkansas.[51] Yet a policy of neutrality could guarantee nothing when opposition came from both sides of the political spectrum, the Southern Tenant Farmers' Union on the left and the Farm Bureau on the right.

When members of the STFU were being evicted in the winter of 1936, the union's friends besieged Washington headquarters with pleas for action. Tugwell, Alexander, and Brooks Hays were anxious to help, promising funds for direct relief and the placement of evicted families on resettlement projects. But in Little Rock the union's pleas did not elicit the same eager response. Washington officials, wrote the union's lobbyist, Gardner Jackson, "either frankly or tacitly admit that they cannot make

47. T. Roy Reid to Will W. Alexander, 7 May 1940, FSA Records, NA, RG 96.
48. H. L. Mitchell to James G. Patton, 11 September 1941, ibid.; see also Mitchell to George S. Mitchell, 2 September 1941, ibid.
49. H. L. Mitchell, Columbia Oral History Project interview, mimeographed, STFU Papers.
50. T. Roy Reid to J. R. Butler, 26 March 1937, ibid.; Reid to C. B. Baldwin, 25 October 1940, FSA Records, NA, RG 96.
51. See the situation which developed at Dyess Colony, in the next chapter.

the local and regional officials in Arkansas carry out" their directives.[52] Even Floyd Sharp of the WPA at first held back aid. Little Rock officials feared the wrath of Senator Robinson if they took the side of the croppers, or so union leaders believed. Perhaps another reason centered on the horror which Socialism inspired in their minds; times may have been hard, but Socialism was not something most people wanted to be identified with.

The assistance the evictees needed, however, was forthcoming. Some of them received standard rehabilitation loans for the coming crop year. Others later found places on resettlement projects. For example, the Twist Cooperative Leasing Association, located in Cross and Crittenden counties, where evictions were most numerous, became a virtual STFU enterprise.[53]

Union leaders also found themselves in disagreement with the New Deal's basic approach to farm tenancy. When the President's Committee on Farm Tenancy recommended privately owned family farms, W. L. Blackstone urged in a minority report the establishment of cooperative farm projects; no doubt Blackstone had in mind Delta Cooperative Farm. Similarly the STFU was cold to the Bankhead-Jones farm tenant bill.[54]

In reality, union leaders thought the New Deal was good as far as it went; the problem was that it did not go far enough. The union was not opposed to a policy favoring small farms, Mitchell later claimed; but he questioned whether many tenants and croppers were ready for small farm ownership, since they had always been accustomed to supervision. To Mitchell, the ideal solution would have been for a group of farmers to rent a plantation, dividing half its proceeds among themselves and, since nothing had to go to a private owner, putting the other half into a pool to pay the rent, buy farm equipment, and eventually purchase the plantation outright. The tenants themselves would select a manager to supervise farm operations. "We wanted . . . a village economy where the

52. Gardner Jackson to Marvin McIntyre, 12 March 1936, quoted in Grubbs, Cry from the Cotton, p. 95; David E. Conrad, The Forgotten Farmers: The Story of Sharecroppers in the New Deal (Urbana: University of Illinois Press, 1965), p. 176; Howard [Kester] to [H. L.] Mitchell, 21 February 1936, STFU Papers; Brooks Hays to Kester, 1 February 1936, Howard Kester Papers, part of STFU Papers; Mitchell, conversation with the author, 9 March 1971; Norman Thomas to Mitchell and Kester, 8 April 1935, Socialist Party Papers.
53. H. L. Mitchell to the author, 29 January 1973; Memphis Press-Scimitar, 3 February 1940; Mitchell, Oral History interview.
54. National Resources Board, Farm Tenancy: Report of the President's Committee (Washington: Government Printing Office, 1937), p. 22.

workers lived in a village and worked out on the farms with a certain small acreage of land where each man could have his own garden and raise his own food," Mitchell explained. "We visualized something similar to what they have in Europe where the workers all live in one central village."[55]

Besides ideological differences, STFU leaders criticized the local administration of the resettlement and rural rehabilitation programs. They complained that the Resettlement Administration's decentralized organization kept it from fulfilling its obligations. Too much authority had been given to local and state committees, committees that helped decide who received loans and other assistance. "If the Resettlement Administration is to adequately serve the people who need its services, political and antisocial officials should be removed and replaced by men who have a broad knowledge of the problems involved and sympathy and interest in the people."[56]

In 1940 the union's sixth annual convention adopted a series of resolutions which summed up their criticisms of the resettlement program. The FSA's "greatest drawback," the delegates said, was "faulty local administration." The convention went on record recommending that 1) "dirt farmers" be put on local administrating committees, 2) Congress appropriate larger sums of money to make the program more effective, 3) more large cooperative projects be set up, 4) special projects be set up to care for migrant farm workers in southern cotton regions, and 5) the FSA be created as a permanent agency independent of the Department of Agriculture. The Farm Security Administration, they were saying, was not doing enough, was doing some things wrong, and could do everything better.[57]

At the same time, the STFU and the FSA moved closer together, and before long they found much common ground. Charles M. Measles, La-

55. Mitchell, Oral History interview.

56. STFU, Executive Council, A Statement concerning Farm Tenancy Submitted to the Governor's Commission on Farm Tenancy, STFU Papers. The Share Croppers' Union (SCU) of Alabama was similarly critical of the Resettlement Administration. In Arkansas, the *Southern Farm Leader* charged, STFU members had been thrown off RA programs after they protested graft. According to the SCU paper, the Resettlement Administration made loans in Louisiana "to people who do not need them and denied them to needy croppers and tenants. Croppers and tenants who do get loans are told what and where to buy and very seldom see the cash. Not one Resettlement farmer we know of has a copy of the Resettlement Contract. The field agents act as complete dictators." *Southern Farm Leader*, May 1936, copy in STFU Papers.

57. "Proceedings of the Sixth Annual Convention, Southern Tenant Farmers' Union," ibid.

bor Relations director for Region VI, sought to improve relations between the two organizations by taking part in the convention. Speaking to the delegates, Measles expressed pleasure that the STFU favored larger appropriations for resettlement work, and promised the union sympathy and cooperation from his office. "I believe that you are fighting for the same things we are," he told the delegates, "and I pledge you our full cooperation. All we need is more money and a chance to help." In a question-and-answer session, some delegates still showed suspicion, but Measles was not easily ruffled. What should we do when local officials of the FSA fail to cooperate? someone asked him. Surprisingly, Measles admitted that some project managers and other officials should be changed.[58]

After their initial difficulties, union and regional officials worked well together; and when Reid left Little Rock in 1941, union leaders felt some trepidation about his replacement, largely because, Mitchell later recalled, A. D. Stewart was from Mississippi. Mitchell saw Stewart a few months after he assumed his new job, and wrote of him, "He appears to be a broken down politician and much less intelligent than T. Roy." This first impression was quite unfair.

The purpose of Mitchell's visit with the new regional director was to get the assistance of FSA county supervisors in building a union organization, including their encouragement to clients to pay union dues as crops were sold. Regional director Ernest S. Morgan of Region V (Alabama, Georgia, South Carolina, and Florida) eagerly cooperated, but Region VI was cool. "That region," Mitchell wrote, "won't play ball with us no matter what Washington says, though quite interesting he [Stewart] betrayed that Washington had made such a suggestion."[59]

C. B. Baldwin had in fact reminded regional directors at Montgomery and Dallas of Secretary of Agriculture Claude Wickard's memorandum dated 21 March 1941, stating that the STFU was a "group to be considered as a worthy effort to improve the position of low income farm people and one . . . which it would be entirely proper for your field people to have a cordial relationship with."[60] Baldwin's reminder apparently did not go to Little Rock. In any event, Stewart remained as cool as ever. Yet as time went on, Stewart and Mitchell became friendly, and in the end he proved to be more helpful to the union's cause than had Reid.

58. Ibid.
59. H. L. Mitchell to the author, 29 January 1973; Mitchell to George Mitchell, 16 June 1941; "Mitch" to Butler, 18 June 1941 (quote); see also Mitchell to John Beecher, 22 June 1941; and Mitchell, memorandum to Mr. and Mrs. J. D. Overholt, 19 July 1941, all ibid.
60. Quoted in C. B. Baldwin to Ernest S. Morgan, 2 July 1941, ibid.

Meanwhile Reid commented that the FSA was already doing everything the STFU currently advocated.[61] Perhaps projects like Terrebonne and Lake Dick were in part concessions to STFU demands for cooperative farming. The land-leasing program, too, was roughly similar to Mitchell's plan, minus the European analogy. But Reid's statement became possible because the union had moderated its demands somewhat. In their eighth annual convention (1942), union delegates passed a resolution "that the STFU seek to preserve the family type farm way of life, to help provide cooperative services for purchasing goods, marketing and preserving farm products, and to fully support all programs designed to reestablish farm people on the land." What had brought the STFU and regional officials together, however, was the threat of a mutual enemy.[62]

The Farm Bureau was just as devoted as the Southern Tenant Farmers' Union to promoting the interests of farmers—but not the same farmers. While some critics have charged that the Farm Bureau did not represent farmers at all, its membership consisted mainly of large-scale commercial farmers—the kind of farmers who benefited most from the Farm Bureau's concern for commodity prices and unconcern for rural welfare programs.

After the depression struck, Farm Bureau leaders quickly defined agricultural problems in terms of national responsibility and looked to Washington for action.[63] Not surprisingly, men like Ed O'Neal rode an inside track in the early New Deal. Henry Wallace consulted with all farm organizations during the Hundred Days, but the Farm Bureau played a crucial role by uniting farmers in both the Midwest and South behind the Agricultural Adjustment Act. While Farm Bureau leaders deserved little credit for helping to formulate agricultural policy, the AAA did favor the interests of landlords and large farmers, which exactly fit the Farm Bureau's idea of whose interests national farm policy should favor. But as the New Deal began responding to the needs of tenant farmers and small farm owners, O'Neal found less and less to be happy about. When President Roosevelt created the Resettlement Administration in 1935,

61. T. Roy Reid, memorandum to C. B. Baldwin, 4 October 1941, FSA Records, NA, RG 96.

62. H. L. Mitchell to C. B. Baldwin, 16 January 1942, ibid. See, for example, "Farm Bureau Advocates Abolition of Tenant Program," *Tenant Farmer* 1 (15 July 1941): 1; Leonard G. Herron, "How Farm Security Administration Is Helping Tenant Farmers, Sharecroppers, Farm Laborers," *Tenant Farmer* 1 (15 August 1941): 2.

63. Christiana McFadyen Campbell, *The Farm Bureau and the New Deal: A Study of the Making of National Farm Policy, 1933–40* (Urbana: University of Illinois Press, 1962), pp. 22–29.

Farm Bureau leaders adopted an indifferent attitude; they were equally unenthusiastic about the Bankhead-Jones bill of 1937.[64] They offered neither active opposition nor active support.

As for Region VI, all farm organizations, Reid wrote in 1940, supported the Farm Security Administration. "The Farm Bureau has probably been less active in its support of the activities of the Administration than any of the other organizations," he conceded.[65] Within a matter of weeks, however, the Farm Bureau launched a vicious attack against the FSA on both the national and local levels.

Before the New Deal, federal assistance to agriculture went to education and research in the form of grants-in-aid. The United States Agricultural Extension Service and the Office of Experiment Stations stood at the top of a ponderous federal-state arrangement which reached down through state land grant colleges, experiment stations, and extension services. At the end of the line was the county agent, who brought the system into contact with the individual farmer. Paralleling this official structure was the American Farm Bureau Federation (AFBF) with its network of state and county Farm Bureaus. Since its inception about 1920, the AFBF had assumed a quasi-public status, developing close ties with the extension service system and monopolizing the machinery of agricultural administration.

When the New Deal revolutionized the federal agricultural landscape, the stage for conflict was set. The Farm Security Administration, like the Resettlement Administration before it, collided with the old-line establishment. So did several other agencies, including the Soil Conservation Service, the Rural Electrification Administration, the Farm Credit Administration, and even occasionally the Agricultural Adjustment Administration. What all of these agencies did "wrong" was simple.

The Agricultural Extension Service had long claimed to be the sole medium of contact for the entire USDA in reaching out to the farmer on his farm, and it looked with little sympathy toward any competition. The New Deal agencies, however, made their own contacts with farmers through their own agents. The FSA's county supervisor, particularly, was seen as an interloper on the private preserve of the county agent; and FSA programs overlapped agricultural extension and home demonstration work, but with a difference. The Extension Service tended to serve well-to-do farmers who could best take advantage of advice, while ignor-

---

64. Grant McConnell, *The Decline of Agrarian Democracy* (Berkeley and Los Angeles: University of California Press, 1959), pp. 97–101.

65. T. Roy Reid to Will W. Alexander, 7 May 1940, FSA Records, NA, RG 96.

ing impoverished farm families that needed help but found it difficult to avail themselves of it. Perhaps farm management and home demonstration work was supposed to "trickle down." The FSA, on the other hand, brought help directly to the chronically impoverished farm families that had been virtually ignored by the agricultural establishment.[66]

While the Resettlement Administration was still in its infancy, Tugwell and the Extension Service signed a "memorandum of understanding." The two organizations agreed that the Resettlement Administration would permit Extension Service officials a large role in the administration of its programs. A short time later Carl C. Taylor, national director of the Rural Resettlement Division, told a conference of extension officials at Fayetteville, Arkansas, that "sooner or later, the Extension Service shall take over entire responsibility" for the rural rehabilitation program; and there were other resettlement officials who would welcome such a move.[67] But they were out of tune with Tugwell's plans, and the memo of understanding became a dead letter.

At first a natural alliance existed between the Resettlement Administration and the region's agricultural establishment—an alliance that was especially close in Arkansas. Reid himself served twelve years as assistant director of the Arkansas Extension Service, and when he left for his federal assignment he brought with him many of his colleagues. He had every reason to expect full and beneficial cooperation.

In order to bring the region's agricultural leadership into general policy planning, Reid in early 1936 set up three state land committees whose memberships included, among others, the dean of the college of agriculture and director of extension work in each state.[68] These committees, as mentioned earlier, approved resettlement areas and made general recommendations in regard to the resettlement program, but they also provided a means of securing the endorsement of agricultural leaders for what he wanted to do. As regional director, Reid no doubt hoped to make use of his ties with the Extension Service, but he ran into trouble where he probably least expected it—in Arkansas.

The Resettlement Administration embittered Dan T. Gray, dean of the Arkansas College of Agriculture and director of the Extension Service, when it established regional headquarters at Little Rock rather than at

66. See Orville Merton Kile, *The Farm Bureau through Three Decades* (Baltimore: Waverly, 1948), pp. 264–69; Campbell, *The Farm Bureau and the New Deal*, chap. 10.

67. Baldwin, *Poverty and Politics*, p. 116.

68. T. Roy Reid to R. G. Tugwell, 11 February 1936, FSA Records, NA, RG 96; see Dan T. Gray to Will W. Alexander, 10 June 1937, ibid.

Fayetteville. In the spring of 1936, still feeling resentful and suspicious, Gray complained that "RA authorities never did consult with authorities of the College of Agriculture before their policies were announced." "The RA," he continued, "has simply announced what is to be done in Arkansas and then come around in a very friendly way and asked cooperation of those associated with the College of Agriculture." "The two organizations—ours and theirs—are, as a matter of fact, just moving along side by side, without any serious attempt at fundamental cooperation."[69]

Specifically, Gray disagreed with the selection of resettlement areas. Concentrate the resettlement program in the hill country of northern Arkansas, he advised, thin out farmers on poor lands, increase the size of farms, and stress livestock production. Disagreeing, Reid argued that northern Arkansas was too thickly settled, good farm land was scarce and high-priced, and much of the land was submarginal. He favored buying up such submarginal land, moving people off (not keeping them on it), and resettling them on alluvial land in the river bottoms. "I do not think that he is critical of our particular purchases," Reid wrote of Gray, "but that he is critical of the fact that we are attempting to resettle farmers on family-size farms rather than on larger commercial farms."[70] But in 1937 and 1938 the College of Agriculture became perhaps even more unsympathetic with resettlement activities, feeling that the program in Arkansas was being carried on with a "lack of capable planning and failure to utilize proven knowledge and experience."[71] They naturally felt they could provide the proper guidance. The seeds of future strife had been sown.

By the time Reid resigned the regional directorship, the FSA and the Farm Bureau were locked in a death struggle, and circumstances demanded a different kind of regional director. By Mississippi standards, A. D. Stewart was a liberal. He was no longer part of the state's agricultural establishment, probably a strong recommendation in his favor. He possessed another quality which came in handy: he was more combative than Reid, more willing to wade into a public fight. Otherwise he fit the familiar mold.

Born on a Mississippi farm, Stewart made agriculture his life's work.

69. Dan T. Gray to Raymond A. Pearson, 20 April 1936, ibid.
70. T. Roy Reid to Will W. Alexander, 15 May 1937, ibid.
71. C. D. Kinsman to M. L. Wilson, 20 July 1937, ibid.

He took an agriculture degree at Mississippi A & M College, like so many other Farm Security employees in the region. While he did not rise as high in the establishment as Reid did, he acquired his Extension Service pedigree during five years as county agent at Mendenhall, Mississippi. He went on to become director of the state Agricultural Service Department, an organization concerned with agricultural production and marketing; then he served as executive director and general manager of the Mississippi Co-operative Cotton Association. He became regional director in February 1941 after a year's apprenticeship as head of the Jackson office.[72]

In Reid's six years the regional office put down deep roots. By the end of 1940 the resettlement projects were complete, and had assumed full operational status. The county supervisors had established themselves in courthouses all over the region, sometimes right next door to the office of the county agent. Rural rehabilitation loans remained their major activity, with the tenant purchase program quite limited. In 1941 the regional organization was rendering assistance to more than fifty thousand farm families in all phases of its program.

Most of the community projects became quiet affairs once the initial excitement died down, but they remained open invitations to controversy. Like all human endeavors, they included some bad eggs. Lake Dick, the cooperative experiment near Altheimer, Arkansas, known locally as Little Russia, fell flat, perhaps flatter than any other project in the region. It just would not work. The rough Arkansas farmers were not ready to submit themselves to the kind of discipline cooperative farming demanded and to forsake their dream of land ownership. They, like regional officials, looked on the project as a transitional stage.

In 1938 or 1939 Will Alexander and M. L. Wilson, then undersecretary of agriculture, inspected Lake Dick, a visit which occasioned an often-repeated story. They were given a tour of the project by one of the clients, who had learned well the mechanics of cooperatives, and he talked enthusiastically about the project. Late that afternoon Alexander got him off by himself. "Now, man to man, how are you getting along here?" Alexander asked. "I'm doing better than I ever done before," he answered. "Look at the house I'm a-living in. My wife don't go to the fields, and my children go to school. I don't have to work as hard as I used do. This co-operative farming is fine. Why, I believe a man could

72. *Arkansas Gazette*, 12 February 1941; E. B. Whitaker to the author, 10 October 1972; T. B. Fatherree to the author, 28 November 1972.

stay around here four or five years and save enough money to go out and buy him a little hill farm all his own."[73]

By 1941 more than a third of the homes stood vacant and the project was deep in unmowed grass. A year later almost two-thirds of the families were gone. They evidently fled to those hill farms or, more likely, to jobs at Pine Bluff. The regional office soon gave up the attempt to operate the project as originally planned; Negro families replaced the few white families that remained, and farmed the land as sharecroppers.[74]

In Louisiana, Transylvania never shook free from embarrassing controversies. On 9 June 1939 the Lake Providence *Banner Democrat* carried a brief front-page story of an automobile accident near Tallulah in which two men and a girl were killed and another girl was hurt. No names and few details were given. George Wolf had persuaded the *Banner* editor to make no mention of the fact that the two men were FSA personnel assigned to the nearby Transylvania project—plus the fact that they were both drunk at the time of the accident. "We have had so much trouble down there," Wolf wrote, "I was afraid the crowning touch would be the project getting the reputation of hiring a bunch of drunks."[75]

His effort to cover up the facts almost worked, as it perhaps did in other cases, but the *Banner* editor apparently forgot to tell a society writer about his agreement with the FSA. There it was, printed on an inside page of the same issue: the story Wolf wanted suppressed, and written with a strong dose of moral disapproval. This version of the accident told what the men did for a living and their names—Leroy Haggerty and J. G. Enright—but not the names of the girls (they were presumably from upstanding local families), called attention to the fact that both men were forty years of age, the girls twenty or less, and pointed out that one man was married. The accident took place, the society writer further revealed, at four o'clock in the morning, after the couples left the Cat Head Club at Tallulah. The men "had no less than ten drinks each," but the girls, readers were assured, had not been drinking at all.

It was a unique incident, but such trouble could no longer be taken lightly. Before 1940 the Resettlement Administration and the Farm Se-

73. Dykeman and Stokely, *Seeds of Southern Change*, p. 220.
74. Henry Reynolds, "High Hopes Crumble on Lake Dick Resettlement Project," Memphis *Commercial Appeal*, 6 July 1941; John L. Fletcher, "Farming Co-op Plan Has Not Been Success—33 of 80 Lake Dick Houses Vacant," *Arkansas Gazette*, 8 July 1941; ibid., 3 December 1942. See also Donald Crichton Alexander, *The Arkansas Plantation, 1920–1942* (New Haven: Yale University Press, 1943), pp. 73–74.
75. George Wolf to Jack [John Fischer], 27 June 1939, FSA Records, NA, RG 96.

curity Administration enjoyed a friendly environment in Region VI, and regional officials worked hard to keep it that way. They sought to minimize conflict through good public relations. When running into opposition, they seemed to play it by ear, answering the Arkansas legislators' charges, trying to divide the opposition in the case of the Mississippi bankers, or giving ground on the race question. The resettlement agencies typically were willing to challenge southern traditions, but only if no objections were raised. They played politics where necessary, maintaining their neutrality in Louisiana politics and in the rivalries among major farm organizations.

If the resettlement program rode on a broad consensus in the mid-1930s, that was clearly evaporating by the end of the decade. After 1939 the tempo of criticism picked up; curiously, the orthodox parts of the program came under fire as much as the more unorthodox. Soon opposition coalesced, and the FSA ran up against a bitter, organized campaign. As this struggle was being joined, the regional office took on a task which could only be a serious liability.

Chapter XII

Dyess Colony: Trouble in Paradise

The houses of Dyess Colony, wrote newspaperman Jonathan Daniels, were like "debutantes in the slums," deliberately emphasizing the squalor of the sharecropper cabins he passed on his way from Tyronza. "I crossed the colony line like a man moving across a frontier," he wrote. Another reporter, Philip Kinsley, who was there about the same time, approached the colony from the opposite direction, through the monstrous Lee Wilson Company plantation, Dyess's well-known neighbor. The Wilson cabins, lined up one after another for miles, reminded him of the standardized poverty of mining towns. Upon reaching the colony, Kinsley felt his spirits lift. "The unprepossessing homes of sharecroppers," he said, "gave way to broad roads bordering neat homes with front yards flaming in purple, feathery flowers that wave like banners of dignity and freedom. The houses are painted and there are barns and out buildings, glimpses of corn and gardens, hay and beans, cows, pigs and chickens."[1] This, it seemed, was the community of prosperous small farms that agrarian dreamers always envisioned. But such fleeting impressions did not reveal what was really happening at Dyess. Amid the purple flowers thrived stories of injustice, mismanagement, and extortion.

During the twelve-year history of the New Deal community program, Dyess Colony generated more internal quarrels and political controversy than any other project in Region VI. When discontent first appeared in 1936, Dyess authorities took the position that the colony offered residents opportunities on a take-it-or-leave-it basis. "No one of you is under any obligation to stay here if he doesn't think he will like it," Lawrence Westbrook told the colonists, "nor is the Corporation under any obliga-

---

1. Jonathan Daniels, *A Southerner Discovers the South* (New York: Da Capo Press, 1970), p. 143; Philip Kinsley, "Communal Farm Plan Hits Snag—Human Nature," *Chicago Tribune*, 25 October 1938.

tion to keep anyone here if its officers feel that that person would not make good and cooperate with the Corporation and with his neighbors. There is no compulsion on either side." Westbrook added: "I merely mention the matter because I have heard that there are a few, a very few, people here in the community who have not understood that the Government was offering them an opportunity they might take on the Government's terms or leave without rancor or prejudice, if they didn't want this particular kind of chance."[2]

Most of the colonists, then and later, put forth an honest effort to take advantage of their new opportunity, made few complaints, and remained confident that the colony administration had their best interests at heart. Harve Smith, one of the original thirteen colonists, was probably typical of the majority of Dyess residents. A newspaper reporter, Frank W. Newell, talked to him after he had lived at Dyess for three and a half years.[3]

"What do you think of this place now?"

"It's the best proposition a poor man ever had," Smith said.

"In what respects?"

"Well, there's nothing against a man here. A man does need more acreage, but still I've got feed enough to do two mules and my other stock this winter. Here, they've given a man a chance when it looked like no one else would."

"Think you'll have any trouble buying your place?"

"Nope. I'll buy it all right."

"What do you think of the cooperative idea for operation of the community center?"

"Swell idea."

"What do you like best about the place?" Newell persisted.

"Well, I've got a home and some good land—best in the world, and an opportunity to buy them. If we boys will just line with them [colony officials] they'll back us, but we wouldn't have a chance without this place. Let me tell you, the sentiment of the farmers is looking up."

"Anything you don't like about it?"

"Well, yes, but it can't be helped. The only thing hurtin' now is this 'PWA' that is putting us on jobs and keeping us off our farms."

Harve worked for the Public Works Administration because he was broke. Having cleared thirty-one acres of land, he lost "near everything"

2. Lawrence Westbrook to Paul V. Maris, 10 August 1936, with enclosures, Hopkins Papers.

3. Little Rock *Arkansas Gazette*, 9 January 1938.

in the flood of 1937: his corn crop, most of his feed, hay, hogs, chickens, and much else. After the flood he tried to make a go of it on a twenty-acre tract. But like many other colonists, he was forced to seek relief work until he could get on his feet again. Smith wanted desperately to get back to farming. He asked: "Why not give me a $25 mortgage on my cow and let me go on my farm and make it back?"

"They've been awful nice to us," Harve concluded. "They've given me a good school for my kids, a good hospital—and a chance."

"I don't suppose you're interested in politics?" Newell asked. In other words, are you part of any dissension movement?

"Nope," Smith grinned. "We ain't interested in politics. I guess we'd just do what 'they' wanted us to."

By 1938, however, a significant number of colonists had indeed developed an interest in "politics." Growing discouraged, many families left the colony when only hard work lay ahead, and the turnover in the early years was excessively large. Other people stayed on and found plenty of things to criticize.

"We came right in the woods," one wife complained to a friend. "Nearly all has cleared their places. The Gov. didnt ask for us to pay anything for 2 years that means food bed clothing, but they have taken all we have made for the last 3 years. We have written letters to our President and we cant get any word to him. We are cut off some where. . . . If there was a Government project that need some one to investigate it surley is this one."[4]

The delay in issuing deeds was a constant source of uncertainty. And when the colonists finally found out how much their homes would cost, many of them thought the price too high. Some families were unhappy with the "furnish" arrangements. Others complained that when they asked for information about their accounts or other matters, they got curses and insults. Their complaints to Washington, they said, were referred back to local officials, getting them in trouble all over again. Still other families felt cheated. They lost mules during the flood in 1937 under circumstances they blamed on the colony management, and they were unhappy with their compensation. A few griped that Dyess Colony, Inc., charged them for hay at twice the price for which it sold in neighboring stores. Throughout 1937 and into 1938 the discontent simmered, waiting for someone to bring it into the open.[5]

4. Edith McCravin to Conrad Espe (copy), 16 January 1938, Sharp Papers. The name McCravin will have more meaning presently.
5. Ibid.; Floyd Sharp to Lawrence Westbrook, 4 April 1938, ibid.

Paul Finch was the first of several dissension leaders, though not himself a colonist. Finch farmed a piece of land adjacent to and partly surrounded by colony property. In 1937 he wrote Dyess officials seeking to buy a piece of the colony's land. They turned him down. He then proposed a land swap which he claimed would benefit both himself and the colony. The answer was still no. This may have increased the antagonism between Finch and colony officials, but he was already unsympathetic with the project. Finch also objected to the establishment of rural free delivery on the colony because he did not want his mail delivered through the Dyess post office. He already knew all he wanted to know about the colony, he said.[6]

On 20 and 21 April 1938, Finch published two articles critical of the colony management in the Memphis *Press-Scimitar*, an afternoon newspaper with a large circulation in northeastern Arkansas.[7] He appeared to be merely a disinterested taxpayer anxious about the well-being of colony families—and perhaps he was.

Claiming that 98 percent of the colonists were dissatisfied, he repeated many of the complaints which circulated through the colony. "The whole trouble," he summed up, "is that the officials have not lived up to what they promised to do, and the colonists have lost all confidence in them." What could be done? Finch believed the colony could be a "paradise" if certain changes were made. Most important, the colonists should have more land, and a real deed with a mortgage behind it. "Cut out these supervisors, riding around telling the colonists nothing, but finding fault with everything they do," he added; "have a manager that can smile and tell them something, and not be cussing them out all the time." He closed both articles with a challenge to any member of the board of Dyess Colony, Inc., for a public discussion at Memphis, Little Rock, or the Dyess community center.

What he really wanted was a chance to speak on the colony itself; but the board chairman, Floyd Sharp, would have nothing to do with it. So Finch began inviting sympathetic colonists to his home just off colony property. Around thirty farmers attended three or four such meetings, and they heard what they came to hear. In one of his newspaper articles

6. Paul Finch to Floyd Sharp, 16 August 1937; E. S. Dudley to H. C. Baker, 18 August, 10 September 1937; Finch to Baker, 6 September 1937; Baker to Finch, 1 October 1937, all ibid.

7. Before turning to the *Press-Scimitar*, Finch had written both Arkansas senators asking for information about the colony, and they in turn made inquiries of Sharp. See John E. Miller to Sharp, 14 May 1938; Sharp to Miller, 11 May 1938; Sharp to Hattie W. Caraway, 4 April 1938, all ibid.

he observed that the colonists would not succeed under the present management. Now Finch called for the replacement of the board of directors with a new colony organization. The colonists, Finch believed, should select their own managers. A board of three men chosen from among the colonists themselves would assume the task of administration at the colony; if their decision were questioned, a jury of twelve men would render the ultimate judgment. The larger body would pass on the eviction of any family.

When Finch saw that his campaign was not getting anywhere, he conceived a plan to provoke an investigation of the colony. He warned Sharp that he was going to speak in several larger towns of Arkansas, and if that did not get results he was going to take his information to big-city newspapers. "There is only one thing," he wrote Sharp on 10 May, "that will stop me from making these speeches to the people of Ark. and this is: for the resignation of your farm and residential Managers together with the supervisors."[8] He demanded that an election be held in which the colonists could vote for whomever they wanted to manage the colony. Sharp did not answer, and Finch's threat turned out to be an empty one.

When he finally did speak on the colony grounds, the evening ended in a free-for-all. On 3 June he went to a schoolhouse where a small crowd waited outside. As he started to read a letter from Sen. John E. Miller outlining the colony's history, five men—two farm supervisors, two colony policemen, and the garage manager—walked up carrying pistols and blackjacks. One of the supervisors, Sam Richardson, ordered Finch to leave the colony. Some name-calling ensued, and Finch knocked Richardson down. The other four then pistol-whipped Finch. The colony physician reportedly stood by without offering any assistance.[9] The incident no doubt confirmed the low opinion of the management in the minds of the dissidents.

From the start Dyess authorities pegged Finch as a troublemaker. To them he had an ulterior motive: he thought he could get himself elected manager. They were just as convinced *they* had the best interest of the colonists at heart. At the scene, resident manager E. S. Dudley gathered information about Finch's activities, keeping tabs on the number who attended his meetings and wondering how his influence could be countered. Dudley dismissed Finch as a "social economist," something apparently very bad.[10]

8. Paul Finch to Floyd Sharp (copy), 10 May 1938, ibid.
9. Notarized statement, dated 18 January 1939, STFU Papers; Floyd Sharp to Sen. Hattie W. Caraway, 6 June 1938, Sharp Papers.
10. E. S. Dudley to H. C. Baker (two drafts), 3 May 1938, ibid.

When Floyd Sharp spoke at the dedication of the new high school in April, he remarked: "Recently some persons residing outside Dyess Colony have been giving some of you a lot of advice—and all of it bad." A man of unquestionable integrity, he consoled himself with the thought that the vast majority of colony families were working hard and had no interest in dissension. In his opinion, the situation was "nothing serious," only "a little wave of criticism" created by "a few agitators." But he also began thinking of ridding himself of the responsibility for Dyess Colony.[11]

Sharp took comfort in another *Press-Scimitar* article, this one written in reply to Finch. The author was Velma Bullard Pittman, a nurse at Memphis. Finch had mentioned her father, Q. A. Bullard, in one of his articles, and the family resented it. In a letter to Sharp, Mrs. Pittman labeled Finch a "fanatic" and "hoodlum."[12] Sharp himself did not want to dignify Finch's articles with an answer, but in a magnificently discreet letter he encouraged her or her father to make a statement refuting Finch's criticism and giving the other side of the story.[13]

Bullard's farm presumably kept him too busy for newspaper work, so his daughter wrote the article. She extolled the opportunity that Dyess Colony provided anyone willing to work hard. "The dissatisfied [colonists] are always listening to outsiders who don't know what they are talking about," wrote Mrs. Pittman, herself an outsider. "The people that are not satisfied," she added, "are those that want everything and are not willing to work for it. You can tell by [the] amount of land they have cleared in the time they have been there."[14]

Privately, however, Sharp did not lay all of the blame on "agitators." One of the most common complaints among colonists had been against rude, abusive treatment; and they had considerable basis for it. In the fall of 1937 the Southern Tenant Farmers' Union conducted an investigation of Dyess Colony, which had a small, struggling union local, and found a "hearty" dislike among the families for the farm manager, Jake Terry. He earned the reputation of being a "typical riding boss." "They say," wrote H. L. Mitchell, "that Terry continually attempts to drive them, cussing them, and that free men from the hills of Arkansas are not accustomed to such treatment." It was, in fact, when Dudley was away on

11. Address of Floyd Sharp, President of Dyess Colony, Incorporated, at the Dedication of the High School, 27 April 1938, enclosed with Sharp to A. D. Stewart, 12 January 1944, FSA Records, NA, RG 96; Sharp to Lawrence Westbrook, 29 April 1938, Sharp Papers; Sharp to Aubrey Williams, 14 May 1938, ibid.
12. Mrs. Velma Bullard Pittman to Floyd Sharp, 21 April 1938, ibid.
13. Floyd Sharp to Mrs. Velma Bullard Pittman, 22 April 1938, ibid.
14. "Reader Answers Dyess Criticism—Fault Is with Malcontents, Not Administration," Memphis *Press-Scimitar*, 2 May 1938.

a trip to Florida and Terry was left in charge that trouble first flared up.[15] Sharp and the board members of Dyess Colony, Inc., had some long sessions regarding Terry. A portion of the unrest among the colonists, Sharp became convinced, resulted from "stubbornness and bad temper on the part of some of our management personnel," meaning in particular Jake Terry. Besides causing dissension among the colony families, Terry did not work well with several members of the administrative force. For a while confusion existed about who was to take orders from whom. Terry claimed to be employed directly by the board and therefore not responsible to the resident manager. When this situation came to the attention of the members of the board in April, they immediately made it clear that Dudley managed "the entire Colony," with Terry and everyone else taking orders from him. This clarification relieved Dudley of an embarrassing situation, and his performance immediately improved.[16]

Dudley in turn suggested that the cooperative bank employ a person to supervise farming operations, using the bank's loans as a motive for farm supervision. Thus Terry could be removed from this area of responsibility and given new duties requiring no direct contact with the families. Sharp endorsed the idea.

Paul Finch was not the only source of dissension at Dyess that spring. In April, Dudley discharged two men, the colony store manager and the dry-goods department manager. His action was taken in order to enable the colony to hire more experienced personnel. "They did not have enough experience in merchandizing to operate the general store," Sharp commented. But 156 colonists signed a petition asking that the two be re-hired; and 200 colonists sent a petition to Eleanor Roosevelt, who had visited and expressed an interest in Dyess, requesting her to investigate the "administrative activities" of the colony. After Sharp refused to re-hire them, the protest gradually subsided, perhaps lost in the more exciting meetings at Finch's home. "As to an investigation," Sharp remarked cagily, "I am sure that the clerks would not welcome one."[17]

The troubled spring of 1938 passed. While Terry's demotion removed a big source of discontent, the dissension movement failed to gather a large following, anyway. It amounted to little, as Sharp said. No more than thirty or forty families of some four hundred actively participated in Finch's meetings, and some attended just for the hell of it. Yet the

15. H. L. Mitchell to Lawrence Westbrook, 11 October 1937, STFU Papers.
16. Floyd Sharp to Lawrence Westbrook, 29 April 1938, Sharp Papers.
17. *Osceola Times*, 25 April 1938; *Arkansas Gazette*, 27 April 1938. Mrs. Roosevelt's visit was reported in ibid., 10 June 1936.

dissension at Dyess Colony was only in its infancy. Less than a year later the colony faced a more serious situation. This time a colonist assumed the lead in protesting against the management.

S. B. Funk was a fifty-two-year-old raw-boned farmer and one-time veterinarian from Haskell in Saline County. On 28 March 1938 colony officials served eviction notices on him and another man, A. J. McCravin, a fifty-two-year-old native of Morrilton, ordering them to vacate their houses within three days. They, like other colonists, had signed contracts with the Arkansas Rural Rehabilitation Corporation to purchase farms on Colonization Project No. 1, agreeing to clear the land, make improvements, and follow the management's supervision. Both men were incompetent, colony authorities now maintained, and had performed insufficient work during the two-year probation period to merit further occupancy.[18] In addition, Funk owed the colony over $1,600 and represented a constant source of trouble. McCravin was in better financial condition, but he continually refused to participate in any of the colony's cooperative enterprises.

Since both men refused to leave, Dyess Colony, Inc., initiated a suit against them for unlawful detainer and cut off their credit at the colony store. But Funk and McCravin obtained credit outside the colony, employed A. F. Barham, an Osceola lawyer, to represent them, and apparently spent their spare time building up support among other colonists. The lawsuit, Funk later claimed, was the start of "open indignation" at Dyess; before then most colonists had been afraid to discuss openly their dissatisfaction. When others saw they might also lose their farms, he said, they "at first bided their time but last fall [1938] decided nothing was to be done about the present management and decided they must interest the public."[19] In 1939 Funk emerged as the new ringleader of a dissident element made up of about a third of the total colony population. "So I am pitching a Boston Tea Party, taxation without representation you know," Funk said. "It seems funny, but there were 13 colonists here originally. And now we have an American revolution."[20]

Dyess Colony reentered the news on 17 March 1939, near the first anniversary of Funk's and McCravin's evictions. After officials refused permission to hold protest meetings at the colony, a group of about 250

18. *Chicago Tribune*, 25 October 1938; *Arkansas Gazette*, 2 April 1939; "*Funk v. Dyess Colony, Inc.,*" *Arkansas Reports: Cases Determined in the Supreme Court of Arkansas from March 1940 to October 1940* (Little Rock: Democrat Printing and Lithographing, 1940), 200:180–93 (cited hereafter in the form 200 *Ark.* 180).
19. *Arkansas Gazette*, 1 April 1939.
20. Quoted in *Chicago Tribune*, 25 October 1938.

Dyess residents—men, women, and children—gathered at the courthouse in Osceola to protest what they called "unfair and discriminatory management."[21] The protestors claimed they had been charged exorbitant prices for the land they occupied at the colony. On 29 March a second mass meeting took place with a crowd of 275 people, this time an all-day affair climaxed with the sending of telegrams to President Roosevelt and Gov. Carl E. Bailey. In the telegram to Bailey, they requested that the governor use his "influence with Mrs. Roosevelt to put an end to the intolerable conditions existing here." "The records of this county show," the telegram read, "that this land was purchased at $2.50 per acre. Our contracts call for its sale to us at its actual cost plus improvements, but officials have now insisted that we agree to pay from $75 to $100 per acre—many times the value of the land." If they failed to pay, they faced the threat of being thrown off the colony. "Unless you can prevent this," they said, "we will lose four years of labor and our last chance for a home. Please help us."[22]

The most vocal dissenter, Funk was probably the author of the telegram. "I bought 38 acres to be paid for over a period of years and thought I was to get it at $2.50 an acre," he complained. "After I had worked it for three years I found out they had charged me $3,900." Colony officials, he further charged, had meted out brutal punishment to dissenters, raising the question of the Paul Finch beating.[23]

Without bowing to the more spectacular charges, officials countered with facts and figures. Dudley denied that anyone had been overcharged. "Prices of the tracts are based on the size and the amount of the improvements," he explained. "The land is appraised and the improvements, such as drainage ditches, roads, schools and other conveniences are figured in as part of the purchase price."[24]

R. A. Lile, colony accountant, admitted that some of the land had been purchased for $2.50 per acre; but that did not represent the entire cost of obtaining title. Lile placed the actual cost at $9.82 per acre—a figure including the cost of land, legal expenses, quit-claim deeds, surveying, and payment of delinquent taxes. For example, Funk's land itself

21. *Arkansas Gazette*, 18 March 1939; *Osceola Times*, 19 May 1939.
22. *Arkansas Gazette*, 30 March 1939; Pine Bluff *Daily Graphic*, 30 March 1939.
23. *Arkansas Gazette*, 18 March, 2 April 1939.
24. Ibid., 18 March 1939. Dudley, however, seems to have been confused about what went into the purchase price, just as some of the colonists were. See Lile's statement in n. 25.

cost $382.88. But counting improvements, he was charged $76.93 an acre for 38.99 acres. The average cost of improvements—five-room house, barn, and poultry house of the type built on the Funk tract—was $2,291.88, while the cost of drainage ditches amounted to $7.18 per acre, or $279.95. "In view of the fact that various tracts were to be sold to the homesteaders as cleared land," said Lile, "$15 per acre was included in the cost price and set up in a reserve for clearing. This added $584.85 to the cost of the land." Thus, Lile said, the cost of the Funk tract was $1,247.68; with improvements, it came to $3,539.56. But he received a $273.90 credit, or $15 per acre, for land he cleared, reducing the cost of the tract to $3,265.66. Finally, allowing him 10 percent off, the sales price to Funk was $2,999.52. Dyess Colony, Inc., added no interest, nor prorated the cost of roads and bridges. Funk's annual payments were $153.03, or about $4 per acre per year; and he had thirty years to pay.[25]

Many colonists, probably most of them, were not involved in the protest. When reporters came around asking about it, they found the most common conversation topics to be where and when they should plant cotton and other crops. Some resented the unfavorable publicity the dissident faction gave the colony. In early April one group, a newspaper reported, planned to send petitions to Roosevelt and Bailey denying all charges in the dissidents' petitions and expressing satisfaction with the opportunity of living at Dyess.[26]

Colonist C. E. Tarpley reflected one school of thought toward Funk and McCravin when he said, "If those two birds were in paradise they wouldn't be satisfied unless they were raising a ruckus." They were "sore because they don't want to get down to work." One reporter found the colonists divided into three groups: those strongly favorable to the colony, those strongly opposed, and those in the middle, not highly favorable but not discontented, either. The majority took the third course. Homer Williams was one of those in the middle. "If they don't like it here," he advised, "I would move." Williams, however, had signed the dissenters' petitions, not because he was dissatisfied, but because he was willing to assist those who asked his help to "improve their condition." Williams had no griev-

25. R. A. Lile (of Russell Brown and Co.) to the Officers and Directors of Dyess Colony, Inc., 8 February 1939, Sharp Papers; *Arkansas Gazette*, 1 April 1939.
26. Ibid., 2 April 1939. See Texarkana *Daily Gazette*, 18 March 1939; Newport *Daily Independent*, 24 March 1939, both clippings in "Scrapbook of Newspaper Clippings about Dyess Colony, 1939," Sharp Papers.

ances against the colony or its management; they always gave him a square deal, he said, and he was making progress toward acquiring his home.[27]

What was really wrong at Dyess Colony? The misconduct of Terry and men like him may have precipitated the original trouble, but the dissension went deeper. The Emergency Relief Administration had made at least two major mistakes which plagued the colony for years afterward. From the beginning, FERA regional engineer Roland R. Payne warned against the danger of not thoroughly acquainting clients with the size of the financial obligations they assumed as colonists. This mistake was never fully corrected, and it did immeasurable harm. A number of colonists, like Funk and McCravin, expected to buy their farms at a far cheaper price than the colony could offer. The colony's developers were in part victims of their own enthusiastic propaganda. Newspaper stories of $2.50-an-acre land and $1,000 homes made such a deep impression that it could never be eradicated. "I know what the cost of this land was —it was $2.50 per acre," Funk declared. "Mr. Dyess told me that."[28]

Equally serious, family selection specialists allowed numerous poor choices to slip through. Although the original intention was to assist persons with farming backgrounds, colony officials admitted many families whose agricultural experience was pretty remote. As a result, such people found adjustments difficult. Homer Williams put it this way: "When this thing started out back in 1934, they brought up here people who hadn't had anything before in their lives. They were on relief. They took them from all walks of life and from all parts of the state, and put them down here on an equal basis, doing the same thing—farming. As time went on, they began to sift down. Some of them couldn't take it. Others made a go of it. You just can't take so many different types of people and set them down doing the same thing without having a little trouble."[29]

The Federal Emergency Relief Administration as well as the Resettlement Administration shared responsibility for selection mistakes at Dyess. But the FERA must take the greatest blame. Funk, who arrived in November 1934, and McCravin, who came in April 1935, were both FERA choices. Dyess Colony, after all, was the Federal Emergency Relief Administration's first colonization effort in Arkansas. No one in 1934 or

27. *Arkansas Gazette*, 2 April 1939. See also R. W. Daniel, "Resident Urges Dyess Colonists to Drop Gossip and Get Back to Producing Crops," *Press-Scimitar*, 7 April 1939.
28. Report of Roland R. Pyne, Regional Engineer, Period Ending 10 November 1934, Hopkins Papers; 200 *Ark*. 188.
29. *Arkansas Gazette*, 2 April 1939.

1935 had the experience in community building available a few years later. Even the Resettlement Administration's family selection staff, young and inexperienced, had undertaken no major selection tasks except for the Mississippi subsistence homesteads. They, too, were still feeling their way.

The sifting-down process was soon at work. Many colony families started with high hopes, worked hard for the first year or two, but, after repeated disappointments, lost their enthusiasm. They found it difficult to adjust to the full-time job of farming, to the "buffalo gnats" common in that part of eastern Arkansas, and to the sticky black gumbo soil that plowed like rubber. The flood of 1937 set back many colonists just as they were getting on their feet. Some people sat on their porches and waited for the "doodlebooks"—their name for the subsistence coupon books issued twice a month and good for an average of $20 worth of groceries.

"Some of them came here under the mistaken impression that they would find Santa Claus," the colony home economist, Fern Salyers, said of families who left the project in its first year. "They expected to have everything done for them, and were not willing to do the really tremendous amount of work that is necessary to make a home and a productive farm under these advantageous conditions."[30] A few colonists, it seems, were unable to understand the legal documents and technicalities involved in purchasing their homes. Thus part of the trouble stemmed from simple misunderstanding and perhaps could have been avoided by a better educational program.

The dissension at Dyess, then, grew out of a set of complex, interrelated mistakes: the misconduct of some of the supervisory personnel, the misunderstanding over the cost of the land, and the selection of families that were ill suited for the colony. Alone, any one of them would have been bad enough, but together they proved almost impossible to correct. Many colonists lost faith in the integrity of the administration; and the administration turned against colonists who complained, labeling them malcontents and troublemakers.

How well S. B. Funk fit the term "troublemaker" is a difficult question. Taking his side, one gains an idea of how complex the situation was. Funk was evidently an industrious man. After becoming a colonist, he cleared thirty-five acres of land and in 1937 raised eight bales of cotton; he accumulated a lot of debts, but he made a start at paying them back.

30. M. C. Blackman, "Uncle Sam Waves a Wand," *Arkansas Gazette Sunday Magazine*, 22 September 1935, p. 3.

He was, after all, offered a deed, a gesture which looked suspicious when colony officials asserted that he had not performed the work expected of him in the probationary period.

Dudley delivered Funk's deed in August 1937. Funk kept it for three weeks and then left it with Dudley's secretary. Looking it over, he decided that it did not correspond with the contract he had made with the Arkansas Rural Rehabilitation Corporation. Nor could he understand, as he put it later, why land costing only $2.50 per acre should be increased to $75 or $80 when he had cleared and ditched it himself. When Funk did not vacate his unit, officials first brought suit to have him evicted and next obtained a writ of replevin to recover colony property in his possession. A deputy took him from his fields and brought him to the community center, where Terry waited. Funk later accused the farm supervisor of being drunk. As A. F. Barham put it, Terry treated Funk "exactly like a negro sharecropper."[31]

While Funk was in conference at the community center, his mules and plow tools were taken away, meaning that he could continue to farm only with the greatest inconvenience and could not pay any more of his debts. He borrowed a team, however, and went on with his farm work while the lawsuit was pending; some of his neighbors helped him in secret, despite their fear of official disapproval. He was cut off at the colony store; he could no longer get decent clothes for his children to wear to school. His wife was barefoot, their home the despair of the home economist.

McCravin was different. He was never offered a deed, and perhaps did not merit one. When suit was filed against him, he owed the colony no money, an indication of frugality but possibly a sign of noncooperation, too. In fact, the colony owned him money for work he had done.[32]

The Funk and McCravin cases dragged on in the courts for two years. Former governor J. M. Futrell, who had resumed his law practice, made a surprising reappearance as legal adviser for the colony. His performance was not particularly competent, and Sharp retained another attorney, Cecil Shane, to help out.[33]

The two cases were decided in the Mississippi County Chancery Court,

31. 200 *Ark.* 188; A. F. Barham to Chancellor J. F. Cautney (copy), 26 July 1939, Sharp Papers.

32. 200 *Ark.* 191; *Arkansas Gazette,* 1 April 1939.

33. J. M. Futrell to A. F. Barham, 31 August 1938; Futrell to H. C. Baker, 5 January, 12 April 1939; Futrell to Floyd Sharp, 11 January 1939; Sharp to Cecil Shane, 31 March 1939, all in Sharp Papers. Sharp did not believe that Barham wanted a trial, preferring instead to gain publicity through the newspapers. Futrell could not bring the case to conclusion.

Osceola District, on 10 August 1939. The defendants, Funk and Mc-
Cravin, lost. The chancellor ruled that Funk's contract with the Arkansas
Rural Rehabilitation Corporation did not require the sale of the property
in question. Such a transaction carried with it certain conditions, and
Dyess Colony, Inc., presumably could judge for itself whether those con-
ditions had been met. Funk and McCravin appealed to the Arkansas
Supreme Court.[34]

After sifting through more than six hundred pages of testimony, the
supreme court affirmed the chancellor's decree, but with a modification.
In 1936 Funk had put up 2,363 cans of tomatoes, believing that he was
acting under contract with Dyess Colony, Inc. If there was any agreement,
it was an oral one; and when he finished sealing the last can, he could not
find anyone who knew anything about it. Since the cans bore the inscrip-
tion "Free—to be given away, and not sold," he was stuck with them.
The supreme court ordered the colony to pay a fair price for the tomatoes
or credit the amount to his account. With that, Funk and McCravin were
sent on their way.[35]

Paul Finch also became involved in an unsuccessful lawsuit with the
colony. After the schoolhouse incident in 1938, he filed charges against
the colony and the farm supervisors who beat him. After dragging on for
two years, Finch's suit came to trial at Osceola only to end indecisively
in a nonsuit motion, with the colony ruled not liable for the action of its
employees.[36]

There was still another element which entered into the dissension movement. Dyess Colony was a potential issue in Arkansas politics, especially
as deficits mounted and the so-called malcontents grew more vocal. At
first the colony's identification with W. R. Dyess was alone enough to
attract controversy. As a large planter and businessman, Bill Dyess had
been involved in politics since coming to Osceola in 1930. The political
situation there was well known. Mississippi County, one of the largest
in Arkansas, was divided into rival northern and southern sections. The
existence of dual courthouses—one at Blytheville in the northern section,
the other at Osceola in the southern section—suggested not only the size
of the county but also the bitterness of the sectional rivalry.[37]

34. 200 *Ark.* 192–93.
35. Ibid., pp. 188, 190–93.
36. J. T. Coston to Floyd Sharp, 19 March 1940, Sharp Papers; Blaine [E.
Treadway], telegram to J. R. Butler, 3 June 1940, STFU Papers.
37. See Mabel F. Edrington, *History of Mississippi County, Arkansas* (Ocala,
Fla.: Ocala Star-Banner, 1962), pp. 171–73, 257.

Since Dyess's home was near Osceola, he built political ties in the southern section with, for example, Ben F. Butler, a farm implement dealer and landowner, and R. E. Lee Wilson, a large planter who owned an entire town and thousands of acres a few miles south of Osceola.[38] In 1932, as a private citizen, Dyess supported J. M. Futrell for governor against Dwight H. Blackwood of Blytheville and did much to win the county for Futrell. Once in office, Futrell backed him for the job as relief administrator; and the following year Dyess threw his relief organization behind the governor's campaign for reelection. As Emergency Relief administrator, Dyess was a powerful force in statewide politics, with large amounts of federal funds to dispense on relief projects and thousands of jobs to fill in every part of the state. When the Works Progress Administration replaced the FERA in 1935, Dyess remained as the head of the Arkansas relief organization, presumably continuing his accustomed political role.

Dyess himself was ambitious for elective office. According to rumors, he planned to run for governor in 1936 after Futrell stepped down—or perhaps for United States senator.[39] He enjoyed the advantages of a favorable popular image as relief administrator and a magnetic personality. Gertrude S. Gates, a state relief employee who was one of his most severe critics, admitted that "he could charm the birds off the trees if he chose."[40] Since he inevitably acquired enemies, his political chances were probably not good. The colony itself was as much a handicap to his political ambitions as he was to its ultimate success. What he had created in northeastern Arkansas was a little Teapot Dome. During the 1934 gubernatorial campaign, Dyess's involvement in local and state politics dragged the colonization project, then only a few weeks old, into the

38. George D. Babcock to Winthrop D. Lane, 13 July 1934, FERA Records, NA, RG 96; Nels Anderson to Lane, 9 July 1934, ibid. Lee Wilson, however, was not always friendly with Dyess. As Anderson told it, they were originally in opposing political camps. When Futrell proposed Dyess's name as superintendent of the state penal farm, Wilson objected to the appointment, and he sent someone to Mississippi, Anderson reported, to dig up something on him. Dyess did not get the job, but before long the opportunity came for the governor to nominate him as state relief administrator. As dispenser of relief funds, Dyess gained in prestige and Lee Wilson became friendly, although he died in late 1933. The Wilson estate passed into the hands of his son, R. E. L. Wilson, Jr.

39. Gertrude S. Gates, memorandum to Winthrop Lane, 18 June 1934, ibid. Dyess denied having any political ambitions, in Blytheville *Courier News*, 6 July 1934; *Arkansas Gazette*, 7 July 1934.

40. Gertrude S. Gates, memorandum to Winthrop Lane, 18 June 1934, FERA Records, NA, RG 69.

primaries as a political issue.[41] A prominent Futrell partisan, Dyess found
himself facing a number of embarrassing questions—questions intended,
the *Osceola Times* said, to "react upon the present state administration."[42]

Had the Emergency Relief Administration shown favoritism to the
southern half of Mississippi County, the less populated part? Why did
most of the relief labor being used at the colony come from Osceola rather
than Blytheville? How, indeed, had the colony itself come to be located
not only in Dyess's home county, but in the very part of that county
where he lived? Was it not true that a substantial part of the land purchased for the colony, if not all of it, had been owned by none other than
his friend's son and heir, Lee Wilson, Jr.? Had Wilson, with Dyess's help,
neatly unloaded a large tract of worthless land on the government at a
handsome profit? What about Dyess's political favoritism, such as the
purchasing of building materials and machinery from his friend Ben
Butler in the initial stages of the colonization project? Why, too, had
relief work crews improved roads running past Dyess's private land in
Mississippi County? Why had there been extensive resurfacing of thirty
or forty miles of formerly gravel roads near Wilson, Arkansas?

As a result of such criticism, three federal officials—Nels Anderson,
George Babcock, and Winthrop D. Lane—spent three days in Mississippi
County conducting a detailed investigation.[43] By improving roads on land
he and Wilson owned, Anderson commented, Dyess committed a clear
indiscretion. Babcock agreed, but he took a generally tolerant attitude toward Dyess's conduct. Where the development of the colonization project was concerned, Babcock saw no "unusual" favoritism toward the
southern section of the county. "That the location of this project," he
noted, "happened to have been in the part of the county which is generally considered as that section in which our executive lives, and almost
surrounded by property owned by one who seems to be one of his strongest friends [Wilson], should not be a particular reason for criticism." "In
fact," he continued, "I believe that if his home had not been located in
this southern region there would have been little criticism of any kind so
far as selection and location were concerned."[44] Dyess's home, Babcock
pointed out, was at least twenty-five miles from the colony and at the
very northern border of the southern section of the county.

41. See *Arkansas Gazette*, 17 June 1934; *Courier News*, 6, 11 July 1934.
42. *Osceola Times*, 6 July 1934.
43. George D. Babcock to Winthrop D. Lane, 13 July 1934, FERA Records, NA,
RG 69; Nels Anderson to Lane, 9 July 1934, ibid.
44. George D. Babcock to Winthrop D. Lane, 13 July 1934, ibid.

Summarizing his colleagues' reports, Lane found "serious indiscretions but no criminal acts or [other] acts justifying removal." He added: "I am still uncertain whether I shall recommend a new state administrator."[45] The man who held the final responsibility, Harry Hopkins, did not fire Dyess, and there was probably never any real danger that he would. While the criticism subsided after Futrell won a second term, the colony was soon back in the news.

In early 1935 the state Emergency Relief Administration came under renewed attack, and rumors flew that Dyess was on his way out. Since relief officials had recently investigated a minor incident of check forging and payroll padding at the colony and fired one or two employees, the House of Representatives of the Arkansas General Assembly passed a resolution calling for the report to be made public. This time Dyess was clear of any wrongdoing, but the colony offered a convenient weakness which anyone unhappy with the state relief organization found hard to resist.[46]

When Dyess was killed in the airplane crash, the colony and its problems fell right into the lap of Floyd Sharp, who succeeded Dyess as director of the Arkansas WPA. For the next few years he worked hard to correct its deficiencies, but he ran up against a series of difficult situations: floods, discontented colonists, protest demonstrations, lawsuits, and threatened investigations. While Sharp knew mistakes had been made on the part of the management, he could not shake off the suspicion that politics also lay behind the dissension movement.[47] W. R. Dyess and Governor Futrell had been political allies, but Sharp and Futrell's successor, Carl Bailey, were soon locked in a bitter political struggle, again dragging the colony into the newspapers.

45. Winthrop D. Lane to Aubrey Williams, 10 July 1934, ibid. See also *Arkansas Gazette*, 6, 7, 8 July 1934. Later Williams remarked that the selection of a new administrator must be made very carefully or else it "would let in all of the political dogs." Williams, telegram to Malcolm Miller, 30 November 1934, FERA Records, NA, RG 69.

46. *Arkansas Gazette*, 1 March 1935. For editorial reactions, see ibid., 2 March 1935; Little Rock *Arkansas Democrat*, 1 March 1935. The FERA Records in the National Archives contain numerous letters praising Dyess and urging that he not be fired; see, for example, Walter E. Winn to Harry L. Hopkins, 2 March 1935, RG 69; J. M. Futrell, telegram to Hopkins, 19 May 1935, ibid.; Neil Brooks to Hopkins, 21 May 1935, ibid. Several months later a Mississippi County grand jury looked into reports of irregularities in the financial operation of the colony and found nothing wrong. *Arkansas Gazette*, 2, 23 October 1935. See a reference made to scandal at the colony in *Congressional Record*, vol. 79, 74th Cong., 1st sess., 22 April 1935, p. 6131.

47. Floyd Sharp to Lawrence Westbrook, 31 March 1938, Sharp Papers.

For a brief time in the late 1930s, as mentioned earlier, Arkansas politics was a contest between two factions, the statehouse crowd led by Bailey and the federal crowd including the United States senators, the congressmen, and most federal officeholders. Although a member of the latter group, Sharp was caught in the middle of this struggle. While answering to Harry Hopkins and administering his relief programs, Sharp also sought to get along with Bailey and to clean up irregularities concerning Dyess Colony before anyone could ferret out more scandal. When the state and federal forces clashed in a special election to fill the late Joseph T. Robinson's Senate seat, the federal crowd won, with John E. Miller pulling off a major upset in defeating the governor. Sharp himself played a neutral role in the campaign, probably casting his own ballot for Bailey.[48] But Sharp's neutrality did not propitiate the governor. According to Bailey's supporters, the Arkansas WPA had become a powerful political machine, and it had been used with deadly effect against him. Smarting from defeat, Bailey was determined to get revenge, and he knew just how to go about it.

In late 1937 the governor began a series of shake-ups in state government, starting with the appointment of one of his supporters to the Arkansas Corporation Commission. "I hope to find it possible in the future," he said, "to give my personal attention to the work of the commission to an extent not possible heretofore because of the press of other duties of state."[49] He did just that. Within a few days all three members of the Corporation Commission were Bailey appointees.[50] No one at Dyess Colony could as yet recognize the ominous implications in this change. Except for naming a new commissioner of education, Bailey saved his next dramatic move until after he had safely won a second term as governor in the 1938 primaries.

48. Aubrey Williams to Floyd Sharp, 2 September 1937, WPA Records, NA, RG 69; Sharp to All Works Progress Administration Employees, 2 October 1937, ibid.; Sharp to Williams, 2 October 1937, ibid. Sharp wrote: "I never wanted anything more sincerely in my life than to be able to keep the unfortunate people on our relief rolls from being made a political football. In my effort to enforce this desire, which really comes from the bottom of my heart, perhaps all that will be left of me when it [the special senatorial election] is over will be a clear conscience. I am sure I will have that." The author is indebted to R. M. Allison (interview on 11 April 1973) for his interpretation of Sharp's political role. Mr. Allison worked behind the scenes in the Miller campaign. For an excellent account of the Miller-Bailey race, see Ernest Dumas, "Arkansas 1937: An Old Political Adage Proves True," *Arkansas Gazette*, 27 December 1970, and part two, "Arkansas 1937: John E. Miller Sweeps On to Victory," ibid., 3 January 1971.

49. *Arkansas Gazette*, 28 November 1937.

50. Ibid., 2 December 1937.

For the previous couple of years, sporadic attempts had been made to remove the director of the Unemployment Security Division of the State Labor Department, W. A. Rooksbery. As it happened, Sharp and Rooksbery were old friends in relief work from before the New Deal, and as head of the National Reemployment Service in Arkansas, Rooksbery provided skilled workers at Dyess Colony and assisted with family selection. In the civil service procedure governing the position, the job of Unemployment Security director was subject to periodic review, with the state labor commissioner filling the position from a list of five names submitted by the governor. In October 1938 Rooksbery, as the current director, ranked first on the eligible register, ahead of four other men, including Eli W. Collins, ranked last, one of the governor's long-time friends. While Bailey was on a trip to the West Coast and Rooksbery was in Washington on official business, labor commissioner Ed McKinley made the political surprise announcement of the year. Probably with a straight face, he revealed that Collins would take Rooksbery's place.[51] All demands for an explanation met with silence. Bailey, known as a strong advocate of civil service, played it cool.

When he returned home, the governor pretended to be unaware of the controversy. Had he heard of Rooksbery's ouster? a reporter asked. "No," grinned the governor. "I hadn't heard anything about it." He added, "How'd that happen?"[52] The next day he declared that he would support the decision of his labor commissioner, and warned that Sharp might seek reprisals, perhaps by pulling WPA workers off state highway construction jobs. Sharp denied any such intention. "This organization," he said, "has never taken any part in politics."[53]

The firing of Rooksbery brought the Bailey-Sharp feud into the open, but Bailey was not through with his vendetta. Next he struck directly at Dyess Colony itself, which was already in an uproar over land prices. During the 1939 legislative session, Representatives B. Frank Williams, L. H. Autry, and Woodrow A. Hutton, all of Mississippi County, introduced an administration-sponsored bill directing the Arkansas Corporation

51. Ibid., 18, 19, 21, 22 October 1938. The incident was full of irony. Collins, a former newspaperman and mayor of Jonesboro, had himself been fired as chief deputy state treasurer for supporting Bailey in a controversy over highway bond refunding. Moreover, it was Rooksbery who had devised the civil service procedure which failed to protect his own job. Arkansas abandoned the civil service system in 1939 after only a brief trial.. See Henry A. Ritgerod, "Arkansas Abandons the Merit System," *National Municipal Review* 28 (April 1939): 296–97.
52. *Arkansas Gazette*, 26 October 1938. See the *Gazette*'s editorial, 22 October 1938.
53. Ibid., 27 October 1938.

Commission to audit the books of Dyess Colony, Inc., while Ivy W. Crawford of Blytheville sponsored a companion measure in the state senate.[54] They called for an investigation "to determine the extent of the State of Arkansas's interest in the establishment, management, and disposition of Dyess Colony." The Williams-Autry-Hutton bill breezed through the house, but in the senate Crawford's bill quickly ran into opposition. Its opponents denounced it as nothing more than a political maneuver.

"I'm going to tell you what's behind this bill," said Sen. Ellis M. Fagan of Little Rock. "I'm speaking for a man who can't speak for himself— Floyd Sharp." The fact that the bill called only for an investigation of Dyess Colony, ignoring its parent agency, Fagan said, showed it was "aimed to embarrass Mr. Sharp and to enliven agitation for his removal." The Corporation Commission was responsible only to the governor, he asserted; it would bring out the report it was told to bring out. Sen. Jeff Bratton of Paragould also opposed the investigation: "Instead of trying to investigate the how and why of Dyess Colony," he said, "we ought to be glad the federal government has given the money to some of our people."[55]

On 7 March, senate opponents amended the bill to place the investigation under the attorney general's office—and out of reach of the Corporation Commission.[56] For an instant it looked as if they had averted any threat of investigation. Then, unexpectedly, Bailey's forces accepted the amendment and lined up enough votes to pass the new version of the bill. But on 8 March, with the legislative session scheduled to end at noon the next day, Fagan and twelve other senators filibustered the bill to death. Together, they kept the floor of the senate for nearly eight hours, the longest filibuster in recent Arkansas history. Fagan read a voluminous report of a federal audit of Dyess Colony, interrupting the narrative with comments on the high cost of living, termites, and the Far Eastern situation. He took almost three hours to read only the first page of the report

54. *Journal of the House of Representatives of the Fifty-second General Assembly, State of Arkansas* (Newark, Ark.: Journal Printing, 1939), p. 986; *Journal of the Senate of the Fifty-second General Assembly, State of Arkansas* (Newark, Ark.: Journal Printing, 1939), p. 1300; *Arkansas Gazette*, 26 February 1939. The subsequent events can be followed in "Scrapbook of Newspaper Clippings about Dyess Colony, 1939," Sharp Papers.

55. All quotes are from *Arkansas Gazette*, 8 March 1939. Fagan's reference to Dyess Colony's "parent agency" meant the Arkansas Rural Rehabilitation Corporation, which had been created by the Emergency Relief Administration in 1934 to oversee rural rehabilitation activities in the state.

56. *Senate Journal*, p. 1408.

and two explanatory letters. The senate adjourned at eleven o'clock that night without taking a vote.[57]

Not one to be outmaneuvered easily, Bailey had held back a trump card. On 16 March, the day before the first mass demonstration of colonists at the Osceola courthouse, he dissolved Dyess Colony, Inc., leaving it without legal authority to do business in Arkansas. In an executive proclamation the governor ordered the dissolution of 153 domestic and 37 foreign corporations which had failed to file reports and pay state franchise taxes for the past three years. The Dyess Colony organization was only one of these, but the intent was clear. Dyess Colony, Inc., Bailey said, failed to pay $33 in franchise taxes due the state. Former governor Futrell had recently advised the Arkansas Corporation Commission that Dyess Colony, Inc., as a federal agency, was not liable for the state franchise tax; and the commissioners accepted this contention. But they soon changed their minds, or someone did for them. They now claimed that Dyess Colony, Inc., possessed the same powers as any other business corporation, with nothing in its articles of incorporation restricting its operations to a nonprofit basis or establishing it as an instrument of the federal government.[58]

Sharp, perhaps a little stunned, declared that the dissolution of Dyess Colony, Inc., was a waste of time if it was an effort to oust him from the project. "I have asked Harry L. Hopkins to be relieved of my duties with the colony," he announced.[59] On 22 March he obtained a new Arkansas charter setting up Dyess Rural Rehabilitation Corporation as the successor to Dyess Colony, Inc. The new organization was a "benevolent, nonprofit corporation" whose major objective was "to rehabilitate individuals and families as self-sustaining human beings." Secretary of State C. G. Hall issued the new charter upon payment of the usual fee of ten dollars. Legally, Dyess Colony was back in business.[60]

These events left Sharp in a mood of depression, particularly when rumors began circulating that Governor Bailey conferred with the president at Warm Springs, Georgia, and possibly with Harry Hopkins. A. F. Barham, along with a former secretary of the governor, traveled to Wash-

57. Ibid., pp. 1412, 1439, 1460; *Arkansas Gazette*, 9 March 1939.
58. Ibid., 17 March 1939.
59. Ibid., 23 March 1939. Sharp, however, stayed on as president of Dyess Rural Rehabilitation Corporation.
60. Articles of Incorporation of Dyess Rural Rehabilitation Corporation, 22 March 1939, Secretary of State, Corporation Department, State Capitol, Little Rock, Arkansas.

ington to see somebody regarding the Dyess matter. Sharp felt that everyone had abandoned him. He warned that Dyess Colony might be "headed for a lot of national publicity next year"—an election year.[61]

Sharp had reason for concern. At the end of March 1939 the colony was in serious trouble; it was on the verge of financial collapse, a third of the colonists were in open revolt, and a state investigation had been barely averted. As Sharp realized, the only way he could safely protect the colony from Bailey's vendetta was to cut all ties between it and himself. Besides, the Works Progress Administration had been under orders since mid-1938 to wind up the affairs of the old state Emergency Relief Administrations, including the liquidation of its interests in three rural community corporations: Pine Mountain Valley, Georgia; Cherry Lake, Florida; and Dyess Colony.[62]

In February 1939, soon after the Bailey feud heated up, Sharp approached T. Roy Reid about the possibility of transferring Dyess Colony to the Farm Security Administration.[63] In August the FSA agreed to take over Dyess, but no one appeared in any hurry to do so. The project was hardly a welcome addition to the FSA's own troubled communities.

Reid warned against moving too rapidly. There was "considerable unrest" at Dyess, he advised, and the FSA's take-over was expected to increase that unrest. The Dyess Rural Rehabilitation Corporation planned to ask forty or fifty families to vacate their units; the present management, Reid contended, should ask them to leave before the FSA took over. It would be hard for the FSA, he argued, to assume control and then demand their withdrawal immediately after taking charge. That was a lesson he had learned at McComb. Nor should the FSA take over until the corporation finished out a final full year for accounting purposes.[64]

Finally the FSA decided to go ahead with the transfer. At a special meeting on 22 November, the board of directors of the Dyess Rural Rehabilitation Corporation—Floyd Sharp, H. C. Baker, and R. C. Limerick—resigned. Then Reid, E. B. Whitaker, and regional finance director James T. Holliday took their places as president, secretary, and treasurer,

61. Floyd Sharp to Lawrence Westbrook, 31 March 1939, Sharp Papers; see also Geneva Holland to Mrs. Roosevelt (copy), 2 April 1938, ibid.
62. H. M. Colvin, memorandum to William E. Linden, 2 February 1939, FSA Records, NA, RG 96.
63. T. Roy Reid to Will W. Alexander, 23 February, 21 March 1939; R. W. Hudgens, memorandum to Monroe Oppenheimer and J. O. Walker, 30 August 1939, all ibid.
64. T. Roy Reid to Will W. Alexander, 15, 21 September 1939; see G. E. Lukas, memorandum to J. O. Walker, 9 October 1939, all ibid.

respectively.[65] Soon afterward the new board of directors transferred their Dyess Corporation stock to the secretary of agriculture, just as the old state rural rehabilitation corporations had done. One of the purposes of this move was to place eviction cases at Dyess Colony in federal court, should such a course prove necessary.[66]

While negotiations were under way, Reid set up a committee under Whitaker to visit the project, report on conditions, and recommend future action. Whitaker found 339 families living at Dyess with a total population of nearly two thousand people, about half being school-age children. The Resettlement Administration's Management Division had selected two-thirds of these families, and about 80 percent of the population had been residents of Dyess three years or longer. The colony contained 518 farm units averaging twenty-five acres each.[67]

Dyess Colony, Inc., had let its farm management program dwindle. Only the basic community services still operated: gin, store, blacksmith shop, schools, hospital, library, and some others. The property had never been restored to first-class condition after the flood of 1937. While the Tyronza River covered the project, about six inches of water stood inside most of the homes; as a result, the pillars sank into the soft soil, leaving floors and walls out of plumb. Very little fencing remained on any of the units, and some no longer had barns or other outbuildings.[68] Roads through the project were in poor condition and sometimes impassable.

"In general, the physical condition of the community and its various structures is good," district engineer Troy C. Donahue reported. "In fact, considering the size of the property and various damaging elements to which it has been exposed, such as the flood of 1937, the cost of putting this large project in good physical condition is comparatively moderate." Yet Whitaker estimated that it would take $830,697.81 to put Dyess on a par with other projects in the region. This represented a cost of $2,770 per unit, assuming the project were finally divided into three hundred units.[69]

65. E. B. Whitaker to Will W. Alexander, 27 November 1939; Mastin G. White, memorandum to Alexander, 4 December 1939; see Alexander to Corrington Gill, 23 October 1939; T. C. Donahue to Baird Snyder, 5 December 1939, an ibid.
66. E. B. Whitaker, memorandums to T. Roy Reid, 20, 22 December 1939; see G. E. Lukas, memorandum to C. B. Baldwin, 20 January 1940, all ibid.
67. T. Roy Reid to Will W. Alexander, 16 August 1939; Dyess Farms: Project Data, n.d.; E. B. Whitaker, memorandums to Reid, 3 January 1940, 29 December 1939, all ibid.
68. Dyess Farms, Inc., Economic Justification, Summary, n.d., ibid.
69. Preliminary Engineering Report on Dyess Community, Mississippi County,

In the spring of 1940 the Farm Security Administration launched a long-range program of reorganization at Dyess. On 19 June the regional office set up Dyess Farms, Inc., a cooperative association composed of the heads of families living on the project.[70] Dyess Farms intended to purchase the entire project, all 15,144 acres and nearly six hundred structures, from Dyess Rural Rehabilitation Corporation, although the latter would retain title for another year.

In the meantime Ray D. Johnston, the new community manager, went ahead with the colony's most pressing need: the reorganization of individual farm units. Whitaker's committee had reported that many of the original farmsteads were too small to support a family, so Johnston resubdivided the farm land, combining many adjacent units, and brought uncleared land into cultivation. He increased the size of the units to an average of 40 acres wherever possible, decreased the total number of farm units to 300, and expanded the amount of available crop land from 9,600 to about 12,000 acres.[71] In addition, the FSA provided Dyess Farms with an $872,820 loan to cover the cost of putting the project structures in good repair and a $30,000 loan for operating capital. As soon as possible, Johnston made necessary repairs to the buildings on all 300 of the reorganized units, improved the drainage system, reconditioned roads, constructed fences, and insured an adequate water supply.[72]

As units were repaired and reorganized, the Farm Security Administration sold them to the occupant families, if they could qualify under the FSA's standards, or to other families selected as residents at Dyess. About two hundred of the families then living on the project already held deeds

---

Arkansas, December 1939, ibid.; E. B. Whitaker, memorandum to T. Roy Reid, 3 January 1940, ibid.

70. By-laws of Dyess Farms, Inc., 19 June 1940, ibid. Under the FSA, Dyess would be known as Dyess Farms, not Dyess Colony. "The name has been officially changed from 'Dyess Colony' to 'Dyess Farms,' " Reid wrote in early 1940, "to give emphasis to the fact that this is a farming enterprise and to remove the general impression that it is a government colony for the segregation of a number of relief clients who are being cared for by the government." The change of name also eliminated a somewhat collectivist-sounding word and substituted one which emphasized the individualistic nature of the project. Dyess had never stressed collective ownership of farm land, but in 1940 the FSA could not afford to take any chances. T. Roy Reid, Quarterly Report, Region VI, January–March 1940, ibid.

71. Dyess Farms, Inc., Economic Justification, Organization and Management, n.d., ibid.; Dyess Farms, Inc., Economic Justification, Summary, n.d., ibid.

72. T. Roy Reid to Will W. Alexander, 22 May 1940, and enclosures; Reid to C. B. Baldwin, 7 August 1940; Loan Agreement, dated 29 June 1940; Alexander to Reid, 29 June 1940; J. O. Walker, memorandum to R. W. Hudgens, 25 June 1940, all ibid.

from Dyess Colony, Inc., although most had made little progress toward purchasing their units. The rest held year-to-year rental contracts. Since Dyess Farms could not make any improvements until the old deeds were canceled, the association requested most of the residents, especially those living on smaller units, to surrender their deeds in return for new sales contracts. The Dyess Farms contracts took into account the increase in size of each farm as well as home improvements; each family received credit for any equity they had built up in their old unit. The cost of the additional land and improvements was based on an appraisal of the earning capacity of each farm.

The conversion from WPA deeds to FSA contracts was an extremely slow process, so great was the suspicion of the government; by July 1943 Dyess Farms had executed only ninety-six new contracts. The board of directors of Dyess Farms and the project manager had to consult with each family, adjust their past indebtedness, and work out the exchange to the satisfaction of the families while protecting the government's interests. To insure the success of farm operations on the new units, Dyess Farms mapped out a new farm and home management plan. As before, each Dyess farmer continued to own and operate his unit individually.[73]

The new management also sought to revitalize the cooperative services program. In 1936 Dyess Colony Cooperative Association had leased the store, cafe, filling station, and blacksmith shop; but every one of its enterprises was a financial disaster. The store failed after only six months, and Dyess Colony, Inc., took it back. Later an individual resident subleased the blacksmith shop; so by 1939 the colony cooperative was reduced to operating only the cafe and filling station, and the cafe sold little more than soft drinks and cigarettes. The store continually suffered from lack of participation. None of the families supported it fully, and when the FSA took charge, only about two hundred of them patronized it at all.[74]

The gin was somewhat better patronized, although some of its three hundred customers had ginned as little as one bale of cotton since it opened. The Dyess hospital had never set up a cooperative medical association; it still operated under an informal association of project fami-

73. Dyess Farms, Arkansas: The First Experiment with a New Kind of Rural Community, dated 7 May 1941; John J. Armstrong to Sen. John L. McClellan, 21 July 1943; John Fischer to Mrs. A. B. Adams, 26 April 1940; Dyess Farms, Inc., Economic Justification, Organization and Management, n.d., all ibid.
74. W. T. Frazier, memorandum to Brice M. Mace, Jr., 19 December 1939, ibid.; U.S. Department of Agriculture, Farm Security Administration, Monthly Narrative Report, Dyess Farms, 1 May 1940, ibid.

lies on a monthly fee basis. Many of the other community facilities were simply not in use.[75]

"One of the main problems that must be overcome before a cooperative association can hope to be successful on this project is the apparent lack of knowledge of cooperative principles and of cooperative spirit among the families now residing on the project," cooperative specialist W. T. Frazier reported. "It is my understanding that the present cooperative association has only about 40 members out of 370 families."[76] The school system represented the only unqualifiedly successful community activity on the project.

The Farm Security Administration streamlined the community program by reorganizing the basic enterprises and eliminating the more superfluous ones. On 1 March 1940, with FSA help, the farmers at Dyess formed the Dyess Cooperative Store Association and borrowed $5,000 for operating capital. The association leased the store building from Dyess Rural Rehabilitation Corporation and purchased the inventory of merchandise on hand for $10,000 with payment to be made over a ten-year period.[77] During the summer the Dyess Hospital and Health Association began operations with a $4,760 grant. Two physicians, a registered nurse, and the community hospital provided members with medical care at an annual cost of $22 per family.[78] On 9 September, Dyess farmers organized the Dyess Cooperative Gin Association, borrowed $6,000 from the FSA, leased the project's gin, and started ginning the current cotton crop.[79] The blacksmith shop, gasoline station, garage, and feed mill also acquired new operators, but no provision was made for the operation of other enterprises. The local school district continued to operate the school system as before.[80]

Finally, on 2 June 1941, Dyess Rural Rehabilitation Corporation and Dyess Farms, Inc., entered into an "agreement for sale of Dyess Colony," covering the farm property but not including the community center and

75. Kate Fulton, memorandum to E. B. Whitaker, 19 December 1939, ibid.

76. W. T. Frazier, memorandum to Brice M. Mace, Jr., 19 December 1939, ibid.

77. Mastin G. White, memorandum to C. B. Baldwin, 2 July 1940; Mason Barr, memorandum to J. O. Walker, 28 November 1940; E. B. Whitaker to Will W. Alexander, 20 June 1940; A. D. Stewart to Baldwin, 26 April 1941, all ibid.

78. Dyess Farms, Arkansas: The First Experiment with a New Kind of Rural Community, dated 7 May 1941, ibid.

79. J. O. Walker, memorandum to R. W. Hudgens, 10 August 1940; E. B. Whitaker to Will W. Alexander, 20 June 1940; J. T. Holliday to Carl H. Bass, 4 October 1940, all ibid.

80. Dyess Farms, Inc., Economic Justification, Summary, n.d., ibid.

cooperative facilities. After the project was fully reorganized, the FSA would appraise the property in terms of its earning capacity and then establish the final purchase price, not to exceed $650,000. While legal possession started immediately, Dyess Farms would not begin making annual installments until ten years after the date of conveyance.[81]

The Work Projects Administration had left a legacy of unrest among the colonists. When the FSA took over, as Reid expected, the unrest increased. "The proposed transfer of the management of Dyess Colony Community to the Farm Security Administration," wrote family selection specialist Kate Fulton in December 1939, "is contributing to the already unsettled state of mind in the Community."[82] Many colonists guessed at how the FSA program would operate. Some were afraid they would no longer be able to supplement their income with WPA work. Some believed they should not have to repay the full amount of their old indebtedness. The Farm Security Administration naturally wanted to end any uncertainty, establish a harmonious relationship with the colonists, and restore their faith in the colony.

Reid and Whitaker made a trip to Dyess in early January 1940 and spoke at a colony-wide meeting in the community center. They invited the colonists to elect an "advisory committee" to consult with the management on matters of mutual concern. Although such committees were standard policy on all FSA community projects, Reid was especially anxious for the Dyess committee to secure the confidence of the people and insure active cooperation on the part of everyone. But soon after the election results came in, he found that the whole idea had backfired: a majority of the new committeemen were members of the Southern Tenant Farmers' Union.[83]

The colony contained a small faction of union members and an energetic leader in Floyd Slayton. Organized in late 1939, Local No. 29 publicly claimed to represent more than two-thirds of the total number of colonists on the project. In early 1940 its membership actually included no more than one-third of the families, but new members joined every day. Whatever its strength, it was active and well organized. The local's major goal was to turn the advisory committee into the collective-bargain-

81. Mason Barr, memorandum to J. O. Walker, 11 March 1941; C. B. Baldwin to A. D. Stewart, 3 April 1941; Agreement for Sale of Dyess Colony, dated 2 June 1941; see Walker, memorandum to R. W. Hudgens, 25 June 1940, all ibid.
82. Kate Fulton, memorandum to E. B. Whitaker, 19 December 1939, ibid.
83. T. Roy Reid to Will W. Alexander, 4 January 1940, ibid.

ing agency for the entire colony.[84] When regional officials issued their invitation for colonists to elect an advisory committee, Slayton got busy. Eight of the new committeemen were union members or had applications pending. These eight were to elect a ninth member, and it was a foregone conclusion that he too would be a union man.[85]

Before the FSA could undertake any reform, the local's president, L. J. Brantley, and its secretary, Slayton, drew up a petition of grievances; the membership passed it unanimously at a meeting on 22 February 1940. "The main element which has been lacking in the operation of the Dyess project heretofore," the petition read, "has been the failure of the management to recognize and encourage Democratic operation of the project." Speaking for the union members, they asked for a greater share in the making of important decisions affecting their welfare. "The colonists have no desire to take away any of the rights of the management to protect the investments of the Corporation," they said. "The colonists desire only the right to be consulted and the right to negotiation of disputed matters as between management and colonists." The election of an advisory committee was a step in the right direction, but they wanted the scope of the committee enlarged and its power extended. "It should become a bargaining agent as between management on the one hand and the committee representing the colonists on the other hand." Specifically, the committee should have power to bargain about such matters as loans and repayment plans, disciplinary action against colonists, equitable settlement of old indebtedness, the right of colonists to be consulted on the plans for management for the coming year, and the right to have a voice in the selection of project supervisors.[86]

On 3 March a delegation of STFU members presented the petition to Farm Security administrator Will W. Alexander at his office in Washington. H. L. Mitchell, one of the founders of the STFU, headed the delegation, and Slayton was there to represent Local No. 29. Mitchell offered evidence that a majority of the families at Dyess were members of the union, and repeated the request that the advisory committee be recog-

---

84. T. Roy Reid to W. L. Ford, Jr., 26 March 1940, ibid.; "Mitch" [H. L. Mitchell] to J. R. Butler, 13 February 1940, STFU Papers; Floyd Slayton to Butler, 14 February 1940, ibid. Slayton gave this breakdown: 328 families lived at Dyess, 114 men were union members, 75 applications were pending.

85. "Mitch" to J. R. Butler, 19 January 1940; Floyd Slayton to Butler, 6 February 1940; Butler to Guy Thomas, 21 February 1940, all ibid.

86. To the Officials of the Farm Security Administration, dated 22 February 1940, FSA Records, NA, RG 96.

nized as the "bargaining committee" of the project. According to news-paper reports the next day—based on an interview Mitchell gave the Associated Press—the STFU won a complete victory: Alexander recognized the union as the bargaining agent for the colonists. "Dr. Alexander said he agreed to bargain with the union because it represented a majority of the project colonists," the AP reported, paraphrasing Mitchell. "He said he would grant similar recognition to any group on any FSA project, whether it be a union or not, as long as it represented a majority." Mitchell added that FSA recognition would pave the way for unionization of sharecroppers and tenants on privately owned cotton plantations.

If the report is correct, Reid moaned, "our actions in attempting to get harmony in the administration at Dyess are nullified."[87] Even more serious, the incident gave the agency the worst possible publicity. One columnist, George Morris, made it seem that the Farm Security Administration was in collusion with the STFU to "bring about universal unionism on the farms of the South," creating a situation where the landowner would negotiate with his tenants through a union spokesman in the same way industry negotiated with workers. After gaining a toehold at Dyess Colony, the union would organize other government projects and then "move in on private landowners."[88]

In reality Alexander granted nothing. Either Mitchell misunderstood what Alexander said or the Associated Press misunderstood Mitchell. "I believe," Alexander wrote Reid immediately, "I made it perfectly plain that such committees are purely advisory, and the responsibility for the management and operations of the project must rest with FSA officials." "I agreed, of course, that the Advisory Committee recently elected at Dyess Colony should be recognized as representing the project residents. . . . It was well understood," Alexander said, "by everyone in the meeting that the Committee could be recognized as representing project residents and not the Southern Tenant Farmers Union."[89]

Two days later, on 6 March, Reid and Whitaker went back to Dyess and, with Ray Johnston, met with the advisory committee. When Reid

87. *Arkansas Gazette*, 3 March 1940; *Arkansas Democrat*, 2 March 1940. See Memphis *Commercial Appeal*, 9 March 1940; T. Roy Reid to Pete [R. W. Hudgens], 3 March 1940, FSA Records, NA, RG 96.
88. *Commercial Appeal*, 9 March 1940.
89. Will W. Alexander to T. Roy Reid, 4 March 1940, FSA Records, NA, RG 96; see William Lightfoot, Jr., to E. P. Coleman, 14 March 1940, ibid. In a conversation with the author on 9 March 1971, Mitchell read this account and conceded that perhaps he had misunderstood Alexander's statement.

asked Tom Hale, chairman of the committee, to preside at the meeting, Hale objected that L. J. Brantley should take charge, since the union was to be recognized as the colony's bargaining agent.

> I immediately advised him [Reid reported] that the Farm Security Administration wanted the advice and counsel of the committee which had been selected by the people, but did not consider any organization or committee from any organization as a bargaining agency. He [Hale] stated that we should so consider it since Washington had authorized such action. I then read your letter. We had about a five minute discussion and the committee seemed to feel that it was all right and that it would be best for us to deal with them as a committee reporting to the residents of Dyess Farms.

The meeting then moved on to a calm, two-and-a-half-hour discussion of the requests listed in their petition.

> The committee seemed pleased that we are taking steps to appraise the farms and rewrite the contracts on the basis of the appraised value or present contract value, whichever is less. . . . They were advised that it would not be possible for them to make changes in our loan policy but we asked for suggestions from them. Apparently they were not insistent on any point; however, they were strongest in their views that we should not take second mortgages on this year's crops to secure their past indebtedness to the Dyess Rural Rehabilitation Corporation, but they seemed to understand the purpose of this and raised no real objection to it.[90]

The basis of the colonists' request for a voice in personnel selection, Reid learned, was the fact that they objected to two men already employed by Dyess, a farm foreman and the clerk in charge of the main office. The foreman had served as a deputy sheriff, and was one of the men who allegedly broke up the Finch meeting in 1938. Reid promised an investigation of both men, and later transferred the foreman and fired the clerk for incompetence.

Regional officials encountered as much trouble with factionalism among the colonists as it did with STFU petitions. Since a group of five men had requested a meeting, Reid and Whitaker stayed overnight at the colony and met with them the following morning. Unlike the other group, these men opposed the announcement that the STFU had been granted bargaining rights at Dyess, and they spoke for a large number of colonists who felt as they did. Reid read Alexander's letter a second time, and they seemed pleased. STFU organizers, they told Reid, were using the news-

90. T. Roy Reid to Will W. Alexander, 9 March 1940, ibid.

paper statement to coerce colonists into the union. Reid left satisfied with the results of both meetings. "I think we made progress in handling our relations with the people on Dyess Farms," he wrote, "and that we can now make more progress."[91]

To further set matters straight, Reid released Alexander's 4 March letter to the press. After this experience, however, he determined to keep Dyess Colony out of the news as much as possible. During the coming weeks, newspaper editors and reporters applied considerable pressure to regional information adviser George Wolf for news about Dyess, but he successfully stalled for time. "Reid is not in favor of any publicity for some time to come," Wolf wrote, "as we have not had time to accomplish anything worth mentioning." Reporters could still go directly to the colony, but, he commented, "Fortunately, the roads into the project are so bad that newspaper men don't drop by there lightly."[92] As for congressional inquiries, FSA policy was to "speak about Dyess only when spoken to" until project affairs reached a more settled state.[93]

Floyd Slayton was another of those colonists who made a career out of dissension. A younger man than Funk, he at first hesitated to speak up. In 1939 he was one of the courthouse demonstrators who complained of exorbitant land prices. About that time, Kate Fulton of the family selection staff reviewed Slayton's case and recommended he be evicted, but no action was taken.[94] After Funk's and McCravin's evictions in 1940, he graduated to ringleader of the dissident faction, serving as both secretary of the STFU local and a member of the advisory committee. Although Local No. 29 soon disbanded, Slayton and four or five others kept up a running battle with FSA officials.[95]

He and most of his clique held old Dyess Colony deeds, and they claimed that Dyess Farms had no right of control over the actions of such deed holders except to collect payments. They insisted they did not have to abide by the rules and regulations of the new management. In January 1943 Slayton circulated a petition, with sixty-eight signatures, proposing

91. Ibid.

92. George Wolf to John Fischer, 16 May 1940, ibid.; Wolf to Nathan W. Robertson, 11 April 1940, ibid.

93. Jack H. Bryan to George Wolf, 7 April 1941, ibid.

94. Homer N. Hall to A. M. Rogers, 3 January 1942, ibid.; B. A. Redwine, memorandum to Miss [Kate] Fulton, 11 February 1941, Miscellaneous Files, Farmers Home Administration, County Office, Osceola, Arkansas; Fulton to Ray D. Johnston, n.d. [ca. 14 February 1941], ibid. (Hereafter cited as Osceola Records. This material is a couple of files left from Dyess Colony days.)

95. See, for example, Floyd Slayton to Brice M. Mace, Jr., 15 October 1940, FSA Records, NA, RG 96.

the removal of the board of directors and the revision of Dyess Farms' land purchase contracts.[96]

"Mr. Slayton's record here shows that he has not cooperated with the organization at any time and that he has gone out of his way to cause dissatisfaction among other members," the new community manager, Homer N. Hall, wrote. "So long as he and his four or five buddies are permitted to carry on as they are now doing, it will not be possible for us to put the program over as it must be put over." With people like Slayton, Hall believed, the FSA had reached an impasse; it was either Slayton or the colony. "This whole thing hinges on whether or not the Farm Security Administration is going to manage the operation of this Project or have it operated by Floyd Slayton, Dewey Smothers, W. M. Hodnett and two or three others." "I think the existence of this Project depends on the elimination of this bunch."[97]

An investigation of Dyess Colony conducted in late 1943 by James I. Hicks, an accountant, supported Hall's judgment. Hicks visited the colony, examined its books, and interviewed the community manager. He found a large percentage of the clients were "problem families" that spent their time fomenting strife and trying to override the management when decisions did not suit them. While some of the colonists complained of a "riding boss" attitude among those in charge, Hicks thought the FSA was guilty of too much leniency. The community manager had a difficult task, but no authority to do such things as move problem families off the project. Hicks had visited other FSA projects, and found the situation widespread. Here, he believed, was the principal weakness of the FSA program.[98]

Between 1943 and 1945, however, the FSA took a number of colonists to court on eviction suits and won. Floyd Slayton was, curiously, not one of them. While he eventually accepted the FSA deed he so distrusted, Slayton later sold any equity he had to an eligible applicant, cutting his ties voluntarily with the colony. So did several others, including Tom Hale. L. J. Brantley and Dewey Smothers also signed new deeds, farmed

96. Homer N. Hall to A. M. Rogers, 3 January 1943, with enclosed copy of Petition for Call of Meeting, signed by sixty-eight people, ibid. Yet when a group of twenty-four persons signed a letter to the Arkansas congressional delegation in March 1942 defending the FSA's management of Dyess, Slayton's name was there along with the others. To the Honorable Senators and Congressmen from Arkansas, dated 23 March 1942, ibid.; Ray D. Johnston to E. B. Whitaker, 6 April 1942, ibid.
97. See Homer N. Hall to T. B. Fatherree, 15 November 1943, ibid.; Hall to A. M. Rogers, 3 January 1943, ibid.
98. James I. Hicks to Select Committee of Congress . . . , 6 December 1943, USHR, *FSA Hearings*, pp. 1667–71.

their units for several years, and sold out at a profit. But the old suspicions died hard. As late as 1945 a group sought to form another STFU local.[99]

Even after allowing for troublemakers, it was increasingly clear that many colonists complained because something existed worth complaining about. In January 1944, just before liquidating Dyess Colony, regional director A. D. Stewart remarked, "Many of the claims of unfair treatment of Dyess farmers arising from conditions existing prior to 1940 . . . are justified."[100] WPA purchase contracts were not only unfair but against the principles of sound agricultural planning. The units were too small for a cotton economy, he pointed out, and cost too much. When the FSA took over, the new management enlarged and reorganized the units and, "in an effort to adjust the unreasonable contracts they had signed," offered colonists additional land at an average of ten dollars an acre. In addition, the FSA marked off the greater part of the indebtedness charged against farmers prior to 1940. But the correction of past mistakes in turn created new problems. "From this reorganization," Stewart said, "has come much discontent and controversy because of the lack of understanding by the farmers of what we were attempting to do." Some did not understand, for example, why old contracts must be exchanged for new ones. "Not understanding that they are bound by the old purchase contract, no matter how unfair, until they relinquish it and sign a new document, some farmers have refused to meet this request and for this reason have yet to receive their deeds."[101] Stewart refused to say the former management was unreasonable, but he stressed that "because of the necessity for changing plans some claims of unfair treatment by occupants were probably justified."[102]

Consider, for example, the hypothetical case of a farmer who came to Dyess in 1934 and lived through every change in management down to liquidation ten years later. When he first arrived, he expected to have a

99. Austin Chaplain to the author, 29 May 1969. Two other old-time "malcontents" who were evicted were A. S. Wheetley and E. C. Webb, both witnesses of the Paul Finch beating. Wheetley to Rep. Clifford R. Hope, 11 February 1945, Osceola Records; Webb to Hope, 11 February 1945, ibid. After a long delay and a final mix-up which lasted over two years, Slayton finally accepted and received his FSA deed. E. B. Whitaker to Alene Ward, 18 December 1946, ibid.; Raymond O. Denham to J. V. Highfill, 11 March 1948, ibid. On the new attempts to set up a union local, see David Burgess, memorandum to H. L. Mitchell, 21 May 1945, STFU Papers.

100. *Arkansas Gazette*, 9 January 1944; A. D. Stewart to Floyd Sharp, 22 January 1944, FSA Records, NA, RG 96.

101. *Arkansas Gazette*, 9 January 1944; see Sen. John L. McClellan to C. B. Baldwin, 10 July 1943, FSA Records, NA, RG 96.

102. A. D. Stewart to Floyd Sharp, 22 January 1944, ibid.

chance to purchase his own farm. He did indeed get a tract of uncleared land and a new home, but he waited two years, until 1936, before learning the price and terms. He was told he must go through a two-year probationary period in order to qualify for a purchase contract. But after finishing his second year at Dyess, he still had no contract. Dyess Colony, Inc., did not issue any sales contracts until after the lapse of three years, in 1937. As farmers began finding out how much they had been charged, unrest broke into the open; but the farmer, let us say, along with about two hundred others, finally received a deed. Then, in 1940, the FSA took control and announced that all old deeds would have to be canceled and new contracts issued. While this process was under way, Dyess Colony went into liquidation, and his new sales contract had to be exchanged again—this time for a deed and mortgage. But at last he did have a deed to his farm; that is, if he had not already been evicted as a troublemaker. "Plans for the sale of units changing at different intervals during the operation have caused some of the occupants who talked to me," Stewart said, "to lose faith in any person offering proposals and to lose faith in all proposals for the final liquidation of this Project."[103]

When the Farm Security Administration started liquidating the resettlement projects in 1943, Dyess's reorganization program remained incomplete. A large number of families, highly dissatisfied with the new sales contracts, simply refused to negotiate with Dyess Farms for the purchase and repair of their units. At the time of liquidation, Dyess Farms had executed only about 125 new contracts, with seventy-five units still occupied under contracts entered into with Dyess Colony, Inc., and the remaining hundred or so units under annual leases.[104]

After several tries and much delay, the Farm Security Administration worked out a liquidation plan satisfactory to all project residents. "Each worthy and eligible occupant now living at the farms," Stewart promised, "will be given an opportunity to buy his unit at a price reasonable to him and fair to the government."[105] The board of directors of Dyess Farms, Inc., stressed the desire of resident families to secure deeds to their farms immediately. On the other hand, the board refused to consider a plan in which Dyess Rural Rehabilitation Corporation would deliver deeds to the residents, and insisted on dealing directly with the government. On 16 June 1944 Dyess Farms held a special business meeting, and about 120 members approved a plan of liquidation. Many of the colonists under

103. Ibid.
104. W. T. Frazier, memorandum to Frank Hancock, 24 March 1944, ibid.
105. *Arkansas Gazette*, 9 January 1944.

eviction suits attended, and they raised no objection. The members passed every required resolution without a dissenting vote; it was the first time everyone at Dyess had been able to agree on anything for years.[106]

Thus, on 17 June, Dyess Rural Rehabilitation Corporation transferred title to the colony's farm land to Dyess Farms, Inc., waiving the payment of $650,000 provided for in the "agreement of sale" of 1941. Then Dyess Farms canceled all purchase contracts and deeds, gave each family a note, deed, and mortgage to their unit, and sold the farm units occupied under rental contracts to applicants eligible for farm ownership under the terms of the Bankhead-Jones Farm Tenant Act. The United States government took a mortgage on the land, and arranged to make all collections from purchasers without the help of either Dyess Rural Rehabilitation Corporation or Dyess Farms.[107]

Next the regional office amended the loan agreement of 29 June 1940 so that, as part of the final arrangement, Dyess Farms could make improvement loans to individual purchasers of farm units. No loan could exceed $1,000 unless personally approved by the regional director. Each farmer's note and mortgage included the amount of the improvement loan, if any were made. Since most of its $872,820 loan was still unspent, Dyess Farms refunded all excess funds (about $325,000) not used for repairs and needed for improvement loans. The association also conveyed its assets—real estate, notes, mortgages, and other property—to the government upon request. By October 1944 Dyess Farms converted to deed and mortgage 220 FSA purchase contracts and 56 old Dyess Colony deeds, leaving only 32 units still unsold.[108]

Since FSA officials did not publish liquidation figures for Dyess Colony, it is impossible to determine the final selling price of the farm units. In an earlier "state of the colony" address, Floyd Sharp remarked that Dyess Colony, Inc., expected to recover $1,275,000 from the sale of individual farms.[109] Yet Dyess Rural Rehabilitation Corporation later agreed to sell them for $650,000, apparently a bargain-basement offer. The latter figure was more in line with the sales price on FSA projects. After disposing of

106. W. T. Frazier, memorandum to Frank Hancock, 24 March 1944, FSA Records, NA, RG 96; A. D. Stewart to C. Stott Noble, 21 June 1944, ibid.

107. Agreement of Transfer between the Dyess Rural Rehabilitation Corporation and the Dyess Farms, Inc., 30 September 1945, ibid.

108. A. D. Stewart to Frank Hancock, 12 February 1944; Robert H. Shields, memorandum to Hancock, 4 April 1944; Hancock to Stewart, 5 April 1944; Dyess Colony, memorandum by A. W. Palmer, 9 October 1944, all ibid.

109. Address of Floyd Sharp, President of Dyess Colony, Incorporated, at the Dedication of the High School, 27 April 1938, enclosed with Sharp to A. D. Stewart, 12 January 1944, ibid.

individual farm units, Dyess Rural Rehabilitation Corporation still owned the community center, containing about forty-five buildings, and 2,596 acres of undeveloped land. In 1945 the corporation began disposing of most of this as surplus property.

The Dyess Health Association paid $1,200 for the hospital building and the block on which it stood. The Dyess Cooporative Gin Association bought the gin building and machinery for $22,500, and the Cooperative Store Association paid $5,000 for the store building and lot. The Arkansas Power and Light Company purchased the electric power distribution system and assumed responsibility for furnishing power to the project.[110] In November 1945 Dyess Rural Rehabilitation Corporation opened bids on the remainder of the community center buildings and land. Lee Wilson Company, which originally sold a considerable part of the project land to W. R. Dyess, submitted the highest bid of $50,100 for the community village as a unit; but the regional office rejected the offer, thinking a much better price could be obtained through negotiations. On the second round Lee Wilson Company again bid high at $60,000, and again the bid was rejected.

By this time some of the families who owned farm units objected that the purchase of the entire village by one large commercial organization would depreciate the value of their small holdings. Conceding their point, the regional office sold the community center piecemeal. By March 1946 the Dyess school district, several churches, and ten individuals had purchased nineteen structures and seven vacant lots for $26,206; still on the market were residences, administration building, community center, three warehouses, and seventeen vacant lots. On 7 May 1948 a notice appeared in the Lepanto *News Record* offering 614 acres of cutover timberland for sale; this tract was all that remained unsold of the Dyess project property.[111]

Before 1940 the Federal Emergency Relief Administration granted Dyess Colony a total of $3,685,224. With these funds Dyess officials bought land, constructed homes, provided community facilities, and operated the project. Over the next five years the Farm Security Administration put $547,820 of its own money into the colony's renovation. From 1934 to September 1946 the project operated at a net loss of

110. Dillard B. Lasseter, memorandum to E. B. Whitaker, 26 July 1946; Dyess Cooperative Gin Association, Annual Report, for Fiscal Year Ending 28 February 1946; Whitaker, memorandum to Lasseter, 1 March 1945; Whitaker to Sen. J. W. Fulbright, 1 March 1946, all ibid.
111. Ibid.; Thirty-four People to Sen. Bill Fulbright, 5 March 1946, ibid.; *News Record* (Lepanto, Ark.), 7 May 1948.

$1,364,890.59. Through 1938 Dyess Colony, Inc., built up a deficit total-
ing $811,546.91, while Dyess Rural Rehabilitation Corporation lost
$553,343.68 from 1939 to 1945. The colony wrote off $252,149.35
through debt adjustment.[112] After 1940 the Dyess Corporation gradually
decreased operations because of the transfer of the farm units to Dyess
Farms, Inc., and the transfer of the store, gin, and hospital to other cooperative associations. Somewhat more successful, Dyess Farms operated
at a profit of $11,432.12 in 1941, but suffered a loss of $2,981.21 in
1942 before going into liquidation.[113]

In total, how much money did Dyess Colony lose? The answer is simple
to estimate. Regional officials finally disposed of the community center for
$50,906. The sale of undeveloped land did not likely bring more than
$50,000. Nor is it probable that the liquidation of the farm units produced
more than the "bargain" price, $650,000. If so, Dyess Colony lost al-
most $3 million.

The Farmers Home Administration (FHA), FSA's successor, wound
up the resettlement program. At Dyess little remained to do. In 1951 both
the Dyess Rural Rehabilitation Corporation and Dyess Farms, Inc., returned their remaining assets to the parent agency of the Dyess project,
the Arkansas Rural Rehabilitation Corporation, which still maintained
a revolving trust fund under the supervision of the secretary of agriculture. Since all government mortgages against Dyess Farms were paid in
full and since Dyess Rural Rehabilitation Corporation had disposed of
its property, the FHA's next step was the dissolution of these two corporations.[114] On 27 June 1951, Dyess Rural Rehabilitation Corporation
dissolved itself—an easy task because the corporation had only three
stockholders, who could easily meet and take the necessary steps for
dissolution.

The Farmers Home Administration consistently maintained that every
FSA cooperative association must be dissolved in order to comply with

112. Audit Report, Dyess Rural Rehabilitation Corporation, Dyess, Mississippi
County, Arkansas, for the Period 22 March 1939 to 30 September 1945, FSA Records, NA, RG 96.
113. W. T. Frazier, memorandum to Frank Hancock, 24 March 1944; Dyess
Farms, Inc., Annual Financial Report, for the Fiscal Year Ended 31 December
1943; Dyess Farms, Inc., Annual Financial Report, for the Period 22 October 1941
to 31 December 1941; Dyess Farms, Inc., Annual Financial Report, for the Fiscal
Year Ended 31 December 1942, all ibid.
114. O. N. Spring, memorandum to D. B. Lasseter, 23 April 1948; Minutes of
Annual Meeting of Board of Directors of Dyess Rural Rehabilitation Corporation,
held 1 June 1951; J. V. Highfill, memorandum to Lasseter, 16 August 1951; Spring
to Highfill, 9 October 1951; Highfill, memorandum to Lasseter, 17 January 1952,
all ibid.

the congressional liquidation mandate. Yet the members of Dyess Farms, Inc., refused this last act of charity. According to Ray Johnston, then FHA county supervisor at Osceola, the current membership list had been lost out of the minute books. In any case, during the previous few years it had been difficult to obtain a quorum (25 percent of the members) at the annual membership meetings, and Johnston doubted that the necessary two-thirds would show up for a meeting of no real importance to them.

Dyess Farms, however, was for all practical purposes already dissolved. It had no debts and no assets, and its membership no longer carried on any business as an organization. In 1951 the Farmers Home Administration simply closed its files on Dyess Colony.[115]

115. Rep. Dan P. Chisholm to J. V. Highfill, 24 April 1952; Highfill to D. B. Lasseter, 28 April 1952; Lasseter, memorandum to Highfill, 15 March 1952, all ibid.

Chapter XIII

From Peace to War: 1941–42

Three months before the Farm Security Administration assumed control of Dyess Colony, Adolf Hitler sent his army across the Polish border and plunged Europe into war. Even though the United States was not yet involved, foreign rather than domestic problems increasingly commanded attention. The depression, which was already on the wane, rapidly lifted as war mobilization gained momentum. Many depression-born New Deal agencies found the transition from peace to war difficult at best. For the FSA, World War II posed not just one but a series of crises. While low-income farmers needed help as much as ever, the agency's leaders found themselves pondering a whole new set of questions: Where could they find justification for their social welfare programs in the matrix of total war? How could they avert the prospect of liquidation which hung over other New Deal agencies and continue to serve the small farmer?

President Roosevelt's declaration that the United States must become "the great arsenal of democracy" suggested the agency emphasize its role in national defense. The FSA could gear the great mass of low-income farm families to the production of food needs for wartime America. Large farmers, it was believed, were already operating at peak capacity, while small farmers could increase their production many times. Soon after Pearl Harbor, FSA chief C. B. Baldwin announced plans not only to encourage regular client families to begin all-out production, but also to assist families not currently participating in FSA programs. The Food for Freedom program, as it was called, could insure small farmers a share in wartime prosperity and, not least of all, give the FSA the viability it needed to survive.[1]

1. Sidney Baldwin, *Poverty and Politics: The Rise and Decline of the Farm Security Administration* (Chapel Hill: University of North Carolina Press, 1968),

Above and beyond its regular activities, the FSA took on emergency defense assignments. Even before the Japanese attack, it relocated farm families who were displaced by defense preparations. Seventy families lost their farms when the U.S. Army acquired an area north of Camp Robinson in Arkansas for use as an artillery range and maneuver ground, and the Little Rock office leased a tract of land to take care of them.[2] More such defense relocation projects soon appeared in the Little Rock area.

With the entry of the United States into the war, many farm people shifted into towns, looking for industrial jobs; and the agency's experience with housing proved invaluable. The Pine Bluff Defense Housing project took care of the migration to jobs at the Pine Bluff Arsenal, some workers perhaps fresh from Plum Bayou and Lake Dick. Other towns of the region—including Jacksonville and Hope, Arkansas; Minden, Louisiana, the site of a munitions plant; and Pascagoula, Mississippi—had FSA-built defense housing.[3]

The Farm Security Administration played a major role in the unpleasant task of removing some 113,000 Japanese from California and relocating them in concentration camps. Two relocation centers were established in southeastern Arkansas, the largest at Rohwer and another near Jerome. The War Relocation Authority (WRA) obtained the land for both camps from the FSA; Rohwer and Jerome were planned originally as resettlement projects, although only Jerome had ever been developed. FSA personnel were prominently involved in the relocation program. E. B. Whitaker became a WRA regional director, and supervised construction of the camps. Ray Johnston transferred from Dyess Colony to take charge of Rohwer; Paul A. Taylor, another old FSA hand, went to Jerome. At their peak the two camps held some thirty thousand Japanese internees and later housed German prisoners of war.[4]

---

pp. 326–32; Walter W. Wilcox, *The Farmer in the Second World War* (Ames: Iowa State College Press, 1947), pp. 46–47.

All resettlement projects adapted their farm program to the war effort. See, for example, Food for Freedom Program, Dyess Farms, S-AK-80, February 1942, FSA Records, NA, RG 96; Homer N. Hall to A. M. Rogers, 27 March 1943, ibid.; *Osceola Times*, 22 May 1943.

2. Little Rock *Arkansas Gazette*, 2 February 1941.

3. The defense housing activities of the agency were transferred to the National Housing Administration in February 1942. Baldwin, *Poverty and Politics*, p. 228.

4. *Arkansas Gazette*, 9 August 1942. See Laurence Hewes, *Boxcar in the Sand* (New York: Knopf, 1957), chap. 14; Ruth P. Vickers, "Japanese-American Relocation," *Arkansas Historical Quarterly* 10 (Summer 1951): 168–76; William C. Anderson, "Early Reaction in Arkansas to the Relocation of Japanese in the State,"

During part of the war, the FSA shared responsibility with the United States Employment Service for the wartime farm labor program. Agriculture faced a major manpower crisis in the early months of the war. The FSA located migrant workers, moved them where they were needed, and looked out for their interests. Controversy, however, dogged the agency even in one of its most humanitarian undertakings. The strict standards of wages, hours, sanitation, and housing in FSA migratory labor camps brought down the wrath of major producer groups, particularly where Mexican workers were concerned.[5]

However meritorious its war service, the Farm Security Administration soon found itself fighting enemies at home as well as abroad. World War II brought a reaction against New Deal reforms, and the FSA was one of the first agencies to come under attack.[6]

"Now comes the New Deal," a Mississippi planter carped in 1942, ". . . with a law to acquire our plantations . . . and divide the land up again into family sized farms of 40 acres and a mule—the same promise the other Yankees made to the negroes during the other Civil War."[7]

The Farm Security Administration and its predecessor, the Resettlement Administration, acquired many critics like this one. Southern landlords and large farm corporations relied on the labor of the very groups the FSA befriended—tenants, sharecroppers, and migrant farm workers. As the FSA took them under its wing, large farm interests began to worry about losing their cheap labor supply. For similar reasons, private processors and retailers—as well as bankers—felt threatened when the FSA made loans to farm cooperatives. And even the agency's war programs aroused the hostility of powerful farm interests that were contemptuous of the productive capacities of small farmers or that preferred to treat

---

ibid. 23 (Autumn 1964): 195–211; Dillon S. Myer, *Uprooted Americans: The Japanese Americans and the War Relocation Authority during World War II* (Tucson: University of Arizona Press, 1971).

5. Baldwin, *Poverty and Politics*, pp. 377–83.

6. Paul K. Conkin, *Tomorrow a New World: The New Deal Community Program* (Ithaca, N.Y.: Cornell University Press, 1959), p. 220. See Hewes, *Boxcar in the Sand*, p. 154; Oren Stephens, "FSA Fights for Its Life," *Harper's Magazine* 186 (April 1943): 479–87.

7. O. F. Bledsoe III, "The Political Aspect of the Delta and Plantation System," political broadside on behalf of James O. Eastland, enclosed with Franklin D. Roosevelt to Eleanor Roosevelt, 9 June 1942, FDR Papers, OF 93, quoted in George B. Tindall, *The Emergence of the New South, 1913–1945* (Baton Rouge: Louisiana State University Press, 1967), p. 707.

their laborers as they had in the past. Most important, the Farm Bureau and its Extension Service ally feared any independent power structure with thousands of clients not under their control.

Unlike many other agencies within the Department of Agriculture, the FSA never dared organize its clientele into a political constituency. In terms of sheer numbers the agency's clientele was impressive, but they came from a class with little experience in political action. Most of the people the FSA helped did not even vote, while southern landlords, large farm corporations, and processors had powerful backers in Congress. The large proportion of Negro families among FSA clients further reduced the possibilities that they could form some kind of political force. True, the FSA had its friends, a schizophrenic collection of groups ranging from the National Farmers Union and Southern Tenant Farmers' Union to the National Association for the Advancement of Colored People and several church-related organizations. But the agency never sought the kind of relationship that existed between the Agricultural Extension Service and the Farm Bureau. When the crisis came, the FSA found itself without political clout.

From 1937 on, a congressional coalition of Republicans and conservative Democrats engaged in a continuous and increasingly successful battle with the Roosevelt administration over domestic policy.[8] The New Deal had actually run out of ideas, but the conservatives in Congress would have made further legislation difficult, anyway. The situation was worse than a stalemate. New Dealers were soon fighting a rearguard action to keep existing programs from being scuttled.

Congressional conservatives like Representatives Clarence Cannon of Missouri, Everett M. Dirksen of Illinois, and Malcolm C. Tarver of Georgia made the FSA a scapegoat for their displeasure with the New Deal. In the budget debates during the spring of 1940, they sought to eliminate all funds for the tenant purchase program and to attach several crippling restrictions to the use of rehabilitation funds. The tenant purchase item was restored in the final Appropriation Act for Fiscal 1941, but only after the personal intervention of several influential individuals, including the president himself. The conservatives' major success was the so-called Tarver Amendment—a bothersome provision of this and subse-

8. William E. Leuchtenburg, *Franklin D. Roosevelt and the New Deal, 1932–1940* (New York: Harper and Row, 1963), chap. 11; James T. Patterson, *Congressional Conservatism and the New Deal: The Growth of the Conservative Coalition in Congress, 1933–1939* (Lexington: University of Kentucky Press, 1967), pp. 250ff.

quent appropriation acts limiting the size and value of farms eligible for purchase with tenant purchase funds. Otherwise, FSA programs came through unscathed, but a showdown was definitely in the offing.[9]

The entry of America into World War II gave the agency's enemies the advantage they needed. The requirements of mobilization lessened the need for federal relief spending, while President Roosevelt did not dare take strong stands on domestic issues and risk alienating congressional support for vital wartime programs. Caught in a cruel dilemma, he watched unwillingly as Congress began to dismantle the New Deal in the guise of economy and nonessential spending. The casualty list of New Deal agencies rapidly mounted—WPA, NYA, and CCC all went under by 1943.

The congressional demands for economy and the end of New Deal "socialism" paralleled the American Farm Bureau Federation's growing hostility toward the Roosevelt administration. At its annual convention in December 1940, the Farm Bureau adopted a scheme for a major reorganization and "decentralization" of the Department of Agriculture, and the rift within the nation's agricultural establishment burst into the open. What the Farm Bureau proposed, if carried out, would have stripped the secretary of agriculture of control over much of his department and turned over the department's "action" programs to the Extension Service, thus eliminating what Farm Bureau leaders described as needless duplication and confusion. As for the FSA, the convention called for a thorough investigation, but the delegates did not have to wait for the results: they went on to propose a curtailment of the agency's activities.[10]

By the time Ed O'Neal placed the Farm Bureau reorganization scheme before the agricultural subcommittee of the House Appropriations Committee in January 1941, he was ready with a bold, even reckless, plan for the FSA. He wanted a dismemberment of the agency—its loan programs transferred to the Farm Credit Administration and its farm and home planning functions to the Extension Service. The reorganization plan was far too sweeping to be taken seriously. It was turned down cold. Although the House Appropriations Committee did approve large cuts in rural re-

9. Baldwin, *Poverty and Politics*, pp. 338–41; 54 *US Stat.* 532.

10. *Nation's Agriculture* 16 (January 1941): 18–20. On the Farm Bureau–FSA conflict, see Christiana McFadyen Campbell, *The Farm Bureau and the New Deal* (Urbana: University of Illinois Press, 1962), chap. 10; Orville Merton Kile, *The Farm Bureau through Three Decades* (Baltimore: Waverly, 1948), pp. 264–73; William J. Block, *The Separation of the Farm Bureau and the Extension Service* (Urbana: University of Illinois Press, 1960), pp. 35–38; Grant McConnell, *The Decline of Agrarian Democracy* (Berkeley and Los Angeles: University of California Press, 1953), chap. 9.

habilitation funds, the New Deal still had strong support in the Senate; and as finally passed, the Agriculture Appropriation Act for 1942 made only modest reductions in FSA funds.[11] O'Neal lost the first round of the fight, but he was full of tricks.

Congressional conservatism and Farm Bureau ambitions converged at the hearings of the Joint Committee on Reduction of Nonessential Federal Expenditures—otherwise known as the Byrd committee, after its chairman, Sen. Harry F. Byrd, the irascible Virginia conservative. The Byrd committee hearings quickly turned into an inquisition of the New Deal. In a preliminary report in December 1941, the conservatives and economizers on the committee put the FSA on their "death list" of New Deal agencies. They proposed that the FSA be abolished and "some more suitable agency" assume its war-related functions.[12]

When Byrd launched his formal investigation of the FSA in February 1942, O'Neal appeared as a star witness and brought others to back him. A shrewd showman, O'Neal created a momentary sensation with the testimony of Robert K. Greene, probate judge from Greensboro, Alabama. The Farm Security Administration, the judge revealed, was engaged in the practice of paying its clients' poll taxes, presumably part of an effort to influence votes and build up a political machine.[13] Having gained the committee's full attention, O'Neal outlined the Farm Bureau case against the FSA. Most Farm Security programs were no longer necessary, he claimed, and the rest should be turned over to other agencies. He went on to make a series of bold charges: the FSA established quotas of clients in order to spend all funds appropriated and to maintain full personnel employment, "solicited" clients to meet those quotas, burdened clients with more loans than they could repay, established "socialistic and impractical farming projects," made emergency grants to enable repayment of overdue loans and conceal the record of failure, used renewal notes and variable payment plans to disguise low payment rates on loans, employed pressure groups to maintain congressional appropriations, wasted funds in excessively high administrative costs, and exercised rigid control of business and farm plans of clients.[14]

11. Baldwin, *Poverty and Politics*, pp. 343–45; 55 *US Stat.* 408.

12. U.S. Congress, Joint Committee on Reduction of Nonessential Federal Expenditures, *Preliminary Report*, Senate Document 152, 24 December 1941, 77th Cong., 1st sess. (Washington: Government Printing Office, 1941), p. 5.

13. U.S. Congress, Joint Committee on Reduction of Nonessential Federal Expenditures, *Hearings on the Reduction of Nonessential Federal Expenditures*, 77th Cong., 2d sess. (Washington: Government Printing Office, 1942), pp. 699–711 (hereafter cited as *Byrd Committee Hearings*).

14. Ibid., pp. 743–45; Kile, *Farm Bureau*, pp. 268–69.

A few days later Donald Kirkpatrick, general counsel of the American Farm Bureau Federation, presented the committee with the results of a "preliminary investigation" which had been the basis of O'Neal's statement. Kirkpatrick had sent six investigators into selected states where the pickings seemed ripest. A Chicago attorney named William G. Carr undertook the most prodigious effort in a whirlwind trip across Alabama, Mississippi, Louisiana, and Arkansas. Whizzing through Region VI in a matter of days, he paid visits to several projects which lay in his path. No matter what their fundamental differences were, he persisted in labeling them all "socialized farming projects." In Mississippi he looked over the Loch Lomond plantation, a tenant purchase project in Leflore County, and the Mississippi Farm Tenant Security project in Sunflower County. He reported that he was unable to find anyone in the whole state other than FSA clients and employees who favored the agency's program.

His visit to Louisiana, taking a single day, was limited to the northeast corner of the state, where he heard the hard-luck story of Transylvania. Heading into Arkansas, he visited the Macon Lake land-leasing project, near Lake Village, and Jerome, the headquarters of Chicot Farms; but Lake Dick with its boarded-up houses was the most exciting find of his trip. He described its troubles in great detail. "The general public in the State of Arkansas," he found after a few days, "feels that the Farm Security Administration is accomplishing nothing but is committing acts the results of which it will take a long time to rectify." In the four states he visited, Carr encountered mismanagement, waste, open solicitation of clients, and trick bookkeeping to cover up poor repayment records.[15]

Baldwin had only three days to prepare his reply, but he vainly tried to answer every criticism. Carr had not appeared before the committee, Baldwin pointed out, and he could not be cross-examined. Since Carr had not revealed with whom he spoke, how reliable they were, whether they were prejudiced, or how they had knowledge of the facts, it was impossible to assess the value of his evidence. All the committee had was Carr's own opinion, a nonexpert one at that.[16] Baldwin was merely blowing in the wind. Although a few friends of the agency testified—H. L. Mitchell was one of them—most members of the committee had already condemned the agency in their own minds.[17]

As soon as the poll tax story broke, it provoked reaction from Region

15. *Byrd Committee Hearings*, pp. 794, 819–38.
16. Ibid., pp. 857–58, 893–905.
17. Ibid., pp. 918–20.

VI. John A. Boutwell, chairman of the agricultural committee of the Mississippi House of Representatives, fired off a long telegram to Sen. Robert M. La Follette, Jr., the only Byrd committee member with any sympathy for the FSA. Trying to turn the tables on O'Neal and the poll tax issue, Boutwell suggested that in Mississippi the Farm Bureau collected its membership dues from AAA payments through an involuntary "set-off" system, particularly where Negro tenants were involved. Many Negroes were not even aware they were members of the Farm Bureau. All over Mississippi, Boutwell said, the Farm Bureau and the AAA county offices were linked together, with the AAA regularly backing Farm Bureau membership drives. Until recently, for example, the AAA office at Clarksdale displayed a large sign reading, "Pay Your Farm Bureau Dues Here. The Farm Bureau Is Responsible for Getting Your Agricultural Adjustment Administration Payments." When La Follette confronted O'Neal with the telegram, O'Neal denied any knowledge of a check-off, and hinted that Boutwell might have some interest in the FSA's cooperative projects.[18]

Carr had claimed that the FSA program in Arkansas included the payment of clients' poll taxes.[19] When Little Rock reporters asked the regional director about it, A. D. Stewart answered much as Baldwin had before the Byrd committee. The FSA did not pay poll taxes for its borrowers, and regional officials "do not attempt to ascertain" whether clients pay poll taxes. Borrowers were encouraged to pay all tax obligations, including the poll tax, but there was no follow-through to see if they had done so. The meeting of tax obligations was necessary for good citizenship and rehabilitation, Stewart continued. When the FSA had mortgages on chattels or land, it made certain that all taxes were paid to prevent the property from becoming delinquent.[20]

At a press conference, Roosevelt himself defended the FSA on the poll tax issue. "These tenant people, these people who come under Federal grants have a budget which includes everything, every necessity of life. It includes food, includes clothes, includes a bed to sleep in, and it in-

18. John A. Boutwell to Hon. Robert M. La Follette, 9 February 1942, ibid., pp. 763–65. The majority of the members of the Mississippi House of Representatives' agricultural committee repudiated the Boutwell statement. Harry A. Jackson et al. to Sen. Harry F. Byrd, 5 March 1942, ibid., p. 765. Ransom E. Aldrich, president of the Mississippi Farm Bureau Federation, also replied to Boutwell, denying all misconduct except that he admitted such a sign had hung in the Clarksdale *courthouse*. "I would like to say that if there ever was a sign telling the truth that this sign spoke the truth." Aldrich to Edward A. O'Neal, 19 February 1942, ibid., pp. 766–74.

19. Ibid., p. 832.

20. *Arkansas Gazette*, 8, 9 February 1942.

cludes taxes of all kinds. And in those budgets they allow people to put down one form of tax, which is a poll tax."[21] "This controversy," he added, "reminds me of the time seven or eight years ago when there was a drive in this country to prevent anybody on W.P.A. from voting." Was the work of the FSA essential? "Our whole food situation for the duration of the war," he had said earlier, "is intimately connected with it. Furthermore the whole problem of security of a large number of individual families is at stake. Of course it is essential."[22] Yet he was powerless to keep Congress from emasculating the FSA's appropriation.

The spring of 1942 saw the struggle over the FSA begin in earnest. The sparring matches of 1940 and 1941 were over. The appropriation bill for the Department of Agriculture, which included the FSA's budget, was the big prize. On both sides the accusations soon became all too familiar, a kind of litany repeated over and over again; even the list of principal witnesses for and against the agency was a familiar parade.

Region VI played a significant role in the sweep of events. Two congressmen from the region—David D. Terry of Arkansas and Ross A. Collins of Mississippi— were members of the agricultural subcommittee of the House Committee on Appropriations. They did not lead the attack. The subcommittee chairman, Tarver, as well as Cannon and Dirksen, assumed that role. When Terry and Collins spoke up, they usually inquired only about matters relating to their home state. More than once, Terry in particular showed a good understanding of the FSA program, and he seemed to possess a sympathetic attitude.[23] Little Rock officials, along with FSA personnel all over the country, watched the proceedings with growing apprehension. The region's activities were often matters of discussion, and occasionally people from the region appeared as witnesses.

One of the most discussed projects was Lake Dick, a perfect example of the "un-American social experiments" and "Communistic communities" which evoked Tarver's bitterest criticism. An orthodox agrarian and self-styled champion of the small-scale farmer, he particularly disliked government projects on which a number of families held land in common rather than individually and shared equally in the proceeds of their com-

21. FDR, *Public Papers* (1942), 11:95–96.
22. Ibid., p. 94.
23. See USHR, *USDA Approp. Hearings, 1942,* 77th Cong., 1st sess., pt. 2, pp. 93–94, 106–7, 123; USHR, *USDA Approp. Hearings, 1943,* 77th Cong., 2d sess., pt. 2, p. 663.

bined efforts. This arrangement constituted a sort of Communism, as Tarver defined the term; it destroyed individual initiative, since no occupant had the opportunity of ever becoming the owner of any part of the land and since everyone earned the same whether he worked or not. "Do you or not consider," he pressed Maston G. White, solicitor of the Department of Agriculture, "that a transaction of that kind is justified under the law and the language under which the appropriation is made?"[24]

Trying to answer the question, White himself mentioned Lake Dick, obviously the type of project Tarver was describing. White would not be trapped into a position of defending Communism; he said, "It does not seem to me that an enterprise involving the joint ownership and operation of a tract of land by several families would necessarily constitute communism. It is somewhat like the joint ownership of a corporation by many people. A corporation is a common enterprise, where the owners all put in money and elect officers to carry on the business. Each stockholder merely owns a share of the whole property of the corporation."[25]

Lake Dick came up again when Baldwin testified a few days later. This time David Terry broached the subject, and Baldwin probably feared the worst. Lake Dick, Baldwin hastily explained, followed "somewhat the plantation day-labor pattern." See, he seemed to say, it was not so unusual after all. "The only difference is that whatever profit they make there will be divided among their own group rather than going to the landowner."[26] He erroneously described the project, however, as getting along "pretty well." Lake Dick had its problems, the FSA chief conceded. An increase in industrial opportunities around Pine Bluff, twenty miles away, accounted for a marked drop in population. Some of the families liked the cooperative arrangement, but others, Baldwin admitted, wanted to get some experience and go out and buy a family-type farm. Trying to justify such projects, Baldwin mentioned the Terrebonne cooperative. Sugarcane, he reminded the subcommittee, was most effectively raised in large-scale operations; and he asked for "tolerance with a certain amount of experimentation."[27]

> I do not know anything more democratic than cooperatives practically carried out [Baldwin said]. I think some of the things that we have heard called by other names reflected other ideologies of government more than

24. Ibid., pt. 1, p. 197.
25. Ibid., p. 198.
26. Ibid., pt. 2, p. 241.
27. Ibid., p. 242.

they reflected the cooperative pattern. I do not know of any reason why we cannot have successful farm-operating cooperatives; and as a matter of fact, I guess they would be perhaps a most democratic type of community if you could get them to work. But now there is one other thing I would like to add, there—

Just as he was warming up to his subject, Tarver cut him off: "Wait just a minute. I think you had better restrict yourself right now to the answering of questions by the committee, and arguments as to the propriety of what you are doing may be deferred until later."[28] That was the kind of intimidation Baldwin received before Tarver's subcommittee; the program in Region VI had provided the occasion for another embarrassing exchange.

"In what respect," Tarver bluntly asked, "does that enterprise [Lake Dick] differ from the system of agriculture practiced in Soviet Russia?" Baldwin may have been taken aback, but he managed to answer that the individual freedom of people living on FSA cooperatives was not in any way abridged. The people at Lake Dick were free to come and go as they pleased, with all the protections guaranteed under the United States Constitution. Tarver snapped: "The distinction you make, as I understand you, is that this is a voluntary collectivism, whereas in Russia it is compulsory."[29]

The Farm Security Administration, Baldwin stressed before the subcommittee, was committed to the family farm, in theory and practice. But the agency dealt with many different types of families, and some of them required closer supervision than others. The cooperative-type project, he said, "serves also as a very good training ground for farmers' families who are later to take their place on family-type operations."[30] This was the most plausible justification for projects like Lake Dick and Terrebonne.

When O'Neal put in his appearance before Tarver's subcommittee, he repeated the testimony he had given the Byrd committee that same morning. Since Judge Greene was still available, O'Neal brought him along for another session on the poll tax, but the reception was surprisingly cooler. As soon as Tarver began to cross-examine Greene, he put the judge on the defensive. Though critical of the FSA's experimentation, Tarver was determined to give the agency fair treatment. When he thought it deserved it, he came to its defense.[31]

28. Ibid., p. 244.
29. Ibid., p. 248.
30. Ibid.
31. Ibid., pp. 628–36.

O'Neal paraded in a number of other witnesses whose job was to collaborate his testimony. Two of them were Farm Bureau state presidents from Region VI; they also ran into stiff cross-examination. Arguing with R. E. Short of Arkansas, Terry maintained that the overall FSA program brought about immense benefits for low-income farmers, as evidenced particularly in their high repayment records; and Tarver flatly contradicted Short by insisting that the agency's methods produced very desirable results.[32]

Ransom E. Aldrich of the Mississippi Farm Bureau was subjected to actual embarrassment. Bringing with him a copy of a speech delivered by Dallas C. Vandevere, FSA state director in Mississippi, Aldrich intended to put one more nail in the poll tax issue. Vandevere had said, according to Aldrich's quotation, "We also insist that all families eligible to vote pay their poll taxes and exercise their voting privilege as citizens." "What is wrong about that?" Tarver shot back. Aldrich could not manage an intelligent reply. There was nothing, Tarver remarked, "contrary to good citizenship in a Farm Security Administration client qualifying himself ... as a voter by paying the poll tax."[33] When O'Neal tried to introduce part of the Carr report as evidence, Tarver ruled that it was not entitled to "any great weight" unless its author appeared before the committee. He would not admit hearsay evidence.[34]

Aldrich and Short later testified before the Senate subcommittee on the agricultural appropriation bill, but this time only Short mentioned the FSA. He claimed to be thoroughly in accord with the primary objective of the Farm Security program—to help worthy farmers. But, he went on, "we are very, very much alarmed about some of the philosophy being expressed by the administration of the Farm Security; not necessarily by the local folks that are administrating the program but by the central agency here in Washington." He referred, he said, to plans for the government to gain control of as much land as possible and to break all land holdings into small units—a theme which also ran through much of the anti-FSA campaign in the region.[35]

Short asked the committee to print in the record a copy of an article he claimed was circulated by the FSA Division of Information at Little Rock. It was Helen Fuller's "Who Speaks for the Farmers?" from the *New Republic*; the article hit the Farm Bureau pretty hard, and was in his

32. Ibid., pp. 656–58.
33. Ibid., pp. 666–67.
34. Ibid., pp. 761–63.
35. USS, *USDA Approp. Hearings, 1943*, 77th Cong., 1st sess., pp. 829–30.

mind prima facie evidence of something sinister. "May be you gentlemen know what the New Republic is," he remarked.[36] They agreed to print it. That summer, after a series of committee fights and compromises, Congress chopped FSA funds by 43 percent, a serious blow to the agency's war efforts. Only the tenant purchase program enjoyed any large degree of congressional enthusiasm. The new appropriation bill for 1943 contained drastic cuts in rural rehabilitation, farm debt adjustment, and migratory labor activities. The resettlement program and related activities were doomed. Congress prohibited any loans to cooperatives, direct land purchases, collective farming, and even the creation of new homestead associations. All resettlement communities were to be liquidated as rapidly as possible, with progress reports filed every six months.[37]

While the committee hearing rooms on Capitol Hill served as the principal battleground for the struggle, the Farm Bureau kept up the attack outside of Congress. In April 1942 Carr published an article on the FSA in *Nation's Agriculture*, the official organ of the American Farm Bureau Federation.[38] It was a distillation of his report. "The South today," he began, "is facing a situation which recalls the reconstruction days following the Civil War." He again used a shotgun attack, moving rapidly from one accusation to another, giving figures here and odd bits of information there, obviously repeating the more sensational stories he had collected from local Farm Bureau leaders and county agents. The land of one project in Arkansas, probably a reference to Plum Bayou, was "unproductive and always will be due to the fact that during the Spring months it is flooded and the clients must keep rowboats tied to their porches in case they want to get about." And Lake Dick, a dead horse, took another beating.

Like other critics, Carr hit the more traditional rehabilitation and tenant purchase programs as hard as the community projects. The charges he repeated were all familiar by then to anyone who followed the congressional hearings. Only a well-organized propaganda machine, he said, enabled the continuation of such deplorable waste and mismanagement.

36. Ibid., pp. 821–33; Helen Fuller, "Who Speaks for the Farmers?" *New Republic* 106 (23 February 1942): 267–68.
37. 56 *US Stat.* 664.
38. William G. Carr, "The Return of the Carpetbagger," *Nation's Agriculture* 17 (April 1942): 7, 9–10. For an interesting contrast, see an earlier article which exhibits a far better understanding of the resettlement program: "For Greater Farm Security," ibid. 13 (April 1938): 8, 14–15.

Within Region VI itself a cold war between the Farm Bureau and the Farm Security Administration had been under way since 1940. After publishing an article critical of the Lake Dick project,[39] the Memphis *Commercial Appeal* received a large number of letters from citizens of Arkansas and Mississippi requesting that its reporters make surveys of other projects and FSA programs in certain counties. Stewart watched and waited; then in early 1941 he summed up what was happening:

> I am afraid that these letters and requested studies are inspired by *"a certain organized"* group that is using this method of attack to offset an inspired public confidence in connection with the Farm Security Administration program in its extension of help to low-income families. The most dangerous attack that could be made would be to have presumably disinterested citizens pick the weak spots in our program and magnify them. We shall then watch every step taken in this direction carefully and prepare to meet the situation when it arises.[40]

Soon the Farm Bureau launched a barrage of criticism in newspapers, through the mail, and in private meetings. In early 1942, Stewart wrote that the Farm Bureau attack had become his "foremost" problem. Farm Bureau opposition, as Stewart saw it, came principally from state Farm Bureau officials, with very little criticism from county officials. He reported receiving resolutions and letters from Farm Bureau members in many counties indicating they did not concur in the FSA fight. "It is quite evident," he wrote, "that state farm bureau leaders did not consult county bureau units before launching the attack on our program. There is abundant evidence to show that farm bureau ranks have broken at many points and that there is clearly much resentment among bureau members over the position some of their leaders have taken."[41] But in this struggle the FSA could take little comfort in the knowledge that its opposition was divided.

Local representatives of the two organizations sometimes engaged in heated exchanges, one of which took place in the Jackson, Mississippi, newspapers. On 26 March 1942, Dallas Vandevere routinely reported that 25,397 Mississippi families with FSA loans had increased their net income from $328 before becoming clients to $571 at the end of 1941— an increase of 74 percent. During the same period, they raised their net

39. Memphis *Commercial Appeal*, 6 July 1940.
40. A. D. Stewart, Quarterly Report, January–March 1941, FSA Records, NA, RG 96.
41. A. D. Stewart, Quarterly Report, January–March 1942, ibid.

worth (all assets, from furniture and clothes to farm equipment) from $443 to $567.[42]

Ransom Aldrich immediately struck back at his nemesis. Vandevere's figures were accurate, a Farm Bureau news release admitted, but misleading. The income increase for FSA families was indeed 74 percent, but all farm income in Mississippi had increased 80 percent during the same period. "Being an FSA client kept 25,000 farmers from getting 6% additional increase in farm income," the Farm Bureau charged. Vandevere's assertion of a gain in net worth was equally misleading, since the FSA had made an average loan of $942 to each client; and it took the entire amount to increase their net worth by $124. For good measure, the Farm Bureau also criticized the high number of FSA employees in Mississippi, excessive administrative costs, misuse of cash grants, collective farming projects, and government policies to acquire "as much land as possible."[43]

It was Vandevere's turn, and he replied promptly. The Mississippi Farm Bureau was out "to discredit the work being done by low income farmers under FSA guidance," Vandevere said. "Like all of the accusations made by the Farm Bureau, the recent outburst is another exhibition of statistical gymnastics and comparison of unrelated facts and figures." When discussing income, he contended, the FSA referred to net increases, while the Farm Bureau used gross increases. He also questioned the accuracy of Farm Bureau figures on farm income. What about charges of overstaffing and excessive administrative costs? Consider Coahoma County, Vandevere said. There the FSA had three field workers, two clerks, and one person on temporary assignment—a force of six to supervise 128 borrowers. In Mississippi, Vandevere said, it cost taxpayers $72 a year per family to administer the FSA programs including all losses and expenses.[44]

When Vandevere replied, the Jackson *Daily News* officially got into the act, taking the Farm Bureau's side. An editorial writer was not impressed by production records of FSA clients. He also accused the agency of overstaffing and administrative extravagance: "A white-collared gentry gallivanting about over the state in expensive automobiles trying to tell farmers how to farm is somewhat akin to teaching bullfrogs how to swim. The truth of the matter about the average tenant farmer in the South is

42. Jackson *Daily News*, 26 March 1942.
43. Ibid., 30 March 1942.
44. Jackson *Clarion-Ledger*, 3 April 1942.

that he isn't farming half as well as he knows how simply because he is too lazy and shiftless to do so, and this condition isn't going to be improved very much by any form of fancy tutoring by FSA agents." According to the *Daily News*, the American people, already burdened with war taxes, were demanding that nonessential spending be stopped.[45]

Pamphleteering was another instrument in the propaganda war. During the spring of 1942 one pamphlet which circulated in Florida and another in both Arkansas and Louisiana consisted of innuendos and exaggerated gossip. The former document bore the heading "FARMERS UNION AND CIO UNITE—Radical Group in Department of Agriculture Urging Triple Alliance of FSA–Farmers Union–CIO." For the Farm Bureau any link between the Congress of Industrial Organizations and agriculture constituted a sinister, unholy union. Specifically, the pamphlet accused Arkansas officials of launching an all-out campaign to organize FSA clients into the Farmers Union.[46]

The Arkansas-Louisiana pamphlet hinted darkly of a plot to confiscate farm lands in excess of acreage sufficient for subsistence. A radical group described as "Modern Carpetbaggers" had come into the South with preconceived ideas about southern conditions, viewing the region's economy through "social-reform eyes." They preached "class distinction, racial distinction in their effort to bring about dissension among Southern farmers and divide them on a racial basis." The document included a blast at Rexford Tugwell. As the new governor of Puerto Rico, the former chief of the Resettlement Administration sought, it was charged, to break up all landholdings in excess of five hundred acres. Although he resigned from the RA in 1936 and never served in the FSA, Tugwell's shadow hung over the controversy.[47]

On its lowest level the Farm Bureau attack was unequaled for bitterness and vituperation. In July 1942, for example, the Tate County Farm Bureau, at Senatobia, Mississippi, adopted a series of resolutions critical of "civilian agencies of alphabetical fame, now being maintained at the expense of the American taxpayer." According to the resolution, such alphabetical agencies "sponsor and support many practices, projects and programs which are economically unsound, socialistic and communistic in their tendency, wholly un-American and contrary to the principles of

45. *Daily News*, 4 April 1942.
46. Wesley McCune, *The Farm Bloc* (Garden City, N.Y.: Doubleday, Doran, 1943), pp. 175–76.
47. Ibid., pp. 177–78.

our form of government, which must be discontinued and the agencies abolished." The Farm Security Administration, "with the cooperation of their socialistic friends," attempted to overthrow the legitimate American farmer and used "approximately forty per cent of their appropriations for administrative costs."[48]

The next month, in a Farm Bureau meeting at Greenville, Mississippi, a speaker insinuated that the FSA opposed private ownership of land and advocated government ownership of all land. If we were fighting World War II to insure this, the speaker said, there was no point in our winning the war.[49] The unthinking and unreasonable quality of this kind of attack made it difficult to deal with. The most spectacular charges, of course, dealt little with hard facts and figures, and in their most extreme form were particularly common in private meetings.

Farm Bureau speakers swarmed all over the states of Region VI, criticizing the FSA in meetings for local Farm Bureau personnel and county agents. On 8 May 1942, Milton Tainter, secretary of the Louisiana Farm Bureau, spoke at Minden, Louisiana. A. E. Robinson, a district rural rehabilitation supervisor in northern Louisiana, attended the meeting to gain firsthand information regarding Farm Bureau activities. His report provides some insight into the nature of such meetings and an example of how the FSA reacted.[50]

Recognizing Robinson as an FSA employee, Tainter explained at the outset that he was not directing his remarks at "any individual or any agency" and specifically not at the Farm Security Administration. Judging from Robinson's report, Tainter made two main points: government agencies helped low-income farmers while neglecting large farmers, and the Extension Service should run all government farm programs anyway. He condemned "certain governmental agencies" for placing too much emphasis on subsistence farming "to the advantage of the tenant farmers and at the expense of the large landowner farmers." Tainter disparaged efforts to aid low-income farm families, a category which, he explained, was "made up of seventy-five per cent negroes and twenty-five per cent fairly low-class white people." He objected to giving such people an advantage denied to the average farmer.

Besides, Tainter added, the Farm Security Administration program was

48. Resolution of Tate County Farm Bureau, Senatobia, Mississippi, enclosed with Sen. Theodore G. Bilbo to C. B. Baldwin, 3 July 1942, FSA Records, NA, RG 96.
49. J. Lewis Henderson to Jack H. Bryan, 20 August 1942, ibid.; *Delta Democrat-Times* (Greenville, Miss.), 2 August 1942.
50. A. E. Robinson to E. C. McInnis, 12 May 1941, FSA Records, NA, RG 96.

"bringing about certain conditions in which negroes in Louisiana were assuming the attitude that the government was endorsing a program whereby they would receive equal rights." Tainter went on to attack what he called "bureautocracy." The Department of Agriculture, he charged, dictated all agricultural work from Washington and eliminated local control of agricultural programs. County and home demonstration agents should handle government programs at the local level. At one point a woman took the floor and stated that "it was time for us to wake up to the fact that our government was turning socialistic." She put it better than he could have, Tainter remarked as she sat down. He had supported President Roosevelt for three consecutive terms, but now, he suggested, the president was too busy with the war and leaving domestic affairs to Mrs. Roosevelt.

After the meeting adjourned, Robinson met Tainter for lunch and tried to set him straight on FSA policies. But again Tainter insisted "that he hoped we [FSA officials] would not assume that his remarks were addressed specifically toward our organization." The purpose of this tactic may have been to throw the opposition off guard or simply to remain on good terms with local FSA personnel.

In March 1942, speaking to the Lafourche Farm Bureau at Thibodaux, Louisiana, Tainter charged that the Farm Security Administration and the Department of Agriculture were permeated with men leaning to the left. With Terrebonne project manager George Harmount sitting in the audience, Tainter explained that he did not mean any FSA men in the field; officials in Washington were the ones leaning to the left. Nor did he have any criticism, Tainter made clear, of the Terrebonne project or the way it was being handled. "You can take this for what it was worth," Harmount wrote Whitaker, "but I think he did not dare, with me being there, to try to start anything."[51]

The Farm Security Administration became involved in a different kind of controversy at Transylvania. On 11 February 1942 the police jury of East Carroll Parish, Louisiana, issued a statement sharply critical of the FSA as a whole and the Transylvania project in particular.[52] With the nation at war, every unnecessary expenditure must be curtailed, they asserted, but the FSA spent money at Transylvania that would never be

51. G. D. Harmount to E. B. Whitaker, 21 March 1942, ibid.
52. A Statement by the Police Jury of East Carroll Parish, Louisiana, regarding the Policies and Administration of the F.S.A., enclosed with Rep. Newton V. Mills to C. B. Baldwin, 23 February 1942, ibid.; Police Jury of East Carroll Parish, Louisiana, to Claude Wickard, 23 February 1942, ibid.

returned to the government. Under FSA management, moreover, Transylvania's cotton yield per acre had dropped far below what the same land produced under private ownership; and the project suffered a reduction in its cotton acreage allotment simply because the land was not kept in cultivation. They backed this charge with a display of research done at the local AAA office. If Transylvania was operated so inefficiently, they asked, how could the government's investment be repaid?

The police jury was even more disturbed over the fear, derived from newspaper reports of congressional hearings on the FSA, that administrator Baldwin "might favor" the exercise of eminent domain or expropriation against absentee owners in order to break up large southern landholdings. "We are also advised," the statement read, "that they . . . plan to dispossess absentee owners of their holdings that they consider large enough to use for F.S.A. projects." This plan was "State Socialism," they asserted.

The regional office faced the charges head-on, conducted some research of its own, and prepared a defense of Transylvania's operations. E. B. Whitaker went to Lake Providence and found that the statement was not an official pronouncement of the police jury, although it did reflect the thinking of some of its members. "It was drawn up by several landowners," Stewart reported to Baldwin, "and circulated over the state in such a manner as to make it appear as though it were a statement from the Police Jury."[53]

Transylvania's board of directors answered the charges in the Lake Providence *Banner Democrat*.[54] True, cotton production was down at Transylvania. Under private ownership, about 250 families had occupied the land, each farming about twenty-three acres devoted exclusively to cotton. But the FSA reduced the number of families to about 150, gave each family about fifty acres, and developed a diversified farm management program. Rather than have the settlers entirely dependent on a single cash crop, the board of directors explained, Transylvania stressed food and feed crops, pasture, garden vegetables, poultry, milk cows, cattle, and hogs. Transylvania settlers produced cotton as their major cash crop, but they had a higher standard of living and more security, whatever the price of cotton.[55]

53. A. D. Stewart to C. B. Baldwin, 6 May 1942, ibid.
54. Lake Providence *Banner Democrat*, 20 March 1942.
55. See also R. W. Hudgens, memorandum to Emery E. Jacobs, 4 September 1942, FSA Records, NA, RG 96; A. D. Stewart to C. B. Baldwin, 7 November 1942, ibid.

At least two local citizens, a landowner and a police jury member, supported the FSA's explanation. Norris C. Williamson, whose property was next to Transylvania, saw part of the project almost every day, he said, and the FSA did a good job operating the land. But since many of the settlers were used to the light sandy soil of the Louisiana hills, they had to learn how to farm the richer delta soil and combat the obnoxious grasses of that area. In addition, the project suffered from heavy rains during recent planting seasons; but despite its disadvantages, he pointed out, Transylvania's cotton yield per acre about equaled the parish average every year with one exception.

F. W. Holt, a police juryman convalescing from an accident when the statement was issued, wrote that he "did not agree with his colleagues on the Police Jury or those sponsoring these charges of communism, socialism, or any other kind of ism." [56] Transylvania settlers operated cooperatives for their mutual benefit; but Socialism, he contended, was a bogus issue since each farmer worked his own land.

The Farm Bureau made so many accusations, and made them so often, that they gained stature by mere repetition, whereas FSA officials found it difficult to keep pace with denials. The constant use of keywords inevitably created the desired image of the agency's activities. Thus government employees became "bureaucrats," administrative procedures "red tape," and supervision of a client "regimentation"; finally projects translated into colonies and communities hinted of Communism.

Stewart managed to find some good resulting from the Farm Bureau controversy. It was "gratifying," he wrote in 1942, "to observe that Farm Security has many supporters which we did not know about before; a large number of editors, civic clubs, preachers, educators, organizations, and individuals have openly expressed their support of the Farm Security Administration." Other groups sided with the Farm Bureau against the FSA, he admitted, but it was a far smaller number. Stewart used the controversy to acquaint many people with the FSA program. People in all walks of life wrote hundreds of unsolicited letters expressing their wholehearted support and endorsement of the FSA. Also, when the Farm Bureau criticized specific projects, FSA clients "have enthusiastically repudiated statements attributed to them and conditions reportedly existing." At Biscoe Farms in Arkansas, the families themselves issued statements answering criticisms. "A strong public reaction has developed

56. Norris C. Williamson to E. B. Whitaker, 15 February 1942, ibid.; F. W. Holt to H. B. Staples, 10 March 1942, ibid.

against the Farm Bureau," Stewart asserted, "because of its attack on the
FSA. This reaction is general, except possibly among certain of the large
farm operators who depend on tenants as day labor."[57] At best, however,
these were only short-term gains.

Stewart fought back, but to no avail. The war was already lost. Only
the last battle lay ahead.

57. A. D. Stewart, Quarterly Report, January–March 1942, ibid. See James F.
Talley to the editor, *Twice-a-Week Arkansas Gazette*, 6 March 1942; Talley to the
editor, *Commercial Appeal*, 15 March 1942; William H. Purkiss et al. to the editor,
ibid., 7 March 1942; see also ibid., 8 March 1942.

Chapter XIV

Losing the Last Battle: 1943–44

As 1942 drew to a close, Little Rock officials made a difficult and dangerous decision. A. D. Stewart authorized the eviction of thirty-three families at Plum Bayou and five at Trumann Farms. It was probably a long-overdue housecleaning. When informed their leases would not be renewed, most of the families voluntarily vacated their homes. Twenty-seven families left Plum Bayou without protest. After negotiations a few of the families signed new temporary agreements, pledging to cooperate fully and mend their ways.[1]

After more than two months the agency filed suit in United States District Court at Little Rock against seven families remaining on their units without authorization. At Plum Bayou two men, Booker McDade and Ernest Priest, retained an attorney and prepared to fight it out. When the five families at Trumann Farms secured the services of an attorney, the FSA dropped its case against two of them—Mrs. May Bloodworth, a widow with three sons in the armed services, and Hubert Davis. The agency went ahead with its suit against W. H. Morgan, Monroe Prince, and W. L. Parnell.

If the experience of Dyess Colony was any guide, Stewart might have expected these evictions to create unfavorable publicity, but he could not have anticipated what happened next. When the FSA appropriation hearings opened in early 1943, Booker McDade, Plum Bayou, and Region VI occupied center stage in the testimony of Oscar Johnston, president of the National Cotton Council.[2] Johnston had once managed the Delta and Pine Land Company, a British-owned super plantation in Mississippi. He had also served as director of the AAA's finance division and later

---

1. Little Rock *Arkansas Gazette*, 4 April 1943.
2. USHR, *USDA Approp. Hearings, 1944*, 78th Cong., 1st sess., pp. 1622ff; Little Rock *Arkansas Democrat*, 28 March 1943; *Arkansas Gazette*, 14 April 1943.

262 Conflict and Controversy

manager of its cotton pool program. One of the "agrarians" within the AAA, his sympathies lay on the side of the larger and more successful farmers.

Still a spokesman for such interests, Johnston launched a personal vendetta against the FSA in late 1942. At several meetings in Mississippi and in Memphis, he sharply criticized the agency, describing its activities as "subversive." The FSA wasted millions of the taxpayers' dollars, he said, and its programs were not administered in accordance with the intent of Congress. "If I tried to sign up my tenants to a contract like that of the FSA," he said in a much-quoted statement, "the government would indict me for peonage and, moreover, they would convict me."[3] This remark elicited a prompt counterattack from the agency's national administrator. When C. B. Baldwin attended a regional Food for Freedom program at Little Rock, he was reminded of Johnston's statement. "Did Mr. Johnston ever sign a contract with one of his tenants?" he asked bitterly.[4]

A couple of days later Johnston, too, was in Little Rock, addressing the annual convention of the Arkansas Farm Bureau Federation, and he elaborated on his earlier remarks. The FSA promoted "land socialism," he flatly asserted, and its practices were "communistic." Citing a recent letter from union leader Phillip Murray in support of increased FSA appropriations, he repeated the rumor that the Farm Security Administration, Farmers Union, and Congress of Industrial Organizations had formed a coalition in order to "drive a wedge into agriculture."[5] In other speeches he expressed the belief that the FSA hoped to retaliate against Farm Bureau criticism by organizing the Farmers Union in Mississippi, which the Farm Bureau monopolized.

Regional officials immediately jumped into the Johnston fight. Stewart challenged him to name the employees supposedly guilty of subversive or Communistic leanings. But Johnston's reply was only a repetition of his previous charges. FSA officials, he added, were not interested in the establishment of family-type farms but sought to acquire "hundreds of thousands of acres of land upon which they propose to settle thousands of farm people, who would . . . be merely serfs or tenants of a paternalistic government."[6]

Next came the unexpected. As a result of Johnston's newspaper publicity, the much-maligned Booker McDade sent him a letter pleading for

3. Ibid., 20 November 1942.
4. Ibid., 22 November 1942.
5. Ibid., 24 November 1942.
6. Ibid., 7 December 1942; *Arkansas Democrat*, 20 December 1942.

help. Johnston had attended Plum Bayou's dedication in 1936, but lost contact with the project in subsequent years. Between speaking engagements he traveled to Plum Bayou and met McDade in preparation for his forthcoming appearance before Malcolm Tarver's Agricultural Appropriations Subcommittee.[7]

McDade, as Johnston told the subcommittee, moved to the project in 1937; five years later, at the end of the usual probationary period, he asked officials about purchasing his unit. Their answer was no. They wanted him to remain one more year and then he could buy his land. That December, in 1942, he was ordered to vacate his home; it was then that he got in touch with Johnston. The Mississippi planter advised him to "sit pat," to make them go a little further. In January 1943 he received formal notification to get out, or he would be forcibly ejected. "What shall I do about that?" McDade inquired. "Sit still, wait until they forcibly eject you," Johnston told him.

On his visit with McDade, Johnston found about twenty more families "in the same shape." They, like McDade, claimed to have paid all their obligations but were being evicted, while other farmers who owed as much as $2,600 were being carried forward the next year.

"McDade is independent," Johnston said. "He does not owe anybody anything and is prepared to pay for his land. I again advised him to sit steady, go ahead with plowing, and make his crop, and if they came out there to evict him refuse to be evicted unless they forcibly did it. They have not done it and he is still farming his land over there. They did not bring an issue." The Plum Bayou project was not an isolated case, Johnston assured the subcommittee; it was a typical example.

Looking over the project, Johnston found "nice houses" with electric lights and running water, and "nice barns." But twenty or thirty of the houses were empty, their windows broken out and doors boarded up. Since the project began, he reported, 129 families had moved in and out of Plum Bayou. "That is almost a 100–per cent turnover." The property had been mismanaged by following a rigid farm program without regard for different qualities of soil. The FSA was proceeding full speed with lease contracts and cooperative operations, and if there was any indication of liquidation he had not seen it.

The agency had, he added, just tried to lease a plantation in Poinsett County, Arkansas. Perking up their ears, the subcommittee members were most concerned about possible violations of anti-land-purchase provisions in the 1943 appropriation law, but Johnston's purpose was to es-

7. USHR, *USDA Approp. Hearings, 1944*, 78th Cong., 1st sess., pp. 1624–27.

tablish a direct link between the FSA and the Congress of Industrial Organizations. The owner of the property in question, a man named Chapin, was informed by CIO officials that they had organized the plantation adjacent to his land and signed up 70 percent of his own tenants. They told him, as Chapin put it, that "I would make *my* contracts with *my* labor on *my* plantation next year through their bargaining committee." A few days later an FSA representative offered to "step in and take my property off my hands and lease it for 10 years." A suspicious series of events, Johnston thought: the CIO organizes farm workers on a plantation, and a day or two later FSA agents offer to lease the property. He also showed the subcommittee a copy of a letter from Phillip Murray of the CIO demonstrating a "direct tie-up" between the union and the FSA.[8]

Another possible violation of the current appropriation law occurred in the case of the Phillipston plantation, near Greenwood, in Leflore County, Mississippi. But for Johnston, it, too, held another interest. Until late 1942, when the FSA acquired the property, the Phillipston plantation was occupied by seventy black families, some having lived there all their lives; and, Johnston reported, they were now old and pitiful. Yet the FSA ordered them to get off the land, and rented their houses to fifty white families.[9]

Johnston was present at the plantation on the day they had to leave. They did not know what to do or where to go. He listened to their lamentations, including the final prayer made by an old Negro preacher who had been there for years. "Has it been answered yet?" Congressman Tarver asked.

"No sir; it evidently was not heard."

"I am not sure that it was not heard," Everett Dirksen commented.

"It may have been heard," Johnston said. "I am hopeful that it is now going to be answered."[10]

The Phillipston incident, in Johnston's view, exemplified FSA cruelty and poor planning. "I am naming you specific cases I saw, and I am telling you that I have in my files innumerable letters from clients and from neighbors of the F.S.A., but primarily I am basing it [his testimony] on clients, people themselves who were hurt and who are suffering and are being unjustly treated, and who are being evicted and not being permitted to buy their land."[11]

8. Ibid., pp. 1622–23, 1630–31. Emphasis added.
9. Ibid., p. 1628.
10. Ibid., p. 1629.
11. Ibid., p. 1630.

The subcommittee spent the next two days going over Johnston's testimony with C. B. Baldwin. As before, the sessions were interminable and the demands for information incessant. Baldwin tirelessly rebutted all of Johnston's charges, but seldom to the satisfaction of the subcommittee members. He gave the agency's side of the McDade story.[12]

After three years as a government farmer, Booker McDade suddenly became "uncooperative." In the latter part of 1940 he left his farm and worked at Camp Robinson. During the next two years he spent considerable time away from the project, working at Jacksonville, Arkansas, and the Pine Bluff Arsenal. Half the crop land on McDade's unit remained idle in 1942; day laborers made a fair crop on a portion of it. Despite Stanley Rhodes's repeated efforts, McDade refused to work with the management in planning a farm program to keep his unit in full production. For a two-year period he refused to make payments on his rehabilitation loan. Only after he was notified to vacate did he come to the manager's office and almost completely pay off his indebtedness, leaving a balance of only $26.84. Clients could not neglect their farming operations, Baldwin remarked, and expect to live in a house on a project. "We must . . . try to protect the farming operations in order to assure full production." "We want to keep people on the land," he added, "and we want them to work that land."[13]

The FSA definitely did not evict families who met their payments as Johnston claimed. "They are the very kind that we are trying to keep," Baldwin remarked. Nor had the agency refused to live up to its promise to sell qualified families their units.

As for the Chapin plantation, it was part of the land-leasing program. The land would be parceled out among rehabilitation clients. Yes, negotiations for the lease were currently under way, but Congress, Baldwin reminded the subcommittee, had renewed the program only the previous year. There was certainly no intention to evade the will of Congress. He assured them the FSA had nothing to do with organizing any farmers into the CIO or any other union.

On the other hand, the Phillipston plantation came under the tenant purchase program, which carried no land purchase prohibition in the current appropriation law. It was acquired on 1 January 1943 and subdivided among fifty individual tenant purchase borrowers. Technically

12. Baldwin's appearances are jumbled in the printed version of the hearings. His testimony on 17 March immediately following Johnston's appearance starts ibid., p. 1690; he returned with more information on 20 March, starting on p. 1648.
13. Ibid., pp. 1657–58.

the FSA did not buy the plantation at all. The agency loaned the families the money with which to pay for it, and they made the purchase directly from the owner, Connecticut General Life Insurance Company, which had put it up for sale. In both cases, Chapin and Phillipston, all clients would come from the county where the project was located. There would be no wholesale relocation of people.[14]

Still unhappy, Tarver expressed concern with the fairness of the Phillipston matter. What was going to happen to the Negro families who lost their homes? Baldwin assured him that the agency found them other, more suitable places to live; their tenure on a plantation already up for sale was insecure anyway. Tarver voiced other complaints. With the program's limited funds, tenant purchase loans typically went to a few families in each county; but the land-leasing projects meant that a single county would get, say, fifty or more loans. The program seemed to be based more on what land could be acquired, Tarver said, than on the real needs of farm families. It also looked like an effort to get around the prohibition against governmental land purchases.[15]

At Little Rock the appropriation hearings put the Farm Security Administration back on the front page, crowding into news of Rommel's impending defeat in Tunisia and American raids in the Solomon Islands. They also made Booker McDade a local celebrity.

When Helene Ward of the *Arkansas Democrat*, Little Rock's afternoon newspaper, went down to Plum Bayou for an interview, the McDade family represented themselves as model clients.[16] McDade was ready and able to make a downpayment on his farm and had tried more than once to do so. Mrs. McDade had her pantry well stocked, with the help of her daughter, LaVerne, who had studied home economics at Arkansas A & M College. They also had a son in the service. McDade bragged about having been the fifth colonist to move to Plum Bayou, but things had not gone according to plans.

> My troubles [as he analyzed his situation] resulted from refusal to borrow and borrow, and to stay in debt to the government. I've paid off and don't owe one cent on the few hundred dollars advanced to me the first couple of years I was here. And, too, I've been too pressing in my demands

14. Ibid., pp. 1665–66.
15. Ibid., pp. 1666, 1683–84.
16. Helene Ward, "Model Farmer Perplexed by Eviction Order," *Arkansas Democrat*, 26 March 1943.

that the government keep its original promise to me to let me buy my place after I'd operated it on a rental basis for five long, hard years to prove my worth. The fellow who owes the government the most money is the fellow who stays the longest, it seems.

The McDades, as Helene Ward described them, were like condemned prisoners with that "sometime between midnight and daylight" feeling. They dreaded every car that came down the road because it might carry a marshal who would order them out. Before coming to Plum Bayou they were "getting along very nicely" on a farm near McGehee, Arkansas, but the hope of owning their own farm lured them to the government project. Having come in search of independence, they now thought of themselves as ironic victims of "regimentation."

McDade was a good carpenter and owned the only car on the project aside from the project manager's.[17] He had taken a job off the project the previous fall (1942) after crops were laid by, and then trouble began. A warning came that outside jobs were forbidden if farm units were neglected. As McDade told it, he had little to do during the winter months, and his family could take care of what few chores must be done. Meanwhile he could earn a little money to square up debts with the government. Before he finally quit his job, he also made a contribution to the nation's war effort. As for the accusation that he neglected his farm, McDade invited anyone to look over his place and inspect his production records.[18]

A. D. Stewart was in Washington when the McDade controversy broke. He was adamant in his decison to go through with the eviction. After returning to Little Rock, he told reporters that all clients were expected to do a good job farming. "McDade didn't do that," Stewart said. "Last year half of his farm grew up in weeds. I saw it myself and that has been true since 1940." McDade did a good job, he admitted, on the other half of his land.[19]

The atmosphere at Plum Bayou changed that spring. At church and social gatherings, the air was charged with tension. Factionalism ran riot. Some clients mumbled about "favoritism," a reference to colonists who worked off the project and got away with it; meanwhile officials complained about "troublemakers." But community spirit, once so strong, did not disappear entirely.

17. Stanley Rhodes, interview with the author, 6 December 1972.
18. *Arkansas Democrat*, 26 March 1943.
19. Ibid., 1, 4 April 1943.

If the dread of evictions created fear in the McDade household, the worry that the Farm Security Administration might be abolished dominated other clients. One night in mid-April a group of Plum Bayou families met and decided to pay for a newspaper ad in defense of the agency, as other FSA clients and friends were doing. "We can read and write down here," Claud J. Bost said, "and there's plenty of us around here bright enough to write our own advertisements, and loyal enough to the FSA to defend it even if we have to pay for doing it." Not only did they fear that they would have to go back to sharecropping, but also reports circulated in Plum Bayou that bankers had inspected the project from one cotton row to another. As one client put it, "capitalist, big bankers, big plantation operators, insurance companies and rich people would buy up all these places, and then where would us little fellows be?" Claud Bost, J. J. Bradshaw, and Tracy J. Sanderlin took up contributions from about a hundred people, and carried an ad to the Gazette Building at Little Rock.[20]

One of the *Arkansas Gazette*'s staff correspondents, Inez Hale Mac-Duff, had just launched a four-part series of articles which came down hard on the Arkansas resettlement program. She began with a dissection of Plum Bayou, contrasting the project's roseate beginning with its current troubles; next took on Lake Dick, an easy mark; returned to Plum Bayou for a second working-over; and finally tried to bring together the financial record of the major resettlement projects in Arkansas. The taxpayers, she said, will have to foot the bill for the New Deal's Arkansas experiments.[21]

Whether by coincidence or design, every time one of her articles appeared the *Gazette* carried a large-sized ad in the agency's defense. "The FSA is the only government agency that has ever stepped out and really helped the farmers who need help," declared some three hundred people of Yell, Logan, Pope, and Conway counties. Their message was, don't condemn all by a few who fail. Businessmen as well as FSA clients had paid for the ad with voluntary contributions. MacDuff's second article was accompanied by two ads, one of them from Plum Bayou. "We feel," their statement read, "that the majority of the families at Plum Bayou

20. Ibid., 24 April 1943; *Arkansas Gazette*, 25 April 1943. See also A. D. Stewart to the editor, *Arkansas Democrat*, 11 April 1943.
21. "Mr. Wallace's Rosy Prophecy Proves a 'Bust': Plum Bayou Not a Promised Land," 18 April 1943; "Government Sponsors Sharecropping after Experiment Fails," 25 April 1943; "New Deal Experiment Placed on Land That Floods Every Year," 2 May 1943; "Taxpayers Will Foot Bill for New Deal's Arkansas Experiments," 9 May 1943, all in *Arkansas Gazette*.

are happy and they are aware of the debt they owe society." Scott and Montgomery County farmers sponsored the second ad in the same issue. The signers included more businessmen than before, particularly proprietors of hardware stores, service stations, and grocery stores. When Mac-Duff's third article appeared, Lincoln County farmers asked, "Why Scrap Here at Home? Do It Over There." The origin of the final advertisement was not revealed.

What happened to Booker McDade and the other clients threatened with expulsion? McDade vacated his unit voluntarily and went to California. No one, after all, Stanley Rhodes recalled years later, was taken to court in eviction proceedings at either Plum Bayou or, presumably, Trumann Farms.[22]

In any event, the McDade story certainly accomplished no good for the agency. It made its friends timid, strengthened its enemies, and provided them with an opportunity for criticism. The *Arkansas Gazette*, once an enthusiastic supporter of the FSA and its predecessors, now seemed to waver, unwilling to speak out forcefully in its favor but unable to forsake it, either. The *Gazette* published an editorial comment on the House appropriations subcommittee suggesting weakly that there was another side to the FSA matter. But the paper did not take a strong stand.[23]

Other old friends, like Edward J. Meeman of the Memphis *Press-Scimitar*, remained loyal and vigorously defended the agency. He served as moderator of a YMCA public affairs forum in which both sides were heard, with Mississippian Owen Cooper representing the Farm Bureau and A. D. Stewart defending the FSA. After conducting his own investigation of FSA activities in the Middle South, Meeman splashed the front page of his paper's second section with articles and photographs showing the agency in the best possible light.[24] It was an able defense, but defenders were always outnumbered by attackers.

In a series of editorials, the *Arkansas Democrat* accused the FSA of trying to squeeze people into a "communal type of farming." The farmer was an individualist, and he could not conform to bureaucratic red tape. "These pink-tinted adventures have no place in the American system," one editorial said of projects like Plum Bayou. In addition, the *Democrat* scored the FSA for ignoring the limits Congress placed on its activities.[25]

22. Rhodes interview.
23. *Arkansas Gazette*, 15 April 1943; see also 14 April.
24. Memphis *Press-Scimitar*, 6 April 1943; Meeman's series may be found in the issues of 15, 16, 17, 19, 20 April 1943.
25. *Arkansas Democrat*, 28 March, 7, 15, 22, 25, 28 April, 12 May 1943; the quote is in 28 April.

As the struggle reached a crescendo, other voices joined in the attack. The Memphis *Commercial Appeal* had given the resettlement program favorable treatment as late as 1939. The original purpose of the FSA—to aid worthy farmers in establishing themselves on their own farms—was still valid, the *Commercial Appeal* now editorialized.[26] "There should be an agency such as the FSA was originally intended to be. The idea was good; the administration of it, terrible." The agency strayed far afield with "social experiments," heading in the direction of "socialists' or collectivists' schemes" which destroyed individual initiative and personal independence. "Included in this category," the paper said, "is the setting up of cooperatives, the acquisition of undeveloped lands, the making of subsistence grants and alleged emergency allotments, the establishing of collective farming practices, and the consistent effort to favor only such 'clients' as proved amenable to the experimentation."

The fault lay in top administrators "vaccinated with the Tugwellian virus," rather than in "any wish on the part of many of the administrative employees on the scene to carry out what they knew were impractical policies." "In other words," the *Commercial Appeal* added, "the FSA appears to have fallen into the hands and under the blight of social gainers, do-gooders, bleeding hearts, and long-hairs who make a career of helping others for a price and according to their own screwball ideas." The agency needed an "operation," it concluded; its leadership with their "foreign" ideas ought to be replaced by sensible, patriotic men.

The Little Rock office once again found help from unexpected sources. After O. E. Jones resigned as regional information adviser and returned to the Batesville, Arkansas, *Daily Guard*, he remained a defender of the FSA. Watching the conflict over his old agency develop, Jones could not hold back his dismay. A year before, he had complained to M. L. Wilson, formerly head of the Division of Subsistence Homesteads and now director of the Agricultural Extension Service. The Arkansas Extension Service, he wrote, was dominated by the American Farm Bureau Federation; and county agents in Arkansas actively solicited Farm Bureau memberships "to swell the coffers of a private lobbying organization." While the Farm Bureau conducted a campaign of vilification and misrepresentation against the FSA, the Extension Service sought to build up the very organization that was "slashing a dagger" at the back of its sister agency. "I am loath," Jones remarked, "to sit idly by and see the Farm Bureau blitzkrieg the Farm Security Administration out of existence."[27]

26. Memphis *Commercial Appeal*, 18 April, 25 May 1943.
27. O. E. Jones to M. L. Wilson, 26 March 1942, FSA Records, NA, RG 96.

He did not sit idly by. In early 1943, as a state senator, Jones complained to Wilson about a Sevier County agent's recruiting for the Farm Bureau. After Wilson checked the matter and replied that no violation had taken place, Jones launched his own legislative investigation of the Arkansas Extension Service. It was an exercise in futility. He called in Romeo Short along with extension officials, and they all denied knowledge of any irregularities. Jones conducted the hearings without the help of any of his senate colleagues, and he had little real evidence to support his charges. After the hearings were over, he continued in his newspaper what had become a one-man vendetta. "The unvarnished truth . . . is that the Arkansas Extension Service is under complete domination, body and soul, of the Arkansas Farm Bureau and therefore is in politics up to its neck," Jones wrote. "Many county agents, whether they like it or not, have been turned into Farm Bureau membership solicitors and fomenters of bad-feeling between low-income and high-income farmers."[28] But Jones's efforts went for nothing.

The agricultural appropriation bill for fiscal 1944 ended the FSA as it had functioned for the past seven years. All cooperative activities as well as land-leasing associations were strictly prohibited. The rehabilitation program was cut almost in half, although the tenant purchase program was retained; but restrictions on the use of funds crippled even these remaining programs. The FSA emerged as only a shell of its former self, virtually powerless and with limited funds.[29]

For the leaders of the FSA, one more indignity awaited at the hands of a vindictive Congress, this one quite anticlimactic. For two years Cong. Harold D. Cooley of North Carolina had sought a resolution calling for an investigation of FSA activities; the House finally passed it in March 1943, setting up a select commitee of the House Committee on Agriculture. The Cooley committee, as it was called, offered an open forum for criticism of FSA programs, and the agency's opponents took a final fling. The Farm Bureau marched out its familiar repertoire of accusations, and most of the agency's friends repeated their testimony, all heard many times before. After hearing witnesses for more than a year, the Cooley committee had accumulated a total of 1,969 pages of testimony and

28. William J. Block, *The Separation of the Farm Bureau and the Extension Service* (Urbana: University of Illinois Press, 1960), pp. 68–69; Batesville *Daily Guard*, 26 April 1943, quoted in Block, *Separation*, 69n.; see *Arkansas Gazette*, 1, 3 February, 12 May 1943.

29. 57 *US Stat.* 392; Sidney Baldwin, *Poverty and Politics: The Rise and Decline of the Farm Security Administration* (Chapel Hill: University of North Carolina Press, 1968), p. 394.

documentation, including an enormous body of factual information on the resettlement program which otherwise might not have existed.[30]

In its report, the Cooley committee found the FSA guilty of ignoring the Bankhead-Jones Act and defying the will of Congress. The FSA, the committee charged, was "financing communistic resettlement projects, where the families could never own homes, or be paid for all that they made or for all the time they worked, and was supervising its borrowers to the extent of telling the borrower how to raise his children, how to plan his home life and, it is strongly suspected in some cases, how to vote." The agency was "an experiment station of un-American ideas," unwisely and dangerously administered, and it duplicated government services no longer needed. The committee wanted the Farm Security Administration abolished outright, but its members did draft legislation creating a Farmers Home Corporation, which would carry on a curtailed program for low-income farmers.[31]

Although the Farm Security Administration lived on for two more years, its primary task was the liquidation of the resettlement projects and related activities. Baldwin resigned in November 1943 in an effort to save some remnant of the agency; Frank W. Hancock, a Democratic congressman from North Carolina, took his place. He became chief liquidator and caretaker. The agency even ceased to be its own master: as the czars and superbureaucrats assumed command of wartime programs, the FSA was placed under the War Food Administration.[32]

The controversies of World War II should not obscure the nature of the resettlement program. The Resettlement Administration and the Farm Security Administration were never as radical as the Farm Bureau and other critics pictured them. The talk of communistic collectives was nonsense. Yet New Deal agricultural policy did break sharply with the past.

30. U.S. Congress, Select Committee of the House Committee on Agriculture, *Hearings on the Farm Security Administration*, 78th Cong., 1st sess., 1943–44, in 4 pts. (previously cited as USHR, *FSA Hearings*).

31. Select Committee of the House Committee on Agriculture to Investigate the Activities of the Farm Security Administration, *Activities of the Farm Security Administration*, House Report 1430, 78th Cong., 2d sess. (Washington: Government Printing Office, 1944), pp. 1–2; see Harold D. Cooley, "Sense and Nonsense in Helping Farmers," *Readers' Digest* 44 (May 1944): 29–32.

32. After leaving government, Baldwin took the job as director of the Congress of Industrial Organizations' political action committee, lending some support to the CIO-FSA conspiracy theory. He later became manager of Henry Wallace's 1948 presidential campaign. Baldwin, *Poverty and Politics*, p. 396.

In the context of depression, federal grants-in-aid for agricultural education, long-term credits, and other traditional devices were totally insufficient. The Agricultural Adjustment Administration, for the first time, made the government a principal force in the regulation and control of agricultural production. The AAA plunged into the uncharted seas of crop destruction and acreage allotments—experiments which old-time agrarians accepted with reluctance. The Resettlement Administration devoted itself to the broad problems of rural poverty and, most important, land reform. Never before had the federal government bought submarginal land, converted it to uses other than crop production, and resettled the families living there on better land. Although Rexford Tugwell soon left government service, the Farm Security Administration continued his experiments with cooperative farming, long-term leases (as opposed to fee-simple ownership), medical care cooperatives, and migrant labor camps. But if New Deal methods were new, what about New Deal objectives?

The Farm Security Administration, the most important and longest lived of the New Deal resettlement agencies, represented a cautious, conservative attempt to deal with the problems of rural poverty. The FSA based its overall program squarely on the agrarian principle of owner-operated, family-sized farms. The ideological heritage of the FSA, Sidney Baldwin has written, gave it "a sense of disadvantage, an optimistic reformist zeal, a nostalgic yearning for restoration of traditional institutions, such as subsistence agriculture and the family farm."[33]

Above all, Region VI officials were not revolutionaries, and the reforms they pushed did not amount to a revolution. As far as they were concerned, the FSA program was fully in accord with American rural traditions. Given the background of the regional leadership (southern birth, agricultural education, and Extension Service experience), it is hard to imagine them caught up in a vision of a "new world" that would eliminate the family farm in favor of cooperative farming. "The funds available to the RA," wrote T. Roy Reid, for example, "are sufficient only to provide a demonstration of the possibilities of rural resettlement. But there is no reason why its methods should not be embodied in a permanent, family-sized owner-operated farm program of the government." The foundation of American agriculture, he devoutly believed, should always remain the family-sized, owner-operated farm.[34] The peo-

33. Ibid., p. 268; for Tugwell's evaluation, see "The Resettlement Idea," *Agricultural History* 33 (October 1959): 159–64.
34. Pine Bluff *Daily Graphic*, 30 August 1936.

ple who became the agency's clients held the same deep faith. On the whole, the resettlement program was designed for people who had always made their own way and who would not need help at all except for the depression. They were the kind of people who would be most concerned with owning their own farms and homes.

Thus the central purpose of the New Deal community program in the Lower Mississippi Valley was farm ownership for tenants, sharecroppers, and submarginal farmers who had no other chance to escape the plight of depression. Virtually all resettlement projects in the region operated on a family-farm basis, whether started by the Subsistence Homesteads Division, Federal Emergency Relief Administration, or Resettlement Administration. Beyond the community projects, the FSA's tenant purchase and rural rehabilitation programs were also aimed at individual farm ownership. The cooperative plantation projects like Terrebonne and Lake Dick were new and startling. But what seemed more important about the New Deal community projects as a whole was that the federal government for the first time operated a program to give direct aid to tenant farmers and sharecroppers.

The liquidation of the resettlement projects across the nation resulted in heavy losses, with the government recovering only about half the program's cost. For a supposedly wasteful program, however, the record of Region VI was quite good. The Resettlement Administration and its successor, the Farm Security Administration, built twenty-six projects of all types, developing 2,809 farm units. These projects represented an investment of $14,347,580.12. In the process of liquidation the government recovered all but $1,557,224.16. The project families and other purchasers signed mortgages obligating them for their farms, and would pay for them in time. On most projects, operating expenses outstripped income, leaving them in the red to the tune of $542,601.75. So total losses came to $2,206,756.36.[35]

Townes, Lonoke, Saint Francis, and Mileston were actually liquidated at a combined profit of $84,658.42. A few other projects left good records, closing with small deficits. Plum Bayou led the pack in poor performance, and many others were in serious trouble.

Those who favored the continuation of the Farm Security Administra-

35. These and the following figures have been drawn from several sources: USHR, *FSA Hearings*, pt. 3; USHR, *USDA Approp. Hearings, 1946*, 79th Cong., 1st sess.; USS, *USDA Approp. Hearings, 1947*, 79th Cong., 1st sess.; FSA, "Resettlement Projects, Region VI." See also Appendix.

tion agreed that the agency's social benefits were more important than the money it spent. Play down the cost, they said; play up the aid given to people. Their point was well taken. One might argue that the losses suffered in liquidation and the deficits accumulated in operation repre- sented the actual cost of the program. If the total deficit is divided by the number of families, the cost of the program per family turns out to be $981.83—a mere $98.18 per year for ten years. That was certainly a mod- est investment in terms of the human potential it salvaged. A far higher amount might have been spent if they had been kept on relief. The pur- pose of the resettlement and rehabilitation programs was, of course, to get away from relief, to rehabilitate rural families on farms, and to help them gain self-respect as worthwhile citizens. While these objectives were accomplished at relatively low cost, it was the lack of business success which became the program's major weakness.

The FSA had not proven that the resettlement projects were sound on a dollars-and-cents basis, and they had not convinced Congress that the nation could afford a heavy outlay for them. As either social experiments or business ventures, the resettlement projects had not lived up to ex- pectations.

The financial records of the Division of Subsistence Homesteads and the Federal Emergency Relief Administration communities were pro- portionally worse than the FSA's, though far smaller in terms of actual expenditures. The Mississippi subsistence homesteads closed with losses totaling $248,274.88. But no single project in the region rivaled Dyess Colony's $3 million loss.

What went wrong with the resettlement program? The answer is dif- ferent for every project, but some generalizations are possible. The two sides—government and clients—were both culpable, but each was ready to lay the blame on the other.

The government made mistakes in the development of the projects— mistakes which they could never outgrow and which eventually would drag down the entire program. Poor planning was often perpetuated by sloppy administration, and many project families paid the price. The spring floods at Plum Bayou were an example of a needless problem. For three consecutive years, before the low-lying areas were finally aban- doned to pasture, water covered part of the project, drowning crops. At Plum Bayou, too, many families were allowed to become burdened with debt, more than they could reasonably hope to repay; and when they fell behind in their payments they were evicted. Many projects were just too expensive, and the average investment per unit was greater than the productive capacity of the land. At every project the most common mistake was the small size of the family units; farmers simply needed more than the thirty or forty acres they were usually allotted. Other serious mistakes may have been made, but these alone wrecked the program.

While government officials may have made selection mistakes, much blame rested on the client families themselves. A disproportionate number of families failed, as the cases of both Dyess Colony and Plum Bayou illustrated. A few families simply became homesick for the hills. Perhaps opportunities on the outside tempted some people. Others fled the load of debt they soon found themselves carrying as resettlement clients. But the problem went deeper.

Contemporaries were fond of observing that the individualism of American farmers frustrated the New Deal's resettlement schemes. It was a misleading observation, but many farmers were distrustful of the government. They were not going to be told what to do. They never caught the cooperative spirit, never worked together as people in any community must do. Project managers found it impossible to sell many families the program. Too much, perhaps, was expected of people who lacked the background and education to adapt to rapid change.

While many people took hold of their new opportunity, other families had accepted failure as a way of life and could not shake off their negative self-images. Whether this applies to the much-publicized troublemakers —the S. B. Funks and the Booker McDades—is difficult to say. They may have been men who harbored the old suspicion that the "big man," or in this case the government, was trying to cheat them. Or they may have simply concluded that they were not getting what was promised.

The resettlement program ended before it could run its normal course. Given time, more of the projects might have proved themselves, but the overall result probably would have been little different. The New Deal was dealing with the difficult problem of rural poverty under impossible circumstances. American agriculture was undergoing vast, even revolutionary, changes, and the resettlement program could never have served as an adequate long-range answer. The FSA tried to keep people on the farm when rural areas already contained too many farmers and would need fewer in the future. True, the cities had only soup lines to offer, but Tugwell was correct when he pointed out the anachronism of the family farm in the age of technology and large-scale, commercial agriculture. Nothing could have brought back the family farm. In this sense the resettlement program was not merely conservative; it was reactionary.

Nor can there be any question of the inadequacy of FSA programs when measured against regional, not to mention national, problems of rural poverty. But criticism of this kind is fruitless. Given the nature of the problem the agency faced, given its own program and the environment within which it operated, the FSA made a quite respectable effort. In Region VI about 146,000 families received rural rehabilitation loans, another 7,000 were tenant purchase borrowers, and the resettlement projects housed 2,800—altogether half a million or more people. There were another 1,100 families that took part in land-leasing associations. The outlay for the three major programs totaled some $182 million.

The forces of twentieth-century change were already providing relief for the masses the New Deal overlooked. The number of southern tenant farmers dropped dramatically during World War II and afterward. In the Lower Mississippi Valley the average rate of tenancy fell from a high of 67.2 percent in 1930 to 59.6 in 1940, 51.0 in 1945, 42.9 in 1950, and 26.4 in 1959.[36] But many of the families who left tenancy became farm laborers, not farm owners; or they left the land entirely during the war and sought defense work in cities and towns. Once the war ended, the movement away from the farm turned into a deluge.

The New Deal did not eliminate rural poverty, just as it did not end the depression. The rural poor today, as Michael Harrington has observed, can be found in certain parts of the South exactly where they were during the 1930s. "The New Deal and post-war prosperity," he wrote, "passed over these areas without really touching them."[37] In the past thirty years the relative number of rural poor has shown remarkable persistence, still remaining around a third of all commercial farmers.

Was nothing achieved in some ten years of effort? While the number of families that participated was small, the resettlement program mattered for those involved in it. The New Deal communities provided homes for some ten thousand families across the nation. In addition, thousands of jobs were created in the construction of the projects. The intangible gains were most important. The resettlement program gave people a renewed hope in the future and restored their faith in their country. That

36. U.S. Bureau of the Census, *Statistical Abstract of the United States, 1942* (Washington: Government Printing Office, 1942), p. 709; *Statistical Abstract of the United States, 1952* (Washington: Government Printing Office, 1952), p. 582; *Statistical Abstract of the United States, 1962* (Washington: Government Printing Office, 1962), p. 619.

37. Michael Harrington, *The Other America: Poverty in the United States* (New York: Macmillan, 1964), p. 46.

type of inspiration, of course, is no small achievement. When Americans again despair of the cities and look toward the country as a source of escape, as many are already doing, the resettlement communities will have even more lessons to teach.[38]

38. News items of the following kind have begun appearing with regularity: David Gumpert, "Living off the Land: Eliot and Sue Coleman Find Life as Pioneers Is Arduous but Happy," *Wall Street Journal*, 12 July 1972 (see also 13 July 1971); James G. Andrews, "The New Settlers," *Mid South* (*Commercial Appeal* magazine), 29 July 1973, is about Ozark homesteaders near Eureka Springs, Arkansas; Stratton Douthat, "Rural Movement Is Thoreau Back to Land," *Commercial Appeal*, 21 October 1973.

Chapter XV

Epilogue: Where Are They Now?

"You are just as wrong as hell when you think I have closed the WPA," wrote Floyd Sharp in 1943. "This thing is harder to wind up than it was to build up."[1] The same was true of the Farm Security Administration's resettlement program.

Maston G. White, solicitor of the Department of Agriculture, ruled that the resettlement projects must not be merely auctioned off; they had to be sold in a manner that would rehabilitate needy families. At the risk of further congressional displeasure, C. B. Baldwin insisted the rate of liquidation not impose a hardship on clients, nor should the government take any greater loss than necessary. The individual farm units were sold, wherever possible, to the families occupying them. Purchasers had to meet the Bankhead-Jones qualifications. Any family with more debts than assets was ineligible, the final disappointment for a few families that had waited years to purchase their homes. If current occupants could not qualify, offers were made to families in the same county, then to families outside the county. Land unsuitable for subdivision into family-sized units was either transferred to the National Forest Service or sold at auction to the highest bidder.[2]

At Little Rock regional officials worked hard to break down the projects and sell the individual homestead units, but it was a slow process. Baldwin originally promised to liquidate the resettlement program by 30 June 1943. With a couple of months to go, a visitor at Plum Bayou quipped, "Looks like the only kind of liquidation they've got down here comes from the drainage ditches." By 1945 most of the individual units were at last in the hands of their new owners. As quit-claim deeds replaced

1. Floyd Sharp to H. P. McGrath, 13 February 1943, Sharp Papers.
2. Paul K. Conkin, *Tomorrow a New World: The New Deal Community Program* (Ithaca, N.Y.: Cornell University Press, 1959), pp. 228–30.

the old lease-and-purchase contracts and project offices closed down, the families that remained looked to the county supervisor for assistance.[3]

After World War II the Farm Security Administration followed its predecessor, the Resettlement Administration, into oblivion. For two years Cong. Harold Cooley sponsored legislation calling for the abolition of the FSA and the substitution of a new agency in its place. The FSA had already been brought to heel, and no one was in any hurry to deliver the coup de grace. But Cooley finally got results. In 1946 Congress created the Farmers Home Administration, which absorbed both the FSA and the Farm Credit Administration's crop and seed program. In the same stroke came the liquidation of the rural rehabilitation program, the FSA's major activity. Only the tenant purchase program, renamed farm ownership, was left. What had been a small part of the FSA became the core of the new agency.[4] The FSA's administrative machinery also underwent a drastic overhaul. The Farmers Home Administration abolished the system of regional offices and made the state offices directly responsible to Washington.

While most of the cooperative associations were dissolved as the resettlement projects went into liquidation, the state rural rehabilitation corporations continued to operate with their own trust funds. In 1950 Congress ordered the liquidation of these corporations, but allowed the state governments to assume control of their assets. Some of the states formed separate organizations to administer the trusts; others absorbed them into existing agencies, usually the state department of agriculture. Today the trust funds are still being used for approved rehabilitation purposes; and they have formed their own organization, the National Association of Rural Rehabilitation Corporations.[5]

The Farmers Home Administration confronted a radically different economic situation than the Resettlement Administration faced ten years before. The gravest worry of Americans during the last months of the war was the possibility of a catastrophic postwar depression, taking up where the Great Depression left off. They knew that World War II rather than the New Deal had revived the economy; perhaps the sudden end of defense spending and the return of millions of jobless servicemen would plunge the nation back into depression. The pessimists could not have

3. Little Rock *Arkansas Gazette*, 20 May 1943; the quote is found in Inez Hale MacDuff, "New Deal Experiment Placed on Land That Floods Every Year," ibid., 2 May 1943.

4. 60 *US Stat.* 1062.

5. T. B. Fatherree to the author, 28 November 1972; National Association of Rural Rehabilitation Corporations, NARRC Newsletter, no. 5, November 1972.

been more wrong. The economy, although shaky at first, soon entered one of the longest boom periods in American history. Without solving the old problems of poverty and deprivation, the United States moved on to the new, more difficult challenges of affluence.

The first task of the agency was to survive. The Farmers Home Administration came to terms with its predecessor's enemies, and congressional conservatives were soon praising it for towing the line. It remained quiescent during the Truman and Eisenhower years, only to come back to life in the 1960s. A revitalized FHA played an important role in the War on Poverty of the Kennedy and Johnson administrations; by the close of the decade it was pumping an average of $1.5 to $2 billion per year into the rural economy. If the character of the agency had changed, so had the rural population.

With the Farm Security Administration's demise, the leadership of Region VI scattered. In 1945 A. D. Stewart left government service entirely, moving to Amory, Mississippi, where he entered private business. E. B. Whitaker spent a little time with the War Relocation Authority during the war, but he was never far from his old post as resettlement director. On 1 January 1945, the long-time number-two man in the Little Rock office succeeded Stewart as regional director. In 1946, when the regional office was abolished, Whitaker graduated to Washington. He moved up to liaison officer in what the FHA called the Southern Region. He later returned to Little Rock to head the Arkansas Rural Endowment Fund, the successor of the Arkansas Rural Rehabilitation Corporation.[6]

T. Roy Reid spent World War II in Washington. He served one year as assistant secretary of agriculture, but then shifted to director of personnel, where he helped trim the department's staff to the bone in the wartime economy drives. For a while he doubled as personnel director of the War Food Administration. When Baldwin was forced out as head of the FSA, a rumor circulated in Little Rock that Reid was in line as possible successor. If so, the appointment never came through. Reid remained with the Department of Agriculture's personnel office until his retirement.[7]

Many of the lower-echelon Farm Security employees, particularly younger men making careers, stayed in the region and rose high in the new Farmers Home Administration. For example, T. B. Fatherree, who

6. E. B. Whitaker to the author, 10 October 1972; T. B. Fatherree to the author, 28 November 1972.
7. *Arkansas Gazette*, 23 May 1943. Reid's obituary is in *Tallahassee* (Fla.) *Democrat*, 17 June 1969.

served in several capacities including regional tenant purchase chief, went to Mississippi as state director. F. L. Spencer, project manager at Mounds Farms, moved to the top in Louisiana; and Herman Hankins, administrative assistant in the regional office, ran the program in Arkansas. George Harmount died soon after World War II. Stanley Rhodes moved to Pine Bluff, where he had business interests; he still keeps a daily eye on the stock market. Another project manager, Cloyd O. Hopkins, who ran the Louisiana Farm Tenant Security project, shifted into the position of county supervisor in Richland Parish, a pattern many of his colleagues followed.

And Floyd Sharp? After winding up the WPA, he became War Manpower director for Arkansas. In 1944 a boom occurred for him as a gubernatorial candidate, but he bowed out when convinced he had no chance to win. After the war he joined the War Assets Administration, which disposed of governmental property and converted war plants to peacetime manufacturing. He later spent a year with the Chicago office of the Department of Health, Education and Welfare. Returning to Little Rock, he accepted a job as vice-president of the Fagan Electric Company. After his retirement in 1964, he resumed his private law practice.[8]

Although the government divested itself of control over the resettlement projects, the communities themselves remained, monuments to the idealism of a nation fighting economic collapse. Some thirty-five years later Dyess is occasionally mentioned as the place where Johnny Cash, the country music singer, grew up, while projects like Plum Bayou and Terrebonne have fallen completely into obscurity.[9]

Dyess today is a run-down community of about four hundred people. The old community buildings still stand, occupied with stores and other uses, though badly showing age and neglect. Out in the fields the old homesteads are abandoned and slowly rotting, and many of them have already been torn down. The people who own the land now live in "town" and they still farm. The Mississippi subsistence homesteads have become small suburbs as the city limits reached out to take them in.

At Plum Bayou, Terrebonne, and most of the other projects, a mere handful of the original settlers remain. They have consolidated their

8. *Arkansas Gazette*, 23 January 1944; *Blytheville Courier News*, 9, 20, 21 March 1944; "Scrapbook of Newspaper Clippings concerning Floyd Sharp, 1943–44," Sharp Papers. For Sharp's obituary, see *Arkansas Gazette*, 20 December 1969. The name Fagan arose during the 1939 legislative battle over Dyess Colony. See above, pp. 221–22.

9. See, for example, Christopher S. Wren, "The Restless Ballad of Johnny Cash," *Look* 33 (29 April 1969): 68–72, 74–75.

original units with adjacent ones, sometimes building up farms of several hundred acres. The former clients are, in fact, just now paying out their mortgages. Most of their neighbors sold out years ago and moved to the city, but those who hung on for a few years earned handsome profits as land values soared after World War II. Their land is now highly sought after. Even the low, wet land at Plum Bayou turned out to be valuable— it is perfect for rice. A few families, particularly the children who came out of these projects, have amazing success stories to tell. For such people the resettlement project did mean security and a brighter future. One can still see at the old project sites what is left of one of the most ambitious efforts in American history to alleviate rural poverty.

Appendix: The New Deal Communities of Region VI[a]

NAME	LOCATION	ACREAGE	UNITS	TOTAL COST[b]	AVERAGE UNIT COST TO EACH FAMILY
ARKANSAS					
Plum Bayou	Jefferson County	9,854	180	$1,589,893.44	$8,052.80
Lakeview	Lee and Phillips counties	8,163	142	892,619.11	4,796.36
Lake Dick	Jefferson and Arkansas counties	4,523	89	661,670.64	6,134.65
Central and Western	Conway and 8 other counties	6,916	82	344,183.93	4,472.72
Northwest Arkansas	Benton and Washington counties	3,233	44	211,711.36	5,919.78
Arkansas Farm Tenant Security	Clark and 3 other counties	4,508	66	476,950.24	6,607.23
Biscoe	Prairie County	4,530	74	372,005.60	4,671.05
Clover Bend	Lawrence County	4,995	86	460,701.28	4,775.62
Desha	Desha and Drew counties	4,422	88	515,039.95	5,207.67
Townes	Crittenden County	1,921	30	163,679.79	4,401.21
Lonoke	Lonoke County	2,903	41	251,964.15	4,675.81
Trumann	Poinsett County	2,224	55	263,229.44	4,446.94
St. Francis	Poinsett County	3,971	72	530,176.20	4,978.36
Chicot	Chicot and Drew counties	13,781	89	568,692.81	3,494.94
Kelso	Desha County	7,582	—	43,333.41	—
Dyess Colony	Mississippi County	15,144	300	4,233,045.00	—

LOUISIANA					
Terrebonne	Terrebonne Parish	5,960	71	505,659.92	5,461.63
Louisiana Farm Tenant Security	Richland and 7 other parishes	7,165	110	612,751.84	5,416.94
Transylvania	East Carroll Parish	10,725	160	845,098.73	4,200.74
Mounds	Madison and East Carroll parishes	11,876	145	795,383.18	3,871.50
MISSISSIPPI					
McComb	McComb	264	20	91,452.52	3,898.11
Magnolia	Meridian	233	25	73,556.46	2,851.47
Hattiesburg	Hattiesburg	130	24	75,648.78	2,521.59
Tupelo	Tupelo	171	35	139,247.12	3,469.91
Northeast Mississippi	Choctaw and 6 other counties	9,283	115	543,315.74	4,862.63
Mississippi Farm Tenant Security	Sunflower and 4 other counties	15,133	295	1,819,136.63	5,652.82
Lucedale	George and Greene counties	5,744	95	397,308.15	3,814.44
Hinds	Hinds County	5,404	73	296,421.67	3,518.72
Mileston	Holmes County	9,350	106	730,510.82	5,283.52
Richton	Richton	7,794	26	215,484.33	7,178.61
TOTALS		187,902	2,738	$18,810,872.23	$5,129.24

a Most of these statistics were compiled (and computed) from data found in USHR, *FSA Hearings*, pt. 3; USHR, *USDA Approp. Hearings, 1946*, 79th Cong., 1st sess.; and ibid, *1947*, 79th Cong., 2d sess.
b Includes costs not charged to client families.

Bibliographical Essay

MANUSCRIPTS

Source materials for this study are abundant. A wealth of correspondence, memorandums, and reports exists in the National Archives, Washington, D.C. The richest collection is Record Group 96, Records of the Farmers Home Administration, which contains 2,433 cubic feet of material on the Division of Subsistence Homesteads, the Federal Emergency Relief Administration, the Resettlement Administration, and the Farm Security Administration. The best available guide is Stanley W. Brown and Virgil T. Baugh, comps., *Preliminary Inventory of the Records of the Farmers Home Administration*, National Archives and Records Service, General Services Administration, Publication no. 118 (Washington, 1959). Unfortunately, Region VI is the only one of the twelve regions with no records for either the regional director's office or the Resettlement Division. Despite this disappointment, the archival records relating to Region VI are still so vast that one person could literally spend weeks in Washington looking through them all. What was lost in the destruction of these records, however, can be glimpsed in Work Projects Administration, Survey of Federal Archives, *Inventory of Federal Archives in the States*, ser. 9, Department of Agriculture, Arkansas (New Orleans, 1938–39).

Four other record groups in the National Archives contain indispensable but relatively small quantities of records on Region VI activities. Since the Resettlement Administration became part of the Department of Agriculture in late 1936, Record Group 16, Records of the Office of the Secretary of Agriculture, contains material relating to the resettlement program. Record Group 48, Records of the Office of the Secretary of the Interior, is disappointing on the early subsistence homesteads program in Mississippi. Record Group 69, Records of the Work Projects Administration, embraces the Works Progress Administration, the Civil Works Administration, and the Federal Emergency Relief Administration. The FERA and WPA records are important sources of material on W. R. Dyess and the rural rehabilitation program in Arkansas. Record Group 207, Records of the Housing and Home Finance Agency, contains material concerning the later years of the Mississippi subsistence homesteads and their liquidation.

Several other manuscript collections supply valuable information. The Franklin D. Roosevelt Library at Hyde Park, New York, provides relevant material concerning the Region VI resettlement program in the president's Official File, the Harry L. Hopkins Papers, and the Rexford G. Tugwell Papers. The Southern Tenant Farmers' Union Papers, deposited in the Southern Historical Collection, University of North Carolina Library, Chapel Hill, are a mine of information. Now available in a convenient microfilm edition, these papers include correspondence dealing with many phases of resettlement activity. The Socialist Party of America Papers in the Duke University Library at Durham, North Carolina, contain material reflecting Norman Thomas's interest in Arkansas sharecroppers. The University of Arkansas Library at Fayetteville has a small but valuable collection of WPA records relating to Dyess Colony. They were formerly in the possession of Floyd Sharp. The Farmers Home Administration office at Osceola, Arkansas, has a couple of small files on Dyess Colony.

As for published primary sources, Samuel I. Rosenman, ed., *The Public Papers and Addresses of Franklin D. Roosevelt*, 13 vols. (New York: Russell and Russell, 1969), is a convenient source for executive orders, speeches, and other official material relating to the resettlement agencies.

GOVERNMENT PUBLICATIONS

Government documents provide a convenient source of descriptive and statistical information on the resettlement program. The Resettlement Administration, *Interim Report* (Washington: Government Printing Office, 1936), is a polished piece of work covering the agency's earliest activities. Equally well done, the RA's *First Annual Report* (Washington: Government Printing Office, 1936) is valuable for its comprehensive summary of every aspect of resettlement work, showing in elaborate statistical tables what had been done to date. The Farm Security Administration's *Annual Reports* (Washington: Government Printing Office, 1937–46) never measured up to the RA's high standards. Descriptive material is sketchy, and sometimes statistical data are nonexistent. The annual reports of the Farmers Home Administration contain the ultimate repayment figures in FSA loan programs, but they are largely silent on the liquidation of the resettlement projects. Of some value for the final disposition of the projects are the annual reports of the United States National Housing Agency (1945–47) and its successor, the United States Housing and Home Finance Agency (1947–53).

The many congressional committee hearings, reports, and documents supply much of the hard factual information on the resettlement projects. The Resettlement Administration prepared an elaborate statistical analysis of its programs for Congress while its resettlement projects were still in the planning stage: U.S. Senate, *Resettlement Administration Program*, Senate Document no. 213, 74th Cong., 2d sess. (Washington: Government Printing Office, 1936). The Cooley committee hearings, or, more properly, the Select Committee of the House Committee on Agriculture, *Hearings on the Farm Security Administration*, 78th Cong., 1st sess. (Washington: Government Printing Office, 1943–44), provide a valuable summary of the resettlement projects. The committee summarized its findings and recommendations in U.S. House of Representatives, *Activities of the Farm Security Administration*, Report no. 1430, 78th Cong., 2d sess. (Washington: Government Printing Office, 1944).

The Byrd committee hearings, or *Hearings before the Joint Committee on Reduction of Nonessential Federal Expenditures*, 77th Cong., 2d sess. (Washington: Government Printing Office, 1942), pt. 3, contain the Carr report on Mississippi, Louisiana, and Arkansas. The annual hearings of the Senate and House agricultural subcommittees of the committees on appropriations for 1941 through 1947 document the growing hostility the FSA encountered in Congress. Especially useful for criticisms of Region VI activities are the House and Senate hearings for 1943 and 1944. The House Agricultural Subcommittee of the Committee on Appropriations, *Hearings on the Agricultural Department Appropriation Bill for 1947*, 79th Cong., 2d sess. (Washington: Government Printing Office, 1946), is the source of the final published figures on the liquidation of almost all resettlement projects, including their total cost, the average unit sales price, operating and maintenance expenses, and income. Many contemporary critics accused the FSA of juggling figures in order to show resettlement projects operating at a profit. This is an exaggeration, but these statistical tables can be misleading if given only a cursory glance. Since so much information is available, however, the occasional omission of vital data is particularly frustrating.

INTERVIEWS

In a study where participants are still living, personal interviews constitute a valuable source of information, second only to archival records and government publications. The passage of time, of course, clouds memories, but much can still be learned about personal attitudes and philosophies. The author had the pleasure of meeting or corresponding with these former officials: Austin Chaplain, T. B. Fatherree, Brooks Hays, J. L. Henderson, Laurence I. Hewes, C. O. Hopkins, the late T. Roy Reid, Stanley W. Rhodes, F. L. Spencer, Horace E. Thompson, E. B. Whitaker, and Claude Woolsey. In addition, H. L. Mitchell looked over parts of the manuscript and provided his observations. The comments of these men were crucial in shaping my view of the nature of the resettlement program. Floyd Sharp and A. D. Stewart died as work on this study was in its early stages.

NEWSPAPERS

The newspapers of the region, both small-town weeklies and large-city dailies, are an invaluable source of information on the local activities of the resettlement agencies. Newspapers not only reflected local attitudes toward resettlement, but also published information about land purchase, family selection, project development, and project operation, although most papers lost interest in local projects once the new wore off and the clients settled down to everyday living. Even the most humble weeklies provide indispensable information, since such papers often served as a kind of "official journal" for the announcements of FSA supervisors. Front-page coverage was the rule.

One example of unusually close cooperation between project officials and a local paper is the *McComb* (Miss.) *Enterprise* in 1934 and 1935. The editor of the paper, J. O. Emmerich, was also the project manager of McComb Homesteads; he of course gave the project big play. Another example is the *Houma* (La.) *Courier*, which followed every move made at the Terrebonne project from 1937 to 1940. The *Richland Beacon-News* (Rayville, La.) showed interest in FSA activities all over the state, but especially at nearby Crew Lake. The Lake Providence *Banner Democrat* and the Tallulah *Madison Journal* were strong boosters of both the Transylvania and Mounds projects in northeast Louisiana. The Columbia *Caldwell Watchman* ran a series of short articles written by Joyce Mullins, Caldwell Parish home management supervisor, under the general heading

"A Few Facts about Resettlement." Both the *Osceola Times* and the Blytheville *Courier News*, the two leading newspapers of Mississippi County, Arkansas, gave excellent coverage on the development of Dyess Colony; but they both seemed to ignore the colony's troubles after 1938.

The Little Rock *Arkansas Gazette* is the single most valuable paper for news about resettlement in Region VI. Located in the same city as the regional headquarters, it carried news releases of region-wide importance. Also important is Little Rock's *Arkansas Democrat*, a paper with more state orientation than the *Gazette*. The large-city dailies offer special advantages not available in the rural weeklies. Their reporters visited resettlement projects to interview officials and clients, and the numerous feature articles they wrote are an important source of firsthand information.

Resettlement projects were the source of much human interest material. The New Orleans *Times-Picayune* published several long stories on the Terrebonne project, as did the *Item-Tribune*. The *Monroe Morning News* gave the Crew Lake project favorable treatment. The Pine Bluff *Daily Graphic*, unofficial spokesman for southeast Arkansas, was in an excellent position to cover resettlement activities, since two large projects, Plum Bayou and Lake Dick, were located just across the Arkansas River. The Jackson, Mississippi, *Clarion-Ledger* and *Daily News* had less resettlement activity to cover, and they became leading critics of the program during World War II. The Memphis *Commercial Appeal* and especially the *Press-Scimitar*, both of which circulated widely in eastern Arkansas, reported news from Dyess, Plum Bayou, and elsewhere; they generally favored resettlement as a means of helping farm tenants. The *Commercial Appeal*, like the Jackson papers, grew more critical as time passed, while the *Press-Scimitar* rose to the defense.

MEMOIRS

The published memoirs of most New Deal insiders give only minimal help. Harold L. Ickes, in *The Secret Diary of Harold L. Ickes*, 3 vols. (New York: Simon and Schuster, 1953–54), makes clear what he thought about the subsistence homesteads program in his account of a trip through Tupelo, Mississippi. Rexford G. Tugwell's *The Democratic Roosevelt* (Garden City, N.Y.: Doubleday, 1957) and *The Brains Trust* (New York: Viking, 1968) furnish insight into the development of the entire Resettlement Administration program. One of Tugwell's protégés, Laurence I. Hewes, tells an engaging story in *Boxcar in the Sand* (New York:

Knopf, 1957). Two other well-known memoirs—Raymond Moley, *After Seven Years* (New York: Harper and Brothers, 1939), and Eleanor Roosevelt, *This I Remember* (New York: Harper and Brothers, 1949)— are of little value so far as this study is concerned.

CONTEMPORARY PERIODICALS

Among the literally hundreds of contemporary articles on the community program, the most helpful are Will W. Alexander, "Rural Resettlement," *Southern Review* 1 (Winter 1936); Oscar Ameringer, "No Thoroughfare to Utopia," *Reader's Digest* 37 (July 1940); M. C . Blackman, "Arkansas's Largest Landlord," Little Rock *Arkansas Gazette Sunday Magazine*, 13 October 1935, and "Uncle Sam Waves a Wand," ibid., 22 September 1935; William G. Carr, "The Return of the Carpetbagger," *Nation's Agriculture* 17 (April 1942); Joanna C. Colcord, "Tenant into Owner: The Dyess Colony Experiment," *Survey Graphic* 26 (August 1937); Mordecai Ezekiel, "Schisms in Agricultural Policy," *Journal of Farm Economics* 24 (May 1942); "FHA [FSA] Helps Construction," *Construction News* 5 (28 September 1938); Richard Hellman, "The Farmers Try Group Medicine," *Harper's Magazine* 182 (December 1940); R. W. Hudgens, "The Plantation South Tries a New Way," *Land Policy Review* 3 (November 1940); Charles P. Loomis and Dwight Davidson, Jr., "Sociometrics and the Study of New Rural Communities," *Sociometry* 2 (January 1939); Rena B. Maycock, "Home Economic Work in the Resettlement Administration," *Journal of Home Economics* 28 (October 1936); Horace G. Porter, "New Farms in the Mississippi Delta," *Louisiana Rural Economist* 2 (April 1940); "Rural Industrial Community Projects: Woodlake, Texas; Osceola, Arkansas; and Red House, West Virginia," *Architectural Record* 77 (January 1935); Oren Stephens, "FSA Fights for Its Life," *Harper's Magazine* 186 (April 1943), and "Revolt on the Delta: What Happened to the Sharecroppers' Union," ibid. 183 (November 1941); Rexford G. Tugwell, "Cooperation and Resettlement," *Current History* 45 (February 1937); George S. Wehrwein, "An Appraisal of Resettlement," *Journal of Farm Economics* 19 (February 1937); Lawrence Westbrook, "The Program of the Rural Rehabilitation Division of the FERA," *Journal of Farm Economics* 17 (February 1935); Elizabeth C. Wherry, "A Chance for the Sharecropper: Farm Colony at Dyess, Ark., Provides a New Start for Farmers Beaten by Depression," *Wallace's Farmer and Iowa Homestead* 63 (7 May 1938); Clarence A. Wiley, "Settlement and Unsettlement in the Resettlement

Administration," *Law and Contemporary Problems* 4 (October 1937); and M. L. Wilson, "The Place of Subsistence Homesteads in Our National Economy," *Journal of Farm Economics* 16 (January 1934).

SECONDARY SOURCES

In recent years New Deal agricultural policy has attracted an extraordinary amount of scholarly attention, a phenomenon paralleling the rediscovery of poverty in the 1960s and the renewal of federal antipoverty programs. Sidney Baldwin, *Poverty and Politics: The Rise and Decline of the Farm Security Administration* (Chapel Hill: University of North Carolina Press, 1968), serves as an excellent administrative history of the resettlement agencies. A political scientist, Baldwin evaluates the FSA through such concepts as institutional survival, goal formation, and goal succession. The most valuable book on the resettlement program itself remains Paul K. Conkin, *Tomorrow a New World: The New Deal Community Program* (Ithaca, N.Y.: Cornell University Press, 1959). Conkin traces the origins of the back-to-the-land movement of the Great Depression, discusses the subsistence homesteads program, the FERA communities, and the RA projects, giving five communities separate treatment. He also stresses the discontinuity of the resettlement program from previous experience. What he says about Region VI, of course, is meager. In "It All Happened in Pine Mountain Valley," *Georgia Historical Quarterly* 47 (March 1963), Conkin deals with an FERA community. Recalling his years with the Resettlement Administration, Rexford G. Tugwell tries to assess what went wrong, in "The Resettlement Idea," *Agricultural History* 33 (October 1959). An early but still valuable study is Joseph W. Eaton, *Exploring Tomorrow's Agriculture* (New York: Harper and Brothers, 1943). Writing under the auspices of the Rural Settlement Institute, Eaton had access to FSA files in Washington, interviewed officials, and visited several projects in early 1941. He attempts specifically to explain the theory and practice of what he calls "cooperative group farms" (like Terrebonne and Lake Dick); but much of what he says about project development, organization, and operation applies to all FSA communities.

The scope of other secondary works on the community program is more limited. Joseph L. Arnold, *The New Deal in the Suburbs: A History of the Greenbelt Town Program, 1935–1954* (Columbus: Ohio State University Press, 1971), is a thorough, scholarly study. And several older works retain their value. Casa Grande Valley Farms, an Arizona cooperative farming project, is the subject of Edward Banfield, *Government Project* (Glencoe, Ill.: Free Press, 1951). Russell Lord and Paul H. Johnstone, eds., *A Place of Earth: A Critical Appraisal of Subsistence Homesteads*, Bureau of Agricultural Economics (Washington, 1942), contains sociological case studies of thirteen individual subsistence homestead communities. Paul W. Wager, *One Foot on the Soil: A Study of Subsistence Homesteads in Alabama* (University: University of Alabama Press, 1945), is limited to five communities in the Birmingham area. Despite the title, Wager deals with FSA projects. How Greenbelt, Maryland, one of the famous Tugwell towns, appeared to an early settler is told in George A. Warner, *Greenbelt: The Cooperative Community* (New York: Exposition Press, 1954). A similar work is Raymond P. Duggan, *A Federal Resettlement Project—Granger Homesteads*, School of Social Work, Monograph no. 1, Catholic University of America (Washington, 1937).

Several recent articles deal with resettlement activities within Region VI: Louis J. Rodriguez, "The Terrebonne Project: Ideological Revolution or Economic Expediency?" *Louisiana Studies* 6 (Fall 1967); Dan W. Pittman, "The Founding of Dyess Colony," *Arkansas Historical Quarterly* 29 (Winter 1970); Donald Holley, "Old and New Worlds in the New Deal Resettlement Program: Two Louisiana Projects," *Louisiana History* 11 (Spring 1970); idem, "The Negro in the New Deal Resettlement Program," *Agricultural History* 45 (July 1971), reprinted in *New South* 27 (Winter 1972); and idem, "Trouble in Paradise: Dyess Colony and Arkansas Politics," *Arkansas Historical Quarterly* 32 (Autumn 1973).

Among doctoral dissertations, Michael Harris Mehlman, "The Resettlement Administration and the Problems of Tenant Farmers in Arkansas, 1935–1936" (New York University, 1970), includes a discussion of the rural rehabilitation program (Arkansas's was the largest in the nation) and land reform activities.

Secondary studies on the subject of sharecroppers and the New Deal begin with M. S. Venkataramani, "Norman Thomas, Arkansas Sharecroppers, and the Roosevelt Agricultural Policies, 1933–1937," *Mississippi Valley Historical Review* 47 (September 1960). David Eugene Conrad treats the subject at length in his award-winning book, *The Forgotten Farmers: The Story of Sharecroppers in the New Deal* (Urbana: University of Illinois Press, 1965); focusing on the AAA and STFU, Conrad does not pursue his subject into the resettlement program. Jerold S. Auerbach, "Southern Tenant Farmers: Socialist Critics of the New Deal,"

Labor History 7 (Winter 1966), and Vera Rony, "Sorrow Song in Black and White," *New South* 22 (Summer 1967), cover the ground again, while Donald H. Grubbs previews his later work in "Gardner Jackson, That 'Socialist' Tenant Farmers' Union, and the New Deal," *Agricultural History* 42 (April 1968). Louis Cantor, in *A Prologue to the Protest Movement: The Missouri Sharecroppers Roadside Demonstration of 1939* (Durham: Duke University Press, 1969) and in an article of the same title, *Journal of American History* 55 (March 1969), describes an episode which saw a clash between the FSA and the union. The STFU has its "official" history in Donald H. Grubbs, *Cry from the Cotton: The Southern Tenant Farmers' Union and the New Deal* (Chapel Hill: University of North Carolina Press, 1971); his partisan approach might have done justice to those who lived through the events he describes. Lowell K. Dyson, "The Southern Tenant Farmers Union and Depression Politics," *Political Science Quarterly* 88 (June 1973), treats the relationship between the union and the Communist party. H. L. Mitchell recalls the 1930s in "The Founding and Early History of the Southern Tenant Farmers Union," *Arkansas Historical Quarterly* 32 (Winter 1973).

A number of new studies provide help in understanding the community program's relation to New Deal agricultural policies. In contrast to most recent assessments of the AAA, Van L. Perkins, *Crisis in Agriculture: The Agricultural Adjustment Administration and the New Deal, 1933*, University of California Publications in History, vol. 81 (Berkeley and Los Angeles: University of California Press, 1969), effectively demonstrates the agency's positive side. Christiana MacFadyen Campbell, *The Farm Bureau and the New Deal: A Study of the Making of National Farm Policy, 1933–1940* (Urbana: University of Illinois Press, 1962), follows the rising conflict between New Deal agencies and the American Farm Bureau Federation but stops before the latter's assault on the FSA. Richard S. Kirkendall, *Social Scientists and Farm Politics in the Age of Roosevelt* (Columbia: University of Missouri Press, 1966), discusses important farm leaders and thinkers in the New Deal, including M. L. Wilson and Rexford G. Tugwell.

Other useful studies are Dean Albertson, *Roosevelt's Farmer: Claude R. Wickard in the New Deal* (New York: Columbia University Press, 1961); Edward L. and Frederick H. Schapsmeier, *Henry A. Wallace: The Agrarian Years, 1910–1940* (Ames: Iowa State University Press, 1969); Russell Lord, *The Wallaces of Iowa* (Boston: Houghton Mifflin, 1947); and Searle F. Charles, *Minister of Relief: Harry Hopkins and the Depression* (Syracuse, N.Y.: Syracuse University Press, 1963). The struggle over the FSA in World War II is recounted in Grant McConnell, *The Decline of Agrarian Democracy* (Berkeley and Los Angeles: University of California Press, 1953). Raymond Wolters, *Negroes and the Great Depression: The Problems of Economic Recovery* (Westport, Conn.: Greenwood, 1970), emphasizes the impact of the New Deal on black Americans. See also Wilma Dykeman and James Stokely, *Seeds of Southern Change: The Life of Will Alexander* (Chicago: University of Chicago Press, 1962); Bernard Sternsher, *Rexford G. Tugwell and the New Deal* (New Brunswick, N.J.: Rutgers University Press, 1964); and William D. Rowley, *M. L. Wilson and the Campaign for the Domestic Allotment* (Lincoln: University of Nebraska Press, 1970).

As a rule, general works on the New Deal treat the Resettlement and Farm Security administrations in cursory fashion. But Arthur M. Schlesinger, Jr., *The Age of Roosevelt*, vol. 2: *The Coming of the New Deal* (Boston: Houghton Mifflin, 1958), includes an exceptionally full account of the early subsistence homesteads program and the Resettlement Administration's activities. William E. Leuchtenburg, *Franklin D. Roosevelt and the New Deal* (New York: Harper and Row, 1963), gives the resettlement program its due. Frank Freidel, *Franklin D. Roosevelt: The Triumph* (Boston: Houghton Mifflin, 1956), discusses Roosevelt's speeches on agriculture during the 1932 campaign. George B. Tindall's magnum opus, *The Emergence of the New South, 1913–1945* (Baton Rouge: Louisiana State University Press, 1967), gives a good summary of Arkansas tenant troubles and the New Deal's response.

Index

Conkin, Paul K., 27, 105
Connecticut General Life Insurance Co.,
    266
Cooley, Harold D., 271–72, 280
Coolidge, Calvin, 11
Cooper, Owen, 269
Cooperative associations: legal status,
    130; purpose, 130–31; rationale, 132–
    33; subsidiary cooperatives, 132
Cooperative farming: advocated by
    STFU, 94, 100, 106–7, 192–93; and
    Tugwell, 106; rationale, 157; at Ter-
    rebonne, 159, 162–63, 165; lack of
    spirit for, 166, 276–77; at Lake Dick,
    199–200; mentioned, 273
Cooperatives, agricultural: history, 133
Copeland, J. T., 57
Cornish, Hilda K., 41
Cotton: changes in farming, 10;
    drought's effect on production, 12;
    prices, 12–13; in Lower Mississippi
    Valley, 6–7
Coughlin, Father Charles E., 65
Counts, Ira W., 144, 151
County supervisor of FSA: conflict with
    county agent, 196–97, 199
Crawford, Ivy W., 221
Creamery Package Co., 35
Credit structure: collapse during Great
    Depression, 13
Crew Lake, La., 111
Cummings, Homer, 93

Daniels, Jonathan, 31, 90, 202
Davidson, Donald, 22
Davis, Chester C., 84
Delta. See Mississippi River delta
Delta and Pine Land Co., 261
Delta Cooperative Farm (Hillhouse,
    Miss.), 106, 192
Depression. See Great Depression
Desha Farms, 112, 284
Dillard University, 180
Dirksen, Everett M., 243, 248, 264
Division of Subsistence Homesteads: in
    Lower Mississippi Valley, 28–29; or-
    ganization, 54; and McComb project,
    55–60, 116–18; abolished, 61–62;

activities assumed by RA, 81, 115–
    21; financial record of projects, 275;
    mentioned, ix, 34, 53, 77, 270, 274
Domestic allotment: agricultural relief
    plan, 24
Donaghey Trust Building, 77, 104
Donahue, Troy C., 224
Doxey, Wall, 101
Drainage District Number 9, 35
Driver, William J., 102
Drought (1930–31), 3, 12
Dudley, E. S.: appointed Dyess Colony
    administrator, 47; areas of responsi-
    bility, 49; and Finch, 206; authority
    clarified, 208; defends price of land,
    210; mentioned, 207, 214
Dunn, Loula, 42
Dupont, Julius, 162
Dyess, W. R.: conceives idea for colony,
    28; dies in plane crash, 30; back-
    ground, 30–31; appointment as relief
    administrator, 31, 216; and Emer-
    gency Relief Administration, 32; in-
    terest in rural relief, 34; investigation,
    37, 217–18; mourned, 45–46; effect of
    death on Colony, 51; political ac-
    tivities, 215–17; and Futrell, 218;
    mentioned, 72, 237
Dyess Colony: population, 28, 44, 224;
    description, 28, 202; cost of land, 35,
    48, 212; construction, 36–40; wage
    scale controversy, 37, 217–18; house
    plans, 39; community center, 40, 45;
    family selection, 40–41, 129, 212–13;
    and family subsistence, 43; dedication,
    45; problems, 46, 204, 212–13, 234–
    35; purchase plans for colonists, 46,
    48, 225–26, 236; use of name, 47,
    255n; family turnover, 50; deficit, 50–
    51, 237–38; discontent among colon-
    ists, 202–5, 211–12, 229, 231–32;
    and 1937 flood, 203–4, 224; and
    Finch, 205–7, 215, 231; store manager
    fired, 208; and eviction suits, 209,
    233; and Funk, 209–15, 232; in-
    volvement in state politics, 215–24;
    irregularities in financial operation,
    218; FSA's reorganization of, 224–